THE PEOPLE'S LIBERATION ARMY
AND
CONTINGENCY PLANNING IN CHINA

THE PEOPLE'S LIBERATION ARMY
AND
CONTINGENCY PLANNING IN CHINA

Edited by
Andrew Scobell, Arthur S. Ding,
Phillip C. Saunders, and Scott W. Harold

National Defense University Press
Washington, D.C.
2015

Published in the United States by National Defense University Press
260 Fifth Avenue (Building 64)
Suite 2500
Fort Lesley J. McNair
Washington, DC 20319

Library of Congress Cataloging-in-Publication Data

Names: Scobell, Andrew, editor of compilation.
Title: The People's Liberation Army and contingency planning in China / edited by Andrew Scobell, Arthur S. Ding, Phillip C. Saunders, and Scott W. Harold.
Description: Washington, D.C. : National Defense University Press, [2015] | Includes bibliographical references and index.
Identifiers: LCCN 2015038587 | ISBN 9780996824903 (pbk. : alk. paper)
Subjects: LCSH: Military planning—China. | China. Zhongguo ren min jie fang jun. | National security—China. | Internal security—China. | China—Military policy. | Sea-power—China—History—21st century. | China—Strategic aspects.
Classification: LCC UA835 .P3773 2015 | DDC 355/.033551—dc23
LC record available at http://lccn.loc.gov/2015038587

Book design by Jamie Harvey, U.S. Government Publishing Office

CONTENTS

INTRODUCTION

The PLA and Contingency Planning in China................................1
Phillip C. Saunders

I. Thinking and Planning for Contingencies

CHAPTER 1

The PLA and Contingency Planning...15
Mark Cozad

CHAPTER 2

PLA Observations of U.S. Contingency Planning:
What Has It Learned? 33
Marcelyn L. Thompson

CHAPTER 3

China Plans for Internal Unrest: People's Armed Police
and Public Security Approaches to "Mass Incidents" 55
Jonathan Walton

CHAPTER 4

Civilian Authorities and Contingency Planning in China 85
Catherine Welch

IV. Maritime Contingencies

Illustrations

Figures

Tables

ACKNOWLEDGMENTS

This volume grew out of a conference on "Contingency Planning, PLA style" co-sponsored by Taiwan's Council of Advanced Policy Studies (CAPS), RAND, the Carnegie Endowment for International Peace (CEIP), and National Defense University (NDU). RAND hosted the conference at its Arlington, Virginia, office. The editors gratefully acknowledge the intellectual contribution of Michael Swaine (CEIP) in shaping the agenda and recruiting paper writers, discussants, and panelists, and the financial support of the four sponsoring organizations. The editors also thank the Taipei Economic and Cultural Representative Office for hosting a dinner in honor of the conference participants.

Yi-su Yang and Polly Shen (CAPS), Cortez Cooper, Lyle Morris, and Heather McLendon (RAND), and Christopher D. Yung, Michael Glosny, Terry Min Jie Zeng, and Deborah Jefferson (NDU) all provided support in organizing the original conference. Dr. Saunders also thanks Gerald Faber, Donald Mosser, Mollie Murphy, Jeanette Tolbert, and Christopher D. Yung (NDU) and Martha Robinson and Patrick Shaw (Joint Staff J7) for their assistance in obtaining permission for NDU's Center for the Study of Chinese Military Affairs to co-sponsor the conference.

In addition to the chapter authors and editors, Ken Allen, Tai Ming Cheung, Bernard Cole, Cortez Cooper, John Corbett, T.X. Hammes, Lonnie Henley, Frank G. Hoffman, John Landry, Oriana Skylar Mastro, Shen Ming-Shih, Yitzak Shichor, Paul Stares, Michael Swaine, Christopher D. Yung, and Yen Tiehlin all provided comments or participated in discussions that improved the chapters in this book. Terry Min Jie Zeng and Adam Jankowski drafted summaries of the chapters for the introduction. Mr. Jankowski also provided additional research to help update Dr. Ma Chengkun's chapter. Drew Casey provided invaluable assistance in reformatting the chapters, tracking down stray references, and standardizing English and Chinese language references.

The editors thank NDU Press Director Dr. William Eliason and Executive Editor Dr. Jeffrey Smotherman for their creativity in squeezing this book into a narrow publication window, Lisa Yambrick and Jane Floyd for copyediting the manuscript, and Erin L. Sindle, Lisa Yambrick, Julia Bowie, and Capt Adam Greer, USAF, for proofreading. Brianna Cappelletti compiled the index. Jamie Harvey at the Government Publishing Office designed the book.

The editors gratefully acknowledge financial support for publication of this book from NDU's Program on Irregular Warfare and Special Operations Studies.

The PLA and Contingency Planning in China

Phillip C. Saunders

ll militaries have a responsibility to plan for contingencies, and China's military, the People's Liberation Army (PLA), is no exception. PLA contingency planning takes place primarily within the General Staff Department's (GSD's) First Department, also known as the GSD Operations Department. China's seven military regions participate in drafting and reviewing the plans relevant to their areas of responsibility, albeit under heavy supervision from the GSD.[1]

U.S. joint doctrine defines a *contingency* as "a situation that likely would involve military forces in response to natural and manmade disasters, terrorists, subversives, military operations by foreign powers, or other situations." U.S. doctrine distinguishes between deliberate planning (advance preparation of campaign[2] and contingency plans in noncrisis situations) and crisis action planning (rapid planning in response to a developing incident or situation). Deliberate planning is typically used to develop campaign and contingency plans for a broad range of activities based on requirements identified in strategic guidance for military commanders. Crisis action planning is conducted with less advance warning (hours, days, or up to 12 months) and focuses on developing alternative courses of action or refining existing campaign or contingency plans to adapt to current circumstances.[3]

Chinese military planning appears to be mostly deliberate planning focused on specific contingencies. Mark Cozad argues that since about 1995, a Taiwan contingency has been the dominant PLA planning scenario, but the PLA also plans for other potential contingencies.[4] The GSD Operations Department also has a contingency planning bureau that works with civilian ministries and agencies on emergency plans for various situations.[5] Chinese documents typically use the same phrase, *yingji jihua* [应急计划], to refer to both military contingency plans and civilian emergency response plans, although other terms are also used.[6] The GSD Operations Department is also responsible for military crisis action planning, although the PLA appears to devote less attention and fewer resources to crisis planning than to deliberate planning. This may be because the PLA rarely deploys outside China's territory in response to crises other than to conduct humanitarian assistance and disaster-relief operations. The few recent exceptions include PLA Navy (PLAN) counterpiracy deployments in the Gulf of Aden (since December 2008), the March 2011 evacuation of Chinese citizens from Libya, and the March 2014 deployment of PLA Air Force, Navy, and Chinese Coast Guard assets to search for the missing Malaysian Airlines flight MH-370.[7]

Some contingencies, such as deployments for disaster relief operations, occur frequently, providing the chance to try out plans and modify them to incorporate lessons learned and correct deficiencies revealed during execution. Others, such as plans to fight major wars, usually sit on the shelf for decades and are reviewed and revised regularly but never executed. In such cases, there is no feedback loop between contingency planning, execution, and revision, so incorrect planning assumptions and faulty operational concepts may go unnoticed and uncorrected. The best that militaries can do is to rely on exercises, wargames, and related operational deployments and make revisions to their war plans based on the results.

A potential fight to prevent Taiwan independence or compel unification clearly represents a high-end contingency that absorbs much attention from PLA planners, especially given the likelihood of U.S. military intervention. Since the Taiwan Strait crisis of March 1996, when President William Clinton deployed two carriers near Taiwan in response to Chinese ballistic missile tests, PLA senior generals have been focused on building the doctrine, trained personnel, and military equipment necessary to have a chance to prevail against a technologically superior and battle-tested U.S. military. Cozad observes that PLA Taiwan contingency planning is a large-scale data- and labor-intensive effort.[8]

However, the PLA must also plan for other contingencies that require different capabilities and are not simply "lesser included cases" that can be adapted from the plans, doctrine, and forces developed for Taiwan contingencies.[9] This is not only a prudent measure, but it also reflects political guidance from Chinese Communist Party (CCP) leaders, including the "new historic missions" [*xin de lishi shiming*, 新的历史使命] that then–General Secretary Hu Jintao gave the PLA in 2004. These give the PLA new responsibilities beyond its traditional role of supporting the CCP, including protecting China's sovereignty, territorial integrity, and domestic security in order to continue national development, safeguarding China's expanding national interests, and helping to ensure world peace.[10] The new historic missions broadened PLA functional roles to increase the emphasis on "diversified military tasks" [*duoyanghua junshi renwu*, 多样化军事任务] and "military operations other than war" [*feizhanzheng junshi xingdong*, 非战争军事行动] and expanded the geographic scope of the PLA's responsibility to safeguard Chinese national interests.

Reflecting this shift in Chinese emphasis, the organizers of the conference that yielded this book considered a wide range of contingencies where PLA involvement is likely or possible. Chapters in this book address domestic contingencies such as disaster response and suppressing internal unrest, border contingencies involving India, Burma, North Korea, Afghanistan, and Central Asia, and maritime contingencies in both the near and the far seas. Although Taiwan is not addressed in detail, it is used to illustrate the range of PLA national-level assets that might be brought to bear in a high-end military contingency.

Given that the PLA does not provide outsiders access to its contingency plans, a major challenge is finding enough information. The authors have used a variety of approaches to overcome this challenge, including examining PLA doctrine, reviewing military writings that discuss particular contingencies, looking at lessons learned from previous Chinese conflicts, reviewing how more accessible Chinese state organs conduct emergency planning, and gleaning lessons from PLA operations where more information about planning and capabilities is available. Some authors have even attempted to "reverse engineer" what PLA plans might look like based on their own military planning experience and open-source information about available local forces and national-level assets.

The effort to examine how the PLA might respond to particular contingencies in particular places produces some interesting insights unavailable from studying doctrine or evaluating new weapons systems. One important insight is the PLA's dependence on mobilizing civilian infrastructure, resources, and personnel to respond to both domestic and international contingencies. A second is how Chinese civil investments in transportation infrastructure— including a national highway system and high-speed rail networks—have given the PLA greater mobility and a new ability to marshal resources from multiple military regions. This new transportation infrastructure even extends to some remote parts of China bordering India, Burma, and Central Asia, increasing the PLA's capability to conduct cross-border operations.

A third insight is that expanded PLA capabilities—which now include space assets and counterspace weapons, cyberattack capabilities, conventional ballistic and cruise missiles, naval power projection capabilities, and a much more capable air force—may make it harder for the PLA to control escalation risks in the event of a crisis or conflict. A fourth, noted in many of the chapters, is that many examples of PLA deployments and contingency responses include explicit efforts to capture lessons learned and to incorporate them into planning and training for subsequent operations. This effort to close the feedback loop and learn from experience is designed to compensate for the PLA's lack of warfighting experience.

A fifth insight derived from observing the PLAN experience in conducting counterpiracy operations in the Gulf of Aden and noncombatant evacuation operations in Libya is that in certain low-intensity scenarios Chinese leaders are now confident enough to deploy PLA forces even if some important planning, training, and logistics support questions are not fully resolved. This suggests that the PLA is becoming a somewhat more flexible political and diplomatic instrument, at least in low-threat environments. A final question posed by several authors—but not fully answered—is whether the PLA's planning processes and command and control system, which have been focused heavily on a Taiwan contingency, will prove flexible and adaptable enough to respond to a more functionally and geographically diverse set of contingencies and operations.

This book is organized into four sections, beginning with an overview of Chinese contingency planning and then considering domestic, border, and maritime contingencies. The first section focuses on contingency planning within the PLA, the People's Armed Police (PAP) and Public Security forces, and the parallel civilian system of "emergency plans" to cover a range of situations. Chapters also consider the role of the Chinese mobilization system in contingency response and how PLA national-level assets might be employed in a contingency.

In "The PLA and Contingency Planning," Mark Cozad of the RAND Corporation examines the PLA's operational planning processes. He begins by reviewing the diverse set of security challenges China faces and the expansion of PLA missions under Hu Jintao's "new historic missions." Cozad details the intellectual framework the PLA uses to identify national interests, military missions, and key threats, focusing on the role of the Military Strategic Guidelines [*junshi zhanlüe fangzhen*, 军事战略方针] and the main strategic direction [*zhuyao zhanlüe fangxiang*, 主要战略方向]. He examines how these strategic concepts influence operational planning at the campaign level, the focus of PLA doctrinal innovation, and he illustrates how doctrine for specific campaigns is translated into the force and functional requirements necessary for operational plans. Cozad concludes by considering whether the PLA's comprehensive but data-intensive and highly centralized planning system, which is heavily focused on planning for a Taiwan contingency, can be adapted to allow planners the flexibility to address the growing range of potential missions and scenarios the PLA may be asked to support in the future.

In PLA Observations of U.S. Contingency Planning: What Has It Learned?" Marcelyn Thompson (U.S. Government) examines what the PLA admires about U.S. contingency planning and how it has influenced their own planning efforts. Reviewing Chinese writings on U.S. operations in Grenada, Iraq, Afghanistan, and Kosovo, she finds that Chinese analysts do not focus on the steps in the U.S. contingency planning process, but they give high praise to the U.S. military's ability to develop, revise, and implement plans quickly. The PLA admires three aspects of U.S. contingency planning in particular: the command, control, communications, computers, intelligence, surveillance, and reconnaissance (C4ISR) capabilities that enable the United States to assess the state of potential threats against which it should plan, the speed at which civilian and military leaders coordinate on the design and approval of contingency plans, and the numerous logistic support options in place around the globe to assist the United States in its contingency operations. Thompson argues that three aspects of the PLA's modernization program—national defense mobilization, logistics, and C4ISR—are likely to improve the PLA's ability to coordinate contingency plans and enable planning for a broad range of scenarios. However, she also suggests that automated decision aids and better C4ISR may deny PLA commanders the autonomy necessary to successfully implement their plans.

In "China Plans for Internal Unrest: People's Armed Police and Public Security Approaches to 'Mass Incidents,'" Jonathan Walton of the University of California, San Diego examines Chinese contingency plans for coping with social unrest. He reviews the nature and scope of unrest in China and then examines available information on the planning to mobilize domestic security forces to respond to unrest and the regulations that guide their responses. Walton describes the legislation that governs PAP and Public Security force responses to unrest and examines two specific contingency plans (the 2010 Xi'an municipal plan and 2006 Ningxia provincial plan) for large-scale mass incidents. He notes that political leaders have choices in how to respond to social unrest, including making concessions, arresting protest ringleaders, hoping unrest will die down, and using repression. Chinese laws and contingency plans focus on larger scale unrest, including provisions for reinforcing public security forces when they cannot handle a local protest, but also requiring higher level authorization for the use of PAP forces and the military. Walton argues that despite significant domestic security challenges, public security forces have been successful thus far in maintaining stability, although challenges may increase as the economy slows down, political reform remains unlikely, and systemic problems go unaddressed.

Catherine Welch of the CNA Corporation introduces China's civilian bureaucratic system of emergency response plans, describes China's approach to emergency response planning, and examines a number of these emergency responses plans in "Civilian Authorities and Contingency Planning in China." She argues that the emergency response planning system is an innovation in response to poor government performance in the avian influenza and severe acute respiratory syndrome crises in 2002–2003. The 2006 National Emergency Response Plan provides insight into the Chinese approach to emergency response planning since the document was approved at a high level, sets requirements and offers guidelines for other emergency plans, and categorizes emergencies by type and level of severity. Welch finds that there are six different types of emergency response plans (including the National Emergency Response Plan itself), that responsibility for emergency response planning is decentralized, that a whole-of-government effort is required to plan and prepare for both moderate and severe emergencies, and that provinces, ministries, and localities have all responded to the requirement to produce emergency plans. She uses China's response to a September 2012 earthquake in Yunnan province to illustrate how emergency plans affect actual crisis response, noting that emergency plans have particular value in specifying who is in charge of response to a particular type of crisis and which other actors have roles to play. Welch argues that studying civilian emergency response plans not only illuminates the PLA's role in particular emergencies, but also may provide insights into PLA planning.

"Converting the Potential to the Actual: Chinese Mobilization Policies and Planning" by Dean Cheng of the Heritage Foundation provides comprehensive information on Chinese defense mobilization policies and planning, which are focused on allowing maximum peacetime development of human, material, and financial power while having in place the mechanisms and plans to exploit them in the event of conflict. He highlights the role of the 2010 National Defense Mobilization Law in establishing peacetime mobilization preparations, guiding wartime mobilization implementation, and defining the coordination structures used at all levels to plan, coordinate, and implement mobilization. In general, Cheng concludes, "The military determines requirements, the National Defense Mobilization Committee implements coordination, and the government fulfills requirements." He notes that it is difficult to assess the performance of this elaborate apparatus because China has not engaged in a full mobilization for war. However, the structure does also provide for partial mobilizations that allow the PLA to mobilize civilian assets for smaller conflicts or contingencies.

In "Employment of National-Level PLA Assets in a Contingency: A Cross-Strait Conflict as Case Study," Mark Stokes of the Project 2049 Institute discusses the role of the Central Military Commission (CMC), the PLA General Staff Department, and the other three general departments in determining how national-level assets would be employed in a contingency. Stokes suggests that national-level PLA assets would likely be employed by a joint campaign command consisting of members from the four general departments, Air Force, Navy, and Second Artillery and reporting to the CMC. Stokes notes that the CMC would issue a "campaign decision" outlining the specific national PLA assets that would be assigned to and employed by a joint campaign command during a contingency. Such assets might include communications systems, intelligence, surveillance, and reconnaissance capabilities, electronic countermeasures, political warfare assets, counterspace systems, and long-range precision strike assets.

The second section of the book considers PLA responses to domestic contingencies. In "China's Armed Forces Respond to Internal Disaster Relief: Assessing Mobilization and Effort," Jeffrey Engstrom and Lyle Morris of the

RAND Corporation argue that PLA participation in internal disaster relief operations provides important evidence about mobilization capacity and manpower effort that can inform understanding of Chinese contingency response capacity across the spectrum of conflict. They begin by reviewing the internal disaster "threat environment" that China's armed forces face, focusing on which types of disasters are most frequent, where they occur, and how much damage they cause. Engstrom and Morris then examine PLA responses to four natural disasters (the 2008 winter storms, the 2008 Wenchuan earthquake, the 2010 Yushu earthquake, and the 2010 Zhouqu mudslides) and determine how much manpower was allocated to each operation, the distance covered to reach the disaster areas, and the amount of time it took PLA forces to arrive. They compare this data to mobilization efforts during the Korean War and 1979 Sino-Vietnamese War and conclude that Chinese mobilization capacity improved three to four times from the 1950s to the 1970s and has improved even more dramatically since then to reach the level of performance demonstrated in responses to the four disasters they examine.

Ma Chengkun of Taiwan's National Defense University details the evolution of the PLA's role in suppressing dissent and protest in his chapter, "PLA Response to Widespread Internal Unrest in the Han Homeland." During the Mao Zedong era, mass riots and protests were seen as counterrevolutionary actions, and the PLA was used to suppress them. Deng Xiaoping had a different view of protests but remained willing to use the PLA if available police forces were insufficient to suppress dissent. After the PLA was employed to suppress the 1989 Tiananmen protests, Jiang Zemin began to build PAP capabilities and made the organization the primary instrument to deal with significant social unrest. Hu Jintao further solidified the PAP's leading role with legislation that called it the "state's backbone and shock force in handling public emergencies." The PLA retains a role in suppressing widespread dissent, and Ma reviews the psychological impact on PLA troops who provided transportation and logistics support to PAP operations and the efforts of PLA political commissars to use political education and control of information to ensure that the PLA remains willing to follow party orders.

Thomas Woodrow, a retired Defense Intelligence Agency and U.S. Pacific Command analyst, argues in his chapter "PLA and Cross-Border Contingencies in North Korea and Burma" that both countries represent special interests for China, the former due to its historical alliance and role as a buffer state and the latter because of resources, longstanding economic and military cooperation, and its position as a strategic gateway to the Indian Ocean. Woodrow suggests that current Chinese plans for cross-border contingencies in North Korea and Burma probably focus on protecting stability and preventing refugee flows, although the PLA must also be ready to deal with issues involving North Korean weapons of mass destruction and potential military intervention by the United States or South Korea in the event of a North Korean collapse. He reviews the available forces and transportation infrastructure that the PLA could employ in the event of a contingency. Woodrow concludes that by the end of the current decade, existing contingency plans will likely be modified to reflect expanding Chinese economic and security interests and a greater Chinese willingness to act unilaterally to protect its interests.

In "PLA Contingency Planning and the Case of India," Larry Wortzel of Asia Strategies and Risks argues that the most likely source of Sino-India conflict is the continuing dispute about the border. He considers the lessons India and China learned from the 1962 border war and how these might affect a future border conflict. The PLA concluded that it is preferable to resolve a border conflict through diplomatic means but that if diplomacy fails, the PLA must be prepared to fight in high altitudes and extremely cold conditions. Given the terrain and conditions, the PLA must conduct independent operations in different areas and directions while also taking advantage of engineers, camouflage units, communications units, weather organizations, artillery and missiles, and specialized reserve forces. Wortzel suggests that unlike the 1962 war, a contemporary conflict would likely expand into the cyber and air domains. He argues that the threat of nuclear weapons use would likely limit escalation but highlights the potential for conventional ballistic missile strikes deep into adversary territory as a potentially destabilizing action.

In "Like a Good Neighbor: Chinese Intervention through the Shanghai Cooperation Organization," Ben Lowsen of the U.S. Army examines how China might use the Shanghai Cooperation Organization (SCO) to intervene in Central Asia or Afghanistan in response to separatist and terrorist threats to its control of Xinjiang. Chinese decisions about whether and how to intervene would be tied to an assessment of China's interests, perceived threats, means available to ameliorate the situation, and political feasibility. Lowsen argues that China has an array of means and approaches it might use, including leveraging multilateral frameworks such as the SCO, supporting regional partners with economic and security assistance or with communications, intelligence, and space-based support, conducting military operations other than war such as training local military forces and participating in peacekeeping operations, and intervening across the border with conventional forces. He concludes that China is likely to seek to minimize its involvement, using indirect means before considering more difficult and risky direct methods such as military intervention.

In "The PLA and Near Seas Maritime Sovereignty Disputes," Alexander Chieh-cheng Huang of Tamkang University describes five types of potential near seas contingencies and reviews three recent examples where People's Liberation Army naval forces have been involved. He examines China's naval strategy and the evolution of PLAN operational thinking and force modernization. Huang describes the role of Chinese maritime paramilitary forces in near seas contingencies and reviews Beijing's efforts to consolidate five separate maritime forces into a new China Coast Guard. He considers the PLAN role in near seas contingencies, noting that the Coast Guard appears to have the leading role in the most likely contingencies, with the PLAN playing a supporting role. Huang concludes that this situation is likely to change in the future, with the PLAN increasing its presence and roles in the near seas.

Michael Chase of the RAND Corporation examines the 2011 Chinese evacuation operation in Libya in "The PLA and Far Seas Contingencies: Chinese Capabilities for Noncombatant Evacuation Operations." The large and growing presence of PRC citizens overseas (often in unstable places) and public expectations that the Chinese government should protect them will generate increasing demand for the PLA to evacuate citizens in danger. Chase notes that the Ministry of Foreign Affairs played the lead role in the Libya operation and that 90 percent of the 36,000 Chinese citizens were evacuated before the first PLAN ships and PLA Air Force (PLAAF) Il-76 transports arrived. He judges the operation as successful but notes that it demonstrated the limited airlift and sealift capabilities of the PLA. Chase notes that the PLA is developing and deploying a number of new capabilities useful for future evacuation missions, such as large amphibious ships, aircraft carriers, and transport aircraft. However, he concludes that it is unclear whether the PLA has developed doctrine to cover evacuation operations and that limitations in lift capability and interagency coordination could prove problematic in more demanding evacuation scenarios.

Kristen Gunness and Samuel Berkowitz of the RAND Corporation discuss naval deployment planning efforts in their chapter, "PLA Navy Planning for

Out of Area Deployments." They argue that changes in doctrine, increased emphasis on at-sea training, efforts to improve political education for long deployments, and a more flexible logistics system all laid the groundwork for the PLAN's successful counterpiracy deployments in the Gulf of Aden. Their case study of how the navy planned for these missions and the challenges it encountered addresses the areas of logistics and replenishment, equipment and maintenance, training, care for personnel, and communications. Gunness and Berkowitz note that the initial group of ships began their deployment in December 2008 without completing all necessary crew training and without having finalized logistics support arrangements, and they describe PLAN efforts to incorporate lessons learned from each deployment into predeployment training for future crews. They argue that the PLAN has improved its expeditionary capabilities and ability to plan for long-term deployments but that substantial logistics and communications challenges remain.

When taken as a whole, the chapters in this volume help illuminate how the PLA conducts deliberate and crisis planning for contingencies, highlight the importance of "whole-of-government" military and civilian responses to both domestic and international contingencies, and examine a wide and expanding range of contingencies where PLA involvement is possible. The chapters document that improving PLA capabilities are giving Chinese leaders new options in responding to domestic and international crises, while noting that the PLA still has significant limitations in projecting and sustaining power, especially at longer distances and in contested environments.

Although China has an expanding array of interests around the world to protect, self-imposed constraints such as no alliances and no overseas bases continue to limit Beijing's ability to employ military power in response to crises and contingencies.[11] There are ongoing debates within China about whether those constraints and China's longstanding foreign policy principles of "nonintervention" and "noninterference in the internal affairs of other countries" still make sense for an emerging global power.[12] Although the chapters in this book focus on the potential for the PLA to become actively involved in a range of contingencies, Chinese leaders remain cautious and wary of taking on responsibility for international problems. The extent to which the PLA becomes more involved in responding to contingencies as opposed to simply planning for them will depend on the extent to which domestic and international developments affect Chinese and CCP interests and on whether Chinese leaders become more willing to employ military power to protect those interests and to shape China's external security environment.

Notes

1   Mark A. Stokes and Ian Easton, "The Chinese People's Liberation Army General Staff Department: Evolving Organization and Missions," in *The PLA as Organization*, 2nd ed. (Vienna, VA: DGI, Inc., 2015).

2   PLA use of the term *campaign* differs from U.S. military use. U.S. doctrine defines a *campaign plan* as "a joint operation plan for a series of related major operations aimed at achieving strategic or operational objectives within a given time and space." Joint Publication (JP) 5-0, *Joint Operation Planning* (Washington, DC: Chairman of the Joint Chiefs of Staff, 2011). In contrast, PLA campaign doctrine focuses on how to employ particular types of forces to achieve narrower operational objectives; several different types of campaigns might need to be executed simultaneously in a conflict.

3   Ibid.

4   Mark Cozad, "The PLA and Contingency Planning," in this volume.

5   Stokes and Easton; and Catherine Welch, "Civilian Authorities and Contingency Planning in China," in this volume.

6   Marcelyn Thompson, "PLA Observations of U.S. Contingency Planning: What Has It Learned?" in this volume.

7   The Gulf of Aden counterpiracy deployment is discussed extensively by Kristen Gunness and Sam Berkowitz, while the March 2011 Libya evacuation is covered by Michael Chase in their respective chapters in this volume. Details on PLA participation in the search for the missing Malaysian airliner are at "PLA in Rescue Mission of Malaysia Missing Jet," China Military Online Special Report, March 2014, available at <http://eng.chinamil.com.cn/special-reports/node_68043.htm>.

8   Cozad.

9   For an earlier look at potential contingencies, see Paul B. Stares et al., *Managing Instability on China's Periphery* (Washington, DC: Council on Foreign Relations, 2011).

10   See Daniel Hartnett, *Towards a Globally Focused Chinese Military: The Historic Missions of the Chinese Armed Forces,* Project Asia (Alexandria, VA: The CNA Corporation, June 2008).

11   For a comprehensive overview of China's global interests and the means available to protect them, see David Shambaugh, *China Goes Global: The Partial Power* (New York: Oxford University Press, 2013).

12   See Mathieu Duchâtel, Oliver Bräuner, and Zhou Hang, *Protecting China's Overseas Interests: The Slow Shift away from Non-interference*, SIPRI Policy Paper No. 41 (Stockholm: Stockholm International Peace Research Institute, 2014).

I

THINKING AND PLANNING FOR CONTINGENCIES

CHAPTER 1

The PLA and Contingency Planning

Mark Cozad

rguably the most significant and pervasive trend during Hu Jintao's term (2004–2012) as chairman of the Central Military Commission (CMC) has been the People's Liberation Army's (PLA's) expanding emphasis on planning and force structure requirements to address what leaders view as an increasingly complex, interconnected, and challenging international security environment. The characteristics and general direction outlined for the PLA are captured in the Military Strategic Guidelines and more specifically detailed in the concept of the New Historic Missions [*xin de lishi shiming*, 新的历史使命].[1] This new direction has generated considerable analysis within PLA strategy and planning circles about future PLA roles and missions, the new requirements necessitated by expanding operational environments and domains, and the increasing importance of nontraditional, nonwar threats. The overall impact on PLA strategic planning remains to some extent uncertain, particularly in the realm of force structure requirements. PLA leaders continue to debate and analyze future scenarios and the related operational requirements. For operational planners, however, these new challenges present both immediate concerns—most notably in the realm of what the PLA terms "diversified military tasks" [*duoyanghua junshi renwu*, 多样化军事任务]—and a host of potential future planning requirements to support China's increasing global presence and continued territorial disputes.[2]

This chapter examines the PLA's operational planning processes and the considerations that have driven planning, particularly since the major doctrinal revisions that took place in the 1990s.[3] It begins by reviewing the diverse set of security challenges China faces and the expansion of PLA missions under the new historic missions. Next, the chapter describes the intellectual framework the PLA uses to identify national interests, military missions, and key threats, focusing on the role of the Military Strategic Guidelines and the main strategic direction. It then examines how these strategic concepts influence operational planning at the campaign level, the focus of PLA doctrinal innovation. The chapter then illustrates how doctrine for specific campaigns is translated into the force and functional requirements necessary for operational plans. The conclusion considers whether the PLA's comprehensive but data-intensive and highly centralized planning system can be adapted to allow planners to address the growing range of potential missions and scenarios the PLA may be asked to support in the future.

The PLA doctrinal revision process yielded numerous publications for both reference and instructional purposes that were largely derived from observations of modern conflicts and foreign planning systems.[4] While universally applicable, this body of work focuses heavily on large-scale conventional conflict of the type reflected in the PLA's Taiwan planning. These doctrinal materials provide insight into PLA strategic and operational thinking on a wide range of emerging security challenges, but they also reveal that PLA planners have not grappled with new challenges in the same detail as they have for Taiwan-centric scenarios. The 2006 edition of *The Science of Campaigns* attempted to incorporate new security issues such as counterterrorism, but it remains heavily focused on conventional conflicts.[5]

The key issue is whether the PLA operational planning system developed over the past 20 years will prove flexible and adaptable enough as China's leaders press the PLA to develop capabilities and operational plans to protect the country's growing interests. The PLA probably will not need to overhaul its entire model to address the new planning problems associated with numerous new requirements. Superficial workarounds, however, are unlikely to alleviate the need for more adaptable processes and for planners with new skills necessary to plan for dynamic situations falling short of major conventional war. The PLA's ability to adapt its planning will be a major determinant of its success in dealing with new operating environments and contingencies.

New Challenges Driving Plans

Over the past decade, the PLA's most important planning scenario centered on Taiwan and fears that Taiwan's political leaders would take actions that would require significant military responses to either reverse pro-independence trends or force unification with the mainland.[6] The defeat of the Democratic Progressive Party (DPP) in Taiwan's 2008 legislative and presidential elections eased Chinese fears and stabilized cross-strait relations. Despite reduced tensions, Taiwan remains the PLA's most significant planning concern and primary operational focus. This emphasis is unlikely to change in the foreseeable future, especially given the DPP's renewed success in 2014 local elections. However, future PLA planning efforts and force requirements cannot neglect the multitude of new security threats and operational requirements that must be considered alongside heavy resource commitments to operational planning for Taiwan. The PLA will have to deal with a much more complex, dynamic set of strategic and operational planning scenarios rather than the Taiwan-focused challenges that dominated PLA thinking from the early 1990s through 2008.

Several recent crises have brought the new dimensions of China's security concerns into focus. Maritime confrontations in 2012 with the Philippines over Scarborough Shoal and with Japan over the Senkaku/Diaoyu Islands highlighted how disputes over maritime and territorial boundaries could present PLA planners with urgent new planning requirements to defend China's claims. Concerns about instability on the Korean Peninsula have also presented PLA planners with another multifaceted problem: maintaining border security and territorial integrity in the midst of a potential crisis with the United States and South Korea over a nuclear-armed neighbor. New diversified military tasks in nontraditional and nonwar areas have also received significant attention from senior PLA leaders.[7] Natural disaster response, internal instability, terrorism, piracy, and energy and resource security have occupied considerable space in the debate about how China should shape its military.[8] There is little evidence that PLA planners are currently devoting significant time and resources to developing comprehensive operational plans for these new scenarios. The level of effort future PLA planners place on developing operational plans for these problems will depend on the degree to which China's leaders perceive these trends as persistent and important threats. Greater emphasis on nontraditional missions and contingencies will challenge PLA planners to be more flexible and force PLA leaders to accept trade-offs between the ability to respond to traditional and nontraditional contingencies.

Most recently, the 2013 version of *The Science of Military Strategy*, an authoritative Academy of Military Science publication, has identified four potential types of conflict the People's Republic of China (PRC) might face in the future: large-scale, high-intensity wars, "relatively large-scale, relatively high-intensity" wars to counter separatism, "small- to medium-scale, low- to medium-intensity" operations for self-defense, and small-scale, low-intensity operations to counter terrorism, maintain stability, and defend territorial rights.[9] This list of potential future conflicts encapsulates the range of security concerns discussed above. The first category is viewed as an unlikely but highly dangerous situation in which the United States seeks to militarily counter China's rise or escalate conflict if it faces losing in a smaller-scale military operation.[10] The remaining three options cover a full range of scenarios that might include Taiwan, North Korea (or other potential instability on China's borders), the South China Sea, the East China Sea, and the protection of Chinese citizens overseas.[11] Though this list provides a broad range of potential future conflict scenarios, this publication does not identify those scenarios for which PLA planners have been directed to develop operational plans.

Central Planning Guidance

The Military Strategic Guidelines (MSG) [*junshi zhanlüe fangzhen*, 军事战略方针] set the PLA's operational planning parameters.[12] This document provides overarching guidance on a wide range of issues that dictate the PLA's future missions and force structure as well as the operational scenarios for which the PLA must plan. It defines the core strategic tasks the PLA must undertake to achieve China's strategic objectives. The guidelines define general trends in the international security situation, current and future trends in warfare, and the critical military capabilities required to meet the challenges presented by modern adversaries and new domains. Its comprehensive guidance defines the PLA's strategic objectives, strategic military tasks, main strategic direction, and other imperatives that give focus to operational planning and development timelines within the PLA.[13] Four areas within the MSG have particular importance for PLA operational planning: the strategic objective, the main strategic direction, strategic deployment, and the patterns of strategic action.

The MSG's strategic objectives [*zhanlüe mudi*, 战略目的] set the direction for PLA planning and development by outlining China's national interests and the PLA's role in securing national objectives. China's general strategic objective is to "ensure the peaceful, stable and good development of the strategic environment at home and abroad" to guarantee national reform and continued modernization.[14] The PLA's role in supporting this objective is to strengthen China's comprehensive national power, promote a peaceful and stable environment, ensure that China's interests will not be encroached upon, prevent invasion by foreign powers, and win future wars and armed conflicts.[15] These strategic objectives set the primary requirements driving PLA strategic and operational planning and are tied to the new historic missions concept promulgated by Hu Jintao.[16] The concept consists of four components: "providing an important guarantee of strength for the party to consolidate its ruling position; providing a strong security guarantee for safeguarding the period of important strategic opportunity for national development; providing a powerful strategic support for safeguarding national interests; and playing an important role in safeguarding world peace and promoting common development."[17] The new historic missions are broad, general statements of strategic intent that provide PLA planners few specifics on future force structure and particular operational scenarios. For outside observers, the new historic missions provide only limited insights for understanding PLA current and future operational planning.

The PLA's specific operational planning efforts rest on the MSG's determination of the main strategic direction [*zhuyao zhanlüe fangxiang*, 主要战略方向], which is the key to realizing strategic objectives and accomplishing strategic tasks.[18] The main strategic direction is determined by the direction and severity of primary threats and is based on the nature and priority of competing interests, the relative strengths of forces, geography, and the overall strategic situation in the region. The delineation between the primary and secondary strategic directions is largely based on the weighting of one threat against others in their respective directions. Multiple simultaneous threats require coordinated planning and deconfliction of resources and efforts among a potentially dispersed set of geographic boundaries. As a concept that applies to both the strategic and campaign levels of warfare, the strategic direction is a crucial link between objectives and warfighting.[19] Understanding which threats are strategic directions—a designation that corresponds to a specific geographical orientation or a particular domain—provides critical information about the focus of PLA operational planning efforts.

PLA operational planning has benefitted from stability in China's strategic focus. As one PLA strategist highlighted, China's main strategic direction has only shifted four times since 1949. Previous strategic directions included a focus against the United States in the early 1950s to early 1960s, toward the

Soviet Union and United States in the mid-1960s and early 1970s, and against the Soviet Union from the early 1970s to the mid-1980s.[20] China's current direction is focused on "improving the strategic situation on the southern front, strengthening the development of border and maritime defense, managing and maneuvering on the high seas, and maintaining our maritime rights and interests."[21] Taiwan has remained the PLA's main strategic direction and the focus of its planning and modernization efforts since the promulgation of the Military Strategic Guidelines for the New Era in 1993.[22] While the PLA has almost certainly planned for other contingencies such as territorial disputes in the South and East China seas and for disaster relief, counterpiracy, and counterterrorism efforts, the weight of these scenarios in PLA planning and modernization is uncertain.[23] Expanding PLA missions, many of which will likely be outside the familiar setting of East Asia, will force PLA planners to adapt to a much more diverse and dynamic set of scenarios and requirements.

The strategic deployment of forces [*zhanlüe bushu*, 战略部署] and the patterns of strategic action [*zhanlüe xingdong yangshi*, 战略行动样式] are two essential concepts derived from the determination of the main strategic direction.[24] Both are meant to place PLA forces in strategically important locations according to the functions key units will be expected to perform in wartime settings. In this context, strategic deployment is the organization and disposition of forces in all directions based on geographic requirements and the relative balance of forces between the PLA and the opposing side. Strategic deployment considerations are designed to bolster both wartime and peacetime strength and disposition in a way that maximizes offensive and defensive capabilities and allows for the most flexible reaction to numerous different strategic challenges and contingencies.

The impact the main strategic direction has on planning and force disposition is clearly demonstrated by the shift in PLA strategic direction in the late 1980s. During the second half of the Cold War, the PLA's main strategic direction was the Soviet threat in the north, and the bulk of the PLA's forces and its most significant capabilities were located in the military regions in northern China. With the shift in main strategic direction to Taiwan in the early 1990s, PLA resources and planning efforts shifted to southeastern China.[25] This example demonstrates two key issues central to PLA planning over the past 60 years. First, the main strategic direction's relative stability allowed PLA planners to place forces in strategically and operationally advantageous locations to respond to one primary threat. PLA forces in these areas were able to focus on their key assigned task without having to address a diverse range of mission requirements. Second, the forward deployment of PLA forces reduced demands on the PLA's logistical capacity and deemphasized the need for long-distance, rapid mobility. These issues highlight a critical tension in the PLA's planning process that may lead to future difficulties. A PLA capable of addressing the traditional and nontraditional security threats China will face as a globally engaged power will require major changes away from a static, continental approach to planning.

Patterns of strategic action accompany the main strategic direction as a link between the strategic and campaign levels of war. Where the main strategic direction is tied to a concrete geographic focus and threat, patterns of strategic action are a manifestation of the PLA's understanding of the key trends in warfare. These trends include emerging and dominant operational concepts—such as noncontact warfare—that the PLA may be required to execute or counter in future conflicts and the specific operational capabilities and technologies supporting these concepts.[26] The PLA's patterns of strategic action address a wide range of characteristics that influence the specific nature of conflicts, including the domains in which they reside, lines of communication and defense, and the types of operations most prevalent in modern warfare. These patterns are tied closely to PLA operational-level thinking, which is built around military campaigns designed as the centerpiece of modern warfare and the primary operational means for achieving China's wartime strategic objectives.

Doctrinal Development for Future Wars

One of the PLA's most significant achievements in the past 20 years has been the development of a broad body of authoritative doctrine to guide operations and planning. This process provides a means for comprehensively studying warfare, developing new operational concepts based on these studies, conducting experimentation, and then codifying the results into operational doctrine.[27] As a system, it captures the most significant components of PLA operational thinking and provides important insights into the types of conflicts for which PLA planners likely spend the most time preparing. The most significant of these documents focus on both the strategic and campaign levels and have been written by teams assembled from the Academy of Military Sciences (AMS) and the National Defense University (NDU). The most noteworthy contribution to the PLA's guiding doctrine on operational planning to come out of AMS is *The Science of Military Strategy*, published in Chinese in 2000 and in an English version in 2006; a revised version was published in 2013. NDU published an analogous document detailing military strategic considerations in 1999 titled *The Science of Strategy*.[28] These documents provide valuable insight into the strategic considerations and decisions that guide PLA operational planning, particularly the strategic assessment of the situation and determination of the main strategic direction. They also provide insight into the national-level requirements essential to the PLA's overall wartime planning such as mobilization, psychological operations, strategic defense, information operations, political work, and deterrence.[29]

The PLA's doctrinal development at the operational level has produced an even more significant body of work. The most authoritative publication for operational art in the PLA remains *The Science of Campaigns*, first published by NDU in 2000 and then updated and revised in 2006.[30] These documents, along with another large volume from NDU entitled *Campaign Theory Study Guide*, capture PLA thinking across the entire campaign level of war and reflect the fusion of the PLA's long process of observation, research, and experience in its own wars and those of others.[31] Campaign studies reflect an essential component in PLA doctrinal development and operational planning derived from a methodology that covers key technical developments, the status of operational art among opponents, historical observations, lessons learned from foreign militaries, and modeling and simulation.[32] This analysis provides a detailed explanation of the joint and single-service ("combined" in PLA terminology) campaigns that are the centerpiece of PLA operational planning and employment.

The principles and campaigns outlined in these texts are viewed by PLA strategists as the most significant operational issues the PLA is likely to confront under the conditions outlined in the MSG. When the earliest version of *The Science of Campaigns* was published in 2000, this condition was understood as "Local Wars Under High-Tech Conditions" [*gaojishu tiaojian xia jubu zhanzheng*, 高技术条件下局部战争].[33] In recognition of the increasing importance of information technology in modern warfare, this statement was later amended to address local wars under conditions of "informationization" [*xinxihua*, 信息化].[34] The relationship between the MSG conditions and the campaigns outlined in these publications demonstrates the degree to which PLA operational thinking and planning are shaped by strategic considerations regarding the international security environment and current trends in warfare. The stability in PLA strategic thinking is reflected in its approach to campaigns. Although *The Science of Campaigns* was updated between 2000 and 2006, there were relatively few major changes to the PLA's overarching campaign structure; the most significant change in the 2006 edition was the addition of the counterterrorism campaign.[35]

The consistency and stability in PLA campaign doctrine should not be viewed as evidence of stagnation. The PLA has demonstrated over the past two decades that it is capable of making substantial changes in both technology and operations. As PLA campaigns remain relatively consistent over the long term, the most significant changes in operational capability occur through the development of new operational concepts and experimentation.[36] New ideas and ways to implement them are performed in a manner consistent with the PLA's understanding of the strategic trends in warfare and their applicability to the campaigns they believe will predominate in modern local wars.

Two examples of critical operational concepts are the development of the "three attacks, three defenses" [*san da san fang*, 三打三防] and "noncontact warfare" [*bujiechu zhan*, 不接触战] concepts following U.S. air operations over Yugoslavia.[37] Both identified key trends based on observations of U.S. capabilities and operations that the PLA viewed as significant new imperatives guiding modern warfare. U.S. advances in airpower; intelligence, surveillance, and reconnaissance (ISR); command and control; and precision guided munitions (PGM) led PLA observers to conclude that fundamental shifts in the nature of warfare had taken place. As a result, the PLA envisioned new concepts of operation that would enable it to "attack" stealth aircraft, cruise missiles, PGMs, and attack helicopters ("three attacks"), and defend against electronic warfare, ISR, and precision attack capabilities ("three defenses") while minimizing direct confrontation between armies (noncontact warfare). Chinese military researchers viewed these new concepts as necessary for success in future wars, particularly against modern adversaries, with the U.S. military identified as the standard. In both cases, PLA strategists performed detailed study of these trends and concepts that culminated in experimentation efforts to operationalize them across the military. The PLA has experimented in a range of areas its leaders view as essential for success in future campaigns, including long-range maneuver, logistics, and joint operations.[38] Understanding the context within these concepts and the specific areas in which experimentation is taking place is essential for analyzing PLA operational planning. Campaigns set the broad parameters for PLA planning, but new operational concepts reflect specific practices and imperatives for conducting the operations necessary to obtain the overall objectives behind the planning.

Diversified military tasks and military operations other than war (MOOTW) [*feizhanzheng junshi xingdong*, 非战争军事行动] have become significant themes in PLA doctrinal discussions due to the new historic missions. The PLA's expanding role in supporting nontraditional military requirements and threats has taken on considerable significance, particularly in countering terrorism and piracy. The PLA will also be expected to provide increasing support to China's foreign policy and domestic stability objectives by increasing military diplomacy and PLA readiness to support disaster relief. The extent to which these new missions will absorb planning resources remains unclear, but the PLA's role in these diversified military tasks is likely to increase with the PRC's expanding global presence. The PLA's success in adapting will rely ultimately on the nature and flexibility of its planning system. The current process is highly centralized and devotes the majority of planning resources to addressing various aspects and campaigns associated with the Taiwan problem. Expanding future missions could generate major challenges for this system if the current process remains highly centralized while the number of these missions expands considerably. However, at this point, there is little evidence to suggest that the PLA is contemplating any significant changes to its planning processes.

Force Requirements, Organization, and Disposition

The forces required to support the PLA's expanding missions depend heavily on two factors: the categories of forces required for campaign operations, and the system-of-systems construct central to PLA thinking about the functional employment of forces. PLA operational art is centered on campaigns. In terms of organization, the type of campaign will dictate operational objectives and the types of forces required to meet those objectives. Campaigns also prescribe the principal structure for command and control and headquarters functions overseeing service forces arrayed in the various operations groups assigned to a specific campaign.[39] Based on the type of joint campaign (island landing, blockade, border counterattack, and so forth), operations groups will provide a hybrid service-functional structure for commanding and controlling the units assigned to them. Geographically, campaign forces will perform their functions within a given strategic direction based on an assigned task.

PLA doctrinal publications outline several categories of forces required for success in modern campaigns including:[40]

- information operations
- firepower
- mobility
- support
- ISR
- precision strike
- electronic warfare
- command and control
- operational support
- logistics and equipment support
- protection.

Based on the specific objectives and types of campaigns, PLA planners can draw on the mix of capabilities best suited to the campaign objectives and geography. PLA modernization efforts over the past two decades have focused on developing the technological and operational capabilities required for each of these specific categories. Experimentation, particularly in the realm of joint operations, has been an essential component of modernization and provides a more detailed understanding of how specific forces are being linked together in operational scenarios.

The other critical employment consideration for PLA forces is the system-of-systems [*tixi*, 体系] approach embedded in the PLA's campaign construct. While campaigns serve as the primary organizing mechanism for PLA forces at the operational level, combat systems are the main method for functionally grouping capabilities. According to the *Campaign Theory Study Guide*, in this dual construct "modern campaigns are the confrontation between combat systems," and "paralyzing the enemy's combat system has become an important means of winning a war."[41] The difference between the forces and systems considerations becomes more apparent when examining a specific campaign such as the joint anti–air raid campaign. From the campaign organizational perspective, service and functional capabilities are brought together and organized within air, ground, naval, and missile operations groups along with associated functional operations groups such as information operations, denial and deception, and special operations added depending on the scope of the campaign's objectives and missions.[42] In terms of a joint anti–air raid combat system, the key capabilities are viewed in terms of the following functions: intelligence early warning, information operations, resistance operations, counterattack operations, and protection operations.[43] Understanding these two characteristics of how campaign forces are arrayed is essential to understanding the types of forces involved in a campaign and how they will fight. These two concepts also highlight the functions PLA planners will emphasize in planning and coordinating the various parts of the campaign and combat system. Coordination among the service operations groups is essential for synchronizing the resources and activities composing the combat system.

Specific force requirements will be determined by the nature of the campaign and the combat systems supporting that campaign, the scale of the conflict, and the adversary's capability and level of technology. In the overall framework of PLA force planning and thinking about future contingencies, U.S. military actions are the most challenging threat planners must confront. In central planning efforts focused on Taiwan, the potential for U.S. involvement has weighed heavily in force modernization and the development of operational concepts designed to counter key U.S. technological advantages. Similar concerns about U.S. intervention are probably factored into planning scenarios for the Korean Peninsula and for maritime disputes in the South and East China seas. The U.S. Air-Sea Battle concept has been a particular focus and concern for PLA observers since the 2010 Quadrennial Defense Review. Developing counters to it will likely serve as the centerpiece for many PLA regional planning scenarios.[44] Other regional powers such as Japan, Vietnam, and India could drive future contingency planning efforts; however, at this point there is limited evidence suggesting that PLA planners have conducted in-depth planning to address these specific operational scenarios.

A critical factor underpinning PLA planning is the requirement for modern logistics and mobility to ensure flexibility in responding to the new security challenges facing China and the PLA.[45] In recent years, the PLA has put extensive effort into improving these two areas based on its perceived shortcomings. When the PLA's planning predominantly focused on the Soviet Union, its overall manpower was considerably greater and geographically focused. Logistics and mobility were important, but positioning and numbers could compensate for many shortcomings. Analyzing the U.S. victory in the first Gulf War and observing military operations in a variety of other theaters, PLA strategists have come to realize that modern wars require improved flexibility and rely more heavily on logistics and maintenance support than at any time in history. Advances in command and control and information technologies now provide military planners significantly greater capability to plan and track the force movements required to fight on an increasingly dynamic battlefield that includes new domains. Joint operations also present opportunities for consolidating logistics and mobility capabilities that were previously service-specific and frequently duplicative. Exploiting these new possibilities is essential in light of PLA efforts to consolidate and streamline forces while meeting an expanded array of challenges such as defending national unity (that is, preventing Taiwan independence), protecting territorial claims in border disputes (against India and claimants along the PRC's southeastern and northeastern borders), defending maritime claims (vis-à-vis Japan and Southeast Asian claimants), and combatting nontraditional threats (piracy, terrorism, and disaster relief).

Conclusion

This chapter has described the intellectual framework that guides PLA planners, integrating strategic factors such as PRC national interests, PLA missions, and geographically oriented threat assessments with operational- and campaign-level factors. Unfortunately, the output of this planning process remains opaque given the lack of access to specific plans and limited information on which contingencies are the primary focus for PLA planners. The process itself, as outlined in PLA doctrinal publications, is comprehensive but also data-intensive and highly centralized. The most pressing analytical question at this time is whether the PLA can adapt its planning system to allow planners to address the growing range of potential missions and scenarios the PLA may be asked to support. The current military strategic framework outlined in *The Science of Military Strategy* and the campaign framework outlined in the two versions of *The Science of Campaigns* demonstrate that while some modifications have been made, PLA leaders appear to still be focused on relatively large-scale conventional operations. In some cases—such as disaster relief and humanitarian operations—PLA planning processes for large-scale movements of forces and equipment appear to translate readily. In other cases, it is unclear whether PLA planners would be able to adapt quickly, particularly to unexpected crises.

PLA doctrine addresses a large range of potential contingencies through discussions on campaigns and on the requirements for the operational level of war. Taiwan scenarios have played a dominant role in PLA thinking about campaigns, and PLA doctrine reflects this focus. Other scenarios involving disputes along China's land borders and maritime disputes in the South and East China seas also fit well into the overall construct that allows for wars of various scales, different levels of enemy capability, and third-party intervention. Within this construct, PLA planners have been exposed to a large body of coherent doctrine over an extended period of time. This thought has guided many aspects of PLA training, exercises, and experimentation and is deeply rooted in a generation of PLA officers.

If Chinese leaders pursue a more globally oriented military posture, a key determinant of PLA success in meeting new requirements will be whether the PLA can modify its doctrine and planning process to address new types of conflicts outside of China's traditional regional confines and adopt a more flexible, and perhaps more decentralized, approach. A long-term, deliberate shift in focus would allow the PLA to adapt to address these issues gradually and comprehensively. However, if China's interests in other areas are under immediate threat, the PLA may be asked to respond with a planning system not suited to the task. The current system has worked reasonably well because China is a central player in regional dynamics—the threats and disputes are well understood, even if not entirely predictable or controllable. A more global posture, which the new historic missions imply, could challenge PLA planners by forcing them to deal with a wide variety of new problems and uncertainties for which they have little historic experience or preparation. Such a posture would also present new logistics and command and control challenges that would need to be incorporated into operational planning. This would test the PLA's operational planning assumptions and the process they underpin. Nontraditional security threats and the diversified military tasks that stem from them could also stress the PLA planning system if not managed adroitly by China's military and political leaders.

Critical questions remain about the suitability of the PLA's planning process for a more diverse and geographically distributed set of challenges. First, if presented with simultaneous crises, will PLA planners be able to adequately plan and provide options for China's senior leaders? The most difficult challenge is not a single crisis with two or three stressing scenarios, but a steady stream of new threats and scenarios that China's leaders feel compelled to address. Second, what effect will these new operational requirements have on the PLA's planning capability across a range of scenarios? Planning for less intense, nontraditional scenarios requires different skill sets in ISR, targeting, and command and control, as well as expertise in subjects such as counterterrorism and international law. A sustained commitment to this type of contingency planning could adversely affect the PLA capability to plan for the large-scale conflicts that it regards as its primary missions. Currently, this prospect appears to be extremely limited. However, future security threats stemming from China's expanding interests and increased global engagement could place the PLA into a situation where its planners are forced to divert resources from the task of in-depth planning for major conventional war to respond to unexpected immediate crises.

Notes

1   David Finkelstein, "China's National Military Strategy: An Overview of the 'Military Strategic Guidelines,'" in *Right-Sizing the People's Liberation Army: Exploring the Contours of China's Military*, eds. Roy Kamphausen and Andrew Scobell (Carlisle, PA: Strategic Studies Institute, May 2007), 82–87; and James Mulvenon, "Chairman Hu and the PLA's 'New Historic Missions,'" *China Leadership Monitor*, no. 27 (Winter 2009).

2   Information Office of the State Council, People's Republic of China, *China's National Defense in 2006* (Beijing: Information Office of the State Council, December 29, 2006). Continued discussion of diversified military tasks is present in all subsequent iterations of *China's National Defense*. In addition, this subject is discussed at length in Andrew Scobell and Andrew J. Nathan, "China's Overstretched Military," *The Washington Quarterly* 25, no.4 (Fall 2012), 135–148.

3   This chapter will not address the entire body of texts but will instead focus on the most significant foundational documents. In-depth studies from various institutions have provided detailed analysis of the specific capabilities and operations outlined in the documents cited in this paper. An in-depth discussion of their findings is beyond the scope of this paper.

4   See Andrew Scobell, David Lai, and Roy Kamphausen, eds., *Chinese Lessons from Other Peoples' Wars* (Carlisle Barracks, PA: Strategic Studies Institute, 2011).

5   Zhang Yuliang [张玉良], ed., *The Science of Campaigns* [战役学] (Beijing: National Defense University Press [国防大学出版社], 2006).

6   Office of the Secretary of Defense (OSD), *Military and Security Developments Involving the People's Republic of China*, 2012, Annual Report to Congress (Washington, DC: OSD, May 2012), iv.

7   Wu Tianmin and Ding Haiming [武天敏, 丁海明], "Key Lies in Building Core Military Capabilities" [关键是打造核心军事能力], *PLA Daily* [解放军报], June 9, 2008.

8   Shan Xiufa [单秀法], "The People's Armed Forces That Are Marching Toward Modernization" [迈向现代化的人民军队], *Liaowang* [瞭望], no. 32 (August 6, 2012), 40–41.

9   Shou Xiaosong [寿晓松], ed., *The Science of Military Strategy* [战略学] (Beijing: Military Science Press [军事科学出版社], 2013), 99–100.

10   Ibid., 99.

11   Ibid., 99–100.

12   Peng Guangqian and Yao Youzhi [彭光谦，姚有志], eds., *The Science of Military Strategy* [战略学] (Beijing: Military Science Publishing House [军事科学出版社], 2005), 167.

13   Ibid.

14   Ibid.

15   Ibid.

16   Mulvenon, 1–3.

17   Jia Yong, Cao Zhi, and Li Xuanliang [贾永, 曹智, 李宣良], "Advancing in Big Strides from a New Historical Starting Point—Record of Events on How the Party Central Committee and the Central Military Commission Promote Scientific Development in National Defense and Army Building" [中国军队打赢信息化条件下局部战争能力不断提升], Xinhua [新华], August 7, 2007.

18   Peng and Yao, 168.

19   Finkelstein, 91.

20   Ibid., 93.

21   Ibid.

22   OSD, 6.

23   Ibid., 21.

24   Peng and Yao, 169–170.

25   OSD, 6.

26   Yun Shan [云杉], "Facing the New Military Transformation Squarely" [直面新军事], *Liaowang*, no. 28 (July 4, 2003), 10–20; and Yang Fan [楊帆], "People's

CHAPTER 1

Liberation Army Rousing Itself to Overtake Others With Major Reforms" [解放軍急起直追大變革], *Wen Wei Po* [文匯報], August 23, 2003.

27 Wu Changde, Wu Guifu, and Yang Chunchang [吴昌德, 武桂馥, 杨春长], "Respond to the New World Revolution in Military Affairs, Walk the Path of Elite Troops with Chinese Characteristics (Experts Weigh In)" [应对世界新军事变革 走中国特色精兵之路（专家议专题）], *People's Daily* [人民日报], July 29, 2003.

28 Wang Wenrong [王文荣], ed., *The Science of Strategy* [战略学] (Beijing: National Defense University Press [国防大学出版社], 1999).

29 Peng and Yao, chaps. 9–18. These chapters cover a range of strategic topics central to PLA war planning efforts.

30 Wang Houqing and Zhang Xingye [王厚卿, 张兴业], eds., *The Science of Campaigns* [战役学] (Beijing: National Defense University Press, 2000); and Zhang Yuliang, *The Science of Campaigns*.

31 Xue Xinglin [薛兴林], ed., *Campaign Theory Study Guide* [战役理论学习指南] (Beijing: National Defense University Press, 2001).

32 Wang and Zhang, 1.

33 Ibid., 16–17.

34 Ibid.; Jia, Cao, and Li.

35 Wang and Zhang.

36 Wang Shenghuai, "Making Innovations in Theory and Practice of the Interaction of 'Fighting, Building, and Training,'" *PLA Daily*, April 7, 2004.

37 Sun Kaixiang and Su Ruozhou [孫開香, 蘇若舟], "The PLA General Staff Headquarters Have Worked Out Plans for This Year's Military Training" [總參部署新年度軍事訓練工作], *PLA Daily*, January 17, 2003; and Wang Shenghuai, "Making Innovations in Theory and Practice."

38 Sun Daifang and Chen Xiaojun [孙代方, 陈小军], "A New Model of Building Modularized Support in the Fujian Provincial Military District" [福建省军区构建模块化融合保障新模式], *PLA Daily*, September 25, 2010; and Wang, "Making Innovations in Theory and Practice."

39 Wang and Zhang, eds., 19–21.

40 Ibid., 4–5.

41 Xue, ed., 66.

42 Ibid., 409.

43 Peng and Yao, eds., 329–332.

44 Dou Chao [窦超], "Big Stick Being Wielded at China—Interpreting the New 'Air-Sea Battle' Operational Concept of the U.S. Military (Part 2)" [挥向中国的大棒 解

析美军新作战概念"空海一体战"(下)], *Modern Weaponry* [现代兵器], no. 8 (August 2, 2011), 46–51.

45   Tang Xiangdong and Fan Juwei [唐向东, 范炬炜], "At the All-PLA Logistic Support Capability Inspection and Evaluation and Warehouse Storage Work Conference, Liao Xilong Calls for Effectively Enhancing the Capability of Logistic Support for Fulfilling Diversified Military Tasks" [廖锡龙在全军后勤保障能力检验评估暨仓库储备工作会议上要求力实提高完成多样化军事任务后勤保障能], *PLA Daily*, September 22, 2012.

PLA Observations of U.S. Contingency Planning: What Has It Learned?

Marcelyn L. Thompson

C hina's People's Liberation Army (PLA) has had generations to observe the U.S. military plan for and go to war, from engagements in China's backyard like the Korean and Vietnam wars to U.S. operations half a world away in Grenada, Kosovo, Iraq, and Afghanistan. As the PLA modernizes to fulfill Hu Jintao's New Historic Missions,[1] what lessons has the PLA drawn from U.S. involvement in these operations? Specifically, has the PLA learned anything about contingency planning from the United States that has influenced how the PLA is designing its own contingency plans for use with its modernizing military?

The easiest way to answer this question would be through a review of Chinese contingency plans—a problematic endeavor from a research standpoint, as any such plans are likely very highly guarded within China. An additional challenge is that despite the PLA's well-established history of analyzing U.S. military operations, there exists a noticeable dearth of PLA research into U.S. contingency planning procedures. Therefore, this chapter focuses on repeated references in Chinese writings to hallmarks of U.S. contingency planning that have piqued the PLA's interest. Notably, these hallmarks are reflected in several steps the PLA is taking to modernize, particularly in the areas of national defense mobilization, logistics, and command, control, communications, computers, intelligence, surveillance, and reconnaissance (C4ISR). The author believes the PLA is aware that these developments can serve as a framework for emulating key components of the U.S. contingency planning process that the PLA admires and perceives as facilitators for the rapid creation, implementation, and revision of contingency plans.

This chapter addresses these hallmarks in detail, focusing first on the different vocabulary Chinese and U.S. practitioners use when discussing contingency planning, and then reviewing Chinese views of U.S. contingency operations since Grenada, with additional insights from recent Chinese contingency operations and the potential influence of the Syria crisis. Finally, a discussion of modernization in China's mobilization, C4ISR, and logistics systems will highlight developments that could serve to build China's contingency planning capabilities.

A Note on Terminology

The primary Chinese term for contingency, in the context of military contingency operations, is *yingji* [应急]. Unfortunately, this is also the word the Chinese government often uses for emergency, as in emergency management.[2] Therefore, when distinguishing the body of research on China's views on contingency planning, it is often necessary to rely upon context to determine whether the sources addressed plans and operations for domestic issues such as social unrest and natural disasters, for which *emergency* is often the best understanding of *yingji*, or externally focused or externally caused events, in which case *contingency* is a more appropriate interpretation. Finally, the phrase contingency plans, often termed *yingji jihua* [应急计划], *yingji yu'an* [应急预案], or *yuxian jihua* [预先计划], is also sometimes referred to as *zhanqian cehua* [战前策划][3] or *zhanqian chouhua* [战前筹划].[4] The lack of standard terminology indicates that the concept of contingency planning is not as systemic and therefore likely less well-developed in China than in the United States.

However, this lack of standardized terminology may have a different cause. It is unclear if the PLA distinguishes either linguistically or conceptually between the U.S. practices of crisis action and contingency planning. The book *Contingency Operations* [*Yingji Zuozhan*, 应急作战], published in 2004 by China's National Defense Industrial Press, does not seem to distinguish between the two, including a study of the U.S operations in Grenada, a crisis action planning-based operation, along with later U.S. operations in Iraq, based on U.S. contingency planning procedures. Therefore, the author has decided to include China's study of Grenada in this chapter, bearing in mind that China's concept of contingency planning may not be limited to the standard U.S. Joint Forces' definition of contingency planning—that is, deliberate planning.

Table 2.1 describes the key Chinese terms used for researching this chapter, and how, depending upon the context in which they have been used in the documents cited herein, they are best interpreted in English. None of these terms convey a clear concept of the timelines used in developing the plans to which they refer. If these phrases are tied to specific steps and timelines for either a Chinese version of what the U.S. Joint Staff would term crisis action or deliberate planning,[5] this is not clear from how they are used in the available sources.

Table 2.1. Key Terms Related to "Contingency Planning" in Chinese and English	
Chinese Term	**Approximate English Definition**
应急 *yingji*	• emergency • contingency
应急计划 *yingji jihua*	• emergency (response) plan • contingency plan • crisis action plan
应急预案 *yingji yu'an*	• emergency (preparations) plan • contingency plan
预先计划 *yuxian jihua*	• preplan • deliberate planning
战前策划 *zhanqian cehua*	• war plan (perhaps one that is thrown together quickly, more akin to crisis action planning than contingency planning)
战前筹划 *zhanqian chouhua*	• war plan

Insights from U.S. Contingency Operations

In general, Chinese writings that relate to contingency planning do not appear to focus extensively on the specific steps of the U.S. contingency planning process as outlined in the U.S. Government's Joint Operations Planning and Execution System. However, when they do, a consistent theme in these writings on the U.S. ability to conduct contingency planning is awe at how often the United States can pull a contingency plan out of seemingly thin air or quickly adjust and approve the use of contingency plans for real-world operations.[6] For example, in a review of U.S. operations in Grenada, the PLA author believes that the United States was a "sledge-hammer" and Grenada a "gnat,"[7] but he is nonetheless impressed with not only the U.S. military's execution of the Grenada operation but also the rapid and comprehensive means by which the United States planned for it. As one PLA publication notes: "The United States was able to respond and succeed quickly with regard to Grenada because its highest levels of strategic policymakers and the supreme command had the capability to respond quickly and decisively to the current state of affairs."[8] This capability refers not only to the ability of America's strategic policymakers and supreme command to arrive at decisions on contingency operations quickly, but also to the country's ability to use strategic reconnaissance to update the Grenada plans swiftly[9] and back these plans up with highly trained and skilled rapid response forces, such as the 82[d] Airborne Division.[10]

On the topic of the U.S. performance in Operation *Desert Storm*, the PLA gives high praise to the level of planning and coordination the United States leveraged in its successes in that conflict,[11] including the use of running multiple scenarios to help in the planning process.[12] This praise also singles out the expansive command, control, communications, and intelligence (C3I) technology the United States employed when coordinating and revising its contingency plans for Iraq, noting that such technology becomes all the more critical in later stages of operationalizing a contingency plan as the fog of war and threats to forces increase, complicating commanders' abilities to make decisions based on reliable data.[13]

Another aspect of U.S. contingency planning for Operation *Desert Storm* that impressed China is the use of prepositioned supplies as well as the large-scale mobilization of commercial transport assets.[14] Chinese commentary on the Gulf War states that the use of prepositioned supplies, particularly petroleum, oils, and lubricants, as well as transport ships already in the region helped the United States save significant time in mobilizing and deploying forces, notably the Marines. The U.S. ability to rapidly mobilize commercial airliners and merchant ships for this effort is also noted, indicating a Chinese belief that massive civil mobilization is something a military should have a plan to do ahead of any potential conflict. This belief was no doubt underscored by China's use of commercial air and maritime transportation during its 2011 non-combatant evacuation operation (NEO) of its citizens from Libya[15] (discussed below in further detail).

The PLA adds further emphasis on the civilian role in preparing for war when reviewing U.S. planning for post-9/11 Iraq operations, stating that the "civilianization" of war preparations is the way of the future.[16] Bringing civilians into the fold from the very beginning of generating contingency plans, adhering to uniform combat theory that is in line with the strategic guidance, and exercising the plans and revising them accordingly are viewed as the vital components of U.S.-style contingency planning for informationized warfare.[17]

In terms of lessons learned from how the United States planned for Afghanistan, PLA analysts again focus on the importance of logistics, notably the integration of all elements of U.S. logistics needs. The PLA notes the top-down scrutiny of and support for logistics requirements, from the Joint Staff addressing logistics as part of revising plans for multiple contingencies to implementation of these plans by the Defense Logistics Agency and logistics departments across the Armed Services.[18]

The U.S. experience in Afghanistan also helped PLA analysts realize China has many steps it needs to undertake when it comes to contingency planning, at least for counterterrorism contingencies: intelligence collection, planning, scenario writing, and exercising against these scenarios.[19]

The one instance in which Chinese writings find clear fault with U.S. contingency planning capabilities is, unsurprisingly, Operation *Allied Force*, due to the mistaken U.S. targeting of the Chinese embassy in Belgrade based on the use of an outdated map. In an article published under the sponsorship of China's National Defense Science, Technology, and Information Center, Chinese authors state that it is not enough simply to conduct intensive intelligence collection; one also has to validate the authenticity and thereby the utility of the intelligence. However, these authors do give the United States some credit for apparently learning from *Allied Force*, referencing significant investments in surveying and mapping local terrain for U.S. operations in Afghanistan and Iraq.[20]

Insights from PLA Contingency Operations

In 2011, the PLA Navy (PLAN) and PLA Air Force (PLAAF) conducted a NEO of Chinese citizens in Libya due to ongoing unrest there. These two services, in conjunction with chartered flights and merchant ships, successfully evacuated over 35,000 people from Libya.[21] To the extent that China's contingency planning for and use of its military in the Libya NEO mirrors any kind of U.S.-style planning, it most closely approximates crisis action planning, similar to what the United States exercised in coordinating between Department of Defense, U.S. Agency for International Development, and Department of State entities located in the Asia-Pacific in response to the 2004 tsunami.[22] For China, coordination during the Libya crisis involved emergency meetings led by the State Council, in addition to emergency communications with the PLAN, PLAAF, and state organs including the Ministry of Public Security, Ministry of Commerce, and Ministry of Foreign Affairs under the oversight of the State Council.[23]

On the civilian side, the State Council's State-Owned Assets Supervision and Administration Commission (SASAC) oversaw the enacting of emergency plans to protect the physical assets and nearly 5,000 Chinese citizen employees of the China Communication Construction Group's (CCCG's) projects in Libya. The CCCG office in Benghazi began emergency preparations on February 8, 2011, after local police notified them of large-scale demonstrations; these preparations included reserving a one-month stockpile of emergency supplies, purchasing a maritime satellite phone, and *beginning* to draft contingency plans. These plans included monitoring reserves of oil and water, procuring materials and teams to establish roadblocks, and assigning CCCG employees to security teams and propaganda and morale duties.[24] CCCG reported that all their employees were successfully evacuated by February 28, 2011.[25]

While this successful NEO, so far from China's borders, was an operational coup for the PLA and by extension for China's civilian leadership, it is unclear what specific impact this event has had on China's contingency planning process. At the very least, the Libya NEO has probably highlighted for China how helpful it is to have a military presence nearby when responding to a crisis; the PLAN frigate used for the NEO was already in the area to conduct escort patrols in the Gulf of Aden.[26] Another lesson it likely provided is the value of relationships with parties nearby that one can leverage in a crisis. In this instance, China's relationship with Greece provided critical supporting infrastructure. Chartered Greek ships helped evacuate at least 2,000 Chinese from Libya, and Greek hotels reserved 6,500 beds for Chinese evacuees.[27] This arrangement may have benefitted from shipbuilding and construction deals that China and Greece agreed to in 2010 whereby China encouraged its businesses to seek investment opportunities in Greece to help that nation overcome its financial problems.[28]

The Libya NEO demonstrated that even though China may have lacked a detailed NEO plan, it still managed to take advantage of nearby resources and regional relationships to coordinate a functional plan in short order. In the wake of the Libya NEO, China created the Strategic Planning Department (SPD) under the General Staff Department in late 2011. Designed to integrate planning and force allocation across all PLA services as well as to improve PLA coordination with civilian entities,[29] the SPD will likely be integral to shaping China's contingency planning process in the future. How the SPD will coordinate with China's nascent National Security Commission (NSC), created late in 2013, and the role the NSC itself will play in drafting and approving future Chinese contingency plans remain unclear.[30]

China has also followed with great interest recent discussions involving U.S. and international experts about how to handle the ongoing unrest in Syria. Observing the United States take time to meet with Turkey to discuss contingency options for improving the situation in Syria[31] likely leaves China wondering if contingency planning always requires extensive diplomatic efforts to coordinate with key regional actors. U.S. advance focus on resolving key issues (such as what will happen to Syria's chemical weapons if the regime falls) may also convince China that mere awareness alone of the possible locations and potential nature of a crisis is insufficient for effective contingency planning. Instead, developing specific scenarios for future possibilities must be a requirement for contingency planning.[32]

Relevant Developments in PLA Modernization

Three areas of the PLA's current modernization, while not necessarily directly linked to contingency planning capabilities, will likely improve the PLA's ability to coordinate contingency plans and enable planning for a broad range of scenarios. The first two areas, national defense mobilization and logistics, are intricately tied to one another, and strengthening each of these capabilities is a priority for China. However, it is in the third area, C4ISR, where the PLA hopes to provide the infrastructure for the type of objective and continuous coordination that enables the kind of U.S.-style planning it admires.

National Defense Mobilization

China's national defense mobilization process was codified in the 2010 National Defense Mobilization Law (NDML), which authorizes Beijing to requisition, with an unspecified amount of compensation, a host of civilian assets, from telecommunications to factories to transportation means, in times of national crisis.[33] The NDML also calls for the military and relevant civilian entities to conduct national defense mobilization training in peacetime, which, if conducted with rigor on a regular basis, would likely provide the PLA an even greater level of mobilization support from the commercial sector than the United States enjoyed during the Gulf War.

China plans for and enforces national defense measures through National Defense Mobilization Committees, which exist from the county level across the country up to the highest levels of government. These committees act upon orders from the president (who is usually also the Chinese Communist Party general secretary) for full or partial mobilization, drawn from a Standing Committee of the National People's Congress decision in response to perceived threats to China's sovereignty, territorial integrity, unity, or security. The State Council and Central Military Commission then undertake joint efforts to create relevant policies and organize the implementation of national defense mobilization work, in keeping with the Standing Committee of the National People's Congress decision on full or partial mobilization and the president's accompanying order.[34]

Recent high-profile civil-military joint exercises in China highlight practicing national defense mobilization, largely for transportation purposes. In exercise Stride [*Kuayue*, 跨越] 2009, the PLA moved a division each from the Shenyang, Lanzhou, Jinan, and Chengdu Military Regions (MRs)—approximately 50,000 troops—across the country to test its strategic projection capabilities for responding to unspecified contingencies.[35] The troops relied upon commercial airliners and high-speed trains to provide strategic projection for part of the exercise, the mobilization of which was coordinated by the PLA headquarters for the event.[36] The PLA also used its *Beidou* [北斗] satellite navigation system to facilitate the PLA's long-distance transit,[37] suggesting that civilian transportation organizations, along with the PLA, are linked into Beidou, which could assist rapid mobilization of their resources for contingency operations. Although Stride occurred prior to the passage of the NDML, it clearly aligned with Article 53 (D) of the NDML, which says that "providing various means of transportation for the armed forces is a priority" once the state has commenced national defense mobilization.[38] The exercise's focus on military use of civilian transport also likely built off the "Regulation on National Defense Mobilization of Civilian Means of Transportation," issued jointly by the State Council and the Central Military Commission in 2003.[39]

Stride also tested other elements of national defense mobilization. For example, the National Defense Mobilization Committee of Luohe Military Sub-District mobilized a local emergency [*yingji*] militia unit to stand guard over nearby freeways in support of the transit for participating Jinan MR troops.[40] In Zhengzhou, not only were local traffic and transportation personnel mobilized, but so were civil affairs, public security, and telecommunications staff along with local militia, for the express intent of practicing civil-military coordination for national defense mobilization purposes.[41]

With the high-profile Mission Action [*shiming xingdong*, 使命行动] 2010 exercise, the PLA again relied upon civilian transportation, using commercial airliners to help move group army–level units from across MRs.[42] Additionally, the movement of forces from Beijing to the Shenyang MR and between the Chengdu and Lanzhou MRs during the exercise indicates Mission Action 2010, in addition to providing additional practice with national defense mobilization, was designed to train the PLA for rapid mobilization in response to specific border contingencies—for example, with North Korea and India.[43]

The extent to which the PLA has used Mission Action 2010—or any of its other exercises, for that matter—to practice specific components of contingency plans is unclear. One PLA training guide notes that designing training based upon operational missions can be handled one of two ways: training programs can either be designed for very specific topics that do not indicate key aspects of operational plans, or they can be designed specifically to align with operational plans. The critical difference between the two methods from an outsider's perspective is that training is usually aligned to operational plans just prior to a war, a tendency that could prove useful for indications and warning of a pending PLA operation. The exception would be following major changes in the world order—possibly including events like the Arab Spring—that merit reviewing and possibly revising a nation's strategies and operational plans.[44]

Whatever the nature of the training program, the PLA does recognize the value of training for contingency planning.[45] In particular, the PLA highlights the lengths to which the United States went to practice elements of contingency plans for operations in Iraq, including exercising units in Israel to acclimate them to the desert conditions they would be fighting in during a war with Iraq, using actors playing Iraqis to provide a realistic opposition during the training, and employing simulators to make training more realistic.[46] Noticeably absent, however, is any indication of the kind of national defense mobilization training China conducts.

Logistics

China is decidedly attuned to the global networks of U.S. troops and military supplies emplaced around the world that enable the United States to respond quickly to contingencies, particularly after observing how such prepositioning benefitted U.S. forces in Iraq.[47] Yet the PLA still lacks the advantage of having its own supplies prepositioned globally, or even regionally, for use in contingency operations. The exception would be its few destroyers dedicated to counter-piracy patrols in the Gulf of Aden, which proved advantageous to China's NEO of its citizens from Libya in 2011, as previously discussed. The PLA may have plans to mobilize these ships for contingencies it may confront in that region, including but not limited to piracy. While the PLA has admitted to considering creating a supply base in the Horn of Africa,[48] as of this writing, the conversation has not moved toward any concrete action.[49]

Regardless, the PLA is changing how it addresses logistics management to create a force that is more prepared to fulfill logistics requirements on short notice and across great distances. In 2011, the General Logistics Department (GLD) issued a framework for the comprehensive building of logistics target tasks, with the aim of establishing a modernized logistics system by 2020.[50] A key focus for this effort is developing logistics commanders who can make the most of newer technological systems that help track and automatically update the status of materiel. This capability is seen as invaluable in an era where information technology causes the battlefield situation to change rapidly, creating chaos that intensifies the need for up-to-date, accurate information about the units being resupplied and the location of materiel.[51]

Additionally, this GLD framework is designed with the understanding that increased civil-military coordination is necessary to develop a logistics capability that can support responses to any contingency on a moment's notice.[52] This fact is what makes the PLA's logistics processes so intricately linked with those of its national defense mobilization. From China's perspective, this is due to a perceived trend of informationized (that is, high-tech and network-dependent) local wars, in which boundaries between military and civilian technology are rapidly collapsing, enabling a much broader population to "support the front" instead of just members of PLA logistics units.[53]

Two items from a June 2012 Small Working Group's work report on civil-military integration of weapons production system construction highlight specific steps China is taking to strengthen the civil-military support relationship. First, the General Armaments Department, in conjunction with Guangdong Province, recently inaugurated a project to demonstrate the applications of Beidou for civilian purposes, termed the "1-2-3 Project." This name is derived from one city—Zhongshan—that will serve as a "Beidou demonstration city," emphasizing the launch of this system for emergency [*yingji*] management, intelligent communications, integration of the city with the administration of law enforcement, and personal security support; two information platforms upon which it will run; and three industries in which it will be demonstrated—including Guangdong's civilian transportation national defense mobilization administration system.[54]

Second, this work report notes the recent establishment, with the support of the GLD, of a civil-military packaging construction work committee. This committee's purpose is to help create a military packaging service that is wholly adaptable to manufacturing products for both peacetime and wartime use, ensuring a rapid response system to the military's needs in wartime.[55]

This expansion of support resources will be best utilized if both the civilian and military sides have a common information system for communicating and coordinating and similar planning and operational procedures to follow. These measures will not be realized overnight but instead are occurring through exercises such as Stride and Mission Action and the above-mentioned information technology training for commanders. If the PLA and their civilian counterparts master all these steps, the PLA will likely be able to plan for the logistics requirements of contingency plans somewhat faster than before and with a far greater array of resources—both physical and intellectual—around the country to support operations of all kinds.

C4ISR

At least since the U.S. Invasion of Grenada, the PLA has envied the U.S. ability to coordinate contingency plans swiftly across civilian and military leadership.[56] A key element in this process of contingency plans coordination, which the PLA is acutely aware it lacks, is the presence of full-time, widespread joint operations staff officers. The PLA would like to expand the number of personnel it can place in this role and dedicate them to reviewing available intelligence and devising initial courses of action for the joint operations command to study and approve.[57]

In terms of the scope of intelligence that the PLA needs for devising contingency plans, at least one author views this as problematic, estimating the PLA would require 5 to 10 years to amass enough information to plan successfully for a possible war.[58] This estimate indicates a strong belief that a well-constructed plan requires a breadth of intelligence data and detailed analysis.

The PLA's need to obtain ever more intelligence to strengthen contingency plans is moderated as the PLA informationizes, a process at the center of PLA modernization. Informationization entails upgrading the information technology capabilities and systems of the force to enable all the military services to exercise the C3I required to function as a joint force that can successfully wage informationized wars. Simply put, informationized wars need "operational systems that can 'see clearly, react quickly, and hit precisely.'"[59] Planning to react quickly and hit precisely during informationized wars requires first and foremost the ability to see clearly and to do so long before the war occurs. The PLA became especially sensitive to this after observing how quickly the United States developed its plan for Grenada, which benefitted from the use of strategic reconnaissance systems to help with planning and targeting for a joint operation.[60] Observations of the U.S. performance in both Operation *Desert Storm* and Operation *Iraqi Freedom* only increased the importance of strategic intelligence, surveillance, and reconnaissance and automated command systems for the PLA.[61]

China's belief in the advantage of strategic ISR for planning is reflected in recent investments it has made in its Beidou satellite coverage, which China expects will provide it global coverage by 2020, improving its mapping and telecommunications abilities.[62] In early 2012, China also launched its Ziyuan-III satellite, designed to provide high-resolution imagery to civilian agencies in China for mapping purposes.[63] China states it has already used the Ziyuan-III to image islands in the South China Sea,[64] and it has also recently begun using its Skynet satellite system to monitor both the South China Sea and the disputed Diaoyu/Senkaku islands.[65]

Using the NDML, China could easily commandeer both civilian and national satellites to assist in providing intelligence for contingency planning in response to a potential or actual crisis. Additionally, China's role in designing and launching communications satellites for Nigeria, Venezuela, Pakistan, Laos, and Bolivia could theoretically provide China additional satellite coverage for any contingency operations it may pursue in those areas of the world.[66]

Once the necessary intelligence is obtained, China still needs a comprehensive C4ISR infrastructure to facilitate dissemination of and coordination on actions in response to the intelligence. In a 2005 discussion on the C4ISR requirements for contemporary special operations, Chinese academics judged that while the overall equipping, training on, and research into China's C4ISR systems have been progressing well, these systems would still fall short of fulfilling the requirements for future contingency operations unless the following issues were addressed:

- weakness in the system architecture and generally low levels of know-how for using the system
- little integration of functions between the applications provided as part of existing equipment, limiting how often the functionality of the whole system can be brought to bear
- vagaries in relationships between modular control operations and weakness in the control capability.[67]

These statements indicate not only a role for the PLA's special operations forces in established PLA contingency plans, but also that these plans rely extensively on C4ISR systems that, at least as of 2005, the PLA had neither fully developed nor mastered.

As of 2010, when the PLA held its Mission Action exercise, the force was still pursuing mastery of high-tech capabilities. In Mission Action, this effort was very noticeable through continued references to the Integrated Command Platform (ICP). Based upon PLA descriptions from Mission Action, the ICP is an information technology system that comprises real-time location tracking, data collection and dissemination, as well as decisionmaking, coordination, and communication tools.[68] In Mission Action, the ICP was used throughout the exercise, where its primary initial task was to facilitate the integration of command staff from all participating units into an automated decisionmaking process to determine which existing operational plan should be followed and which relevant command decisions should be issued.[69]

In a 2011 exercise in Shenyang MR, a PLA division used the ICP to build a three-dimensional map of the battlefields in under 3 minutes and also used it to sift through and identify critical information from the combat scenario as well as previously collected data on weather and terrain, according to *PLA Daily* [解放军报].[70] Having all these capabilities available for rapid use would be very helpful to any unit or command element for creating, coordinating, and revising contingency plans.

However, while the PLA will likely continue training intensively with the ICP and similar technologies to provide improved C3I and C4ISR capabilities comparable to what the United States uses in wartime, this does not necessarily equate to a direct improvement in or standardization of the PLA's contingency planning process. The PLA does value contingency planning, noting that in the integrated operations it hopes to fight in the future, winning on the battlefield is not as good as winning via preplanning.[71] Yet as the PLA evolves rapidly from a mechanized force to an informationized one, the PLA's traditional approach to contingency planning may be perceived as a relic of mechanization, in which the PLA is limited to a few very select, rigid options, deviation from which only causes chaos.[72] Informationization, however, is discussed as providing the PLA a truly cohesive joint operations capability, in which contingency planning will not become extinct but will take on a more dynamic, rapidly self-adjusting nature, based upon systems and processes that enable nimbly reorganizing operational units and actions to address a variety of operational goals.[73] Essentially, the PLA's contingency planning process, informed to some extent by the goal of developing C4ISR capabilities similar to those of the United States, may become less of a process and more of an experiment in how the PLA can use modern communications systems to integrate forces to respond to current, not potential, crises.

Conclusion

Broadly speaking, the PLA seems to admire three aspects of U.S. contingency planning: the C4ISR capabilities that enable the United States to assess the state of potential threats against which it should plan, the speed at which civilian and military leaders coordinate on the design and approval of contingency plans, and the numerous logistic support options in place around the globe to assist the United States in its contingency operations.

While the PLA may want to replicate all these contingency planning strengths itself, global prepositioned logistics resources will likely remain aspirational for the near term. The specific impact of the ICP on contingency planning is unclear at this time, although PLA employment of it to aid in planning and mobilization of forces for a real-world situation, such as a noncombatant evacuation operation, would help the force better understand what specific contingency planning benefits it provides, as well as help ameliorate any undiscovered issues with the software and the command staff's ability to operate it.

The PLA's reliance on national defense mobilization appears to be an asset for China's contingency planning process, forcing civilian and military institutions across China to think through the transportation and C4ISR requirements of any number of sectors for any number of scenarios. The PLA itself values the role of civilians in the process very highly and would actually characterize their role in contingency planning as the foundation of a successful war, perhaps second only to high-technology communications systems that allow for ongoing coordination and revision of contingency plans. What remains less clear at this point is how much emphasis either the PLA or China's civilian leadership places on developing decisionmaking procedures between civilian and military elements that can move as quickly as the new communications and C4ISR systems emerging throughout the country.

Analysts seeking to learn more about the extent to which the PLA's approach to contingency planning mirrors aspects of U.S. planning methods should pay close attention to the role of civilian elements and how well they coordinate with the PLA through National Defense Mobilization Committees and other means. Tracking progress in integrating civil-military technologies and processes in peacetime that also have wartime applications, such as Beidou and logistics supply chains, will also elucidate how the PLA's contingency planning process is modernizing and the extent to which it is evolving into or away from one like that of the United States.

Finally, PLA advances in recent years in adopting automated decisionmaking software across the force suggest that PLA leaders recognize that the military will not always have the luxury of long lead times for contingency planning but instead will need the ability to react quickly to crises as they emerge. To the extent that the PLA has derived lessons about contingency planning from the United States, the question now is which aspects of the U.S. system it seeks to emulate, and especially whether it seeks to develop what the United States would term a crisis action planning process. An emphasis on the latter would require greater realism and command autonomy in PLA exercises. This leads to a critical contradiction: commanders need autonomy in a crisis, but automated decisionmaking aids such as the ICP can deny PLA commanders that autonomy even as it seeks to enable them to make better decisions and exercise command over their forces. Therefore, even as the PLA's contingency planning process seeks to better support crisis action planning, this does not guarantee that the PLA will develop commanders who can help see their forces through a crisis amidst potential failures with the ICP or other components of China's C4ISR architecture and planning procedures.

Notes

1   Jian Cheng, Mo Jun, and Lan Li Qing [程坚, 莫军, 蓝立青], "An Important Discussion on the Value and Meaning of the Historic Missions of the New Era and New Century for the PLA" [新世纪新阶段我军历史使命重要论述的价值和意义], Xinhua Online [新华网], September 27, 2009, available at <http://news.xinhuanet.com/mil/2005-09/27/content_3548905.htm>. This article states, "Chairman Hu told the military earnestly that it should serve as a powerful guarantee to consolidate the Party's rule, provide a strong security guarantee to protect the nation's development during the period of strategic opportunity, serve as a strong means of strategic support to provide the country's benefits, and play an important role in protecting global peace and advancing mutual development" [胡主席向安全郑重提出，军队要为党巩固折证地位提供重要的力量保证，为维护国家发展的重要战略机遇期提供坚强的安全保障，为维护国家利益提供有力的战略支撑，为维护世界和平与促进共同发展发挥重要作用].

2   "Emergency Management" [应急管理], Central People's Government of the People's Republic of China, official web portal, October 28, 2012, available at <www.gov.cn/yjgl/index.htm>.

3   Yang Qingchuan and Fan Yunzhao [杨晴川, 潘云召], "Bush Admits the U.S. Made Errors in Assessing the Situation in Iraq" [布什承认美国对伊拉克形势的判断出现过失误], Xinhua Online, April 25, 2006, available at <www.annian.net/show.aspx-?id=18304&cid=5>; and Wang Jianfen [王建芬], "New Information on the Iraq Attacks: Saddam Drew Up Attack Plans Before the War" [伊拉克袭击新说：萨达姆在战前制定游击战计划], Sohu News Channel [搜狐新闻频道], October 30, 2003, available at <http://news.sohu.com/30/51/news215005130.shtml>.

4   "The U.S. Military Disestablishes Joint Forces Command, Indicating the Difficult Cost-Saving Measures It Needs to Achieve" [美军撤销联合部队司令部 被指省钱目标难达成], Phoenix Online [鳳凰網], August 13, 2010, available at <http://news.ifeng.com/mil/4/detail_2010_08/13/1947152_0.shtml>.

5   Joint Chiefs of Staff, Joint Publication 5-0, *Doctrine for Planning Joint Operations* (Washington, DC: The Joint Staff, April 13, 1995), ix, available at <www.bits.de/NRANEU/others/jp-doctrine/jp5_0(95).pdf>.

6   Wang Wenrong [王文荣], ed., *The Science of Strategy* [战略学] (Beijing: National Defense University Press [国防大学出版社], 1999), 285–286; Huang Bin [黄彬], *Army, Navy, and Air Force Operational Command under High-Tech Conditions* [陆海空军高技术条件下作战指挥] (Beijing: National Defense University Press, 1993), 228, 235; and Li Houmin [李厚敏], *High Technology—Local War and Battle Tactics* [高技术局部战争与战役战法] (Beijing: National Defense University Press, 1993), 131, available at <www.doc88.com/p-494079297.html>.

7   Ning Ling [宁凌], ed., *Contingency Operations* [应急作战] (Beijing: National Defense Industrial Press [国防工业出版社], 2005), 29.

8   Ibid., 28.

9   Ibid.

10   "The 82nd Airborne Division" [第82空降师], Knowfar Institute for Strategic and Defence Studies [知远战略与防务研究所], November 6, 2003, available at <www.defence.org.cn/article-1-42009.html>; and "Airborne Troops in the U.S. Military's History" [美军历史上的空降部队], August 28, 2008, accessed at <www.chinamil.com.cn/site1/2008b/2008-08/28/content_1446589.htm>.

11   Huang, 235.

12   Wang, 285.

13   Huang, 235; Li, 219–220.

14   Huang Zhijie [黄治茂], ed., "The Gulf War 20 Years On: The Military Transportation of Truly and Falsely Strong Countries—Part 2" [海湾战争20年启示录: 真伪强国的军事运输，第2期], *NetEase News* [网易新闻], available at <http://war.163.com/special/gulfwar1/>. Although the publication date is unavailable, the fact that this is a 20-year retrospective of the Gulf War likely places it sometime in 2001.

15   "The Motherland Helps Me Return Home" [祖国援我回家], *People's Daily* [人民日报], February 24, 2011, available at <world.people.com.cn/GB/8212/191606/214871/index.html>.

16   Liu Jianggui [刘江桂], "The Iraq War—the 'Invariable' and the 'Variable'" [伊拉克战争的"不变"与"变"], *China Military Science* [中国军事科学], no. 4 (2003), 16–21.

17   Ibid., 6–7.

18   He Mingyuan [何明远], ed., *The War in Afghanistan* [阿富汗战争] (Beijing: PLA Press [中国人民解放军出版社], 2004), 172.

19   Ibid., 203–204.

20   Hao Yuqing, Cai Renzhao, and Cai Shichuan [郝玉庆, 蔡仁照, 蔡世川], "Military Surveying and Mapping is the Precursor to Building an Informationized Military" [军事测绘是军队信息化建设的先导], *Conmilit* [现代军事], no. 6 (2003). Conmilit Magazine Publication Bureau is sponsored by China National Defense Science, Technology, and Information Center.

21   "The Motherland Helps Me Return Home."

22   Office of the Press Secretary, Executive Office of the President, "Fact Sheet: Continuing Support for Tsunami Relief," February 9, 2005, available at <http://georgewbush-whitehouse.archives.gov/news/releases/2005/02/20050209-20.html>.

23   Ibid.; Gabe Collins and Andrew S. Erickson, "Implications of China's Military Evacuation of Citizens from Libya," *China Brief* 11, no. 4 (March 10, 2011).

24   "On-the-spot Report of China Communications Construction Group's Protection and Rescue of its Suluq, Libya Project" [中交集团利比亚苏卢格项目自保自救

纪实], State-owned Assets Supervision and Administration Commission of the State Council, People's Republic of China, March 2, 2011, available at <www.sasac.gov.cn/n1180/n12534878/n13079015/n13079383/13079521.html#>.

25 Ibid.

26 Royston Chan and Tom Miles, "CORRECTED—China evacuates 12,000 from Libya, sends frigate to help," Reuters, February 25, 2011, available at <www.reuters.com/article/2011/02/25/libya-china-evacuations-idAFTOE71O00420110225?pageNumber=2&virtualBrandChannel=0&sp=true>.

27 "Vessels with Chinese Evacuees from Libya Aboard Due in Greece's Crete Thursday Afternoon," *CCTV Online*, February 24 2011, available at <http://english.cntv.cn/20110224/109819.shtml>.

28 "China, Greece Sign Deals, Want Stronger Business Ties," Reuters, June 15, 2010, available at <uk.reuters.com/article/2010/06/15/greece-china-business-idUK-LDE65E0MU20100615/>.

29 Peter Mattis, "Chinese Military Creates Strategic Planning Department," *China Brief* 11, no. 22, (November 30, 2011).

30 "Deciphering the 'National Security Committee'" [解读"国家安全委员会"], *Communist Youth Online* [中青在线], November 21, 2013, available at <http://news.cyol.com/content/2013-11/21/content_9335509_2.htm>.

31 "The U.S. and Turkey Consult over an Operational Plan to Oust Bashar" [土美商议 推翻巴沙尔 '行动计划'], *Wen Wei Po* [文匯報], August 25, 2012, available at <http://roll.sohu.com/20120825/n351497526.shtml>.

32 Jiao Xiangshe [焦翔摄], "U.S. Already Researching Contingency Plans, Non-Military Intervention for Downfall of Syrian Regime" [美国已研究叙政府台应急预案或不军事干预], *People's Daily*, August 7, 2012, available at <www.chinanews.com/gj/2012/08-07/4087999.shtml>.

33 National Defense Mobilization Law of the People's Republic of China [中华人民共和国国防动员法], February 27, 2010, available at <www.mod.gov.cn/policy/2010-02/27/content_4127067.htm>.

34 "How Is the National Defense Mobilization Guiding Structure for the 'National Defense Mobilization Law' Regulated?" [对国防动员的组织领导体制是如何规定的?], *Ministry of Defense Network*, February 27, 2010, available at <www.mod.gov.cn/reports/201002/gfdyf/2010-02/27/content_4126697.htm>. Also see Article 9 of "The People's Republic of China's National Defense Mobilization Law (Full Text)" [中华人民共和国国防动员法（全文）], February 26, 2010, available at <www.chinanews.com/gn/news/2010/02-26/2141912.shtml>.

35 "'Kuayue-2009' Military Exercise Raises the PLA's Contingency Operations' Capability" ['跨越一2009'军演提升我军应急作战能力], *China Broadcasting Online*

[中国广播网], August 12, 2009, available at <http://mil.news.sina.com.cn/2009-08-12/2251562320.html>; and "The Beidou Communications System Goes into Battle for the Kuayue '09 Military Exercise; It Can Defend Against Leaks" [跨越09军演北斗系统上阵可防通信 '泄密'], *Sichuan News Network* [四川新闻网], August 13, 2009, available at <http://mil.huanqiu.com/china/2009-08/545720.html>.

36   "The Beidou Communications System Goes into Battle."

37   Ibid.

38   National Defense Mobilization Law.

39   The State Council and Central Military Commission of the People's Republic of China, "Regulation on National Defense Mobilization of Civilian Means of Transportation" [民用运力国防动员条例], September 13, 2003, available at <www.gov.cn/zwgk/2005-05/23/content_178.htm>.

40   Hua Xinding and Wei Zhiqiang [华新定, 魏志强], "Luohe Militia Company Supports 'Kuayue-2009' Military Exercise" [漯河民兵应急连保障'跨越—2009'军演], *China Military Online* [中国军网], August 24, 2009, available at <www.gfdy.gov.cn/arm_m/2009-08/24/content_4916695.htm>.

41   "In Zhengzhou City, Both Civilians and Military Enter Battle Together; Ensuring 'Kuayue-2009' Unfolds Smoothly" [郑州市军民齐上阵 保障'跨越—2009演习'顺利进行], *Xilu Online* [西陆网], August 18, 2010, available at <http://junshi.xilu.com/2009/0818/news_56_10268.html>.

42   "'Mission-Action-2010' Chengdu Military Region Units Launch Long-Distance Three-Dimensional Delivery" ["使命行动-2010"成都军区部队展开远程立体投送], "Examining the Future Trends In PLA Modernization Based on 'Mission Action-2010'" [从 '使命行动—2010' 军演审视解放军未来发展趋势], October 15, 2010, Xinhua Online, available at <http://news.ifeng.com/mainland/detail_2010_10/15/2798520_0.shtml>; and Li Jing [李靖], ed., "'Mission Action-2010' Cross-Region Mobility Exercise Ends Satisfactorily" ['使命行动—2010' 跨区机动演习圆满结束], *PLA Pictorial* [解放军画报], no. 813, November 2010, available at <http://web.archive.org/web/20120726003232/http://www.plapic.com.cn/txt/201011b/20101107-3B.htm>.

43   Ibid.

44   Zhu Rongbang [朱荣榜], ed., *The Science of Campaign Training* [战役训练学] (Beijing: National Defense University Press, 1997), 60–62.

45   Ning, 28; Liu, 6–7.

46   "Deciphering Integrated Operations" [解读一体化作战], *PLA Daily* [解放军报], May 3, 2004, available at <www.china.com.cn/chinese/junshi/557013.htm>.

47   Wang Xuhe [汪徐和], "Comments on the Readjustment of U.S. Military Strategy" [美国军事战略调整评析], *American Studies* [美国研究], no. 2 (1994), available

at <http://ias.cass.cn/show/show_mgyj.asp?id=628&table=mgyj>; and Han Xudong [韩旭东], "The 'Globalized Battlefield' is Drawing Near, Internet War Sounds the Bugle" ['全球化战场'逼近 网络战吹响号角], *Liaowang* [瞭望], July 12, 2010, available at <www.chinanews.com/gj/2010/07-12/2396546.shtml>.

48   Lucy Hornby, "Talks of a PLAN Overseas Naval Base," *China Defense Blog*, December 30, 2009, available at <http://china-defense.blogspot.sg/2009/12/talks-of-plan-overseas-naval-base.html>.

49   Daniel J. Kostecka, "Places and Bases: The Chinese Navy's Emerging Support Network in the Indian Ocean," *Naval War College Review* 64, no. 1 (Winter 2011), 61, 64, available at <www.dtic.mil/dtic/tr/fulltext/u2/a536636.pdf>; and Christopher D. Yung and Ross Rustici with Scott Devary and Jenny Lin, *"Not an Idea We Have to Shun": Chinese Overseas Basing Requirements in the 21st Century*, China Strategic Perspectives 7 (Washington, DC: NDU Press, 2014).

50   "Building Modern Logistics—Four Successes in National Defense and Military Construction" [全面建设现代后勤—国防和军队建设成就综述之四], Xinhua [新华], September 11, 2012, available at <www.gov.cn/jrzg/2012-09/11/content_2222135.htm>.

51   Li Wenlong, Guo Yijun, and Wang Gencheng [李文龙, 郭义军, 王根成], "Study the Technical Ability of the Integrated Command Platform: With a New 'Gun' You Can Break a Few 'Links'" [学用一体化指挥平台技能: 用新 '枪' 你能打击 '环'], April 13, 2012, available at <www.gxnews.com.cn/staticpages/20120413/newgx-4f87cd95-5061060.shtml>.

52   "Building Modern Logistics."

53   Ren Min [任民], *Science of National Defense Mobilization* [国防动员学] (Beijing: Military Science Publishing House [军事科学出版社], 2008), 468.

54   "General Armaments Department and Guangdong Province Together Promote the First Engineering Construction of the Beidou Navigation System Application Demonstration" [总装备部和广东省政府共同推进首个北斗导航示范应用工程建设], *Civil-Military Integration Civil and Military Weapons Armament Scientific Research Production System Construction Department Small Working Group Work Briefing* 3 (June 29, 2012), 8, Civil-Military Promotion Headquarters of the Industrial and Informationization Department, Internal Materials, June 2012, available at <http://jmjhs.miit.gov.cn/n11293472/n11295193/n13373876/n14805156/n14806597.files/n14845597.pdf>.

55   "The Civil Military Fusion Packing Development Construction Work Committee is Established in Beijing" [军民融合包装发展建设工作委员会在京成立], *Civil-Military Integration Civil and Military Weapons Armament Scientific Research Production System Construction Department Small Working Group Work Briefing* 3 (June 29, 2012), 8, Civil-Military Promotion Headquarters of the Industrial and

Informationization Department, Internal Materials, June 2012, available at <http://jmjhs.miit.gov.cn/n11293472/n11295193/n13373876/n14805156/n14806597.files/n14845597.pdf>.

56   Ning, 23, 28.

57   Dang Chongmin [党崇民], ed., *Joint Operations Staff Officer Work* [联合作战参谋工作] (Beijing: PLA Press, 2006), 2.

58   Li Jijun [李际均], *Military Strategic Thinking* [军事战略思维] (Beijing: Military Science Publishing House [军事科学出版社], 1998), 93–94.

59   Liu Jian [刘建], "Wireless Technologies: Military Applications of Wireless Sensor Networks" [无线技术：无线传感器网络在军事的应用], *Chinabyte.com* [比特网], January 31, 2010, available at <http://network.chinabyte.com/248/11119248.shtml>.

60   Ning, 28.

61   Li, 220; Yao Wang and Wang Xiangjiang [姚旺,王湘江], "From Stalingrad to Fallujah—the Development and Transformation of Urban Operations" [从斯大林格勒到费卢杰:市作战的发展和变化], *International Military Art* [外国军事学术] (2005), 55–59, available at <www.360doc.com/content/14/0403/11/10106911_366043813.shtml>.

62   "China's Satellite Navigation System is Online," Agence France-Presse, December 27, 2011, available at <http://news.discovery.com/space/china-navigation-satellite-system-111227.html>.

63   "Hi-res Mapping Satellite Expands Coverage," *ChinaDaily.com.cn*, May 24, 2012, available at <www.chinadaily.com.cn/china/2012-05/24/content_15372204.htm>.

64   Ibid.

65   "China's Satellite is Already Conducting Surveillance on the Diaoyutai and South China Sea" [中国卫星已开始动态临视钓鱼岛和南海海域], *Phoenix Satellite Television* [凤凰卫视], September 4, 2012, available at <http://news.ifeng.com/mainland/special/diaoyudaozhengduan/content-3/detail_2012_09/04/17327444_0.shtml>.

66   Stephen Clark, "Chinese Rocket Launches Powerful Nigerian Satellite into Orbit," *Spaceflight Now*, December 19, 2011, available at <www.space.com/13975-china-rocket-launching-huge-nigeria-satellite.html>.

67   Wang Jianhong, Zhang Yaohong, and Li Xin [王建宏, 张耀鸿, 李新], "Research into C4ISR Systems for Special Operations" [特种作战 C4ISR系统], *Fire Control and Command Control* [火力与指挥控制] 30, no. 4 (August 2005), 48–50, available at <www.defence.org.cn/aspnet/vip-usa/uploadfiles/2006-6/20066114449161.pdf>.

68   Li Jing, ed., "'Mission Action-2010' Cross-Region Mobility Exercise Ends Satisfactorily," and Joe McReynolds and James Mulvenon, "The Role of Informatization in the People's Liberation Army Under Hu Jintao," in *Assessing the People's Liberation*

Army in the Hu Jintao Era, ed. Roy Kamphausen, David Lai, and Travis Tanner (Carlisle Barracks, PA: U.S. Army War College Press, 2014).

69   Liu Yonghua and Cai Pengcheng [刘永华, 蔡鹏程], "The PLA's Cross-Region Exercise Achieves Full Visualization and Real-time Dynamic Monitoring" [我军跨域演习实现全程可视化及实时动态监控], Xinhua Online, October 13, 2010, available at <http://mil.huanqiu.com/china/2010-10/1166308.html>.

70   Liu Jianwei and Chang Xiexue [刘建伟, 杨勤学], "Shenyang Military Region's Integrated Command Platform Spawns 8 Functions in the Command Personnel" [沈阳军区部队一体化指挥平台催生指挥员8种能力], *PLA Daily*, March 28, 2011, available at <http://mil.sohu.com/20110328/n280022801.shtml>.

71   "Deciphering Integrated Operations."

72   Zhang Lingjun [张领军], ed., "Integrated Joint Operation: Theory Development and Practical Exploration" [一体化联合作战理论发展与实践探索] (Beijing: Military Friendship Literary Press [军事谊文出版社], 2006), 4.

73   Ibid.

China Plans for Internal Unrest: People's Armed Police and Public Security Approaches to "Mass Incidents"

Jonathan Walton

The domestic security forces of the People's Republic of China (PRC)—primarily the national police force managed by the Ministry of Public Security and the paramilitary People's Armed Police (PAP)—have a broad mandate to uphold the stability of the country and the continued rule of the Chinese Communist Party (CCP).[1] Under this mandate, they have been specifically assigned a number of tasks and areas of responsibility, which cover such diverse duties as maintaining public order, investigating crimes, securing borders, handling customs, fighting fires, combating drug and human trafficking, conducting counterterrorism activities, guarding important leaders and locations, monitoring the Internet, operating certain prisons and detention centers, directing traffic, and so forth.[2] All of these responsibilities are generally viewed as part of the larger goal of preserving social stability in China as it attempts to transition toward becoming a developed country.

While the majority of Chinese domestic security personnel have day-to-day responsibilities in monitoring or administrative work, Public Security and PAP units are also regularly mobilized in response to certain contingencies, including natural disasters, violent crimes, and other emergency situations. Over the last decade or more, handling mass incidents [*quntixing shijian*, 群体性事件] has become an increasingly common task facing security personnel activated for such emergencies. *Mass incident* in Chinese security jargon refers to a protest, riot, or other gathering of a large number of people without prior approval from the appropriate government organs.[3] Such incidents reportedly occurred approximately 74,000 times in 2004 and 87,000 in 2005 (the last years for which official numbers were released), which averages to 238 mass incidents per day, or roughly 30 incidents per year for every county-level subdivision in

China. Current annual estimates vary widely due to the lack of official numbers, but nearly all proposed figures are upwards of 100,000.[4]

In 2005, then–Minister of Public Security Zhou Yongkang indicated that "actively preventing and properly handling" mass incidents was the main task facing his office.[5] That same year, the central government issued the National Contingency Plan for Large-scale Mass Incidents, a landmark document that local governments at the provincial, prefectural, and county levels were required to use as a model for their own contingency plans regarding unrest.[6] This focus by the PRC government on the core task of *stability preservation* [*weiwen*, 维稳]—another increasingly ubiquitous term in Chinese security jargon—is not particularly new, at least not by itself. Indeed, the majority of the contemporary PAP is composed of forces officially designated as *internal security* [*neiwei*, 内维], which are primarily meant to respond to mass incidents and other disturbances. The more novel aspect, beginning in the mid-2000s, has been the convergence of two major trends: the advent of robust emergency planning and crisis-response capabilities within various parts of the state bureaucracy and the strengthening of heretofore inconsistent attempts to provide a legal basis for Chinese police work.

Following the poorly coordinated response to the 2002–2003 severe acute respiratory syndrome (SARS) outbreak, the PRC government made extensive efforts to develop a more effective crisis-response system, including mandatory contingency planning throughout all levels of government. Many of these plans propose a whole-of-government approach that involves domestic security organs and the People's Liberation Army (PLA) in addition to civilian government offices. For example, the 2005 General Contingency Plan for National Public Emergencies asserted that "the PLA and the PAP are the backbone and shock forces for managing public emergencies and participate in emergency response work according to the relevant regulations."[7]

These efforts to create contingency plans that include Public Security and PAP personnel have drawn on and benefited from reformist efforts to standardize and regulate Chinese policing, which have—among other things—generated more explicit guidelines for how police should respond to various contingencies, beginning with the 1995 Police Law. Spurred on by preparations for the 2008 Olympics and the 60th anniversary of the PRC in 2009, as well as the 2008–2009 large-scale unrest in China's western regions, the central government released the 2008 Regulations on the Handling of Mass Incidents by Public Security Organs and the 2009 People's Armed Police Law, the latter representing the first time that extensive regulations for paramilitary activities had been publicly released.[8] The availability of these and other relatively recent planning and regulatory documents means that outside observers of Chinese policing have a much better understanding of how domestic security forces are expected to operate in crisis situations.

This chapter outlines how Chinese domestic security institutions think about, plan for, and attempt to respond to incidents of social unrest. Where possible, this examination identifies the government and party leaders responsible for many major policing concepts, plans, and decisions, since Public Security and PAP forces are supposed to be subservient to civilian political leaders. It also leverages analyses by scholars based outside of China in an effort to overcome ideological or political concerns that may hamper Chinese security personnel and PRC-based scholars from accurately perceiving or publicly describing certain aspects of the problems China confronts in the domestic security domain.

The chapter opens with a discussion of the nature and scope of unrest in China. This is followed by an examination of the publicly available information on the planning for mobilization of domestic security forces to respond to unrest and the regulations that guide their responses. The chapter then explores a number of the most commonly discussed issues facing domestic security forces in responding to unrest. It closes with a few thoughts on the importance of studying mass incidents, given their regular occurrence and persistent importance in the minds of China's highest-ranking leaders.[9]

The Nature and Scope of Unrest in China

The authoritarian government of the world's most populous country is attempting to manage an astonishingly rapid but still lengthy and complex transition to developed country status. While the PRC has many advantages as a late developer—notably the opportunity to learn from the experiences, development models, technological advances, and institutional innovations of other, more developed countries—it also faces many challenges that are the product of its own unique history and context, including substantial challenges in the area of domestic security.

The reforms promoted by Deng Xiaoping have inspired dramatic changes in the structures and incentives in Chinese society, leading to a breakdown of village and family relations in rural areas due to labor migration, a huge influx of people into the cities, the decline of the state's former systems of monitoring and social control, the empowerment of social institutions outside of government, and a number of other developments that have increased what the CCP calls "contradictions among the people" (social tensions and increasing disparity). In addition, the state's encouragement of unbridled economic growth and its limited efforts to strengthen popular political participation have contributed to increased tensions between local populations and local government, as citizens feel aggrieved by land seizures, widespread official corruption, corporate poisoning of the environment, abuses of power, and—in some cases—suppression of basic human rights and lack of adherence to China's own laws. Such suppression happens throughout the country but appears to be more extreme in the minority regions of Tibet and Xinjiang, where semi-colonial government policies promote Han in-migration and restrict the religious and cultural practices of native ethnic groups. Paired with the absence of clear, effective channels for political participation and redress, all these complaints have contributed to an immense and apparently steady increase in the number of mass incidents whereby citizens seek to air their grievances and create enough trouble for local, regional, or even national government officials that some intervention and/or compromise is made.

According to PRC guidelines on bringing complaints to government offices, it is improper to petition with a group of more than five people. In practice, however, petitioners find that much larger groups—known as "collective petitions"—obtain better results. A common saying is that "a small disturbance leads to a small solution, a large disturbance leads to a big solution, [and] no disturbance leads to no solution."[10] Given the complexities of managing a crowd or mob, distinctions between collective petitions, protests, riots, and other mass incidents are often unclear. Chinese security writings recognize that mass incidents can take a variety of different forms, including collective petitions, demonstrations, marches, strikes, surrounding or obstructing government offices or transportation routes, blocking construction work, holding officials hostage, and so on.[11] The scale of mass actions and degree of premeditation also vary significantly, as does the level of unruliness exhibited by participants and the level of experience with past incidents.

Motivations for organizing or participating in a mass incident are likewise diverse. However, China's domestic security literature and policing regulations typically only recognize a few broad categories of motivations, as their main goals are to create a typology of participant motivations and assist security personnel in analyzing situations and rationalizing differential treatment of participants. Such simplified models typically discuss:

- *legitimate motivations*, such as seeking redress of specific grievances or expressing frustration with circumstances or the actions of local leaders, though having good intentions does not necessarily absolve such participants of the crime of organizing an illegal protest
- *illegitimate, criminal, or political motivations*, such as the desire to commit violence, create chaos, or sabotage China's aspirations for a "harmonious society," making such participants significantly more dangerous and guilty of major crimes
- *no particular motivations*, but simply being caught up in things, misled by protest organizers, or excited to be an onlooker, which in most cases is assumed to apply to the majority of participants, who will likely face only mild consequences for their involvement.

The officially reported number of 87,000 mass incidents for 2005 generated a significant buzz in the international press, and some scholars think that China's central leaders have attempted to artificially lower (that is, underreport) the number of protests since then. Sun Liping of Tsinghua University, for example, estimates that China may have experienced 180,000 mass incidents in 2011, rather than the roughly 100,000 estimated in other accounts, which would indicate that protests are growing exponentially rather than linearly.[12] Even 100,000 mass incidents a year would be the equivalent of roughly three incidents per month for every county-level subdivision in China, though the occurrence is spread heterogeneously rather than evenly.

Under the administration of former President Hu Jintao and former Premier Wen Jiabao, the central government increasingly acknowledged that many if not most instances of unrest are inspired by legitimate grievances on the part of local citizens, rather than the desire for political subversion or general opposition to the CCP regime, a theme that has so far continued under Xi Jinping. As a recent example, in February 2012, Wen visited the site of a major 2011 protest by farmers and said, "What is the widespread problem now? It's the arbitrary seizure of farmers' fields, and the farmers have complaints about this, and it's even sparking mass incidents. . . . The root of the problem is that the land is the property of the farmers, but this right has not been protected in the way it should be."[13] While this shift in policy toward acknowledging popular grievances is a positive development, it also appears to be partially tactical, an attempt to preserve the legitimacy of the central government by throwing local leaders under the bus for carrying out extractive or development-first policies that in many instances were required or encouraged by the center. For example, following an explosive 2008 incident in Guizhou's Weng'an county, the provincial party secretary argued that the situation was exacerbated by the mishandling of previous incidents:

> In the development of local mineral resources, resettlement, building demolition and other such work, situations frequently occurred that infringed upon the interests of the masses. In the process of disposing of these contradictions, disputes, and mass incidents, some cadres used a brash style, simple methods, and were cavalier about calling on police suppression. In this regard, the Weng'an party secretary, county government, county public security bureau, and the leading cadres of the relevant departments cannot avoid responsibility [for the 2008 incident].[14]

As illustrated in this example, the responsibilities placed on local leaders by the central government are often both contradictory (pursue rapid economic development but preserve social harmony) and underfunded (in effect, encouraging local leaders to use improper fundraising methods such as seizing agricultural lands and selling them to developers). Facing such pressures, many local leaders have chosen to serve the center's goals (and the cause of their own enrichment) over the interests of their local constituents. That is the surest path to promotion or transfer and officials typically have few ties to the locale over which they are appointed, limiting potential qualms about using their financial and administrative authority over security forces to suppress any local dissent. But while both the center and local protesters often frame all problems as the responsibility of local leaders, the systemic nature of such problems means that the central PRC government cannot avoid responsibility either.

Meanwhile, Public Security and PAP leaders tend to be less sympathetic to popular grievances in their own writings. This is particularly true of high-level domestic security leaders, who do not fear the consequences of using too much force in suppressing a local incident as much as they fear domestic security forces refusing to obey orders or, worse, choosing to side with a group of protesters. The failure of police organs to effectively handle the 1989 Tian'anmen protests still casts a shadow over such thinking,[15] and as China enters what may be a more difficult stage of its development—where it can no longer count on 10 percent annual economic growth rates—there have been frequent speeches by central leaders that emphasize the necessity of ensuring the police (and PLA) remain loyal and obedient to the CCP above all else. This is accomplished in part by demonizing potential targets of suppression, obscuring many of the legitimate motivations of protesters and dissenters, and claiming that they are active or unwitting pawns of foreign or domestic enemies that desire China's downfall. For example, the director of the Sichuan Provincial Public Security Department wrote an article in 2011 for the PRC's leading journal of policing, *Public Security Studies,* claiming that:

> hostile foreign and domestic forces manipulate, incite speculation about, and directly provoke contradictions within our people in increasingly prominent ways. . . . *Taking advantage of our instabilities to stir up trouble.* The economic transition and social transformation that have accompanied our country's reform and development have brought about a profound adjustment of the pattern of interests and, objectively speaking, have provided the conditions for hostile elements to meddle. They seize on some controversial and sensitive domestic issue, "rights protection" incident, or judicial case and openly meddle, wantonly speculate, and attempt to instigate the ignorant against the party and the state, damaging our excellent situation of prosperity and stability. . . . *Meddling in our mass incidents to intensify contradictions.* This specific stage of our country's economic and social development exhibits a wide range of social contradictions and major disputes; if these are improperly handled, they can easily lead to mass incidents. Hostile forces do everything in their power to meddle in our country's internal mass incidents in a vain attempt to exacerbate the situation, scale, destruction, and impact; the incidents in Guizhou's Weng'an County and Yunnan's Menglian County are typical examples. . . . *Seeking every opportunity to directly create chaos.* An increasingly powerful China creates great uneasiness for the hostile forces both inside and outside its borders. They directly rouse their

domestic forces into action and take advantage of the portion of the masses that do not know the truth; increasingly common incidents of vandalism, arson, and other destructive activities—such as the March 14 incident in Lhasa, the March 16 incident in Aba, the July 5 incident in Xinjiang, and others—are certainly [the responsibility] of Western anti-China forces and hostile foreign and domestic forces.[16]

While it is tempting to speculate on the extent to which China's leading domestic security leaders believe such convenient fictions about the omnipresence of foreign saboteurs promoting unrest—something that dramatically exaggerates the reach of U.S. intelligence services, for one, even if they were interested in local events such as the 2008 Weng'an crisis—it may be presumptive to dismiss all of this as intentional misinformation. To draw a comparative example, when protest leader Wael Ghonim met with high-level Egyptian officials at the height of the Arab Spring, just before President Hosni Mubarak agreed to stepped down, he was stunned by the extent to which government and security leaders believed their own propaganda about the Tahrir Square protests being caused by foreign subversion and people with ulterior motives, rather than recognizing the many reasons citizens had to denounce the regime.[17] Similar messages are repeated so often in PRC security circles that even top leaders may find it difficult to fully appreciate that China's unrest is overwhelmingly caused by systemic domestic problems and not foreign subversion.

The desensitization of security forces to the legitimate demands of Chinese citizens is also aided by the relatively recent trend of periodic violent outbreaks, such as mass knifing attacks. Knives have long been a weapon associated with ethnic minorities from the Western regions of Tibet and Xinjiang, male members of which traditionally carry knives, and the gangland violence of organized crime, as they have often been the weapon of choice for gang members due partially to the relative difficulty of obtaining firearms in China and Hong Kong. However, knife attacks seem to have spread beyond those limited demographics, such as in a number of disturbing attacks on school children between 2010 and 2012. In 2010, in the midst of those attacks, the drunken and enraged Li Xianliang used a tractor to kill 17 people in Hebei province. There was also the case of Yang Jia, who in 2008 directly attacked a police station in suburban Shanghai with gasoline bombs and a knife, murdering multiple officers (and receiving a surprising amount of popular sympathy for his actions).

In 2013–2014, there were multiple attacks outside of Xinjiang—in Beijing, Kunming, Urumqi, and Guangzhou—that apparently involved ethnic Uighurs, perhaps indicating an intensification of ethnic tensions related to Xinjiang.

Such attacks are not mass incidents but can easily become linked with them in the minds of Chinese security forces, since in official accounts they are often associated with similar motivations to those that are supposedly held by protest leaders. Particularly in the case of Xinjiang and Tibet, there is not often a clear distinction drawn between the dynamics behind the 2008 and 2009 outbreaks of mass unrest in those regions and violent crimes or terrorist attacks that involve ethnic Uighurs and Tibetans. Instead, a strong sense of confirmation bias appears to be in play; violent and destructive actions by individuals or groups—be they ethnic minorities, the religious fringe,[18] the mentally ill, violent criminals, or mobs of protesters—fuel the widespread belief that China is under siege from foreign and domestic opponents.

In summation, the sheer number of mass incidents in China is enormous, and while each one has its own idiosyncratic causes and situation, they are collectively driven by systemic problems related to the immense changes that China is undergoing and the limitations of the social and political institutions that are supposed to manage these changes. Additionally, the conspiratorial ideology incessantly repeated in political and domestic security circles focuses blame on largely imaginary foreign forces that are incapable of being reasoned with, which frames these problems as being insolvable except by tougher and better police work. Hence, the already difficult task of managing China's unruly transition toward being a developed country is made more difficult by institutional inertia and inaccurate views of the problems at hand.

Mobilizing Security Forces in Response to Unrest

During the Hu-Wen administration, local officials were encouraged—both through public pronouncements and by revisions to the cadre evaluation system—to address the concerns of citizens before they led to mass incidents that had to be dealt with by the police. Local party leaders were supposed to get ahead of a problem, be responsive to local needs, control the "spin" of a particular issue in the local media, and otherwise handle problems in a much more sophisticated way than in the past. Hand in hand with this, Hu and Wen placed greater emphasis on the need for a multifaceted and whole-of-government approach to unrest. After all, local party and government leaders have many other tools to draw on other than just local Public Security and PAP units. The media control and propaganda system, petitioning system, mediation system, legal system, household registration system (for tracking people), state-owned enterprises, state-run labor unions, a number of different detention systems, and a wide variety of other bureaucratic mechanisms and offices can all play important roles in monitoring and redirecting aggrieved citizens in such a way that social order is maintained, either before, during, or after a mass incident. While coordinating all these offices is a logistical nightmare, this process is made easier in China by the pervasive nature of the CCP. While it may sometimes be difficult to convince different government offices to work together, especially if both are on the same level and there is no clear hierarchy, the hierarchical relationships of officials within the CCP are much clearer. Furthermore, many party officials wear multiple "hats" on the government side, so the head of one office may also be the head or a member of several other offices, knitting the government together and enabling coordination across the various bureaucracies.

In addition to individual party leaders, the center also mandates coordination through a number of "leading groups" established directly by the Politburo, many of which have offices down to the local level. Such groups hold semi-regular local meetings to discuss issues and incidents and include members from a variety of local government offices. In terms of domestic security, the most important of such groups are probably the Central Leading Group on Stability Preservation and the Central Leading Group on Dealing with Evil Cults (originally established in 1999 for the campaign against Falun Gong and popularly known as the "6-10 Office" due to the date of its establishment), as well as the Public Security System's secretive Domestic Security Department, which reportedly works closely with the two mentioned leading groups. The Domestic Security Department, according to leaked documents, conducts "regularly scheduled domestic security report meetings, serious incident analysis meetings, and specialized work coordination meetings; these meetings ensure the timely communication of intelligence and the coordination of command mechanisms."[19] Such meetings involve both civilian government and security leaders.

While central directives encourage local leaders and security committees to prevent mass incidents by practicing good governance and conducting strong "grassroots work," getting close to their constituents and earning their trust, local leaders have not proven to be successful at reducing the annual number of mass incidents in the PRC. Consequently, many are confronted with what to do about a mass protest or other large-scale event once it occurs, with the main options being making concessions to at least partially appease the protesters, making some concessions but also disciplining or imprisoning the ringleaders, tolerating and managing the unrest for a while without responding directly to see if it loses steam, and repressing the unrest using formal or informal methods, whether by employing hired local thugs or calling upon the police. Hong Kong–based scholar Yongshun Cai has observed that local governments evaluate the costs of these various options in a semi-rational fashion, weighing such issues as the economic and political costs of concessions, the possible risks associated with showing weakness and losing/gaining legitimacy through compromise, the uncertainties of repression, the presence or absence of violence, media exposure, the number of protesters involved, and the history of previous problems with this group of protesters or this particular issue.[20]

In recent years, when making decisions about repression, local governments have also been able to draw on a number of widely available laws and regulations on deploying Public Security and PAP forces to handle mass incidents, in addition to a large body of internal documents that are not public. Several of the most important are discussed below.

2008 Regulations on the Handling of Mass Incidents

The most pertinent portions of the 2008 Regulations on the Handling of Mass Incidents are articles 6, 7, and 8, which describe when Public Security personnel should become involved in managing an incident of social unrest and what authorization is needed for responses of varying scope.[21] Article 6 describes mass incidents that Public Security organs should not confront directly but rather should leave to local government authorities to manage (unless things become violent or destabilized). Such incidents include assemblies, processions, and demonstrations that occur within school campuses or places of employment; collective petitions; protests related to legitimate concerns such as land acquisitions, layoffs, unpaid wages or pensions, pollution, or corruption; and other public disturbances that have not yet become destructive or challenged the social order by blocking major roads or the entrances to important buildings. However, even in cases such as these, the regulations instruct Public Security organs to "dispatch plainclothes police or a small number of uniformed police to the site to grasp the situation, maintain order, and

promptly report the dynamics on the ground; work with local Party committees, government offices, and relevant departments to resolve contradictions;
and prepare to quickly mobilize police to manage the situation." In contrast,
Article 7 describes incidents that are much more immediately pressing, such
as protests or collective petitions that disrupt the social order in a serious way
or endanger public safety; incidents organized by "evil cults or other illegal
organizations"; and those that:

> impact Party and government organs, judicial organs, military organs,
> important guarded targets [such as facilities or high-level officials],
> radio and television stations, communications hubs, foreign embas-
> sies or consulates, as well as other vital parts or offices; and those that
> involve mass blocking of public transport hubs, traffic routes, and
> ports . . . or illegally occupying public places.

Under these more dangerous conditions, the regulations state that "public
security organs should—in accordance with the decisions of local party committees and governments, and under their unified leadership—rapidly mobilize police personnel, rush them to the scene, and take measures to properly
dispose of the incident according to the law."

Article 8 describes the authorization needed for mobilizing different
numbers of police personnel to respond to a mass incident. Mobilizing fewer
than 100 personnel can be approved at the county level, mobilizing between
100 and 300 personnel must be submitted for approval at the prefecture level,
mobilizing more than 300 personnel must be submitted for approval at the provincial level and reported to the Ministry of Public Security so it can be officially
recorded, and cross-regional mobilization must be approved by a higher-level
public security organ with authority over all the regions involved. In addition
to limiting mobilization numbers without higher-level authorization, Article
8 offers the following guidance:

> The application for and approval of police force mobilization should
> be submitted and authorized in writing in the name of the public
> security organ at the same level [that is, the same level as the party
> organ required to approve the mobilization]. In especially urgent cir-
> cumstances, oral submission and approval can be done, with written
> authorization later being obtained and applied retroactively.

The existence of the oral authorization clause raises more questions about the inability of domestic security forces to respond in a timely fashion to the 2008 and 2009 outbreaks of unrest in Tibet and Xinjiang, though the clause may not have been fully in use at the time of those riots. It is also possible that party and public security leaders may be hesitant to give even oral authorization for police actions that may come back to haunt them later, since applications for retroactive authorization would seem either to lay the blame for any misman-agement at their feet if they sign them or to require them to throw their subor-dinates under the bus if they later claim not to have given oral authorization.

2009 People's Armed Police Law

In terms of involving paramilitary forces rather than just increasing the num-bers of Public Security personnel responding to an emergency, the 2008 Regu-lations on the Handling of Mass Incidents unhelpfully state that "mobilization involving the use of the PAP to handle mass incidents must be in accord with the relevant regulations." Until 2009, this would have meant considering a number of different regulations that touch on the PAP in passing and extensive internal regulations unavailable to open-source researchers. Luckily, while secret internal regulations likely provide much more detail, the public release of the 2009 People's Armed Police Law dramatically improves the transparency of this process. An interview with then–PAP commander Wu Shuangzhan on the day the law was released confirmed that it was based at least partially on unifying existing guidelines and transforming classified internal regulations into something that could be made public.[22]

In early drafts of this law, the PAP were described as potentially intervening in any "incident which threatens social stability," a very vague and amorphous description that some lawmakers suggested might make it easy to abuse the use of armed force. Consequently, in the final draft, this language was tightened up to limit PAP involvement to "riots, turbulence, severe violent crimes, terrorist attacks, and other social security incidents."[23] While the last term is something of a catch-all, its comparability to the previous terms indicates that only severe or highly disruptive situations require intervention by the PAP.

If the law is still somewhat vague on when it is appropriate to deploy para-military forces, it is much clearer than previous regulations about who needs to authorize deployment and the relationship between PAP and Public Security personnel when cooperating to handle an incident. First, Chapter II, Article

10, notes that the PAP can be "deployed to perform security tasks according to the Public Security organs of People's Governments above the county level."[24] Essentially, the latter part of this means that party and government leaders at or below the county level cannot call upon the PAP without higher-level authorization, limiting abuse of paramilitary force—at least in theory—to the prefectural level and higher, where it is apparently hoped that ambitious leaders will consider the broader policy effects of such a course of action, beyond their own parochial interests. However, it is unclear if this actually puts a brake on the use of the PAP in situations where less violent methods could be more effective.

Perhaps more interestingly, in the course of conducting policing tasks—such as "taking necessary measures to stop or disperse a mob that is attempting to harm the social order or the safety of your assigned target [that is, an important person or location]"—the PAP must operate according to the will of the Public Security organs supervising the situation (who will of necessity be prefecture level or higher if the PAP has been called in). This theme of treating the PAP in a manner similar to normal Public Security officers is repeated elsewhere in the law, with PAP personnel being required to turn over all detainees to Public Security or State Security officers (Article 11) and also, surprisingly, the PAP being told to follow the same weapons and equipment procedures as Public Security organs (Article 15).[25]

Previously—and even after the passage of this law—one of the main things that differentiated the PAP from Public Security officers had been their access to military-grade weapons and equipment (hence the "armed" in "People's Armed Police"). This was especially noticeable in decades past, when Public Security officers were hardly ever authorized to carry guns in the course of their normal duties. This lack of firearms was standard practice until very recently, but beginning in 2014, several cities have experimented with allowing police to carry guns while on patrol, a practice that seems likely to spread.[26] The PAP was originally intended to be reserved for rare situations where armed force might be necessary. However, in recent years, due to the arming of Public Security officers, first as part of fast-response SWAT-style teams, the distinctions between Public Security and PAP are less cut and dried than they once were.

Contingency Plans for Large-scale Mass Incidents

While the 2005 National Contingency Plan for Large-scale Mass Incidents is no longer publicly available, the 2010 Xi'an Municipal Public Security Bureau

Contingency Plan for Large-scale Mass Incidents and the 2006 Ningxia Hui Autonomous Region Contingency Plan for Large-scale Mass Incidents[27] are examples of local contingency plans written up in response to the national plan. The Xi'an plan includes both an Emergency Command [*yingji zhihui*, 应急指挥], led by the Party Secretary of Xi'an (who is also head of the Political and Legal Affairs Committee, which oversees security issues), and an Office of Emergency Response [*yingji xiangying bangongshi*, 应急响应办公室], led by the Deputy Secretary of the Municipal Public Security Bureau. During a crisis, the headquarters of the Emergency Command is set up in the command center of the Municipal Public Security Bureau, where it coordinates efforts by the Office of Emergency Response to implement its directives. There is also an Emergency Response Working Group composed of all the county- or district-level Public Security sub-bureaus, all Bureaus of Education (which oversee students), all Bureaus of Letters and Visits (which oversee petitioning), and all Ethnic Affairs Commissions (which oversee minority affairs). The working group is described as being specifically responsible for responding to a large-scale mass incident.

In terms of tailoring an appropriate response, the Xi'an plan identifies three general categories of mass incidents: Grade Three (general) [*yiban*, 一般], Grade Two (large) [*jiaoda*, 较大], and Grade One (significant) [*zhongda*, 重大]. This plan reflects a rating scale for emergencies similar to those seen in contingency plans for natural disasters and other types of situations:

- Grade Three events include small gatherings of Falun Gong practitioners, other cult members, or members of illegal organizations; unregistered assemblies or protests; blocking traffic; or large-scale gatherings involving sporting events, commercial activities, or entertainment. During such events, the police are instructed to use caution when using coercive measures, announce the relevant laws and regulations, issue verbal warnings to the leaders of the gatherings, and dissuade people from causing trouble.
- Grade Two events include large gatherings of cult or illegal organization members; large illegal assemblies with more political purposes, such as processions, demonstrations, and rallies; strikes and similar events that "harm society"; the blocking of major traffic hubs; and mobs that become violent. If such events require cooperation across districts or regions, a field command should be set up to coordinate the response. During such incidents, the police are instructed to quickly and resolutely

break up the event and restore social order, moving people away from the scene (especially the core troublemakers), stop the distributions of "reactionary propaganda" materials [*fandong xuanchuan*, 反动宣传] and record the incident using photos and video to identify the individuals involved.

- Grade One events, following the established pattern, are not different in type, just in scope: larger assemblies that cause greater social harm or are more violent. In order to manage multiple incidents across the city and prevent the situation from escalating out of control, the city will be divided into six emergency districts, each with its own District Working Group, which will cooperate with the Emergency Response Working Group in managing the situation. The municipal Working Group is supposed to inform the municipal Office of Emergency Response when the situation has expanded beyond its control, and then the office will mobilize the District Working Groups to assist in management.

Notably, the Xi'an plan is silent on what happens if the municipal and district working groups prove unable to handle the situation (presumably there is an internal document that specifies what happens at that point, or the situation is then bumped up to the provincial level, since Xi'an is a prefecture-level city). After the incident is resolved, the plan tells Public Security forces to use the criminal law and mass incident mediation system, prosecuting some leaders but releasing the rest and also working to resolve the problems facing the masses. In addition, the Emergency Response Working Group is supposed to submit a full report of the incident that includes lessons learned and areas that need improvement to provide the basis of an improved response in the future.

In comparison to the municipal plan, the Ningxia provincial-level plan also includes establishing an emergency command structure but suggests doing so at the level of the entire province, the city where the disturbance originated, and the site of each individual incident. Similar to the municipal plan, each of these commands is given coordinating responsibility over their jurisdiction and is composed of representatives of government organs at each level, including not just party leadership and Public Security organs but also—especially at the provincial level—the local wings of various ministries that might be involved (development, investment, education, religious affairs, minority affairs, labor, public health, and media, as well as PAP and PLA representatives).

In terms of categorizing incidents, the Ningxia plan uses the same three grades as the Xi'an plan, though they are described somewhat differently: Grade One (extremely serious incidents or those of over 1,000 people), Grade Two (serious incidents or those of between 500 and 1,000 people), and Grade Three (incidents of between 100 and 500 people), since, presumably, incidents of fewer than 100 people are not considered serious enough to demand the involvement of the provincial government. Noticeable in this section are the characteristics that can push an incident up to a higher grade without requiring higher numbers of people: causing deaths or directly attacking party, government, or military interests; incidents that involve religious or ethnic issues; prison riots; those that take over college campuses; those obstructing major transport thoroughfares; and those being publicized by information technology.

The Ningxia plan provides extensive guidelines only for Grade One incidents, presumably because those are the ones that are most likely to involve the provincial government directly. Notably, the response guidelines for Grade One incidents specifically mention mobilizing the PAP, though they simply say this should be done "strictly according to the relevant procedures." Because this plan was written for the provincial government, rather than for the Public Security organs (as the Xi'an plan was), much of the plan involves information control, both in terms of coordinating among various state units involved in emergency response and also in terms of controlling the message about what is happening in news media reports. Since the Ningxia plan dates to 2006, this information control aspect may have become even stronger in more recent plans, as there have been notable initiatives in recent years to promote this aspect of incident management among local governments and Public Security departments.

Bringing in Security Forces from Neighboring Regions

One issue worth noting in discussions of contingency planning is the guidelines for mobilizing units from other regions in response to incidents, which includes the PAP, militia/reserve units, and PLA support units. For example, PAP units from Jiangsu, Fujian, and Henan were dispatched to assist with the 2009 unrest in Xinjiang.[28] According to the regulations examined above, it is likely that the decision to move these forces across provincial boundaries was taken at the level of the Ministry of Public Security, the Central Military Commission, or even higher (such as the Politburo Standing Committee) because no lower level has authority over both the eastern provinces and Xinjiang. Requiring such high-level approval for cross-provincial transfers of security forces may be partially to blame for the lack of a rapid and adequate response by the PAP to the original disturbance and for Hu Jintao pulling out of the Group of Eight summit to return to China to attend to the matter. While the PLA was also mobilized to provide support in Xinjiang, most authoritative sources suggest it is unlikely that they were directly involved, though there were reports to the contrary, as there were in Tibet in 2008.[29]

Intervention by the PLA

Notably absent from any publicly available regulations, laws, or plans is any notion of when the PLA might have to step in to resolve an incident of domestic unrest or, more likely, a series of linked incidents or a general lawlessness engulfing a city or region. While China's military has avoided direct involvement in domestic security activities since the period immediately following their intervention in the 1989 Tian'anmen Square protests, the PLA still provides the ultimate guarantee for the continued rule of the CCP and could conceivably be called on if domestic security forces proved insufficient, were unable to respond, or proved disloyal. PLA responsibilities in the event of massive, uncontrolled unrest may be detailed in internal documents, but it is also possible that PLA and civilian authorities both wish to avoid making concrete promises about military intervention, leaving that instead as a special mission to be invoked only if circumstances require. Certainly, Lin Biao's invocation of emergency powers and use of the PLA in internal CCP politics near the end of the Cultural Revolution, including his purported failed attempt to execute a coup against Mao Zedong, still cast some shadow over creating any formal method for one or more high-level political leaders to call in the PLA for a domestic crisis.

China's Security Forces Discuss Difficulties and Challenges in Responding to Mass Incidents

The writings of Chinese domestic security personnel on the handling of mass incidents emphasize a number of areas in which responses could be strengthened. These include:

- acting quickly and decisively
- acting with the appropriate authorization

- acting with appropriate strength
- being deliberate in the use of force
- targeting the leadership as opposed to the masses
- controlling the narrative
- working to resolve problems in the aftermath
- conducting post-incident "grassroots" work to avoid future problems.

The first two issues are complicated, since they are largely dependent on the decisions of civilian government actors, not those of security personnel. Public Security, PAP, and militia and reserve forces are essentially under local party and government administration—though they also have to answer to higher-level authorities in their own institutions. This can lead to delays in response time, since local leaders can be reluctant to step up and take responsibility for a crisis lest they get blamed for it, though eventually the same leaders will earn the attention of higher-level CCP officials if the problem gets worse and they are not seen as responding appropriately or effectively.

Particular emphasis has also been placed on handling incidents correctly the first time, rather than suppressing protests too harshly and thereby radicalizing protesters and perhaps creating future problems. A separate problem that Chinese security writers identify is using insufficient numbers of security personnel at the outset and allowing a clash with protesters to escalate to lethal force or an uncontained riot. These concerns are reflected in the efforts of recent regulations to more clearly specify the number of police needed for particular kinds of circumstances, though this may make it more difficult for security forces to respond dynamically to the situation at hand, particularly if they need authorization to bring in more personnel.

In terms of managing the use of violence, central authorities are also clearly worried about local leaders using the PAP haphazardly to enforce their will in situations where the deployment of Chinese security forces may not actually be required. Ultimately, to encourage local officials to use the other means at their disposal rather than just calling in security forces at the first sign of trouble and wielding force indiscriminately, the central government has attempted to place tighter restrictions on the ability of local officials to bring in the PAP in particular and security forces more broadly. This has led to newer developments such as control over PAP deployment being restricted to local governments above the county level.

A stickier problem may be that suppression in general is not a viable long-term solution in instances where the real problem is lack of good governance and poor relations between local officials and their constituents. In the aftermath of the 2008 Weng'an incident, Shen Guirong, the former head of the local Public Security Bureau, suggested in an interview that the police had been unable to solve serious crimes due to collusion between the police and local criminal organizations. In addition:

> Shen blamed the non-police uses to which public security forces had been put over the years for causing deep social discontent. There had been five mass incidents "in recent years" in which more than 100 public security personnel had been dispatched. The instances were occasioned by conflicts over mine rights, migration and relocation, and the demolition of houses. "We have infuriated almost everyone."[30]

The persistence of mistreatment, torture, and even mysterious unexplained deaths in police custody also exacerbates current and future conflicts with protesters long after the initial response to a mass incident has been completed.[31] If citizens lack even the basic confidence that they can be detained by police without being murdered, trust in the system becomes virtually impossible and protesters may increasingly radicalize or escalate their own efforts to match the new threat level (death) posed by the state.

Beyond inappropriate levels of violence, Chinese domestic security scholars and personnel note the importance of targeting repressive measures against the "backbone" organizers of a particular incident of unrest [*gugan fenzi*, 骨干分子] rather than the broader mass of people who may just be upset about a variety of problems, misled by the protest leaders, or caught up in events. Broad or poorly targeted violence or other forms of suppression tends to produce popular resentment and a decrease in the legitimacy of the local government, party leaders, and Public Security personnel in the eyes of citizens. However, identifying, isolating, detaining, and punishing protest leaders are often easier said than done. In urban areas, police sometimes cultivate informants from within unruly groups of citizens or even dispatch plainclothes officers to observe and report, though this is more difficult in rural communities where everyone knows each other. Additionally, the removal of key protest leaders does not always succeed in dispersing and minimizing unrest, particularly if new leaders step up to take their places and perhaps take the movement in a new direction or battle with other potential challengers for authority.

Two other challenges commonly mentioned in the literature are controlling the narrative of a particular incident, especially in the media, and conducting good "grassroots" work in the aftermath to prevent recurrence. Discussions of the former often focus on weaknesses in early identification and response to problems, which makes it more difficult to control the information that gets out about it. Often, by the time local party leaders are mobilizing resources and personnel to respond to a problem, it is already being discussed in online forums and more traditional media outlets such as newspapers and television. Efforts to address this lack of control of the portrayal of an incident often suggest that local leaders get in front of an issue, releasing extensive information through government offices and using media controls to shape the way the incident "plays" and the information that is available on it. Under Xi Jinping's presidency, there have already been a number of new regulations released that further restrict news reporting on negative or sensitive topics, often requiring higher-level permission to do so or holding publications responsible for the release of anything that might harm social stability—at least in the eyes of the party. Other efforts involve new restrictive measures for information technology, an area that deserves a more extensive discussion.

The PRC—along with other authoritarian and democratic regimes all over the world—is still struggling with how to respond to the growing use of information technology and the increasing ease with which disaffected persons can communicate and organize collective action, whether protests or terrorism. While Chinese government sources blamed the Arab Spring largely on the failure of authoritarian regimes in the Middle East and North Africa to institute reforms and provide tangible benefits to the majority of their populations, PRC leaders did not miss the critical role played by cell phones and the Internet in enabling activists and dissidents to connect with a broad range of people across different walks of life. In addition, as with China's domestic unrest, bogeyman claims of Western masterminds being behind these movements were often repeated. Consequently, senior Public Security and PAP officials are increasingly worried about "hostile foreign and domestic forces [that] increasingly use the Internet and other emerging media as important tools and channels for various strategies to promote a color revolution against us, forming various parties and groups to compete for the battlefield of public opinion, the people's hearts and minds, and the support of the international community."[32] Prior to the Arab Spring, the PRC already possessed perhaps the most sophisticated control system for information technology in the world, but Chinese leaders have since doubled down on strengthening these capabilities to avoid a recurrence of the "Beijing Spring" social atmosphere that spawned the Tian'anmen protests in 1989, an atmosphere that was partially driven by improved access to cultural products and information sources from the West.

Prior to the Arab Spring, domestic security forces were concerned about the Internet, but mostly as a site for "online mass incidents" where thousands of posters could rant about their political concerns on message boards or in online games before state-backed censors were able to silence them, potentially even allowing this anger to lead to a protest in the real world. However, beginning in the late 2000s and further validated by the Arab Spring, more sophisticated ideas began to be developed about the potential interconnectedness of online and real-life activities. In 2011, police analysts argued that "online and offline activities related to mass incidents are synergistic and intertwined. In the information age, Internet media can cause mass incidents by gaining the attention of a vast number of Internet users."[33] The analysts added that:

> First, online mass incidents are a significant trend. . . . On active forums, communities, blogs, and other sites, a few posts are reproduced repeatedly or spread by instant messaging, email, and other methods, quickly forming a network of public opinion. . . . Internet users draw on the large-scale dissemination power of the Internet to release and spread certain kinds of information, venting their discontent and relying on networked IT [information technology] to communicate with each other in a long chain, planning, organizing, and liaising, easily evolving into a mass incident based around specific demands.

> Second, Internet media can accelerate the development of mass incidents. Currently, stories involving the wealthy, corruption, police cases (or incidents), or other subjects can easily become hot topics for Internet public opinion, and some have even been used to create massive crises.[34]

Finally, in terms of "grassroots" work to prevent future incidents, the domestic security literature frequently suggests that this, like many of the other measures listed here, is the responsibility of local party leaders and state organs, though Public Security forces also have a role to play. The idea of grassroots work is an older communist concept that essentially means that party and state leaders and personnel need to build strong ties with their local communities, understanding their desires and concerns, gaining their trust and obedience, cultivating informants and a general spirit of cooperation with the state, and doing other things to make sure problems are solved—or at least brought to the party's attention—before they blow up into major incidents. Unfortunately, this is often discussed in instrumental terms: party leaders must conduct good grassroots work in order to gain cooperation and compliance from citizens, not because it actually informs or alters what party and government leaders were already planning to do. It is essentially more a matter of proper marketing and relationship-building than learning how local leaders can actually address citizens' concerns.

Overall, it is fascinating that the security literature often sees problems on the side of the party-state rather than with Public Security organs themselves, though this may indicate a bias in these sources. Non-police sources, for example, are more prone to complain about how the police often fail to follow proper procedures and legal regulations. However, as China continues to seek reform of both local government (particularly on the financial side) and the domestic security apparatus, hopefully the decisionmakers will remain aware of how intertwined these issues are. It is difficult to imagine significant improvements to China's domestic security situation without improvements to both local government and how the local police and other security forces conduct their activities.

Conclusion

Despite its significant domestic security challenges, China has not been debilitated by sustained internal insurgencies that render large portions of the country ungovernable or result in areas of relative impunity and independence. Even in light of the principal-agent problems noted above, provincial or regional leaders are not able to ignore central mandates and operate as they please (a point emphasized by the recent downfall of Bo Xilai), and there have been no popular revolutions that threaten to overthrow the current regime, nor have there been serious threats of a coup, direct intervention by the military or, worst of all, the prospect of civil war. In this sense, despite its various weaknesses and problems, the CCP has been significantly more successful than many regimes in charge of managing the progress of a developing country. Remarkably, the central government continues to enjoy a robust level of domestic legitimacy in the eyes of the general populace, at least as measured by multiple national-level surveys designed by U.S. scholars.[35] This sustained legitimacy most likely derives from the CCP's historical dominance, pervasive ideological influence through strict media controls and the education system, systematic elimination of all political alternatives, and—not insignificantly—the ability to deliver on economic development, a better quality of life for many people, the promise of a stable and prosperous future, and China's rapid increase in status and capabilities on the international stage. However, whether this legitimacy can be maintained in future decades is an open question.

This question is especially important now because of additional changes appearing on the horizon. Among the most critical of these changes, both economists and political leaders have signaled that China is rapidly approaching or has already reached the point beyond which its recent decades of 10 percent annual growth can no longer be sustained by a booming low-skilled manufacturing sector powered by labor migration from the countryside and foreign direct investment (including a sizable portion "round-tripped" through Hong Kong). The Chinese economy will have to shift to higher-end manufacturing and services as its advantages in cheap labor diminish in relation to markets in Southeast Asia and elsewhere. Such a transformation will not be easy and may include significant increases in unemployed or underemployed young people, a near-universal recipe for increased crime and unrest, as well as greater economic uncertainty for Chinese citizens at a time when the state needs them to consume more and save less.

The PRC's national police and paramilitary institutions have undergone numerous reforms since the death of Mao Zedong, many of them aimed at "professionalizing" these forces—making them better educated, better trained, and more sophisticated in the use of tactics and equipment. However, as much as China's domestic security forces have attempted to change, Chinese society has changed and will continue to change even faster and more dramatically, challenging the ability of domestic security forces to adapt to new conditions.

As domestic unrest continues to grow, the economy slows down, political reform remains unlikely, systemic problems go unaddressed, and the long-avoided costs of unrestrained development come due, mass unrest in China appears likely to remain a major concern for decades to come. While multiple scholars have noted that political revolutions occur when "the impossible becomes possible" through a confluence of factors that is nearly impossible to predict beforehand, popular disaffection in China is not entirely dissimilar to that in Egypt or other countries involved in the Arab Spring, despite the greater confidence Chinese citizens seem to have in the PRC's central leadership. Mass incidents in China are at present almost universally framed around specific grievances rather than broader opposition to CCP rule, though this may be a tactical choice on the part of protesters as much as a reflection of true feelings. Certainly, Chinese leaders are concerned about domestic security, as recently indicated by ongoing reforms to this sector following the removal of Zhou Yongkang and by the decision by Xi Jinping to chair the new national security commission himself.

Focusing on mass incidents is the easiest way to see China's domestic security forces in action. In terms of contingency planning, this allows outside observers to examine how domestic security forces and their civilian superiors attempt to implement plans in the event of a crisis and later adapt plans based on lessons learned from China's near-constant experience of unrest. Unlike many other contingency plans that are on the books or perhaps even trained for through exercises, China's contingency plans for mass incidents have the potential to be put into practice upwards of 100,000 times a year. Moreover, aside from a handful of international missions, such as contributing to United Nations peacekeeping, conducting antipiracy operations in the Gulf of Aden, and policing drug trafficking on the Mekong River,[36] domestic security incidents provide one of the few opportunities to observe Chinese security units (including the PLA, in supporting roles) actually execute the missions for which they have trained and prepared, including their interaction with real opposition, albeit civilian and typically unarmed.

While China has gradually improved its counterterrorism capabilities, fighting terrorism remains a secondary mission with a much lower priority. Multiple recent attacks outside of Xinjiang that apparently involved ethnic Uighurs may motivate China to devote more resources to this mission, as may the potential for radicalism among contemporary Tibetan youth. However, the fact remains that the vast majority of unrest in China occurs among the Han majority living in the more heavily populated eastern and central provinces. Even if Chinese policing, ethnic suppression, and counterterrorism in minority regions increase dramatically, the bulk of Public Security and PAP work will still be focused on Han populations and more highly assimilated ethnic minorities.

Notes

1   The Ministry of Public Security (MPS) is a national bureaucratic organ under the State Council that oversees all of China's police and co-administers the PAP with China's highest military decisionmaking body, the Central Military Commission. The national Public Security bureaucracy is broken down into various subdivisions at the provincial level and below, each of which is responsible to both the party committee on the same level and the Public Security body at the level above. As Harold M. Tanner describes, "within the government of each province, autonomous region, and centrally administered city [is] a department of public security [*gong'an ting*, 公安厅], while each city or county government include[s] a bureau of public security [*gong'an ju*, 公安局] and each city district [*qu*, 区] a public security sub-bureau [*gong'an fenju*, 公安分局]. At the base level— town, street, busy urban areas—[are] the public security stations [*gong'an paichusuo*, 公安派出所]." See Harold M. Tanner, *Strike Hard! Anti-Crime Campaigns and Chinese Criminal Justice, 1979–1985* (Ithaca: Cornell University East Asia Program, 1999), 33. All lower level Public Security offices—and the police in general—are colloquially known as Public Security Bureaus [*gong'an ju*, 公安局], regardless of their scope. Local PAP units are also in theory subject to local party committees and Public Security offices, but only those at the county level and above. The local party committees that oversee local police organs, called Political and Legal Affairs Committees (PLACs), are all subject to the Central PLAC that is, in turn, responsible to the Central Committee of the Communist Party of China. Local PLACs are typically headed by one of the highest-ranking local party leaders, often the party chief. The head of the Central PLAC was in years past a member of the all-powerful Politburo Standing Committee, though this changed when the Standing Committee was reduced from nine to seven members at the 18th Party Congress in November 2012. The previous and current heads of the Central PLAC (Zhou Yongkang and Meng Jianzhu, respectively) previously held the position of Minister of Public Security, so there does seem to be a direct route from heading the MPS to heading the Central PLAC. However, the purge of and ongoing criminal proceedings against Zhou Yongkang and the establishment of a new national security commission headed by Xi Jinping may alter the manner in which China's leading domestic security organs operate.

2   Note that some of these missions are shared with other bureaucratic ministries and administrations under the State Council.

3   Obtaining official approval to hold a protest is incredibly difficult. The act of applying mostly serves to earn the applicant attention from the government and

police. Notable exceptions are anti-Japan and sometimes anti-U.S. protests, which are often passively or actively supported by the state.

4   For data on protest numbers, see Jae Ho Chung, "Assessing the Odds Against the Mandate of Heaven: Do the Numbers (on Instability) Really Matter?" in *Charting China's Future: Political, Social, and International Dimensions*, ed. Jae Ho Chung (Lanham, MD: Rowman & Littlefield, 2006), 112; "China's Spending on Internal Police Force in 2010 Outstrips Defense Budget," Bloomberg, March 5, 2011; and Xuezhi Guo, *China's Security State: Philosophy, Evolution, and Politics* (New York: Cambridge University Press, 2012), 246–247.

5   "Protests in China: The Cauldron Boils," *Economist*, September 29, 2005. Zhou Yongkang was later promoted to head of the Central Political and Legal Affairs Commission—the "security czar" position on the all-powerful Politburo Standing Committee—before that position was demoted during the contraction of the Standing Committee from nine to seven members in 2012. Since late 2013, Zhou and some of his associates have been under investigation for corruption and other abuses of power, due at least in part to Zhou having been formerly supportive of purged Chongqing party chief Bo Xilai.

6   State Council of the People's Republic of China [中华人民共和国国务院], "National Contingency Plan for Large-Scale Mass Incidents" [国家大规模群体性事件应急预案] (2005). This document is unfortunately no longer available, but its contents can be extrapolated from the various provincial, municipal, and county-level plans that were required to propagate its core concepts.

7   Central People's Government of the People's Republic of China, "General Contingency Plan for National Public Emergencies" [国家突发公共事件总体应急预案], August 7, 2005, available at <www.gov.cn/yjgl/2005-08/07/content_21048.htm>.

8   Ministry of Public Security, "Regulations on the Handling of Mass Incidents by Public Security Organs" [公安机关处置群体性事件规定], Public Security Document, no. 56 (2008); and "People's Armed Police Law of the People's Republic of China" [中华人民共和国人民武装警察法] August 2, 2009, available at <www.gov.cn/flfg/2009-08/27/content_1403324.htm>.

9   The author would specifically like to thank several of the "deans" of Chinese policing studies in the United States—Murray Scot Tanner, Harold M. Tanner, Kam Wong, George Xuezhi Guo, and Ivan Sun—whose scholarship has strongly influenced this chapter, even in instances where their work is not directly cited.

10   Elizabeth Rosenthal, "Workers' Plight Brings New Militancy in China," *New York Times*, March 10, 2003.

11   Wang Xianlin [王先琳], "Methods, Planning, and Exercises Regarding the Handling of Mass Incidents" [群体性事件处置方法与预案制定及演练], *Police Practical Combat Training* [警察实战训练研究], no. 2 (2008).

12   See "Protests in China: The Cauldron Boils," *Economist*, September 29, 2005; and "China's Spending on Internal Police Force in 2010 Outstrips Defense Budget."

13   Chris Buckley, "China's Wen Says Farmers' Rights Flouted by Land Grabs," Reuters, February 5, 2012.

14   "Weng'an Party Secretary and County Head Are Removed from Office" [贵州瓮安县委书记和县长被免职], Xinhua, July 4, 2008.

15   See, for example, Murray Scot Tanner, "The Institutional Lessons of Disaster: Reorganizing China's People's Armed Police After Tian'anmen," in *The People's Liberation Army as Organization*, ed. James C. Mulvenon and Andrew N.D. Yang (Washington, DC: RAND Corporation, 2002).

16   Zeng Shengquan [曾省权], "Inquiry into the Ability of Public Security Organs to Enhance the Safeguarding of National Security and Social Stability in the New Era" [新时期公安机关提升维护国家安全和社会稳定能力探究], *Public Security Studies* [公安研究] 196 (2011), 12.

17   Wael Ghonim, *Revolution 2.0: The Power of the People is Greater Than the People in Power—A Memoir* (Boston: Houghton Mifflin Harcourt, 2012), 267, 271.

18   For an introduction to accusations of violence among fringe Christian sects in China, see Joseph Kahn, "Violence Taints Religion's Solace for China's Poor," *New York Times*, November 25, 2004. The PRC executed the main leader of Three Ranks of Servants, Xu Wenku, in 2006, along with several of his followers. They were convicted of supposedly murdering 20 members of the Eastern Lightning sect.

19   Yang Guangwei [杨光伟], "Follow the Path of Staying Close to the Masses, Strengthen the Foundation of the Domestic Security Department" [走群众路线 实国保根基], translated in "Internal Document of the Domestic Security Department of the Public Security Bureau (Part I)," *China Digital Times*, January 26, 2010, available at <http://chinadigitaltimes.net/2010/01/internal-document-of-the-domestic-security-department-of-the-public-security-bureau-part-i>.

20   Yongshun Cai, *Collective Resistance in China: Why Popular Protests Succeed or Fail* (Stanford: Stanford University Press, 2010), 5, 6, 12, 50.

21   "Regulations on the Handling of Mass Incidents by Public Security Organs."

22   An Interview with PAP Commander Wu Shuangzhan on the Promulgation Day of the 'People's Armed Police Law'" [《武装警察法》颁布之日专访武警部队司令员吴双战], Xinhua, August 28, 2009, available at <www.china.com.cn/military/txt/2009-08/28/content_18419479.htm>.

23   Yuning Wu, Ivan Y. Sun, and Aaron Fichtelberg, "Formalizing China's Armed Police: The 2009 PAP Law," *Crime, Law, and Social Change* 56, no. 3 (2011), 250.

24   Central People's Government of the People's Republic of China, "People's Armed Police Law of the PRC" [中华人民共和国人民武装警察法], Eleventh National

People's Congress Standing Committee, 10th Meeting, August 27, 2009.

25   "People's Armed Police Law;" and Wu, Sun, and Fichtelberg, 252–253.

26   James T. Areddy, "Shanghai Police Officers to Begin Carrying Guns, Move Illustrates Perception Violence from Crime and Terrorism are Growing in Expanding Urban Areas," *Wall Street Journal*, April 21, 2014.

27   See Xi'an Municipal Public Security Bureau, "Xi'an Municipal Public Security Bureau Contingency Plan for Handling Large-Scale Mass Incidents" [西安市公安局处置较大规模群体性治安事件应急预案], March 23, 2010; and People's Government of Ningxia Hui Autonomous Region, "Ningxia Hui Autonomous Region Contingency Plan for Large-Scale Mass Incidents" [宁夏回族自治区大规模群体性事件应急预案], July 24, 2006.

28   "Map of People's Armed Police Troops Dispatched to Xinjiang," *China Digital Times*, July 10, 2009, available at <http://chinadigitaltimes.net/2009/07/map-of-peoples-armed-police-troops-dispatched-to-xinjiang/>.

29   For a serious examination of whether PLA forces were involved in suppressing the 2008 unrest in Tibet, see Murray Scot Tanner, "How China Manages Internal Security Challenges and Its Impact on PLA Missions," in *Beyond the Strait: PLA Missions Other Than Taiwan* (Carlisle, PA: Strategic Studies Institute, 2009).

30   Joseph Fewsmith, "An 'Anger-Venting' Mass Incident Catches the Attention of China's Leadership," *China Leadership Monitor*, no. 26 (Fall 2008), 7.

31   See, for example, Cai, 42.

32   Zeng, 10–11.

33   Jia Dongjun [贾东军], "The Impact of the Rapid Development of Internet Media on Social Stability and Some Brief Comments on Responsive Measures" [网络媒体迅猛发展对社会稳定的影响及应对措施略论], *Public Security Studies* [公安研究] 199 (2011), 6.

34   Ibid.

35   See, for example, Martin King Whyte, *Myth of the Social Volcano: Perceptions of Inequality and Distributive Injustice in China* (Stanford: Stanford University Press, 2010); and Teresa Wright, *Accepting Authoritarianism: State-Society Relations in China's Reform Era* (Stanford, Stanford University Press, 2010).

36   For an overview of the latter two missions, see Andrew S. Erickson and Austin M. Strange, "Ripples of Change in Chinese Foreign Policy? Evidence from Recent Approaches to Nontraditional Waterborne Security," *Asia Policy*, no. 17 (January 2014).

CHAPTER 4

Civilian Authorities and Contingency Planning in China

Catherine Welch

This chapter introduces the People's Republic of China's (PRC's) civilian emergency response planning system, reviews some plans in this system with an eye toward understanding the PRC's approach to emergency response planning, and examines one recent instance in which emergency response plans were activated. In doing so, the chapter illustrates a few of the ways that these plans can be examined and highlights the value of analyzing their content.

Insights into China's civilian emergency response planning system are of value in understanding Chinese military contingency planning for two reasons. First, it is reasonable to expect similarities between Chinese civilian and military approaches to certain kinds of emergency or contingency planning because many of the problems the government may face, such as injuries and displacements, will be similar whether the government is preparing for a natural disaster or a domestic military contingency. For that reason, information on the civilian system of emergency plans should be viewed as useful background for understanding the People's Liberation Army's (PLA's) contingency planning.

Second, there is evidence that civilian emergency response planning and military and national defense mobilization planning are linked. The PRC's National Defense Mobilization Law states that "the national defense mobilization plan(s) should be linked together with the sudden incident emergency response and management plan(s) in aspects of command, the use of force, information, and support, etc."[1] Additionally, articles released in 2006 at the time of the Central Military Commission's promulgation of the Comprehensive Emergency Response Plan for the Military's Handling of Sudden Incidents noted that the military's plans for such events are related to the corresponding civilian plans.[2] One article states that the military's emergency plans are an important component of China's civilian system of emergency response plans, and that these documents provide a legal basis for the military to be involved in local disasters.[3]

This evidence, which suggests linkages between civilian and military contingency planning and national defense mobilization, reinforces the value of understanding China's civilian emergency planning in the context of military contingency planning and highlights an area worthy of future research.

This chapter draws on a range of primary and secondary sources. Official Chinese government Web sites have detailed information about emergency management including plans, news about emergencies, and information on emergency training and exercises.[4] Another source is a paper by Chinese researchers posted on the Organisation for Economic Co-operation and Development Web site that provides an overview of China's emergency response planning system and gives details on how the system is intended to improve China's response to emergencies.[5] Articles posted on Xinhua Online, the *People's Daily Online*, and the *China Daily Online* that include background information on China's efforts to improve its management of emergencies supplement information on the release of emergency response plans and provide insight into recent activations of plans.

China's Emergency Response Planning System

In the wake of the 2003 severe acute respiratory syndrome (SARS) outbreak, the Chinese government launched efforts to improve its crisis management capabilities.[6] Development of an emergency response planning system was a central part of broader government efforts to improve the management of emergencies.[7] The system is designed to improve China's ability to handle myriad emergencies and institutionalize a management approach that is integrated vertically (national to local), horizontally (multi-ministerial and departmental), and institutionally (with other laws and regulations).[8]

China's emergency response planning system is described in a broad national plan, released in January 2006, called the National Comprehensive Emergency Response Plan for Sudden Public Incidents, hereafter referred to as the "National Emergency Response Plan."[9] The plan identifies six key types of PRC emergency response plans, develops a taxonomy for categorizing emergencies by type of crisis and level of severity, and provides a national template for emergency response plans, including key sections that should be included and issues that ought to be addressed. The six types of emergency response plans include:[10]

- The National Emergency Response Plan. This plan is the State Council's "guiding document for addressing extraordinary emergencies."[11] These include emergencies that cross provincial boundaries.
- Emergency response plans for specific contingencies. The State Council and its related departments (ministries, commissions, and so forth) draw these up to address a given type of emergency. These plans typically address an emergency that requires a multi-institutional response, such as an earthquake. (Note: In the rest of this document, these are referred to as *contingency plans*.)
- State Council departmental emergency response plans for sudden public incidents. State Council departments draw up these plans based on the National Emergency Response Plan, relevant contingency plans, and departmental duties (that is, those of a particular ministry or commission) in addressing an emergency. They typically address emergencies that fall exclusively, or almost exclusively, within the domain of a particular ministry (for example, the Ministry of Health's avian flu plan).
- Local emergency response plans for sudden public incidents. These include provincial-level equivalents of the National Emergency Response Plan, contingency plans, and departmental plans as well as city, prefecture, and county emergency response plans drawn up by local people's governments and related departments.
- Enterprise, institution, and work unit emergency response plans. The National Emergency Response Plan does not describe these, but they appear to include plans developed by individual companies and non-governmental institutions such as hospitals.[12]
- Emergency response plans drawn up by units holding large-scale exhibitions and cultural, sports, or other events. Recent examples where such plans appear to have been in place include the 2008 Beijing Olympics and the 2010 Shanghai Expo.[13]

Exactly how many plans fall into these six key types is unclear. Early news reporting on the national-level plans described the inclusion of the National Emergency Response Plan, 25 contingency emergency response plans, and 80 departmental emergency response plans.[14] One academic paper stated that as of March 15, 2006, China had developed 24,293 emergency response plans.[15]

The paper indicated that these included a single National Emergency Response Plan, 25 contingency and 80 departmental emergency response plans, 971 plans from various "sectors in the State Council,"[16] 158 plans from "central enterprises,"[17] and 23,058 regional or local plans.[18] Given that the National Emergency Response Plan calls for plans to be continuously updated and refined, these numbers have likely changed since then.

The National Emergency Response Plan defines an emergency as "an incident that occurs suddenly and causes or has the potential to cause enormous casualties or fatalities, loss of property, and environmental or ecological damage; and to pose a severe threat to society or endanger public security."[19] It divides emergencies into four main categories and classifies them according to severity. The four categories of emergencies are:

- natural disasters, which include floods, droughts, other weather hazards, earthquakes, and forest and grassland fires
- accidents, which include safety incidents at industrial, mining, commercial, or trading enterprises, traffic or transportation incidents, incidents at public facilities or installations, environmental pollution, and damage to the environment
- public health incidents, which include epidemics, food safety and occupational hazards, animal diseases, and incidents that seriously affect public health and safety
- public security incidents, which include terrorist attacks and emergencies involving economic security and/or foreign countries.[20]

The National Emergency Response Plan also establishes a four-level, color-coded warning system to convey the severity of an emergency, including "a very serious emergency" (Level I), "a serious emergency" (Level II), "a relatively serious emergency" (Level III), and "a general emergency" (Level IV).[21] It provides no more details on the criteria for determining the severity of an emergency.[22] However, a Chinese paper on emergency management states that as the severity of an emergency increases, the level of the national authority with oversight of the emergency's management also increases. Level I natural disaster emergencies are overseen by the vice premier of the State Council (and director of the National Commission for Disaster Reduction); Level II emergencies are overseen by the minister of civil affairs; Level III emergencies are overseen by the vice minister of civil affairs; and Level IV emergencies are overseen by the Department of Disaster and Social Relief, Ministry of Civil Affairs.[23]

Much of the National Emergency Response Plan is dedicated to providing a template for use in other emergency response plans. The template includes:

- a description of the organizational structure of the PRC civilian emergency management system
- an outline of the basic steps in any PRC civilian emergency response
- identification of the kinds of support that may be needed
- recommendations on training, raising public awareness about emergency response, and ensuring accountability in an emergency.

Most of the plans examined address these elements of emergency response.

Organizational Structure of the Civilian Emergency Management System

The National Emergency Response Plan divides the organizational structure of the emergency management authorities into five layers. The first layer is the State Council as a whole, which the plan states is the highest leading authority in emergency management. Under State Council leadership, the State Council Standing Committee and "National Related Sudden Incident Command Organizations" (not further described in the plan) are responsible for handling emergencies.[24] The second layer is the State Council Emergency Management Office.[25] This office, established in 2006, is described as playing a pivotal role in emergency response. (Because of its importance, a detailed description is provided below.) The third layer includes State Council ministries and departments, which are responsible for developing plans for, and actually handling, emergencies that fall within their areas of responsibility. The fourth layer is local authorities at each successive administrative level (province, municipality, county, and so forth), which are responsible for handling emergencies within their administrative areas. Only when emergencies exceed a certain level or cross administrative areas does a higher authority get involved. The fifth and final layer is expert or specialist groups. Authorities are permitted to hire specialists and experts to assist in decisionmaking and handling emergencies if necessary.[26]

One of the most important players in PRC civilian emergency response planning, the State Council Emergency Management Office, appears to be composed of one office and four committees.[27] Each committee is responsible for managing one of the four categories of emergencies in the PRC emergency response system (natural, accidental, public health, and public security emergencies), as illustrated in table 4.1.[28] Each committee consists of a director, a vice director or administration vice director, and committee members. The people occupying these positions come from different government institutions.[29] This enables various institutions to better coordinate their response to emergencies.

Table 4.1. Committees of the State Council Emergency Management Office	
Committee	Responsibility
National Commission for Disaster Reduction	Natural disasters
National Committee on Work Safety	Accidental disasters
National Committee for Patriotic Health	Public health disasters
Central Committee for Comprehensive Management of Public Security	Public security disasters*
* The Central Committee for Comprehensive Management of Public Security is a Chinese Communist Party body. The same article also refers to this body as the National Committee for Integrated Management. See Peijun Shi et al., "Integrated Disaster Risk Management," 7–8.	

The National Commission for Disaster Reduction's Web site provides an organizational chart illustrating broad institutional membership in the committee (see table 4.2).[30] More than 30 institutions participate in this particular committee, illustrating the multi-institutional nature of emergency response in China.

Basic Steps of Any Civilian Emergency Response

The National Emergency Response Plan describes four basic steps involved in any PRC civilian response to an emergency: forecasting and early warning, emergency response, recovery and reconstruction, and releasing information.[31]

All regional and departmental authorities are responsible for creating forecasting and early warning systems. These systems enable authorities to identify an emergency early on and to report and act on the emergency. One example of the actions that may follow identification of an emergency is announcing it to the public. For example, the plan says that warning announcements can be made, updated, or lifted via radio, television, newspapers, mail, information networks, alarms, propaganda vans, and door-to-door notifications.[32]

Table 4.2. Organizational Chart of the China National Commission for Disaster Reduction

| 国家减灾委员会 China National Commission for Disaster Reduction | | 办公室 General Office |
| 专家委员会 Board of Experts |

中央宣传部 The Communist Party of China Central Committee Propaganda Department	国务院办公厅 General Office of the State Council	外交部 The Ministry of Foreign Affairs	发展改革委 The National Development and Reform Commission
教育部 The Ministry of Education	科技部 The Ministry of Science and Technology	工业和信息化部 The Ministry of Industry and Information Technology	公安部 The Ministry of Public Security
民政部 The Ministry of Civil Affairs	财政部 The Ministry of Finance	国土资源部 The Ministry of Land and Resources	环境保护部 Environmental Protection Department
住房城乡建设部 Housing and Urban-Rural Development	交通运输部 The Ministry of Transport	水利部 The Ministry of Water Resources	农业部 The Ministry of Agriculture
商务部 The Ministry of Commerce	卫生计生委 The National Health and Family Planning Commission	国资委 The State-Owned Assets Supervision and Administration Commission	新闻出版广电总局 The State General Administration of Press and Publication, Radio and Television
安全监督总局 The State Supervision and Administration of Production Safety Administration	统计局 The National Bureau of Statistics	林业局 The State Forestry Administration	中科院 The Chinese Academy of Sciences
地震局 Seismological Bureau	气象局 The Meteorological Administration	保监会 The Insurance Regulatory Commission	自然科学基金会 The National Natural Science Fund Committee
海洋局 The State Oceanic Administration	测绘地信局 The National Geographic Information Bureau of Surveying and Mapping	总参谋部 The Chinese People's Liberation Army General Staff Department	武警总部 Headquarters of the Chinese People's Armed Police Force
中国科协 China Association for Science and Technology	中国红十字总会 Red Cross Society of China	中国铁路总公司 China Railway Corporation	

The next step is emergency response, comprised of four main stages. When a Level I or Level II emergency occurs, regional authorities and departments must report it within 4 hours (the plan suggests that these authorities must report to the next higher level, though this is not specified) and notify other localities and departments affected by the emergency. Second, authorities are to take measures such as activating their emergency response plan and making preliminary efforts to address the emergency (at this point, the response may involve only one, or a limited number of, departments or authorities). If such measures are insufficient to control the emergency, other emergency response plans may be activated and higher level authorities, such as the relevant State Council–related emergency command organization or a State Council task force, may become involved.[33] Departments that specialize in handling a particular type of emergency (for example, the Ministry of Health in a public health incident) lead the response and other departments provide assistance. This stage continues until the emergency concludes and the on-site emergency command organization is discontinued.[34]

The third step is the recovery and reconstruction period. This is marked by actions to remedy or ameliorate the conditions of individuals and work units that suffered losses. It can include provision of psychological, legal, and financial support. An investigative effort is also launched to assess the causes, nature, impact, and lessons learned during the emergency. Reconstruction efforts may also begin.[35]

The final step addressed in the plan is the release of information. Authorities are advised to release information in a timely, accurate, objective, and comprehensive manner. They are to do so throughout the emergency management process, with an emphasis on announcing the emergency soon after it has occurred and including information on authorities' assessment of it, measures adopted by authorities to handle it, and any preventative measures individuals should take in light of the occurrence.[36]

The National Emergency Response Plan addresses a number of types of support that may be necessary in an emergency and stipulates that relevant departments must be prepared to provide support if called on to do so. These areas of support are fairly comprehensive in the tasks described and are rarely associated with specific bureaucracies. There is overlap between some of the categories. Table 4.3 lists them as they appear in the National Emergency Response Plan.[37]

Table 4.3. Contingency Support Requirements of the National Emergency Response Plan	
Human resource support	Providing emergency response personnel (the PLA and the People's Armed Police are the only two specific institutions mentioned)
Financial support	Providing funds for preparation and relief for emergencies as well as providing compensation to victims after an emergency occurs
Material support	Establishing an emergency material monitoring network, an advance-warning system, and systems for material production, storage, allocation, and delivery
Support of essential needs	Ensuring that victims have food, water, clothing, shelter, and medical care
Medical and health support	Enabling the deployment of medical teams that can rush to emergencies to provide first aid, disease prevention and control, and other medical services (public health departments are specified as responsible for these tasks)
Traffic and transportation support	Prioritizing emergency-related traffic and transportation needs, including access to supplies and roadways as well as imposing traffic control measures on areas affected by the emergency, if necessary
Maintaining public order	Strengthening security for certain areas, premises, groups of people, materials, and installations; deterring criminal activities
Protecting victims and emergency response personnel	Constructing emergency refuge centers, overseeing evacuations or relocations, and protecting emergency response personnel
Communications support	Refining emergency communications, television, broadcasting, and public communications networks as well as setting up an emergency communications system
Provision of critical supplies and services	Maintaining adequate supplies of water, coal, electricity, oil, and gas and continuing to dispose of waste materials
Technological support	Developing better technologies and equipment for emergency monitoring, forecasting, early warning, prevention, and emergency management

These areas of support provide an outline for the kinds of responsibilities identified in what is designed to be an inter-institutional approach to emergency management. However, in any given emergency, not all of these kinds of support would necessarily be required.

Finally, the National Emergency Response Plan encourages rehearsals of the plans, propaganda, and training efforts and the use of rewards and disciplinary measures. Regional authorities and departments are to rehearse or train for carrying out their emergency response plans. Propaganda, education, culture, broadcasting, news, and publication departments are to raise awareness about and increase public knowledge of emergency response prevention, mitigation, and preparedness. "Relevant authorities" are to train emergency rescue forces. Individuals who make contributions should be recognized, and those responsible for negligence or dereliction of duty should be punished.[38]

Examining PRC Emergency Response Plans

The PRC government has released the full text of a small number of national-level emergency response plans (18 contingency and 2 departmental).[39] While this sample is not necessarily representative of the entire PRC system of civilian emergency response plans, it can still reveal useful information about Chinese emergency response plans, including variance in the specificity of certain kinds of plans, insights on the simultaneous activation of multiple emergency response plans, and identification of important players in emergency response.

PRC civilian emergency response plans vary widely in how specific they are. Some plans appear to be written to address broadly defined contingencies (for example, the National Emergency Response Plan on Sudden Public Health Incidents). Other plans appear tailored to a fairly unique range of events (for example, the Emergency Response Plan on People Infected with Avian Influenza) or to a particular ministry or commission (for example, the Ministry of Railways' Emergency Response Plan on Destructive Earthquakes).

More than one emergency response plan may be activated for the same emergency. This is noted in the National Emergency Response Plan, but looking at other emergency response plans or their titles provides insight into which types of emergencies may require the activation of multiple emergency response plans. If, for instance, there was a health incident on a train, the Ministry of Railways could activate its emergency response plan on health incidents. If this failed to control the incident, presumably the Ministry of Health would activate its emergency response plan on public health incidents. One example of an emergency where more than one emergency plan was activated is in the response to an earthquake in Yiliang County, Yunnan, which is discussed in the final section of this chapter.

Identification of Important Players in Emergency Response Plans

Several types of groups appear to play important roles in leading the management of emergencies, providing expertise, and ensuring coordination within or between ministries. Most plans describe groups that have important responsibilities associated with leading and coordinating the management of emergency response.[40] These groups are sometimes formal bodies, such as the State Flood Control and Drought Relief Headquarters (located in the Ministry of Water Resources). At other times, the groups appear to be informal bodies convened on an as-needed basis, such as the Leading Small Group for Urban Subway Accidents and Disaster Emergency Response.

Some plans or articles provide insight into the institutions represented in these leading groups. The composition of these groups suggests that the government can reach across civil-military and state-enterprise boundaries to coordinate emergency responses. The National Emergency Response Plan on Communication Support, for example, states that the Ministry of Industry and Information Technology (MIIT) is responsible for setting up a National Leading Small Group for Emergency Communication Support.[41] This group is to be responsible for leading, organizing, and coordinating the protection and restoration of communications during emergencies in China. An article posted on the PRC government Web site notes that leaders from the following institutions comprise the National Leading Small Group for Communication Support:

- the ministries of Civil Affairs, Finance, Transport, and Railways
- the National Development and Reform Commission
- the General Administration of Customs
- the Administration of Work Safety
- the Civil Aviation Authority
- the State Council Information Office
- the PLA General Staff Department's Operations Department and its Informationization Department [*zongcan xinxihua bu*, 总参信息化部]
- three state-owned telecommunications companies (China Telecom, China Mobile, and China Unicom).[42]

The composition of this group and the responsibilities associated with it in the National Emergency Response Plan on Communication Support suggest that both communication emergency response operations and decisionmaking about communication emergencies will be multi-institutional in nature.

Some plans describe groups that are primarily responsible for providing expertise in emergencies, illustrating how the PRC government might tap the knowledge of nongovernmental experts. The National Emergency Response Plan on Maritime Search and Rescue, for instance, calls for a National Maritime Search and Rescue Expert Group to be made up of experts in shipping, maritime affairs, aviation, firefighting, medical services, environmental protection, petrochemical engineering, maritime engineering, maritime geography, meteorology, security management, and other areas to provide maritime search and rescue–related technical consulting.[43]

A smaller number of plans refer to inter- or intra-ministerial working groups. The former appear to be bodies set up to encourage horizontal communication and coordination of emergency response, which is probably not a surprise given how many institutions may be involved. The latter appear to be formed within a particular ministry (for example, the Ministry of Civil Affairs) and to sometimes deploy to the site of an emergency to provide on-the-ground support and an on-site, national-level presence for a ministry.

Recent Activation of Emergency Response Plans

Chinese civilian authorities have invested a great deal of effort in the PRC system of emergency response planning, but actual bureaucratic response in a real-world emergency situation is a different matter. In order to gain some sense of how plans play out in practice, it is instructive to look at the response to the earthquakes in Yunnan and Guizhou in September 2012.[44]

Beginning on September 7, 2012, multiple earthquakes and aftershocks, ranging in magnitude from 4.8 to 5.6, hit the Yiliang County and Zhaotong City areas in Yunnan and the Bijie City area in Guizhou. As a result of the quakes, 81 people died, more than 800 were injured, and over 200,000 had to be relocated.[45] More than 6,600 homes were destroyed and approximately 430,000 buildings sustained damage.[46] Direct economic losses incurred from the quakes were estimated to be equal to U.S. $552 million.[47] While the quakes did not cause nearly as many casualties or as much damage as the 7.9-magnitude earthquake that struck Sichuan province in May 2008, they were severe enough to require national-level response.

National-, provincial-, and local-level authorities activated emergency response plans,[48] as did institutions including the China Earthquake Administration, the Yunnan Bureau of Agriculture, the Bureau of Public Security's Fire Prevention Team, the PLA's Chengdu Military Region, a power company, and others.[49]

Articles about the emergency response to the earthquake show the ways that high-level party, state, and military officials were involved and give details about the many departments that responded. Then-President Hu Jintao and then-Premier Wen Jiabao were among the high-level officials who got involved in the response, with Wen even visiting the site of the quake.[50]

PLA leaders, including then–Vice Chairman of the Central Military Commission Xu Caihou, met to discuss how to handle the emergency and to provide instructions on response. The General Staff Department and the General Political Department assisted in rescue and relief-related tasks, and the General Logistics Department and the General Armament Department assisted with earthquake supply and logistics support.[51] The PLA's Chengdu Military Region provided air support, sending 13 tons of quake-relief materials and transferring a number of severely wounded people.[52]

Then–Minister of Public Security Meng Jianzhu issued instructions on handling the emergency response. The ministry mobilized fire and rescue equipment, dispatched police and search and rescue teams, and supplied equipment such as generators and other relief supplies.[53]

Other ministries and government agencies also contributed to the response. The Ministry of Civil Affairs facilitated the distribution of supplies such as tents, blankets, and coats. The China Earthquake Administration dispatched a working group to the area. The Ministry of Land and Resources sent experts to assist in rescue and relief and to investigate the prevention and early warning of aftershocks. The Ministry of Health sent experts in intensive care, epidemiology, food safety, and mental health. The China Civil Aviation Administration helped charter flights to transport rescue workers and supplies.[54]

State telecommunications providers China Unicom, China Mobile, and China Telecom provided telecommunications support. Various local power departments organized teams to repair damaged power grids.[55]

Looking at PRC emergency response to this particular disaster provides more details about the specific responses that government officials, individual ministries, and parts of the PLA carried out. The array of institutions and levels of government involved demonstrate how widely emergency management responsibilities are distributed in China and why high-level groups are needed to lead and coordinate the many institutions involved. In this case, because the National Emergency Response Plan for Earthquakes was activated, national-level coordination between these bureaucracies may have taken place via the State Council Headquarters for Earthquake Relief and possibly the National Commission for Disaster Reduction.

The case study suggests that the planning requirements levied in China's National Emergency Response Plan have translated into concrete emergency plans at the local, provincial, and national levels of government and within specific ministries, military regions, and companies. Many of these plans were activated as part of the emergency response effort. Although a full assessment of the effectiveness of the response is beyond the scope of this chapter, the existence of an emergency response mechanism and emergency response plans likely facilitated the involvement and coordination of a wide range of government, military, and business actors in responding to the crisis. This is notable given bureaucratic stovepipes and the difficulty the Chinese government has in coordinating across bureaucratic boundaries. It demonstrates progress in the PRC's efforts to institutionalize a vertically and horizontally integrated approach to emergency management since the SARs epidemic in 2003.[56]

Conclusion

China's National Emergency Response Plan, other Chinese emergency response plans, and news coverage of Chinese responses to disasters are valuable resources for understanding PRC civilian government approaches to emergency response planning. There are several reasons for this.

First, the National Emergency Response Plan is an authoritative document issued by the State Council. It describes a system of emergency response plans designed to improve China's abilities in handling myriad emergencies and to institutionalize an approach to emergency management that is vertically (national to local), horizontally (multi-ministerial and departmental), and institutionally (with other laws and regulations) integrated.[57]

Second, the National Emergency Response Plan articulates requirements for other plans to be created. A careful reading of the plan indicates that there are six different types of plans: the National Emergency Response Plan itself, contingency plans, departmental plans, local plans, enterprise and work unit plans, and plans for large-scale events. The real take-away from this broad range of required plans is that responsibility for emergency response planning is not centralized but is instead widely shared. This distribution of responsibilities is evident in other Chinese emergency plans as well as in news coverage of disasters. Not every type of emergency requires a whole-of-government response, but there does appear to be a whole-of-government effort to plan and prepare for disasters. It is unclear whether the distribution of emergency planning responsibilities produces a dearth or a proliferation of functional expertise in emergency management.

Third, the National Emergency Response Plan provides a taxonomy for categorizing emergencies by type and level of severity. Other emergency plans and news coverage of disasters provide more granular insight into how this taxonomy is applied for specific kinds of emergencies. Such data can be used to adopt a common frame of reference when speaking with counterparts about the commonalities and differences in U.S. and Chinese approaches to emergency response planning.

During the conference that produced this volume, a number of speakers and panelists touched on the involvement of the PLA in broader governmental response to certain domestic disasters and on civil-military cooperation in preparing for and carrying out other disaster response missions. Many remarked on how little information is available with regard to the PLA's contingency planning. By contrast, the Chinese government *has* made information about civilian bureaucracies' emergency planning available. Understanding how Chinese ministries and commissions respond to emergencies provides a civilian-sector complement to the limited knowledge of how the PLA responds to emergencies. A better understanding of China's approach to civilian emergency response planning may contribute to a better understanding of the Chinese military's approach to contingency planning for disaster response and other domestic operations.

The author would like to acknowledge the following individuals for their assistance with this chapter: Maryanne Kivlehan-Wise, Ian M. Easton, and James A. Bellacqua.

Notes

1 Ministry of National Defense, People's Republic of China, *People's Republic of China National Defense Mobilization Law* [中华人民共和国国防动员法], February 26, 2010, available at <www.mod.gov.cn/policy/2010-02/27/content_4127067.htm>. See Part Three, Article 16.0.

2 See Li Yun [黎云], "Explanation of the 'Comprehensive Emergency Plan for the Military's Handling of Sudden Incidents'" [《军队处置突发事件总体应急预案》解读], Xinhua Online [新华网], November 14, 2006, available at <http://news.xinhuanet.com/mil/2006-11/14/content_5329033.htm>; "The Promulgation and Implementation of the 'Comprehensive Emergency Plan for the Military's Handling of Sudden Incidents'" [《军队处置突发事件总体应急预案》颁布实施], Xinhua Online, November 14, 2006, available at <http://news.xinhuanet.com/mil/2006-11/14/content_5328431.htm>; "'The Comprehensive Emergency Plan for the Military's Handling of Sudden Incidents' Reflects a People-Oriented Approach" [《军队处置突发事件总体应急预案》体现以人为本], Xinhua Online, November 14, 2006, available at <http://news.xinhuanet.com/mil/2006-11/14/content_5328890.htm>.

3 "'The Comprehensive Emergency Plan for the Military's Handling of Sudden Incidents' Reflects a People-Oriented Approach."

4 This section of the Web site is available at <www.gov.cn/yjgl>.

5 Peijun Shi et al., "Integrated Disaster Risk Management," Organisation for Economic Co-operation and Development, Session III: Financial Management: Role of Insurance Industry, Financial Markets, and Governments, Part B: Developing Country Perspective, Hyderabad, India, February 26–27, 2007, available at <www.oecd.org/finance/insurance/38120232.pdf>.

6 While the SARS outbreak was not the sole emergency that sparked these efforts, it was a culminating event and is frequently cited in articles highlighting the need to improve China's crisis management capabilities. Other examples of emergencies that occurred in China in the early and mid-2000s that got domestic or international attention include: the Nanchang nursery fire in 2001, the Nandan mine accident in 2001, food poisoning in Nanjing in 2002, an avian flu outbreak in 2004–2005, and the Songhua River benzene spill in 2005. For articles discussing the significance of the SARS outbreak specifically, see "Sudden Public Incident Emergency Management" [突发公共事件应急管理], Xinhua Online, January 17, 2006, available at <http://news.xinhuanet.com/ziliao/2006-01/17/content_4062615.htm>; "Xinhua Viewpoint: Perspective on Sudden Public Emergency Plan Framework System" [新华视点: 突发公共事件应急预案框架体系透视], *People's Daily Online* [人民网], February 25, 2005, available at <www.people.com.cn/GB/14576/28320/44506/44513/3207170.html>; Gao Xiaoping [高小平], "Achievement and Development of the Emergency Management System Construction with Chinese Characteristics" [中国特色应急管理

体系建设的成就和发展], *People's Daily Online*, December 2, 2008, available at <http://theory.people.com.cn/GB/49150/49152/8448741.html>; and Peijun Shi et al., 3.

7   China's system of emergency response plans is known formally as the National Sudden Public Incident Emergency Response System [*quanguo tufa gong-gong shijian yingji yu'an tixi*, 全国突发公共事件应急预案体系]. A Xinhua article documents a series of important dates in the evolution of this system of emergency planning. In December 2003, the Office of the State Council established an emergency response plan working group [*yingji yu'an gongzuo xiaozu*, 应急预案工作小组]. In January 2004, a work conference was called to draw up a plan for public emergencies for all State Council departments and units. In January 2005, the Politburo Standing Committee of the Chinese Communist Party approved, in principle, the State Council's report on the formulation of a national plan for emergency response. In February 2005, the State Council reported on the status of the national plan for emergency response to the National People's Congress. In April 2005, the State Council decided to adopt and implement the National Comprehensive Emergency Response Plan for Sudden Incidents. In May-June 2005, the State Council published and distributed 25 special contingency plans and 80 departmental emergency response plans and provincial-level plans began to be released. See "Sudden Public Incident Emergency Management."

8   Peijun Shi et al., 3, 7, 13–15. An example of a law with which any PRC emergency response would need to be institutionally integrated is the Emergency Response Law of the People's Republic of China. Emergency Response Law of the People's Republic of China, Order of the President of the People's Republic of China, no. 69, August 30, 2007, National Peoples' Congress Web site, available at <www.npc.gov.cn/englishnpc/Law/2009-02/20/content_1471589.htm>.

9   In Chinese, *guojia tufa gonggong shijian zongti yingji yu'an*, 国家突发公共事件总体应急预案.

10   The descriptions are primarily excerpts from section 1.6 in the National Comprehensive Emergency Response Plan for Sudden Public Incidents.

11   Ibid.

12   News coverage of the activation of emergency plans in early October 2012 documents the activation of emergency plans by a private bus company, the Hangzhou Changyun Group, and a hospital, the Tianjin Wuqing District People's Hospital. See "Four Big Hangzhou Bus Stations Grant Over 200,000 Passengers Free Ticket Exchanges or Refunds Within a Three Day Period" [杭州四大汽车站发送旅客20万余人次　三天内可免费退换票], *Zhejiang Online News* [浙江在线新闻], September 30, 2012, available at <http://zjnews.zjol.com.cn/system/2012/09/30/018849364.shtml>; and "6 Dead and 14 Injured in Car Accident of a Delegation of German Doctors to Tianjin; Passengers Had to Smash Windows to Escape" [德国医生代表团天津遇车祸6死14伤 乘客砸窗逃], *People's Daily Online*,

October 2, 2012, available at <http://ah.people.com.cn/n/2012/1002/c227130-17545417.html>.

13   See "Meteorological Emergency Plans Activated for the Start of the Beijing Olympic Games Closing Ceremony" [北京奥运会闭幕式气象应急预案启动], Xinhua Online, August 23, 2008, available at <http://news.xinhuanet.com/newscenter/2008-08/23/content_9639947.htm>; and "Shanghai Municipal Vice Mayor: The World Expo is to Pay Close Attention to the Preparation and Implementation of Medical, Security, and Other Emergency Plans" [上海市常务副市长：世博会正抓紧编制和实施医疗、安保等应急预案], Xinhua Online, September 29, 2009, available at <http://news.xinhuanet.com/politics/2009-09/29/content_12127618.htm>.

14   The existence of 25 contingency emergency plans and 80 departmental emergency plans is documented in "Sudden Public Incident Emergency Management;" and "16 Big Recent Administrative Reform System Achievements, Inspirations, and the System's Deficiencies" [16大以来行政体制改革成就、启示和现行体制的不足], Xinhua Online, July 16, 2012, available at <http://news.xinhuanet.com/legal/2012-07/16/c_123416297.htm>.

15   See Peijun Shi et al., 11. All of the authors are Chinese researchers affiliated with disaster management research institutes or authorities in China.

16   This total does not include the 80 departmental plans.

17   This was the English term the authors used. Presumably this term refers to state-owned enterprises.

18   Peijun Shi et al., 11.

19   National Comprehensive Emergency Response Plan for Sudden Public Incidents, section 1.3.

20   Ibid.

21   Ibid., section 3.1.

22   Some individual plans do provide more insight. For example, the National Emergency Plan on Flood Control and Drought Relief differentiates between the types of floods and droughts that qualify as a Level I, II, III, and IV incident. See section 4.2, "National Emergency Plan on Flood Control and Drought Relief (Full Text)" [国家防汛抗旱应急预案（全文）], *People's Daily Online*, January 12, 2006, available at <http://politics.people.com.cn/GB/1026/4021376.html>.

23   Peijun Shi et al., 11.

24   The Chinese term for State Council Standing Committee is *guowuyuan changwu huiyi*, 国务院常务会议. It could also be translated as State Council Executive Meeting, or Executive Meeting of the State Council. Regardless, the participants appear to be the same. They include the premier, four vice premiers, five state councilors, and the secretary general of the State Council. The sudden incident command

organizations are not described in this plan; however, pages 89–90 of this chapter provide an example of what such groups might look like.

25   The Chinese term for this office is *yingji guanli bangongshi*, 应急管理办公室.

26   National Comprehensive Emergency Response Plan for Sudden Public Incidents, section 2.

27   Peijun Shi et al., 7.

28   A diagram of these institutions is provided at Peijun Shi et al., 8.

29   Ibid., 7.

30   China National Commission for Disaster Reduction, People's Republic of China, "Organizational Structure," available at <www.jianzai.gov.cn//DRpublish/jggl/00010008-1.html>.

31   The plan calls these steps "operations mechanisms" [*yunxing jizhi*, 运行机制]. See National Comprehensive Emergency Response Plan for Sudden Public Incidents, section 3.

32   Ibid., section 3.1.

33   The Chinese term for "State Council-related emergency command organization" is *guowuyuan xiangguan yingji zhihui jigou*, 国务院相关应急指挥机构, and "State Council task force" is *guowuyuan gongzuozutong*, 国务院工作组统.

34   National Comprehensive Emergency Response Plan for Sudden Public Incidents, section 3.2.

35   Ibid., section 3.3.

36   Ibid., section 3.4.

37   Ibid., section 4.0.

38   Ibid., section 5.0.

39   See the emergency management section of the PRC government Web site with lists of contingency plans available at <www.gov.cn/yjgl/2006-01/11/content_21049.htm> and departmental plans available at <www.gov.cn/yjgl/2005-08/07/content_21051.htm>. See also "National System of Plans for Sudden Public Incidents, Full Text" [国家突发公共事件预案体系全文], *People's Daily Online*, January 12, 2006, available at <http://politics.people.com.cn/GB/8198/57347/57350/4021527.html>.

40   Broadly speaking, leading small groups are important mechanisms for the Chinese Communist Party to make decisions and maintain control over various parts of the government. See Kenneth Lieberthal, *Governing China: From Revolution to Reform* (New York: Norton and Company, 1995), 209, 213.

41   The Chinese term for this group is *guojia tongxin baozhang yingji lingdao xiaozu*, 国家通信保障应急领导小组. The plan was issued in 2006, when MIIT had

not yet been created. The reference in the plan is to the Ministry of Information and Industry, the predecessor to MIIT. See National Emergency Response Plan on Communication Support [国家通信保障应急预案], *People's Daily Online*, January 24, 2006, at <http://politics.people.com.cn/GB/1026/4059051.html>.

42   Ministry of Industry and Information Technology, People's Republic of China, "Ministry of Industry and Information Technology Holds 2012 National Inter-Provincial Emergency Communication Drill" [工业和信息化部举行2012年国家应急通信跨省演练], September 4, 2012, available at <www.gov.cn/gzdt/2012-09/04/content_2216401.htm>.

43   National Emergency Response Plan on Maritime Search and Rescue [国家海上搜救应急预案], *People's Daily Online*, January 23, 2006, available at <http://politics.people.com.cn/GB/1026/4055359.html>.

44   This is just one of many examples of the Chinese government activating emergency plans in response to a disaster. Also, given the scale of the disaster, it may have attracted a higher level of participation from, and scrutiny by, national-level officials. Additional research comparing how the response to this disaster was handled in comparison to other larger and smaller scale disasters would provide more insight into the regularity with which these plans are activated, how the plans may actually affect emergency response, and how frequently higher level officials are involved in responding to local-level emergencies.

45   Zhao Yinan, "Donations Pour in for Yiliang Quake Victims," *China Daily Online*, September 11, 2012, available at <www.chinadaily.com.cn/china/2012-09/11/content_15748654.htm>, and Chen Zhi, ed., "Earthquake Aftermath in Yiliang Yunnan," Xinhua Online, September 8, 2012, available at <http://news.xinhuanet.com/english/photo/2012-09/08/c_131837014.htm>.

46   Chen Zhi.

47   Ibid.

48   For the national level for example, see "Rolling Broadcast: 5.7 Level Earthquake Occurs in Yiliang, Yunnan, with 16 Aftershocks" [滚动播报：云南彝良发生5.7级地震 发生余震16次], *China Daily Online*, September 7, 2012, available at <www.chinadaily.com.cn/dfpd/dfshehui/2012-09-07/content_6946786.html>. At the provincial level, for example, see "Yunnan Province Earthquake Bureau: Yunnan Province Earthquake Bureau Activates Level IV Emergency Response" [云南省地震局：云南省地震局启动IV级应急响应], September 7, 2012, available at <www.gov.cn/gzdt/2012-09/07/content_2219140.htm>. At the local level, for example, see "Yiliang County, Yunnan Province Earthquake Kills 64 and Injures 715" [云南省彝良县地震已造成64人遇难 715人受伤], September 7, 2012, available at <www.gov.cn/jrzg/2012-09/07/content_2219201.htm>.

49   For the China Earthquake Administration, see "Rolling Broadcast: 5.7 Level Earthquake Occurs in Yiliang, Yunnan, with 16 Aftershocks;" for the Yunnan Bureau

of Agriculture, see "Yiliang Agriculture Seriously Affected by Disaster: Yunnan Activates Agricultural Disaster Prevention Emergency Plan" [彝良农业受灾严重 云南启动农业减灾防灾应急预案], September 8, 2012, available at <www.gov.cn/jrzg/2012-09/08/content_2219581.htm>; for the Public Security Bureau Fire Prevention Team, see "Yunnan Province Public Security Fire Prevention Team to Mobilize Many Local Fire Team's Rescue Forces to Rush to the Area of the Earthquake" [云南公安消防总队调集多地消防支队地震应急救援力量赶赴震区], *People's Daily Online*, September 7, 2012, available at <http://society.people.com.cn/n/2012/0907/c223276-18949820.html>; for the Chengdu Military Region, see the summary of "Chengdu Military Region: More than 1,000 Soldiers Rush to the Rescue at the Sichuan-Yunnan Border to Assist with Earthquake Relief" [成都军区千余兵力驰援川滇交界抗震救灾], provided in "Hu Jintao and Others' Instructions: Rapidly Organize for Earthquake Relief and Ensure the Safety of People's Lives and Property" [胡锦涛等指示: 迅速组织力量抗震救灾确保人民生命财产安全], *China Daily Online*, available at <www.chinadaily.com.cn/micro-reading/mfeed/hotwords/20120907963_3.html>; and for the power company, see summary of "Yunnan Power Rapidly Activates Emergency Plan to Restore Power" [云南电网迅速启动预案响应全力组织抢险复电], provided in "Hu Jintao and Others' Instructions: Rapidly Organize for Earthquake Relief and Ensure the Safety of People's Lives and Property."

50   "The Power of a Cohesive Rescue Effort—Every Locality and Every Department Rushes to the Area of the Earthquake" [力量在救援集结号下凝聚——各地各部门驰援震区], September 8, 2012, available at <www.gov.cn/jrzg/2012-09/08/content_2219925.htm>.

51   "Armed Forces and Armed Police Devote Their Full Effort to Doing Yunnan Earthquake Relief Work" [全军和武警部队全力以赴投入云南抗震救灾工作], September 8, 2012, available at <www.gov.cn/jrzg/2012-09/08/content_2219883.htm>.

52   "Rescuers Make an All-Out Effort in Yiliang, Yunnan," *Sina English*, September 9, 2012, available at <http://english.sina.com/china/p/2012/0909/504807.html>.

53   "Ministry of Public Security and Related Organizations Begin Earthquake Relief Work in Yunnan and Guizhou" [公安部部署组织开展云南贵州地震抗震救灾工作], September 8, 2012, available at <www.gov.cn/jrzg/2012-09/08/content_2219837.htm>.

54   Ministry of Civil Affairs, People's Republic of China, "Ministry of Civil Affairs Dispatches 10,000 Tents to Earthquake Stricken Areas in Yunnan" [民政部向云南地震灾区紧急调运1万顶救灾帐篷等], September 8, 2012, available at <www.gov.cn/gzdt/2012-09/08/content_2219813.htm>.

55   Ibid.

56   Peijun Shi et al., 3, 7, 13–15.

57   Ibid.

CHAPTER 5

Converting the Potential to the Actual: Chinese Mobilization Policies and Planning

Dean Cheng

For the People's Republic of China (PRC) and the People's Liberation Army (PLA), the nature of modern war has evolved as a result of major shifts in the larger global political and technological context. Consequently, Chinese concepts of mobilization have also been refined and taken on greater importance as a means of reconciling military and national economic modernization efforts. Where mobilization once focused on maximizing the amount of human, material, and financial power that could be brought to bear in a major conflict, the PRC now views mobilization as an essential means of allowing maximum peacetime development of those same resources while having in place the mechanisms and plans to exploit them in the event of conflict.

This chapter examines current Chinese policies on mobilization in the era of "Local Wars Under High-Tech Conditions" [*gaojishu tiaojian xia jubu zhanzheng*, 高技术条件下局部战争] and "Local Wars Under Informationized Conditions" [*xinxihua tiaojian xia jubu zhanzheng*, 信息化条件下局部战争]. It reviews the 2010 law governing national defense mobilization and the organizational structures that have been put in place to manage any mobilization effort.

Evolving Concepts of Modern Warfare

Since the early 1990s and the Gulf War, the PLA has been reforming its conception of how modern wars will be fought. At the same time, it has also had to deal with the ongoing process of economic reform, which has altered its relationship with the larger economy and polity. This has involved a revision of not only doctrine and operational concepts, but also of the PLA's approach to "army-building."

From a focus under Mao Zedong on preparing for "early [imminent] war, major war, nuclear war" [*zaoda, dada, dahe zhanzheng*, 早打, 大打, 打核战

争], the PRC has shifted to an assumption that major wars are unlikely in an international system that is largely peaceful. Consequently, there is less need to concentrate all national resources on military purposes, but there is a corresponding increase in emphasis on national defense mobilization [*guofang dongyuan*, 国防动员], also known as wartime mobilization [*zhanzheng dongyuan*, 战争动员]. National defense mobilization (hereafter simply referred to as mobilization) entails "the set of actions undertaken to shift from a peacetime stance into a wartime stance, for the unified activation of manpower, material power, and financial power."[1]

Under Deng Xiaoping, civil-military integration became an essential part of both national defense and national development efforts. Deng created the 16-character formulation of civil-military integration that still underpins much of the Chinese thinking on mobilization: the military and the people are united; wartime and peacetime (functions) are united; military goods are given preference; civilian resources are used to support the military [*junmin jiehe, pingzhan jiehe, junpin youxian, yi min yang jun*, 军民结合, 平战结合, 军品优先, 以民养军].

In the course of the 1980s and 1990s, the PRC revised its outlook on both future wars and economic development. According to PLA theorists, the previous assessment of conflicts had been that they would be "Local Wars" and "Local Wars Under Modern Conditions." By the late 1990s, this had shifted to "Local Wars Under High-Technology Conditions," and in 2004 it evolved into "Local Wars Under Informationized Conditions." These shifts required the PLA to prepare not only for mechanized warfare [*jixiehua zhanzheng*, 机械化战争], but also for warfare involving information technology (or *informationized*) warfare [*xinxihua zhanzheng*, 信息化战争]. This, in turn, placed a higher premium on the incorporation of science and technology into both weapons and training, in order to field both advanced weapons and a force whose personnel could handle the new weapons.

Providing trained personnel and advanced weapons could not come at the expense of economic modernization, however. Indeed, national development [*guojia jianshe*, 国家建设] continues to be accorded higher priority than purely military development or "army-building" [*jundui jianshe*, 军队建设]. Consequently, the PLA and the overall Chinese leadership also began to pay renewed attention to the issue of mobilization.

Growing Role for Mobilization

Mobilization is the means by which the full array of comprehensive national power, including economic and financial wherewithal as well as scientific talent and technological capacity, can be brought to bear on an enemy after some period of mobilization. Given the priority accorded national economic development, the PLA must rely upon mobilization to gain maximum military power from China's national potential.

The short notice and decisive nature of "Local Wars Under Information-ized Conditions" place a premium on being able to mobilize promptly and effectively. This is further complicated by the emphasis on advanced weaponry and technical capability in fighting "Local Wars Under Informationized Conditions," which makes mobilization much more complex than simply arming the masses with basic weapons. Proper mobilization for such conflicts requires mobilizing not only industrial plants but also transportation assets. In order to deal with high-tech wars, mobilization also entails exploiting science and technology. There must also be adequate mobilization planning and training in order to fully convert the disparate elements of comprehensive national power into effective military capability. These considerations also require, in turn, that national construction efforts should incorporate mobilization elements in order to improve mobilization response, should it be necessary.[2] This also extends to the financial realm; mobilization is not simply a command system for acquiring civilian facilities and assets but also involves mobilizing the wherewithal to pay for wars.

For all of these reasons, PLA analyses note that mobilization is not something that can be improvised, but instead requires extensive advance peacetime preparations. In order to undertake proper mobilization, the PRC leadership created a separate bureaucracy, in the form of the National Defense Mobilization Committees, and a set of supporting laws, including the Reserve Officers Law (1995), the People's Air Defense Law (1996), the National Defense Law (1997), and the National Defense Education Law (2001), culminating in the Defense Mobilization Law of 2010. These laws, and the attendant mobilization organization, are essential elements for mobilization planning and implementation.

Components of Mobilization[3]

For the PLA, mobilization involves the conversion of several broad categories of resources from potential sources of national strength to actual military power.

These include armed forces mobilization, People's Air Defense (PAD) mobilization, political mobilization, information mobilization, national economic mobilization, transportation combat preparations mobilization, equipment mobilization, and mobilization of science and technology (S&T).

Armed forces mobilization [*wuzhuang liliang dongyuan*, 武装力量动员] refers to the shift of military and other armed organizations from a peacetime structure [*pingshi tizhi*, 平时体质] toward a wartime structure [*zhanshi tizhi*, 战时体制] and is considered the core of national defense mobilization. Once mobilization is ordered, the first task associated with armed forces mobilization is the rapid expansion of active-duty PLA units and the transition of reserve forces to active duty. At the same time, other elements of the armed forces (for example, the People's Armed Police) should shift to a wartime footing, with corresponding mobilization of military equipment and resources, so that forces are at their notional table of organization and equipment.

PLA writings indicate that armed forces mobilization comprises three separate strands: troop mobilization [*bingyuan dongyuan*, 兵员动员], weapons and equipment mobilization [*wuqi zhuangbei dongyuan*, 武器装备动员], and logistics and material mobilization [*houqin wuzi dongyuan*, 后勤物资动员]. This last aspect involves mobilization of suitable petroleum, oil, and lubricants (POL), transport, and medical assets to support military expansion and sustain operations.[4]

People's Air Defense mobilization [*renmin fangkong dongyuan*, 人民防空动员], also termed "mass-style defensive mobilization" [*qunzhongxing fangwei dongyuan*, 群众性防卫动员] or "civil defense mobilization" [*minfang dongyuan*, 民防动员], refers to the national organization of defensive preparations for the civilian population against enemy air attack. Key components of PAD include:

- protective measures for the population at large. This includes not only construction of shelters, dispersal sites, and decontamination facilities, as well as stockpiling necessary equipment for repairs, but also propaganda and education regarding air defense measures and knowledge.
- creation of specialized air defense units for rescue operations, damage repair, firefighting, road clearance, and preservation of public safety
- establishment of an early warning network and safeguarding capacity.[5]

Political mobilization [*zhengzhi dongyuan*, 政治动员] refers to those organizational measures and broader activities that will create a good political environment for conducting a conflict or responding to a crisis or emergency. Successful political mobilization will help safeguard and ensure the smooth implementation of all the other elements of mobilization. The goal is to ignite patriotic fervor among the broad military and civilian populations, inspire the military to greater heroism and sacrifice, and mobilize the population toward greater support for national efforts.[6]

It is important to note that political mobilization includes efforts not only to enhance domestic support but also to attract foreign support, and therefore includes diplomatic mobilization. Political mobilization measures include:

- adjusting national political structures to accommodate wartime requirements
- orchestrating broad patriotic support, conducting national defense education, and strengthening national spirit and will
- activating various social organizations to provide support for the war effort
- engaging in diplomatic activities and foreign propaganda, so as to strengthen and broaden international support from both foreign nations and populations.

Information mobilization [*xinxi dongyuan*, 信息动员] refers to those activities and organizational measures undertaken to ensure that there are sufficient information resources, facilities, technology, and talent to meet military requirements. It involves mobilizing manpower and material assets involved with the collection, transmission, storage, and/or management of information, as well as management of the electromagnetic spectrum.[7] Information mobilization measures include not only wartime conversion of civilian and commercial assets, but also incorporating considerations of wartime requirements into peacetime development of national information industries and infrastructure, at both the national and local levels.[8]

Because of the increasingly central role of information and information technology, especially in the context of informationized warfare, information mobilization has correspondingly assumed greater importance. Aspects of information mobilization include:

- expanding information equipment production capacity
- organizing information personnel and facilities and adjusting communications networks to support front-line military requirements

- ensuring that communications and information networks are secure and functional through the creation of safeguarding, repair, and construction units
- employing civilian information resources [*shehui xinxi liliang*, 社会信息力量], including personnel and equipment, in electronic combat and network offense and defense.[9]

National economic mobilization [*guomin jingji dongyuan*, 国民经济动员] refers to the transition of economic resources from peacetime to wartime production and the attendant shift of economic departments and their corresponding structures from a peacetime stance to a wartime stance. Economic mobilization is considered a special form of economic activity, distinguished by the fact that it affects almost all aspects of the nation's economy and is intended to promote national security.[10] Successful economic mobilization requires a unified national leadership to oversee plans for the coordinated mobilization of industry, agriculture, natural resources, transportation, finance, communications, science and technology, and other such material areas.

Transportation combat preparations mobilization [*jiaotong zhanbei dongyuan*, 交通战备动员] involves mobilization of all forms of national transportation, including railways, highways, waterways, and airways. Transportation mobilization is essential for redeploying military forces, personnel, and equipment and for ensuring that vital industries are sustained, that industrial production reaches its intended consumers, and that personnel and equipment can be dispersed and moved as necessary.

As with other forms of mobilization, Chinese concepts of transportation mobilization include organizational components as well as mobilization measures and activities. Thus, they include shifting government ministries associated with transportation from a peacetime to a wartime footing, as well as organizing safeguarding units that can repair and defend key transportation assets and lines. Transportation mobilization measures also include, at the order of higher levels, cutting off [*zheduan*, 折断] certain regions.[11]

Equipment mobilization [*zhuangbei dongyuan*, 装备动员] refers to the incorporation of civilian and commercial equipment, associated facilities, and other assets to support wartime requirements. It includes the organization and activation of stockpiles of equipment and raw materials; the drafting of civilian equipment; and the redirection of both production and research capabilities toward wartime ends. It also includes the mobilization of relevant technical personnel to provide maintenance, support, and other safeguarding functions for these assets. Equipment mobilization, like national economic mobilization, allows for maximum peacetime reliance on the market for efficient allocation of resources, while also meeting those national requirements that arise in wartime or in event of crisis or emergency.[12]

Science and technology (S&T) mobilization [*keji dongyuan*, 科技动员] refers to organizing and adjusting civilian, commercial, and governmental scientific research departments to undertake military research and development, while incorporating specialists, scholars, engineers, and technical personnel to support such research and to supplement military technical operations. The purpose of S&T mobilization is to concentrate available scientific research capabilities to apply extant scientific advances to military operations and wartime production, while also accelerating research and development so as to create new advantages in weapons, equipment, and technology.

According to PLA assessments, the mobilization of science and technology effectively acts as a force multiplier for human and material power, substantially increasing the ability to generate real military power.[13] They highlight S&T mobilization as a major factor in the development of the atomic bomb and the V-1 and V-2 rockets, as well as more recent developments such as the Patriot surface-to-air missile and the F-117 stealth fighter.[14]

Guiding Thoughts and Principles of Mobilization

PLA analyses note that mobilization is no different from other aspects of military science, insofar as there are scientific abstractions that constitute the foundation for national defense mobilization. These abstractions take the form of guiding thoughts and principles that, once derived, should guide mobilization activities.

As noted earlier, the guiding thought for PLA mobilization thinking remains rooted in Deng Xiaoping's 16-character general guideline [*zong-fangzhen*, 总方针], which calls for the shifting of technological and industrial resources from the defense sector to the civilian side, in order to facilitate national economic construction.[15] Under Jiang Zemin, this general guideline was modified to "link the military and civilian, link peacetime and wartime, embed the military in the civilian" [*junmin jiehe, pingzhan jiehe, yu bing yu min*, 军民结合, 平战结合, 寓兵于民].[16] The modification would seem to reflect a further shift toward emphasizing national economic construction, with the military's needs embedded within it. Hu Jintao, in turn, further emphasized the integrated nature of the civilian and military economies by adding "melded-style development" [*ronghe shi fazhan*, 融合式发展] to Jiang's formulation.[17]

Under this evolving set of broad general guidelines, the PLA sought to develop a set of principles [*yuanze*, 原则] to govern mobilization planning and organization consistent with the broader PLA approach to military science, which involves determining guidelines and principles to help guide policy. In line with the passage of the National Defense Mobilization Law, it would appear that the following constitute consensus principles regarding mobilization.[18]

Unified leadership [*tongyi lingdao*, 统一领导]. Given the complexities associated with mobilization, it is essential that there be a streamlined, unified leadership structure for planning and implementing mobilization. According to Chapter 2, Section 9 of the National Defense Mobilization Law, as well as the Chinese constitution and National Defense Law, the State Council and Central Military Commission (CMC) will together exercise unified leadership over all aspects of mobilization work, including planning, preparation, and implementation. The State Council is responsible for leading and managing national defense construction (as well as national economic construction), while the CMC is responsible for managing the nation's armed forces. The two together will lead mobilization preparation and implementation work.[19]

As specified in the National Defense Mobilization Law, however, between the national and county levels (that is, at the provincial and prefectural levels), mobilization activities are the responsibility of the state, consistent with legal authorities and higher-level directives, and not the Chinese Communist Party (CCP) or the military.[20] This is consistent with the earlier National Defense Law, which specified the same allocation of authority.[21]

Population-wide participation [*quanmin canyu*, 全民参与]. From the Chinese perspective, despite the growing importance of information technology, the support of the population remains a vital factor in determining wartime victory. It is therefore still necessary to mobilize the populace. This involves two aspects.

First, it is essential to actively integrate the broad civilian populace and associated resources into the planning and implementation of mobilization efforts. Successfully linking civilian resources (including manpower) with military requirements combines the sustainment of fewer military forces in peacetime with the ability to field more forces in time of war.[22] Thus, national defense mobilization work includes not only military forces, but also political, economic, S&T, education, culture, health, and many other resources.

Second, it is vital to ensure popular support for a conflict, especially in the face of potential enemy attacks. Thus, Chinese mobilization writings also note the need for engaging in political mobilization, including such measures as political propaganda and encouragement of patriotic fervor and sentiment.[23] National defense education [*guofang jiaoyu*, 国防教育] and specifically national defense mobilization education [*guofang dongyuan jiaoyu*, 国防动员教育] are considered essential parts of mobilization efforts. Such efforts are intended to establish a firm foundation of national defense theory within the entire populace, so that every person, no matter their position or occupation, will feel a personal sense of responsibility and a stake in defending the nation and thus will support mobilization activities.[24]

Importance of planning and oversight [*tongchou jiangu*, 统筹兼顾]. PLA writings emphasize that army building [*jundui jianshe*, 军队建设] remains subordinate to national economic construction. Equally important is the idea that only by expanding all of the facets of comprehensive national power can the military enjoy sustainable, long-term growth. Consequently, planning for long-term military security requires concomitant, coordinated planning for economic development, including the forging, in turn, of a strong scientific and technological base.

As the hallmark of the times remains "peace and development," there must be a focus on developing the broad national economy without neglecting defense modernization. Mobilization work occurs within this context, consistent with both economic and military construction. Mobilization preparations will increase comprehensive national power, but only if they are organically integrated into both economic and military construction in a coordinated manner. Thus, only by firmly holding to the principle of undertaking planning and oversight of both elements can mutual support between national defense mobilization work and economic construction be realized. Interestingly, over the last several years, there has also been additional emphasis placed on linking mobilization planning and implementation structures to crisis response and disaster relief.

Long-term development [*changqi fazhan*, 长期发展]. According to Chinese assessments, because it includes manpower, material, and financial aspects, mobilization is a major piece of systems engineering, requiring the coordination of a disparate range of capabilities and efforts. Mobilization can be successfully implemented only if national economic construction [*guojia jingji jianshe*, 国家经济建设], national defense construction [*guofang jianshe*, 国防建设], and armed forces construction [*wuzhuang liliang jianshe*, 武装力量建设] are linked from the outset.

To this end, mobilization preparations encompass a wide range of measures that must be integrated into the earliest stages of project planning and budgeting. Many aspects of mobilization require either sustained commitment of resources, such as the creation and maintenance of strategic stockpiles, or else regular refreshing, such as mobilization planning, calculating mobilization potential, and mobilization training.[25]

Key point construction [*zhongdian jianshe*, 重点建设]. The complement to long-term planning is key point construction. Long-term planning can succeed only when there is a persistent focus on the essentials. Thus, according to PLA writings, successful mobilization requires focusing efforts on key points. The starting key point for all mobilization preparations is supporting the ability to fight and win "Local Wars Under Informationized Conditions." Another key point is mobilization of armed forces strength [*wuzhuang liliang*, 武装力量], which is considered the core of national defense mobilization. The extent and level of armed forces construction will directly affect the likelihood of victory.

Another key point for mobilization construction is developing national S&T levels. The rapid development of science and technology has deeply influenced modern warfare; the concept of "Local Wars Under Informationized Conditions" has further increased its impact.[26] Consequently, the ability to mobilize scientific and technological assets, facilities, and personnel will directly affect a nation's ability to fight and win modern conflicts—which are seen, at one level, as a contest between respective arrays of high technology.

According to this principle, then, effective national mobilization efforts must establish priorities. These include the provision of immediate mobilization support to the armed forces and support of the mobilization of scientific and technical assets and talent.

Sequencing and effectiveness [*youxu gaoxiao*, 有序高效]. This principle calls for improving the effectiveness of mobilization planning and implementation. Sequencing refers to the idea that mobilization preparations, planning, and demobilization must be carefully coordinated, so as to minimize mutual interference. One aspect of sequencing is ensuring that mobilization occurs first along the key point strategic direction [*zhongdian zhanlüe fangxiang*, 重点战略方向]. That is, mobilization should begin where conflict or crisis is most likely so that mobilized resources are promptly at hand while national disruption is minimized. Another aspect of sequencing is that there must be proper coordination among the disparate elements of mobilization, so that there is minimal mutual interference as the various components of mobilization are activated. High effectiveness refers to shifting the focus of mobilization from sheer mass to quality and from numbers of people to levels of science and technology.[27]

Legal Structures of Mobilization

The enactment of the National Defense Mobilization Law in 2010 put in place a long-missing piece of China's legal structure governing mobilization. In the PLA's conception, mobilization laws and regulations [*dongyuan falü yu fagui*, 动员法律与法规], often shortened to *dongyuan fagui* [动员法规] provide the framework for peacetime mobilization preparations as well as wartime mobilization implementation.[28]

The key point of mobilization laws and regulations is to lay out explicitly what missions need to be accomplished for successful wartime mobilization and what lines of authority exist to fulfill those missions [*zhanzheng dongyuan zhong de quanli he yiwu*, 战争动员中的权力和义务]. Mobilization laws and regulations serve to inform the populace as a whole, as well as all levels of government, the military, and relevant organizations, of these missions and lines of authority. Furthermore, mobilization laws and regulations codify and institutionalize the means for implementing wartime mobilization [*dongyuan gongzuo tiaolihua he zhiduhua*, 动员工作条例化和制度化].[29]

Thus, according to PLA writings, the body of mobilization laws and regulations should include the range of guidelines, policies, missions, mechanisms, processes, timing, and organizational structures governing mobilization. It should also clearly delineate organizations' and masses' assignments and duties as well as the people's rights and responsibilities.[30] By creating a single, coherent, consistent body of mobilization laws and regulations, and thoroughly inculcating this throughout the mobilization structure and apparatus, it is hoped that mobilization, if called for, can proceed smoothly.[31]

According to Chinese analyses, a comprehensive, formal system of laws and regulations to govern mobilization nationwide is essential in order to create consistency across provinces, across different levels of government, and across different components of mobilization. Moreover, the system of laws and regulations helps ensure that each level of government and military command understands its missions and responsibilities. Furthermore, the National Defense Mobilization Law also allows for the imposition of penalties and the awarding of bonuses, depending on the level of compliance with mobilization mandates and directives.

In this context, the longstanding absence of a National Mobilization Law constituted a serious problem for Chinese mobilization planners. As one Chinese general observed, without a National Mobilization Law it was extremely difficult to adopt an overall perspective or develop principles upon which to ground mobilization work. It also made it very difficult to formulate more specialized mobilization laws for such areas as armed forces mobilization or economic mobilization.[32]

The 2010 National Defense Mobilization Law remedied many of these problems. According to one Chinese account:

> The National Defense Mobilization Law has 14 sections and 72 parts, and encompasses overall principles; organization and leadership structures and their authority; national defense mobilization planning; methods for implementing solutions and potential strength calculations and investigations; as well as how to link national defense construction areas and vital products. It also includes reference to reserve personnel call-up and registration; strategic resource stockpiles and use; military item R&D, production, and maintenance safeguarding. In addition, there is wartime disaster preparation and rescue, national defense logistics, civil-use resource call-up and compensation, propaganda and education, special measures, and legal responsibilities.[33]

Not surprisingly, given its broad purview, the National Defense Mobilization Law did not come about easily. Chinese accounts suggest that, despite being considered a priority and placed on a fast track for development, the law took perhaps 12 years from when it was first conceived (in 1998) until it was finally approved. This time period included convening various study groups to analyze specific aspects of the law, soliciting views from disparate parts of the Chinese bureaucracy, including such elements as the Guangzhou Military Region and the Ministry of Finance, and the apparent submission of a draft in 2005, which was not accepted by the State Council and the Central Military Commission.[34]

Organizational Structures of Mobilization

One of the most significant aspects of the National Defense Mobilization Law was its specification of the lines of authority vested in the various organizations that manage China's mobilization activities.[35] While these had been implicitly understood and even explicitly discussed (for example, in the PLA's *Mobilization Encyclopedia*) prior to the law's passage, PLA analyses had emphasized the need for a formal, definitive clarification. This was provided in the National Defense Mobilization Law.

Chinese analysts view national defense mobilization as a two-part process. In peacetime, the PLA lays out its requirements; the state, in cooperation with the commercial sector, will develop plans and policies to meet those requirements and incorporate them into defense construction and economic construction plans. There should be steady deconfliction of any competing demands and requirements that emerge.[36] In wartime, those plans are then implemented so that, ideally, only the inevitable exigencies of war have to be addressed.

To achieve these aims, PLA analyses conclude that the mobilization structure is comprised of three essential elements:

- mobilization decisionmaking—the formulation of mobilization plans in peacetime and the decision to implement them in wartime
- mobilization coordination—the coordination of various mobilization-related activities across the various levels of government and among the various organizations and bureaucracies involved in both the planning and implementation phases, so as to resolve any contradictions that arise
- mobilization implementation—the actual execution of mobilization policy.[37]

Each of these tasks, in turn, has its own structure: there is an organization responsible for the decisionmaking associated with mobilization, an organization charged with coordinating the various parts of the state, party, military, and economy, and finally, a structure for executing or implementing mobilization.

Mobilization Decisionmaking Structure

China's mobilization decisionmaking structure [*dongyuan juece jigou,* 动员决策机构] governs mobilization planning and implementation. PLA writings describe the mobilization decisionmaking structure as the basic nervous system of the mobilization system. This structure has several fundamental responsibilities:

- to assess the strategic environment and to undertake mobilization preparations and implementation based on that assessment
- to create and promulgate the guidelines, principles, and policies to govern peacetime mobilization preparations and wartime implementation
- to monitor the development of mobilization guidelines and plans and ensure that they provide enough time for the national leadership to undertake mobilization
- to issue the directives for peacetime mobilization preparation and wartime mobilization implementation as well as to ensure that mobilization will be regularized [*guifanhua,* 规范化] and orderly
- to inspire the nation to improve production and to be ready to convert latent power to combat power.[38]

According to PLA writings, the decisionmaking structure for Chinese mobilization is primarily vested in the state, in the form of the National People's Congress (NPC) and State Council, and in the military, in the form of the PLA's Central Military Commission (CMC). Both bodies, of course, are comprised of members of the CCP, so all mobilization (or, for that matter, defense) decisions ultimately occur under the aegis of the CCP. Nevertheless, within the legal framework, it is primarily the state and the military that are responsible for key decisions. This was formally codified in the 1982 PRC constitution and the 1997 National Defense Law, which state that the State Council and the CMC together are charged with undertaking mobilization preparations and mobilization implementation.[39] These laws, as well as the National Defense Mobilization Law, "specify that the [mobilization] decisionmaking structure resides within the National People's Congress, and the highest leadership structures are the State Council and the Central Military Commission."[40] Specifically, for peacetime mobilization planning, decisionmaking rests primarily with the State Council, which is responsible for decisions regarding national economic construction (including provisions for economic mobilization), and the CMC, which is responsible for decisions regarding military construction (including provisions for military mobilization).[41] In wartime, the mobilization decision-making structure is responsible for concluding that mobilization is necessary and then issuing the requisite orders.

Once mobilization is determined to be a necessity, a mobilization order or proclamation [*dongyuan ling*, 动员令] must be issued. In line with Article X of the National Defense Law, the NPC (or its Standing Committee if it is not in session) is responsible for determining whether to proclaim mobilization and whether such mobilization should be local or national. Article XI of the National Defense Law states that the premier, based on the NPC's (or Standing Committee's) determination that mobilization is necessary or that a state of war exists, will proclaim a state of war and issue the mobilization proclamation. He will then have conferred upon him additional authority, as specified by the Chinese constitution.[42]

Chinese writings note that the decision to undertake mobilization can be made only by senior, national-level officials. There are several reasons for this. First, the decision to undertake mobilization [*jinxing dongyuan juece*, 进行动员决策] is momentous, with repercussions for politics, military affairs, the economy, and diplomacy. Moreover, it must be properly timed. If the proclamation is issued too early, it will disrupt overall national economic affairs and affect societal order. On the other hand, if it is issued too late, the nation might be forced into a passive, reactive position in a crisis or conflict.[43] In addition, the proclamation is highly complex; it must indicate the timing and scale of mobilization as well as respond to likely military requirements. For all of these reasons, Chinese writings emphasize, such a decision requires national-level authority and the involvement of the most senior officials. It cannot be made by local authorities (even those at the military region level). Mobilization-related activities cannot commence without the explicit order of national-level decisionmakers.[44]

Mobilization Coordination Structure

Chinese writings suggest that the PLA considers coordination of activities in both the planning and implementation phases to be a vital part of the mobilization process. It is important in peacetime, when mobilization must be planned and conflicts between various goals and among various bureaucracies must be resolved. It is even more essential in wartime, when problems will inevitably arise; thus, the mobilization coordination structure [*dongyuan xietiao jigou*, 动员协调机构] is required. Chinese writings have noted that defense mobilization requires multiple forms of coordination.

Consistent with the overall guideline, for example, there must be coordination between peacetime and wartime needs—specifically, between the demands of defense mobilization and those of economic construction. This includes both material requirements and financial resourcing. Such coordination, moreover, is necessary not only at the national level, but also at the local level, between local officials and their military counterparts. There must also be coordination between levels—that is, between the national and local authorities (both military and civilian).[45]

In order to effect this coordination, in November 1994 the PRC replaced the unwieldy agglomeration of various commissions, including the National People's Air Defense Commission, the CMC Militia Commission, and the State Council and CMC Transportation Combat Preparations Leading Small Group, with the system of National Defense Mobilization Committees (NDMCs) [*guofang dongyuan weiyuanhui*, 国防动员委员会].[46] This system of committies is responsible for coordinating and implementing mobilization-related activities. The purpose of the system is to provide a single, unified leadership structure for coordinating mobilization efforts of the relevant agencies, departments, and key positions of the military and the state, in conjunction with the party.[47] For each layer of party, state, and military authority, there is a corresponding layer within the NDMC structure.

The overall system serves to provide an institutional basis for senior leaders at each level of authority to meet their counterparts from the party, the state, and the military. By instituting a mobilization-related set of regular meetings, the system is expected to coordinate everyone's needs and resolve issues. The implication of creating an institutional basis for cross-bureaucratic discussions seems to be that the cross-staffing that already occurs (especially between the party and the state) is insufficient for the purposes of mobilization.

National-level NDMC. At the apex of the system is the national-level National Defense Mobilization Committee, which reports to the CCP Central Committee, the CMC, and the State Council. It is headed by the premier of the State Council, while its vice chairmen are the vice premier of the State Council and one of the vice chairmen of the CMC. Its membership includes representatives from the ministries of State Security, Finance, Commerce, Railways, Transportation, Health, and Posts and Telecommunications, as well as the Civil Aviation Administration of China (CAAC), and other national ministries (most of which are also part of the State Council), as well as officers from the relevant departments of the General Staff Department (GSD) (the Mobilization Department), the General Political Department (the Mass Work Department), and the General Logistics Department (GLD).

Finally, the NDMC includes a specialized national defense education element. In 2002, the State Council and the CMC formally created the National Defense Education Office within the General Political Department (GPD), to help lead nationwide national defense education work. This was seen as an important move to smoothly link national defense mobilization and national defense education.[48]

At the national level, the NDMC is responsible for the following tasks:

- providing guidance to lower levels on relevant matters of mobilization work, including setting forth policies and promulgating directives, based on the decisions of the party's Central Committee, NPC, and CMC
- organizing and setting down laws, regulations, and methods for mobilization work
- organizing mobilization planning
- overseeing compliance with defense mobilization laws, including undertaking inspections
- coordinating military, economic, and societal aspects of mobilization work
- organizing and leading preparations for armed forces mobilization, economic mobilization, political mobilization, People's Air Defense work, and defense transportation work
- implementing other relevant directives set forth by the party's Central Committee, NPC, and/or CMC.[49]

Military Region–level Defense Mobilization Committee.[50] Military region defense mobilization committees (MRDMCs) are the organizing and coordinating structures for national defense mobilization work within the PLA's various military regions, responsible for the regions' mobilization work. Under the leadership of the military region's party committee and commander, and within the national-level NDMC's guidance, this layer coordinates the strategic regions, including the defense mobilization committees (DMCs) of the various component provinces, autonomous regions, and municipalities, in their national defense mobilization work. The MRDMC's chair is the military region commander. The vice chairman of the MRDMC frequently is a military region deputy commander responsible for mobilization work.

The rest of the MRDMC membership will include relevant provincial, autonomous region, and municipality senior leaders, including commanders from the MR headquarters, as well as its political department, joint logistics department, equipment department, and provincial military district commanders. An MRDMC will also include relevant personnel from the provincial, autonomous region, and municipality leadership, as well as leaders from those services and branches stationed in the region. The secretary of the MRDMC will be the deputy chief of staff for the MR. The MRDMC's organization will include a general office [*zonghe bangongshi*, 综合办公室], People's Armed Forces mobilization office, national economic mobilization office, PAD office, transportation combat preparations office, and national defense education office. Some MRDMCs have apparently also created an information mobilization office and equipment mobilization office.

The tasks of the MRDMC are essentially identical to those of the NDMC, adjusted for the lower level of responsibility. Thus, like the NDMCs, the MRDMCs are responsible for incorporating national-level guidance into their mobilization activities. They are also responsible for implementing national laws in mobilization, while also creating suitable laws and regulations adapted to the conditions of their specific military region.

Service and branch DMCs. Each service and branch has DMCs that serve as the organizational coordinating structures for their respective mobilization activities. The ground forces' defense mobilization committee was created in 1998.[51] These service- and branch-based defense mobilization committees are often chaired by key leaders of the respective service and branch or by deputy commanders, while the vice chairman is usually the service or branch deputy commander or in some cases the service or branch headquarters, political department, logistics department, or armaments department leader. Service and branch DMCs contain a general office, the People's Armed Forces mobilization office, the national economic mobilization office, transportation combat preparations mobilization office, equipment and technology mobilization office, and political mobilization office.

These DMCs are responsible for developing mobilization-related activities by their respective service or branch.

DMCs at various local levels. Local government DMCs are the organizational coordination structures between the provincial level and the county level, with their main role being to administer provincial-, prefectural-, and county-level defense mobilization work. Beginning in 1995, provinces, regions, and counties all established DMCs. These lower levels of the defense mobilization committee system are considered essential because mobilization cannot simply be ordered in a top-down manner based on the assumption that instructions and plans will be blindly obeyed. While the higher levels need to make clear what is required of lower levels, mobilization plans must also incorporate local realities into their formulation and execution. Moreover, lower levels of government are more likely to have a grasp of the actual resources potentially available for mobilization.

Consequently, the national defense mobilization structure must have a strong presence at these lower levels, to ensure that coordination is sufficient to bring about smooth mobilization planning and implementation. One PLA article notes, for example, that the efficacy of provincial-level defense mobilization will directly impact the effectiveness of national-level mobilization.[52] The overall NDMC structure therefore serves to link not only the party, the state, and the military at the national level, horizontally, but also national to local authorities, vertically.

Meetings at the provincial DMC level and below are apparently headed by the corresponding government-level leader, and the vice chairs are from the respective state levels' deputy leaders and equivalent-level military leaders.[53] Thus, the provincial DMC is usually headed by the governor as chair, with the provincial party secretary as first chairman and the provincial military district commander and first party secretary (formerly the "first political commissar") as vice chairs. To support their work, local DMCs rely on the corresponding People's Armed Forces Departments (PAFDs) [*renmin wuzhuang bu*, 人民武装部] to help implement plans and policies.[54] These include:

- organizing and (when necessary) implementing regional and local mobilization laws
- establishing the mobilization laws, plans, and programs, based on higher-level determinations
- overseeing the implementation of national and local defense mobilization plans within their area of responsibility

- coordinating military, economic, and social work with defense mobilization requirements
- organizing and leading People's Armed Forces mobilization, national economic mobilization, People's Air Defense work, and transportation and communications preparedness.[55]

Each of these lower levels of defense mobilization committees includes an office structure, with assigned personnel typically drawn from other governmental departments and agencies, giving them a dual-hatted role. The various levels of local government DMCs and their counterpart party People's Armed Force committees therefore typically operate under a "one structure, two nameplate" system. There is usually a general office, People's Armed Forces mobilization office, national economic mobilization office, PAD office, transportation combat preparations office, and national defense education office. Some lower level DMCs have also created political mobilization offices, S&T mobilization offices, and information mobilization offices.[56]

Mobilization Implementation Structure

While the NDMC structure is expected to coordinate defense mobilization efforts, mobilization implementation structures [*dongyuan zhixing jigou*, 动员执行机构] mostly rely on the government, and its bureaucratic structure, to execute and fulfill mobilization decisions. This allocation of authority is described as "the military determines requirements, the NDMC implements coordination, the government fulfills requirements."[57]

The mobilization implementation structure comprises those governmental ministries, offices, departments, and so forth, as well as corresponding military commands and relevant businesses whose functions are integral to the implementation of mobilization decisions.[58] For each layer within the bureaucracy, the mobilization implementation departments are responsible for implementing decisions issued by the next higher level, while simultaneously leading their own layer's enterprises and governmental departments. Thus, each layer of the mobilization implementation structure is charged with planning for subordinate units within its "stovepipe" (in peacetime) and executing its portion of the overall mobilization plan (in wartime), while ensuring that those plans and activities are compatible with higher-level intent.

In general, the PLA seems to have four categories of mobilization leadership and implementation structures: government, military, nongovernmental (or social) groups, and mass defense.

The government mobilization implementation structure is the main body responsible for mobilization. It builds upon the government's various bureaucracies, which exist at every level of governance and which have extensive reach into the economic, educational, administrative, and other aspects of the nation as a whole. There are two components to the governmental portion of the mobilization implementation structure. One is at the national level, wherein various government ministries and departments have mobilization implementation offices. The other portion is at the local levels of government. Operating under national-level guidance and directives, local government structures organize the implementation of their specific area's defense mobilization work.[59]

As one PLA assessment notes, it is the task of each level of government to set mobilization policy, oversee mobilization work, sensibly reconcile peacetime and wartime construction requirements, maintain a focus on the overall situation, and incorporate defense mobilization work into national economic construction efforts as well as developments in broader society. It is also the responsibility of the government to reconcile mobilization work with regional party-government leadership tasks, as well as relations with the corresponding military organizations.[60] Thus, each local government is expected to cooperate with local military forces in coordinating responses to any friction that might arise in mobilization planning (and, presumably, in other areas of civil-military disagreement).

The military mobilization leadership and implementation structure is the military structure responsible for mobilizing active-duty, reserve, and militia forces.[61] According to PLA writings, troop mobilization [*bingyuan dongyuan*, 兵员动员] is overseen and directed by the State Council and the CMC but relies on the local/regional governments and associated military structures [*difang zhengfu he junshi jiguan*, 地方政府和军事机关] for actually mobilizing troops. The GSD is responsible for the overall troop mobilization structure, mostly in terms of planning and management of the overall process and laying out broad targets. The military regions' mobilization departments, as well as the provincial military districts and county-level PAFDs, then work to achieve these GSD-administered goals for troop mobilization.

Each level has the following responsibilities:

- following the next higher level's guidance, policies, laws, and directives [*fangzhen, zhengce, fagui, zhiling*, 方针, 政策, 法规, 指令]
- ensuring that its own level is following the troop mobilization plans for that level
- monitoring the next lower level's implementation of troop mobilization plans
- managing troop mobilization work in peacetime.[62]

Thus, each military region, service, provincial MD, military subdistrict, and so forth is responsible for raising troops within its own purview. This includes not only the active-duty armed forces, but also the reserves and militia.[63]

A key part of the troop mobilization structure is the system of PAFDs, also referred to as the People's Armed Forces Work Organizational Structure [*renmin wuzhuang gongzuo zuzhi jigou*, 人民武装工作组织机构], as well as by the contraction *renwu bu* [人武部]. At the provincial military region, military sub-district, and county level, the PAFD is also the corresponding level's party committee military department, as well as the government's military service office.[64]

All levels of the PAFD are supposed to help organize reserve and militia support in such areas as air defense and chemical defense (both of which are also part of the People's Air Defense mission) in the event of attacks. They are also responsible, at the local level, for national defense education, military training, and some teaching and research in military theory in peacetime, and for support to the frontlines and drafting of additional troops in wartime.[65]

The PRC has several categories of reserve forces. Reserve units were established for all its services in 1983. These forces are organized as divisions [*shi*, 师], brigades [*lü*, 旅], and regiments [*tuan*, 团]. The objective was to enable the PLA to field more units for the same given expenditures.[66]

In addition, there are reserve personnel (both reserve officers and reserve enlisted personnel). According to the 1995 Law of the PRC on Reserve Service Officers [*zhonghua renmin gongheguo yubeiyijunguan fa*, 中华人民共和国预备役军官法], there are four kinds of reserve officers, based on their roles:

- military affairs officers [*junshi junguan*, 军事军官]
- political officers [*zhengzhi junguan*, 政治军官]

- logistics officers [*houqin junguan*, 后勤军官]
- specialized technical officers [*zhuanye jishu junguan*, 专业技术军官].[67]

Finally, there is also militia mobilization [*minbing dongyuan*, 民兵动员]. Although this follows the same chain of command as active-duty and reserve mobilization, militia mobilization above the county level is under the dual control of the party and the state, requiring cooperation between the local PAFDs and DMCs.[68]

There appear to be a variety of militia organizations that can be mobilized, depending upon the exigencies and requirements of the situation.[69] There are specialized militia units, including artillery, missile, communications, engineering, chemical defense, and other capabilities, available in time of war or in response to crises. There are also "corresponding" [*duikou*, 对口] militia units, first established in 1997 and expanded since 2004. These appear to organize civilian specialists into units that take advantage of their unique knowledge, such as information and communications units, medical and health units, and petroleum product safeguarding units. Another type of militia unit is the crisis response unit, which supports the People's Armed Police, Ministry of Public Security, and the PLA in maintaining public order. Finally, there are frontline support militia forces, which may undertake combat, combat support, and combat service support tasks, allowing the reallocation of active-duty units.

Social groupings are considered a necessary part of the mobilization structure as well. Interestingly, they are accorded importance in PLA writings because it is noted that the state can only apply so much authority in order to compel support from the population in the course of mobilization. By contrast, social organizations, because they are essentially voluntary, by their very nature organize and command support to a far greater degree than is possible from compelled mobilization.[70]

There are three broad elements of the social groupings portion of the mobilization implementation structure. The first are those based on social entities and civilian organizations, such as youth leagues, student committees, and religious organizations. Second are those centered on enterprises and businesses. These are often based upon contractual relations between these companies and the military and include not only production of goods and services, but also the provision of vital scientific research. Finally, there are grassroots level mobilization implementation structures, such as rural villager committees, which can undertake mobilization implementation at their level of activity.[71]

Finally, there is the civil defense mobilization system [*renmin dongyuan*, 人民动员] or People's Air Defense mobilization system [*renmin fangkong dongyuan xitong*, 人民防空动员系统]. The core organization for implementing PAD mobilization in wartime is the People's Air Defense Committee (PADC) [*renmin fangkong weiyuanhui*, 人民防空委员会]. There is apparently a PADC at the national level, at the military region level, in the provinces (including autonomous regions and autonomous cities), and in certain key cities and sub-districts.[72] The PADC operates under the State Council and the CMC, which are responsible for national civil air defense work [*renmin fangkong gongzuo*, 人民防空工作].

Assessing Chinese Mobilization

This chapter has reviewed China's mobilization structure and theoretical underpinnings, but it cannot assess the likely performance of that structure. Indeed, whereas the Chinese military last saw combat in 1979, it has arguably not engaged in mobilization since even before the rise of Deng Xiaoping—and China's economy and society have changed radically since then. China has conducted some mobilization exercises, but while this allows the various organizations to meet and review practices, it remains unclear how well the system would actually function in time of crisis. It may require a national emergency (for example, a major natural catastrophe) to gain real insight into how well the system can and will respond. The chapter by Jeffrey Engstrom and Lyle Morris in this volume provides some insights into Chinese mobilization capacity, albeit within a peacetime disaster response context.

What seems clear, however, is that the Chinese leadership has gone to great effort to establish a mobilization structure, including a legal foundation, in recognition that it cannot simply demand compliance and access to materials, people, or facilities. Indeed, the fundamental shifts in Chinese society and economics since 1979 have compelled the CCP to accommodate them, if it wishes to access the fruits of those changes in time of crisis.

At the same time, it would appear that there has been a systematic attempt to plan for mobilization, integrating it into physical, societal, and legal aspects of economic development. This spans the Chinese economy and polity from the national to the local level. Consequently, in the event of a more protracted or extensive conflict, it is likely that the PLA would be able to call upon a substantial mobilization base—and do so more smoothly, precisely for having spent time thinking about possible pitfalls and shortcomings.

Notes

1   Hu Tianjiang and Huang Gang [胡田疆, 黄刚], *PRC National Defense Mobilization Law Study Questions and Answers* [《中华人民共和国国防动员法》学习问答] (Beijing: National Defense University Press, 2010), 1.

2   Wang Wenrong [王文荣], ed., *The Science of Strategy* [战略学] (Beijing: National Defense University Press, 1999), 405.

3   Unless otherwise noted, this section is based upon Hu Tianjiang and Huang Gang, 12–16.

4   Ren Min [任民], *The Science of National Defense Mobilization* [国防动员学] (Beijing: Military Science Publishing House [军事科学出版社], 2008), 42.

5   Hu Guangzheng [胡光正], ed., *Chinese Military Encyclopedia* [中国大百科军事], 2nd edition, v. 26, *Wartime Mobilization* [战争动员] (Beijing: Encyclopedia of China Publishing House [中国百科全书出版社], 2007), 186.

6   National Defense Mobilization Knowledge Supplemental Material Editorial Group [国防动员知识辅导材料编写组], *500 Questions about National Defense Mobilization Knowledge* [国防动员知识500问] (Beijing: Long March Press [长征出版社], 2002), 6; and Ren, 58.

7   Hu, ed., 44.

8   Ren, 253.

9   Hu, ed., 44.

10   Zhu Qingling and Li Haijun [朱庆林, 李海军] et al., *Research on Chinese National Economic Mobilization Studies* [中国国民经济动员学研究] (Beijing: Military Science Publishing House, 2005), 3.

11   Hu and Huang, 15.

12   Ren, 359.

13   *500 Questions about National Defense Mobilization Knowledge*, 57.

14   Hu, ed., 41, 42–43.

15   Mobilization Encyclopedia Editorial Committee [中国战争动员百科全书本书编委会], *China Mobilization Encyclopedia* [中国战争动员百科全书] (Beijing: Military Science Publishing House, January 2003), 38.

16   Jiang Zemin [江泽民], "Regarding the Historical Experience of Twenty Years of Army Building" [关于二十年来军队建设的历史经验], speech to an enlarged session

of the Central Military Commission, Beijing, December 25, 1998, available at <www.wxyjs.org.cn/GB/186508/186515/231588/16912321.html>; and Hu Tianjiang and Huang Gang, 24–26.

17   Hu and Huang, 24–25.

18   The following, except where otherwise noted, is drawn from Hu Tianjiang and Huang Gang, 26–29.

19   Ren, 22.

20   The following, except where otherwise noted, is drawn from Hu Tianjiang and Huang Gang, chap. II, sec. 10–11.

21   *National Defense Law of the People's Republic of China* [中华人民共和国国防法], August 2009, art. II, sec. 15.

22   Ren, 24.

23   Ibid., 58.

24   Hu and Huang, 221.

25   Ren, 168.

26   Ibid., 466.

27   Ibid., 24.

28   Wu Ziyong [吴子勇], *Wartime Mobilization Studies Course Materials* [战争动员学教程] (Beijing: Military Science Publishing House, 2001), 93.

29   *China Mobilization Encyclopedia*, 50.

30   Ibid., 320.

31   Wu, 93.

32   General Qian Guoliang [钱国梁], "On Innovation and Development of the National Defense Mobilization System" [试论国防动员体系的创新与发展], *China Military Science* [中国军事科学] 16, no. 4 (2003), 78.

33   Liu Wanping and Chen Xiaoqing [刘万平, 陈小菁], "National People's Congress Standing Committee Passes National Defense Mobilization Law" [全国人大常委会审议通过国防动员法], *PLA Daily* [解放军报], February 27, 2010.

34   "National People's Congress Legal Work Committee Introduces National Defense Mobilization Law and Provides Detailed Explanations" [全国人大常委会法工委介绍国防动员法制定细节], *People's Daily Online* [人民网], February 26, 2010, available at <http://npc.people.com.cn/GB/11038758.html>.

35   "What Effects Will the 'National Defense Mobilization Law' Have on Mobilization Organization and Leadership Structures?" [《国防动员法》对国防动员的组织领导体制是如何规定的?], Ministry of Defense of the People's Republic of China, February 27, 2010, available at <www.mod.gov.cn/reports/201002/gfdyf/2010-02/27/

content_4126697.htm>.

36   Wei Yuxiang [魏玉祥], "Several Issues Regarding Strengthening National Economic Mobilization Preparations" [加强国民经济动员准备的几个问题], *National Defense* [国防], no. 8 (2003), 60.

37   Wu, 82–92.

38   Ibid., 85–86; and Hu and Huang, 31.

39   Wu, 85.

40   Hu and Huang, 34.

41   Wu, 85.

42   Gao Hongchun [高鸿春], ed., *Defense Education Teaching Materials* [国防教育教材], vol. 3, *Defense Knowledge* [国防知识] (Beijing: Military Science Publishing House, 2003), 81.

43   *China Mobilization Encyclopedia*, 322.

44   Gao, 80.

45   Qian.

46   To avoid confusion, only the national-level entity will be called the National Defense Mobilization Committee (NDMC). The lower level commissions will be referred to as defense mobilization committees or DMCs. Where possible, they will be more specifically referred to as provincial defense mobilization committees (PDMCs), local defense mobilization committees (LDMCs), and so forth.

47   Major General Fan Xiaoguang [范晓光], "Theoretical Discussion of Strengthening National Defense Mobilization Policy, Push Forward the Building, Creation, and Development of National Defense Mobilization" [加强国防动员政策理论研究 推进国防动员建设创新发展], *National Defense* [国防], no. 2 (2003), 10–15.

48   Hu and Huang, 35.

49   Ibid., 37; *China Mobilization Encyclopedia*, 258.

50   This section is drawn from Hu and Huang, 35–38.

51   Ibid., 36.

52   Yang Guodong [杨国栋], "An Initial Discussion of Issues Regarding Provincial Level Mobilization Structure Commencement" [省级国防动员机构启动问题初探], *National Defense*, no.1 (2003), 32.

53   Information Office of the State Council of the People's Republic of China, China's National Defense in 2002 (Beijing: Information Office of the State Council, 2002), 31.

54   *China Mobilization Encyclopedia*, 299; Hu and Huang, 36.

55   *China Mobilization Encyclopedia*, 298–299.

56   Hu and Huang, 36.

57   Ibid., 38.

58   Ren, 420.

59   Ibid., 420–421.

60   Hu and Huang, 41.

61   Wu, 88.

62   *China Mobilization Encyclopedia*, 212.

63   Ibid.

64   Hu and Huang, 41.

65   Wu, 60.

66   Hu and Huang, 101, 102.

67   Fang Ning [方宁], ed., *Defense Education Teaching Materials* [国防教育教材], vol. 9, *National Defense Laws* [国防法规] (Beijing: Military Science Publishing House, 2002), 222.

68   *China Mobilization Encyclopedia*, 212.

69   Ren, 269–271.

70   Wu, 89.

71   Ren, 421–422.

72   *China Mobilization Encyclopedia*, 258–259.

Employment of National-Level PLA Assets in a Contingency: A Cross-Strait Conflict as Case Study

Mark A. Stokes

The Chinese People's Liberation Army (PLA) is transforming into a modern military force capable of responding to an increasingly diverse set of contingencies. In the wake of the Third Plenum of the 18th Central Committee of the Chinese Communist Party (CCP) in November 2013, official press releases indicated an intent to adjust the PLA's organizational structure in a manner that would enhance its jointness and ability to respond to contingencies, while at the same time reducing the relative size of noncombat forces.[1] The General Staff Department (GSD), guided by the CCP and its Central Military Commission (CMC), remains the principal PLA organization responsible for employing national-level PLA assets in contingencies. National-level assets include those assigned to GSD, as well as those managed by three other first-level PLA General Departments and units subordinate to the PLA Navy, Air Force, and Second Artillery Force.

What would it look like if the CMC directed the PLA to mobilize for a major contingency in the Taiwan Strait? How would command and control be exercised, and what national-level capabilities could be allocated to a theater command in a major crisis? This chapter begins by outlining a notional organizational structure for national-level contingency planning and provides a preliminary assessment of command and control of assets at the strategic and operational levels. After a brief review of GSD's peacetime contingency planning organization, the chapter addresses a possible PLA joint operational-level command structure. Discussion then turns to national PLA assets that could be assigned to and employed by a joint campaign command. As a baseline for assessing how the PLA could operate increasingly farther from Chinese shores over time, the discussion focuses on an illustrative scenario involving PLA coercive use of force against Taiwan.

Contingency Planning Organization and Management

The CCP Central Committee Political Bureau (Politburo) exercises control over PLA through the CMC.[2] The CCP general secretary is usually dual-hatted as CMC chairman. The CMC chairman and the two military CMC vice chairmen serve as Politburo members. The chairman, vice chairmen, and CMC members exercise authority over the PLA through four first-level departments—the GSD, General Political Department (GPD), General Logistics Department (GLD), and General Armaments Department (GAD)—and through the Ministry of National Defense, Navy, Air Force, and Second Artillery Force. As a CMC member, the GSD director, also known as the chief of the General Staff (COGS), has a grade equal to the minister of defense, directors of the other three General Departments, and commanders of the PLA Navy, Air Force, and Second Artillery Force (see appendix for table providing information about the grades and ranks for organizations and personnel discussed within this chapter). The CMC chairman, under advisement from the Politburo and the CMC, functions as the national command authority for PLA employment, including nuclear weapons.

The CMC relies heavily on a dedicated staff for day-to-day management of its affairs. The staff is centered upon the General Office, which wields considerable influence as the administrative window of the CMC. It also provides for the personal security of national leaders. Within the CMC General Office, the Comprehensive Investigation and Research Bureau coordinates policy studies and analysis. Broad, long-range force building plans most likely are coordinated on behalf of the CMC by the PLA Strategic Planning Department (SPD).[3] The department conducts long-term analysis of the international security environment, including net assessment of evolving national security challenges, force balances, and capabilities required to meet future challenges. The department could have a role in developing defense planning and policy guidance, including illustrative scenarios as a basis for contingency planning, programming, and budgeting. SPD's role, if any, in coordinating nuclear force modernization is unknown at the current time.[4]

Under CMC guidance, and in coordination with the three other General Departments, GSD likely would determine how national-level assets are to be employed in a contingency operation.[5] GSD encompasses a large, complex bureaucracy consisting of a General Office and at least 12 second-level departments (see figure 6.1).[6] GSD departments are responsible for contingency planning, real-time emergency management, and control of a wide range of national-level PLA assets.

The GSD First Department (Operations) manages the National Joint Operational Command Center and oversees a specialized contingency office that appears responsible for coordination with civilian authorities during emergencies.[7] The Operations Department also controls the national navigation and positioning system, meteorological and hydrological assets, and dual-use airfields. The Operations Department's Readiness and Force Development Bureau is responsible for a range of planning and security functions, including coordination of dual-use airfields.[8]

Figure 6.1. General Staff Department Organizational Structure

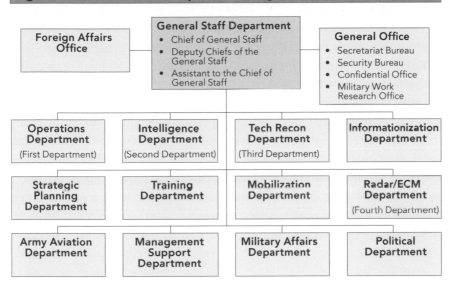

GSD's nationwide joint command and control communications system, managed by the GSD Informationization Department, comprises at least two communications commands that support GSD leaders in Beijing and link authorities there with military regions and GSD units throughout China.[9] Each command oversees a number of communications regiments.[10] In addition to fiber optic, microwave, and satellite communications networks, the GSD Informationization Department reportedly leverages long-range unmanned aerial vehicles (UAVs) and helicopter assets for radio relay.[11] The PLA is enhancing interoperability of GSD's national-level backbone network and operational-level networks managed by the PLA Navy, Air Force, and the seven military regions. Based on a "system of systems" approach, a newly fielded integrated command platform is intended to facilitate interoperability between national- and operational-level commands.[12]

National-level assets subordinate to the GSD Radar and Electronic Countermeasures (ECM) Department (the GSD Fourth Department) likely would be allocated to a theater command in the event of a contingency. In addition, GSD Army Aviation Department rotary wing assets may also be made available to theater commanders. The GSD Mobilization Department presumably would coordinate with civilian authorities for mobilization of reserve and militia assets.[13]

In addition to the General Staff Department, GPD, GLD, and GAD have peacetime management authority over other national-level PLA assets that could be employed in a contingency.[14] As the operational command responsible for space launch, tracking, and control, GAD identifies and monitors foreign space assets that could affect PLA operations.[15] The GAD space surveillance system, under Base 26 headquartered in Weinan (Shaanxi Province), probably fuses space tracking data from sensors managed by the GSD Technical Reconnaissance Department, PLA Air Force (PLAAF), and civilian authorities such as the China Academy of Science Space Target and Debris Observation and Research Center. The lead organization within the PLA for counterspace operations remains an open question. However, command and control of space operations appears to reside outside of the GSD system. Likewise, command and control of nuclear forces likely is separate and distinct from the GSD system. The Second Artillery functions as the central custodian for nuclear weapons under direct CMC command and control.

Finally, the PLA's national-level intelligence system that could be leveraged in a contingency situation consists of three departments. Each department carries equal status as a corps leader–level organization. First, the GSD Intelligence Department (also known as the GSD Second Department) carries out human intelligence collection operations, provides indications and warning and other analysis to the CMC leadership, and manages intelligence produced by dedicated PLA space reconnaissance assets. Secondly, the GSD Technical Reconnaissance Department (also known as GSD Third Department), roughly analogous to the U.S. National Security Agency, has control over a vast signals intelligence (SIGINT) and computer network operations (CNO) infrastructure. SIGINT and cyber assets target foreign satellite, line of sight, and over-the-horizon communications, as well as computer networks.

The GPD Liaison Department (GPD/LD) comprises the third component of the PLA's national-level intelligence system. As the principal PLA organization responsible for political warfare, GPD/LD collects and analyzes intelligence information regarding senior-level officers from the United States, Taiwan, Japan, and other defense establishments of interest. The PLA Navy, Air Force, Second Artillery, and the seven military regions all oversee independent departments with similar responsibilities.

In short, the CMC, under advisement from GSD, likely would play a major role in determining how national-level assets would be employed in a contingency operation. The GSD develops policies, plans, and programs, establishes requirements, and allocates resources to support the PLA mission. The GSD is responsible for day-to-day joint operations, intelligence, strategic planning and operational requirements, training, and mobilization. Assets that are subordinate to GSD during peacetime (and possibly those subordinate to other general departments such as GAD) could be made available to a theater command in the event of a crisis.

Contingency Command and Control

Employment of national-level PLA contingency assets would most likely be exercised through a Joint Campaign Command (JCC).[16] National and military region assets assigned to a JCC likely would be specified in a CMC directive outlining strategic intent. These directives might be in the form of campaign principles [*zhanyi fangzhen*, 战役方针] and a campaign decision [*zhanyi juece*, 战役决策]. The campaign decision would include a campaign resolution [*zhanyi juece*, 战役决心], which would identify national PLA assets available to the JCC, define the campaign phases, delineate responsibilities, and establish timelines for achievement of operational objectives.[17]

The JCC would execute contingency plans and exercise authority over national-level PLA assets and corps-level component commands within a defined theater of operations. The seven military regions have established geographical boundaries. In the event of a contingency, the theater of operations could transcend peacetime military region boundaries and PLA forces could

139

deploy from other military regions to the combat theater as needed. A JCC staff could consist of CMC representatives and personnel from the four General Departments, Navy, Air Force, and Second Artillery Force. Direct CMC oversight of, and integration with, the JCC ensures an orchestrated political-military strategy with access to government resources.[18]

Administrative organs under a JCC would probably include a Headquarters Department, Political Department, Logistics Department, and Equipment Department. The CMC chairman, in consultation with the Politburo Standing Committee, may assign a CMC vice chairman, the COGS, or a Deputy Chief of the General Staff (DCOGS) to command the JCC. Other CMC members or their organizational representatives could serve as JCC deputy commanders and the chief of staff, who presumably would oversee the JCC command and control system.[19] A second CMC vice chairman, GPD director, or GPD deputy director probably would be designated as JCC political commissar and secretary of the JCC party committee. In a Taiwan scenario, a JCC Headquarters Department staff may consist of officers from the GSD Operations Department and the Nanjing Military Region Operations Department.[20]

Employment of national assets probably would be directed through the JCC's primary command post, which might be supported by reserve and rear command posts and, if necessary, a forward command post. The forward and rear command posts, which would be responsible for logistics support, likely would report to the primary command post. The reserve post would assume duties as the primary command post in the event the latter was neutralized.

A primary command post may consist of a communications center, firepower coordination center, intelligence information center, ECM command center, and a weather center. The primary JCC command post might specify the levels of command that have skip echelon authority and include representatives from corps-level Navy, Air Force, and conventional Second Artillery component commands. JCC communications authorities, most likely assigned from the GSD Informationization Department, would leverage dedicated PLA assets and the civilian telecommunications infrastructure as needed to establish a joint operational command communications network.[21]

The GSD Operations Department may assign officers to a firepower coordination center, which notionally could be directed by a JCC deputy chief of staff. Air Force, Second Artillery, special operations, and ground force representatives may also be attached to carry out necessary liaison with their respective corps-level headquarters. In addition to cells responsible for coordinating with corps-level component commands, the firepower coordination center may consist of operational planning, targeting, and airspace coordination cells.[22]

A targeting intelligence cell may coordinate with the JCC intelligence information center, maintain target folders, carry out battle damage assessment, and develop a target sequence schedule for the operational planning cell. An airspace coordination cell, perhaps directed by a career Air Force officer from the GSD Operations Department's Air Traffic Control or Air Force Bureau, would coordinate with the operational planning cell on airspace management issues and resolve conflicts in air operations with the Second Artillery and other service operations. Possibly directed by a DCOGS, an intelligence information center would probably integrate sensor information from strategic- and operational-level intelligence, surveillance, and reconnaissance assets. A firepower coordination center presumably would work closely with the intelligence and ECM centers, as well as political warfare entities, in developing a general firepower plan.

Leaders and staff officers from the GSD Radar and ECM Department (also known as the GSD Fourth Department), subordinate brigade/regiments, military region headquarters ECM staff and units, and assets under component commands would likely man the ECM Center. ECM Center responsibilities may include collection management and analysis of electronic intelligence, development of an ECM concept of operations and electronic attack plan, assignment of responsibilities and targets, transmission of orders to ECM units, and coordination with the JCC leadership and other centers. An ECM Center may be subsumed into a broader information operations center that could consist of three sub-centers: an ECM sub-center, a network warfare sub-center, and a physical destruction sub-center.

The CMC may direct formation of PLA Navy, Air Force, and conventional Second Artillery corps-level component commands. Navy and Air Force component staff positions likely would be filled by representatives from their respective general headquarters in Beijing and military regions/fleets (for example, the Nanjing Military Region Air Force and East Sea Fleet). The JCC's primary command post would direct operations through component-level command centers. Division-level Navy and Air Force units (and conventional Second Artillery brigades) from throughout China may be resubordinated to a JCC component command in the event of a contingency. In a Taiwan scenario, as many as four communications commands that are subordinate to the Nanjing Military Region Informationization Department during peacetime presumably would form the backbone network linking a JCC with component-level command centers.[23]

The Air Force component command likely would bear primary responsibility for integrated air defense, one of the most complex JCC tasks. The operational-level air defense command center would rely upon national-, operational-, and tactical-level assets for air and space surveillance. An air surveillance command structure may be divided into sectors, presumably along the lines of peacetime Air Force command posts (or bases).[24] Radar tracking data could be transmitted to air and/or fighter units that may engage aircraft flying within a defined air defense identification zone (ADIZ).[25]

Selected conventionally capable ballistic and land attack cruise missile brigades and support regiments, which are under direct authority of the Second Artillery during peacetime (rather than military regions), may be apportioned to a JCC's Second Artillery component command in a contingency. However, the CMC chairman can be expected to retain exclusive control over the allocation of nuclear warheads through the PLA's central warhead storage and handling complex (known as Base 22), which is headquartered deep in Shaanxi's Qinling Mountains. The nuclear command and control system most likely would be separate and distinct from that of the JCC.[26]

Assigned Forces

Any assessment of the national-level PLA assets or units that could be mobilized and apportioned to a JCC is a speculative endeavor. However, the following discussion offers a tentative baseline that could be refined over time. National-level PLA assets most likely would include selected GSD, GPD, GLD, and GAD units, conventional brigades and support regiments subordinate to the Second Artillery Force, as well as Air Force and Navy units that report directly to headquarters in Beijing.

Intelligence, Surveillance, and Reconnaissance Assets

In addition to intelligence, surveillance, and reconnaissance assets subordinate to the Nanjing and perhaps the Guangzhou military regions, selected units under the GSD Second and Third Departments could be apportioned to a JCC intelligence information center in a contingency situation. For example, the GSD Second Department oversees a network of satellite remote-sensing ground stations that could provide direct support to a JCC. The GSD Second Department oversees at least one UAV regiment that could be apportioned to the JCC intelligence information center. GSD UAVs would augment assets organic to Air Force, Navy, and Second Artillery component commands.[27]

Selected offices subordinate to GSD Third Department technical reconnaissance bureaus could be resubordinated to a JCC for signals intelligence and cyber reconnaissance support. Candidates could include selected offices under GSD Third Department 2nd and 12th Bureaus in Shanghai, 3rd Bureau in Beijing, and 4th Bureau in Qingdao. The Third Department 1st Bureau and/or a subordinate division of the Beijing North Computing Center may support a JCC's network information center with threat assessment and computer network defense.[28] These units likely would augment technical reconnaissance bureaus that are under military regions during peacetime. For example, the Nanjing Military Region oversees two technical reconnaissance bureaus, one of which focuses exclusively on Taiwan. The PLAAF likely would assign selected assets subordinate to its three technical reconnaissance bureaus to the theater air force component as well.[29]

GSD units responsible for navigation, surveying, mapping, and weather could provide other forms of operational support. The GSD Navigation and Positioning Command likely would provide valuable operational support. During peacetime, survey and mapping groups are garrisoned in the Beijing and Xi'an areas.[30] GSD Survey Bureau Survey Information Center could be allocated to the JCC for military geographic information systems support.[31] The Xi'an Institute of Survey and Mapping may be equipped with mobile laser range-finding systems, which could be tasked with responsibility for satellite dazzling. The GSD Meteorological Center likely would provide weather support for joint contingency operations.[32]

ECM Forces

Forces subordinate to the GSD Fourth Department during peacetime could be allocated to the JCC ECM command center. The Fourth Department Air Defense ECM Brigade may be assigned for jamming support to strategic air defense.[33] Dedicated satellite jammers subordinate to the GSD Satellite ECM Command, including a subordinate element on Hainan Island, also likely would be apportioned to the JCC in a major contingency. GSD's Spectrum Management Center would ensure minimal red-on-red electronic fratricide.

Battalions subordinate to the Fourth Department ECM brigade at Qinhuang-dao in Hebei Province could be allocated as well.[34]

Political Warfare Assets

In a notional Taiwan scenario, GPD/LD psychological warfare units such as Base 311 in Fujian Province could provide political support for a contingency operation. Among other missions, Base 311 manages broadcasting stations, such as the Voice of the Taiwan Strait.[35] Specialized units for concealment, camouflage, and deception could also be assigned, such as the GSD Camouflage Engineering regiment.[36]

Counterspace Assets

Assuming the capability is operationally available, the CMC may grant the JCC authority over kinetic counterspace systems. The PLA has demonstrated an ability to engage targets in space as part of a broader effort to field a national aerospace security system.[37] The lead organization within the PLA for counterspace operations remains an open question. Chinese writings tend to link counterspace with the ability to track and engage all flight vehicles transiting space, including ballistic missiles.[38] Some Chinese analysts have advocated in favor of an independent space force that would centralize space operations under a unified command.[39] The GAD Headquarters Department, or China Launch and Tracking Control, oversees China's space launch, tracking, and control network. PLAAF and Second Artillery representatives have also argued in favor of adopting the counterspace mission. Theoretically, existing medium, intermediate, and intercontinental ballistic missiles could be adapted for a space intercept role by reprogramming missile guidance and fusing.[40] Should former PLAAF commander Xu Qiliang's concept of integrated air and space (aerospace) operations bear fruit, a future Air Force component command might oversee an evolving aerospace defense system under a JCC.[41]

Long-range Precision Strike

National PLA assets subordinate to the Second Artillery would constitute the centerpiece of the JCC and its Firepower Coordination Center. In enforcing sovereignty claims in the Taiwan Strait over the last 20 years, conventional ballistic missiles have been one of the most effective tools of CCP political and military coercion. As a symbolic metric of intent, the PLA's expanding arsenal of conventional ballistic missiles across the Taiwan Strait is intended to deter political support in Taiwan for formal independence and coerce the island's population to support unification on Beijing's terms.

In the event of a crisis, selected brigades, support regiments, and staff elements under Second Artillery general headquarters and one or more missile bases would comprise a corps-level Second Artillery conventional missile component under a JCC. The JCC's conventional Second Artillery component command likely would be comprised largely of officers from Second Artillery's Base 52, a corps-level organization that ensures the peacetime readiness of missile brigades and support regiments under its purview.

Under the authority of the Second Artillery chief of staff or Base 52 commander, key Headquarters Department staff, selected support regiments, Base 52 staff, and Base 52 support regiments may be assigned to form the Second Artillery corps-level component. Base 52's six conventional missile brigades could notionally also be assigned to the Second Artillery component command. The command could be augmented by an anti-ship ballistic missile (ASBM) brigade that appears to be subordinate to Base 53 during peacetime, as well as by a land attack cruise missile (LACM) brigade subordinate to Base 55.[12]

Units reporting directly to Second Artillery headquarters during peacetime also could be apportioned to the component command. For example, a regiment-sized unit north of Beijing specializes in imagery and all-source intelligence and would likely be deployed as the command intelligence cell.[43] At least one and probably two ECM regiments would support the JCC Second Artillery corps-level component commander.[44] The Second Artillery Technical Reconnaissance Bureau would likely be the service-level cryptologic authority and could engage in computer network operations.[45] A separate nuclear corps–level group, reporting directly to the CMC, could be comprised of Base 22 and intercontinental ballistic missile (ICBM) brigades subordinate to Bases 54, 55, and 56.[46]

In sum, the employment of national-level PLA contingency assets would most likely be exercised through a JCC. The JCC would execute contingency plans and exercise authority over national-level PLA assets and corps-level component commands (Navy, Air Force, and conventional Second Artillery) within a defined theater of operations. National and military region assets to be assigned to a JCC likely would be specified in a CMC directive outlining strategic intent. A JCC staff may consist of CMC representatives and personnel from the four General Departments, particularly the GSD. Integration of CMC and

GSD staff elements with the JCC would ensure an orchestrated political-military strategy with access to national-level resources.

Conclusion

The PLA is transforming into a modern military force capable of responding to an increasingly diverse set of contingencies farther from its shores. Guided by the CMC, GSD would be the principal organization responsible for commanding and employing national-level PLA assets in a contingency situation. National-level assets include those assigned to GSD, GPD, GLD, as well as the Second Artillery and units directly subordinate to the PLA Air Force and Navy.

The GSD Operations Department manages peacetime contingency planning and operations and would likely form the basis of a JCC, the leading authority for a military contingency. Under command by a CMC and/or GSD leader, JCC staff elements (for example, Headquarters, Political, Logistics, and Equipment Departments) would be drawn from the four General Departments, relevant military region(s), and representatives from the Air Force, Navy, and Second Artillery. The JCC's primary Command and Control Center would include a subordinate Communications Center, Firepower Coordination Center, Intelligence Information Center, Information Operations or ECM Command Center, and a Weather Center. An Intelligence Information Center theoretically would access sensor data, navigation, survey, mapping, and weather information through the Integrated Command Platform developed by the GSD Informationization Department. Second Artillery, Air Force, and Navy component commands under the JCC would coordinate long-range precision strike operations through the JCC Firepower Coordination Center.

In its campaign decision, the CMC would outline specific national PLA assets that would be assigned to and employed by a JCC during a contingency. In a notional Taiwan scenario, national PLA assets apportioned to a JCC would include a range of GSD elements, including units subordinate to the GSD First, Second, Third, Fourth, and Informationization Departments. Selected Second Artillery brigades and support regiments would be assigned to a Second Artillery component command. Conventional missile operations would be integrated with Air Force, Navy, and Military Region ground force strike elements through a JCC Firepower Coordination Center. This sampling of national-level PLA assets that could be employed in a contingency is speculative in nature but offers a tentative baseline that could be refined over time.

Appendix
PLA Grade and Rank Structure

Grade	Positions (Ranks)
CMC Member [*junwei weiyuan*, 军委委员]	Minister of Defense; Chief of the General Staff; General Political Department (GPD) director; General Logistics Department (GLD) director; General Armaments Department (GAD) director; Navy, Air Force, and Second Artillery commanders (General [GEN])
Military Region (MR) Leader [*zheng dajunqu zhi*, 正大军区职]	Deputy Chiefs of the General Staff (GEN/Lieutenant General [LTG]); GPD deputy directors; Navy, Air Force, and Second Artillery political commissars; MR commanders/political commissars (GEN/LTG)
MR Deputy Leader [*fu dajunqu zhi*, 副大军区职]	MR deputy commanders, political commissars, chiefs of staff, and MR Political Department directors; MR Air Force; Navy Fleets; Assistants to the Chief of the General Staff (LTG/Major General [MG])
Corps Leader [*zhengjunzhi*, 正军职]	MR deputy chiefs of staff; GSD, GPD, GLD, and GAD Second-level Department Directors; Second Artillery Force Base 52, 54, and 55 commanders/political commissars (MG/LTG); military district commanders/political commissars (MG/LTG)
Corps Deputy Leader [*fujunzhi*, 副军职]	GSD, GPD, GLD, and GAD Second-level Department directors and some Third-level Bureaus and Directors (MG/Senior Colonel [SCOL])
Division Leader [*zhengshizhi*, 正师职]	Third-level Departments/Bureaus and Directors and some Third-level Bureau Deputies (SCOL/MG)
Division Deputy Leader [*fushizhi*, 副师职]	Third-level Department/Bureau Deputies

Source: Directory of PRC Military Personalities, March 2013.

Notes

1   "Decision of the Central Committee of the Communist Party of China on Some Major Issues Concerning Comprehensively Deepening the Reform," Xinhua [新华], November 12, 2013, English translation available at <www.china.org.cn/

china/third_plenary_session>; and "Decision Directive: Deepen the Military System's Organizational Adjustment and Reform" [《决定》指出: 深化军队体制编制调整改革], Xinhua Online [新华网], November 15, 2013.

2   Tai Ming Cheung, "The Riddle in the Middle: China's Central Military Commission in the Twenty-first Century," in *PLA Influence on China's National Security Policymaking*, eds. Phillip C. Saunders and Andrew Scobell (Stanford: Stanford University Press, 2015), 84–119.

3   This new second-level department was founded on the basis of the GSD Operation Department's Strategic Planning Bureau until its conversion to a corps leader–grade organization nominally under GSD. For example, see Yao Yijiang, Lü Zhengtao, and Zhang Xuege [姚忆江, 吕正韬, 张雪歌], "Think Tank Construction: A New Center of Gravity in China's Military Reform" [智库建设: 中国军改新重心], *Southern Weekend* [南方周末], January 4, 2012.

4   The Strategic Planning Department may be linked with the CMC Strategic Committee [*zhanlüe weiyuanhui*, 战略委员会] or Strategy Small Working Group [*zhanlüe xiaozu*, 战略小组]. The department reportedly has five subordinate bureaus and two directly subordinate research centers. A review of available information indicates that the subordinate bureaus include Development Planning, Strategic Resources, Strategic Research, and Statistical Assessment. The Strategic Planning Department could oversee a GSD International Situation Study Group [*zongcan guoji xingshi yanjiu xiaozu*, 总参国际形势研究小组], although little is known about the organization. Major General Chen Shoumin [陈守民] was identified as deputy director in March 2012. See Zhou Feng [周峰], "The Formation of the Strategic Planning Department Moves Our Military to Adapt to the New Revolution in Military Affairs" [组建战略规划部是我军适应新军事变革之举], *PLA Daily* [解放军报], December 1, 2011; Xue Litai [薛理泰], "PLA Increasing Focus on Strategic Planning" [解放军愈益重视战略规划], *Phoenix Net* [凤凰网首页], November 24, 2011, available at <http://news.ifeng.com/opinion/zhuanlan/xuelitai/detail_2011_11/24/10873044_0.shtml>; and Xue Litai, "Xue Litai: CMC Set Up Strategic Planning Department to Avoid War" [薛理泰: 中央军委设战略规划部以避免打仗], *21ccom.net*, November 30, 2011, available at <www.21ccom.net/articles/qqsw/zlwj/article_2011113049577.html>.

5   Among various sources, see Liu Feng'an [刘逢安], "Strive to create a 'national army' with responsive strength" [全力打造应急力量"国家队"], *PLA Daily*, September 6, 2012.

6   See GSD chapter in *The People's Liberation Army as Organization: Reference Volume v 2.0* (Vienna, VA: DGI, Inc., 2015).

7   The Contingency Response Office [*yingji bangongshi*, 应急办公室], which is a corps deputy leader organization, may have an association with Unit 61683. For example, Tian Yixiang [田义祥] was identified as director of Unit 61683 and director of the Contingency Response Office in the 2008 timeframe. For reference to Tian as

director of Unit 61683, see "Authorized release: List of Nationwide Model Earthquake Responders" [授权发布: 全国抗震救灾模范名单], Xinhua, October 8, 2008, available at <http://news.xinhuanet.com/newscenter/2008-10/08/content_10167205_1.htm>. More recently, Unit 61683, directed by Dai Cunbing [戴存兵] in the 2013 timeframe, has been affiliated with analyzing weapons effects, bomb damage assessment, and civil engineering. See "Defense Engineering Branch Weapons Effects and Damage Assessment Experts' Committee 2013 Annual Academic Conference convenes in Beijing" [防护工程分会武器效应与毁伤评估专业委员会2013年学术年会在北京召开], China Civil Engineering Society [中国土木工程学会], September 27, 2013, available at <www.cces.net.cn/guild/sites/tmxh/detail.asp?i=xshdxshy&id=39182>. Until 2013, the Emergency Response Office was directed by Major General Li Haiyang [李海洋]. Li formerly directed the Lanzhou Military Region Operations Department. See, for example, "China Earthquake Administration Vice Bureau Chief Zhao Heping, General Staff Operations Department Contingency Response Office Director Li Haiyang arrive at Lanzhou National Land Search and Rescue Base to Inspect and Direct Work" [中国地震局副局长赵和平、总参作战部应急办主任李海洋到兰州国家陆地搜寻与救护基地检查指导工作], China Earthquake Administration [中国地震局兰州地震研究所], April 1, 2012. Contingency Response Office deputy director, Senior Colonel Wu Xihua [吴喜铧], may have filled the position.

8   As of March 2014, the Readiness Bureau [*zhanbei jianshe ju*, 战备建设局] director was Ma Yifei [马翼飞]. See, for example, "Ma Yifei leads Joint Military Installation Protection Law Enforcement Evaluation Team to Luoyang for an Inspection" [马翼飞率国家军事设施保护联合执法检查组来洛检查], *Luoyang Online* [洛阳网], June 21, 2011, available at <http://news.lyd.com.cn/content/2011/6/21/941331.shtml>.

9   Major General Wang Kebin [王克斌], born in 1961, was assigned as GSD Informationization Department director in 2013. He replaced Chen Dong [陈东]. Before his current assignment, Wang Kebin directed the GSD Joint Operations Command Center [*zongcan moubu zuozhan bu lianhe zuozhan zhihui zhongxin*, 总参谋部作战部联合作战指挥中心] and was subsequently promoted as GSD Operations Department deputy director. He was also dual hatted as deputy director of the State Civil Defense Office [*guojia renfang ban*, 国家人防办]. Communications Departments of services and military regions were also renamed Informationization Departments. Among various sources, see Guo Yuandong [郭媛丹], "PLA Sets up Four New Departments in One Month" [解放军1月内成立4个新部门], *Legal System Evening Post* [法制晚报], December 22, 2011, available at <www.fawan.com/Item/140667.aspx>.

10   The First Communications Command [*zongcan diyi tongxin zongzhan*, 总参第一通信总站] (Unit 61623) is headquartered in Beijing and consists of at least six regiments that are primarily concentrated in the Beijing area. Regiments possibly subordinate to the First Communications Command include: Unit 61035 (First Regiment, Beijing's Changping District, Yangfang Village); Unit 61416 (Third Regiment,

Beijing Wanshou Road); Unit 61932 (Fifth Regiment, Beijing Wanshou Road); Unit 61468 (Sixth Regiment, Xinzhou City, Dingxiang County); Unit 61516 (11th Regiment, Lengquan Village in the Beijing suburb of Xibeiwang); and Unit 61593 (possibly the 10th Regiment, although indications exist it has been closed). The Second Communications Command (Unit 61068) is headquartered in Xi'an and appears to manage satellite communications (SATCOM). Regiments under the Second Communications Command [*zongcan di'er tongxin zongzhan*, 总参第二通信总站] (Unit 61068) that appear to support the SATCOM mission include: Unit 61345 (Second Regiment in Shaanxi's Ankang City); Unit 61655 (Fourth Regiment in Chongqing, previously Unit 61256); Unit 61413 in Wolong Village, near Hubei's Xiangfan City); and a SATCOM engineering regiment near Henan's Xuchang City. Both commands appear to be division leader–level organizations.

11   At least one source asserts that the GSD Informationization Department also leverages UAVs. See, for example, Andrei Chang, "Application of Strategic Reconnaissance UAVs in Chinese Armed Forces," *Kanwa Asian Defense Review*, no. 86 (December 1, 2011), 6–7.

12   Among various sources, see Cortez A. Cooper, "Joint Anti-Access Operations: China's 'System-of-Systems' Approach," testimony presented before the U.S.-China Economic and Security Review Commission, January 27, 2011, available at <www.rand.org/content/dam/rand/pubs/testimonies/2011/RAND_CT356.pdf>; Larry M. Wortzel, "PLA Command, Control, and Targeting Architectures: Theory, Doctrine, and Warfighting Applications," in *Right-Sizing the People's Liberation Army: Exploring the Contours of China's Military*, eds. Roy Kamphausen and Andrew Scobell (Carlisle, PA: Strategic Studies Institute, September 2007), 191–234. For discussion of the Integrated Command Platform [*yitihua zhihui pingtai*, 一体化指挥平台], see "Army implements comprehensive visualization and real-time trend monitoring in exercise spanning multiple military districts" [我军跨区演习实现全程可视化及实时动态监控], Xinhua, October 13, 2010, available at <http://mil.huanqiu.com/china/2010-10/1166308.html>.

13   The director of the GSD Mobilization Department is dual-hatted as director, National Defense Mobilization Committee Office [*guojia guofang dongyuan weiyuanhui zonghe bangongshi*, 国家国防动员委员会综合办公室].

14   For overviews of the GLD logistics system, see Lonnie D. Henley, "PLA Logistics and Doctrine Reform, 1999–2009," in *People's Liberation Army After Next*, ed. Susan M. Puska (Carlisle, PA: Strategic Studies Institute, 2000), 55–77; and Dennis J. Blasko, "Chinese Military Logistics: The GLD System," *China Brief* 4, no. 19 (September 29, 2004), available at <www.jamestown.org/single/?no_cache=1&tx_ttnews%5Btt_news%5D=3678>.

15   Base 26 (63750 Unit) likely functions as a space and missile surveillance center. In years past, the Base 26 network included the 7010 space and missile radar

system mounted on the side of Huangyang Mountain in Xuanhua County, north of Beijing. The PLA Air Force originally operated the system when first entering initial operational capability in 1976, but it later was resubordinated to Base 26 (old military unit cover designator of Unit 89851). The system was dismantled in the late 1980s/early 1990s. For an excellent overview of Base 26, see "The Leaker: Overview of Xian Measurement and Control Center" [漏斗子：西安测控中心概览], *Wangchao Online* [王朝网络], October 10, 2005, available at <www.1n0.net/Article/Print.asp?ArticleID=6279>.

16   For reference to an initial exercise on transitioning to a JCC [*lianhe zhanyi zhihui bu*, 联合战役指挥部] in 2009, see Feng Chunmei, Wei Guo, Yang Jilong, and Ding Feng [冯春梅，魏国，杨继龙，丁峰], "Spotlight on the First War Zone-Level Joint Campaign Training" [聚焦我军首次战区级联合战役训练], Xinhua Online, August 18, 2009, available at <http://news.xinhuanet.com/mil/2009-08/18/content_11901638.htm>.

17   For a brief discussion of the campaign resolution in the context of a combined exercise with Russia, see "Shanghai Cooperation Organization Exercises Carried Out to Set Resolute Practice of Campaign Action" [上合军演进行定下战役行动决心演练], Xinhua, August 13, 2007, available at <http://military.china.com/zh_cn/djjl/sh2007/01/11062721/20070813/14273408.html>.

18   For further discussion of various operational-level organizational structures, see Dennis J. Blasko, *The Chinese Army Today: Tradition and Transformation for the 21ˢᵗ Century* (New York: Routledge Press, 2012), 115–138.

19   If organized along similar lines as in peacetime, deputy commanders would manage individual portfolios, such as operations, logistics, and equipment.

20   Among various sources addressing a JCC, see Nan Li, "The PLA's Evolving Campaign Doctrine and Strategies," in *The People's Liberation Army in the Information Age*, eds. James Mulvenon and Richard Yang (Santa Monica: RAND, 1999), available at <www.rand.org/pubs/conf_proceedings/CF145/CF145.chap8.pdf>; Jianxiang Bi, "Joint Operations: Developing a New Paradigm," in *China's Revolution in Doctrinal Affairs: Emerging Trends in the Operational Art of the Chinese People's Liberation Army*, eds. James Mulvenon and David Finkelstein (Arlington, VA: CNA Corporation, 2005), 47–55; Dean Cheng, "Zhanyixue and Joint Campaigns," in *China's Revolution in Doctrinal Affairs*, 101–117; Mark A. Stokes, "The Chinese Joint Aerospace Campaign: Strategy, Doctrine, and Force Modernization," in *China's Revolution in Doctrinal Affairs*, 221–306; John Wilson Lewis and Xue Litai, *Imagined Enemies: China Prepares for Uncertain War* (Palo Alto, CA: Stanford University Press, 2006); and Kevin Pollpeter, "Towards an Integrative C4ISR System: Informatization and Joint Operations in the People's Liberation Army," in *The PLA at Home and Abroad: Assessing the Operational Capabilities of China's Military*, eds. Roy Kamphausen, David Lai, and Andrew Scobell (Carlisle, PA: Strategic Studies Institute, 2009), 193–236.

21   Among various sources, see Zhang Yuliang [张玉良], ed., *The Science of Campaigns* [战役学] (Beijing: National Defense University Press [国防大学出版社], 2006), 124.

22   Within traditional PLA operational lexicon, an integrated joint firepower campaign would consist of strike aviation, theater missile assets, and/or long-range artillery. PLA analysts view an air campaign as an integral component of *joint firepower warfare* operations involving the coordinated use of PLA Air Force strike aviation assets and Second Artillery conventional theater missiles. Officers from the GSD Operations Department Joint Command Operations Bureau Targeting Control Center [*mubiao kongzhi zhongxin*, 目标控制中心] most likely would play a prominent role.

23   For further discussion, see Stokes, "The Chinese Joint Aerospace Campaign: Strategy, Doctrine, and Force Modernization." The Nanjing Military Region communications commands, probably division deputy leader organizations, are based in Nanjing, Fuzhou, Xiamen, and Nanchang. Command automation and network control hypothetically would be provided by the Nanjing Military Region Computer Network Information Center [*jisuanji wangluo xinxi zhongxin*, 计算机网络信息中心] (73685 Unit).

24   See Zhang Yuliang, ed., 312–330. Existing Air Force command posts (bases) affiliated with the Nanjing and Guangzhou Military Regions are headquartered in Shanghai, Fuzhou, Zhangzhou, and Nanning. Air Force radar brigades and regiments subordinate to these command posts/bases may represent air surveillance sectors. However, East Sea Fleet and South Sea Fleet Naval Aviation radar brigades appear responsible for air surveillance sectors around Ningbo and Hainan Island.

25   For example, the East China Sea air defense identification zone appears to consist of two air surveillance sectors. The PLA Air Force Third Radar Brigade (Unit 94969) likely is responsible for flight tracking in the northern sector and PLA Navy Second Radar Brigade (Unit 92602) for the southern sector.

26   See organizational charts in Yu Jixun [于际训], ed., *Second Artillery Campaign Science* [第二炮兵战役学] (Beijing: PLA Press [中国人民解放军出版社], 2003), 149–151. For another perspective, see John W. Lewis and Xue Litai, "Making China's Nuclear War Plan," *Bulletin of the Atomic Scientists* 68, no. 5 (September/October 2012), 45–65.

27   The GSD Second Department's Space Reconnaissance Bureau [*zongcan hangtian zhencha ju*, 总参航天侦察局] (Unit 61646) may oversee the remote sensing network. The unit may also be designated as the GSD Second Department Technical Bureau [*zongcan er bu jishu ju*, 总参二部技术局] and/or the Beijing Institute of Remote Sensing Information [*Beijing yaogan xinxi yanjiusuo*, 北京遥感信息研究所]. The UAV regiment (Unit 61135) appears to be garrisoned in the northern Beijing suburb of Shahe.

28   For example, Nanjing MR's Network Information Center [*wangluo xinxi zhongixin*, 网络信息中心] (Unit 73685) could become a JCC's network information center during a crisis.

29   The three PLA Air Force technical reconnaissance bureaus are headquartered in Beijing (Unit 95830), Nanjing (Unit 95851), and Chengdu (Unit 95879). Each oversees 8 to 12 subordinate offices/workstations.

30   The GSD Navigation and Positioning Command [*zongcan dingwei daohang zongzhan*, 总参定位导航总站] carries a cover designation of Unit 61081.

31   The GSD Survey Bureau Survey Information Center [*cehui xinxi zhongxin*, 测绘信息中心] carries a cover designation of Unit 61512.

32   The Weather Center [*qixiang zhonxin*, 气象中心] carries a cover designation of Unit 61741.

33   The Air Defense ECM Brigade [*fangkong dianzi duikang lü*, 防空电子对抗旅] (Unit 61906 or former Unit 58046) hosts elements in Langfang (Hebei Province), the northern Miyun County township of Beizhuang, Huaibei (Anhui Province), and Yingtan (Jiangxi Province).

34   The Satellite ECM Command [*dianzi duikang weixing zongzhan*, 电子对抗卫星总站] carries a cover designation of Unit 61276. The element on Hainan Island carries a cover designation of Unit 61764. Unit 61251 appears to be a Fourth Department brigade based in the Qinhuangdao area. The unit's Second Battalion appears to be in Funing County.

35   The GPD unit, including the Voice of the Taiwan Strait [*haixia zhi sheng*, 海峡之声], carries a GSD military cover designation of Unit 61716. Another element unit affiliated with Base 311 is Unit 61275, in Fujian's Ningde City.

36   The GSD Camouflage Engineering Regiment carries a cover designation of Unit 61606.

37   "Establishing a National Aerospace Security System" [建立我国的空天安全体系], *Science Times* [科学时报], February 24, 2002, available at <www.cas.cn/xw/zjsd/200202/t20020224_1683499.shtml>.

38   See, for example, "Present and Future of Foreign Air and Space Defense Equipment" [国外防空防天装备发展现状与趋势], *Aerospace Electronic Warfare* [航天电子对抗] 26, no. 3 (2010), available at <http://d.wanfangdata.com.cn/periodical_htdzdk201003002.aspx>. Also see "PLA Air Defense Unit Has Anti-Missile Capabilities, Changing Air Defense" [解放军防空部队具备反导能力,将向防天转变], *Liexun Military Intelligence Online* [猎讯军情网], June 8, 2011, accessed November 2012 at <www.1n0.net/Article/zhjs/114708.html>.

39   For a comprehensive discussion of PLA operational space theory, see Larry C. Wortzel, "The Chinese People's Liberation Army and Space Warfare: Emerging

United States-China Military Competition," *AEI Online*, October 17, 2007, available at <www.aei.org/papers/foreign-and-defense-policy/regional/asia/the-chinese-peoples-liberation-army-and-space-warfare/>.

40   For one discussion of use of ballistic missiles, see Paul B. Stares, *Space and National Security* (Washington, DC: Brookings Institution, 1987), 97–99. One analysis explains that the aerospace defense domain would be divided along the Karman Line: the PLA Air Force would assume the air defense mission for threats below 100 kilometers, while Second Artillery would be responsible for threats above 100 kilometers.

41   Xu Qiliang now serves as CMC Vice Chairman. For an overview, see Kevin Pollpeter, "The PLAAF and the Integration of Air and Space Power," in *The Chinese Air Force: Evolving Concepts, Roles, and Capabilities*, eds. Richard P. Hallion, Roger Cliff, and Phillip C. Saunders (Washington, DC: NDU Press, 2011), 165–190. Also see "Establishing a National Aerospace Security System" [建立我国的空天安全体系], *Science Times*, February 24, 2002, available at <www.cas.cn/xw/zjsd/200202/t20020224_1683499.shtml>; "Xu Qiliang: The Chinese Air Force Must Have an Aerospace Security Perspective" [许其亮: 中国空军必须树立空天安全观], Xinhua Online, November 1, 2009, available at <http://mil.news.sina.com.cn/2009-11-01/1424572155.html>; "General Xu Qiliang: The PLA Air Force Will Develop an Integrated Air and Space Operational Capability" [许其亮上将: 中国空军将发展空天一体作战能力], Xinhua, November 11, 2009; Zhu Hui [朱晖], "China's Aerospace Security Facing Threat of Full Range of Stealthy Unmanned Vehicles and Other Weapon Systems" [我国空天安全面临隐形战机无人机等武器威胁], *PLA Daily*, December 3, 2009, available at <http://mil.eastday.com/m/20091203/u1a4853820.html>; "PLAAF Deputy Commander Chen Xiaogong Calls for Attention to Aerospace Security" [解放军空军副司令员陈小工呼吁关注空天安全], *China News Online* [中国新闻网], March 9, 2010, available at <www.chinanews.com/gn/news/2010/03-09/2160134.shtml>; and Zhong Shan [钟山], "Discussion of Information Age of the Aerospace Century" [论信息时代的空天世纪], *China Space News* [中国航天报], February 4, 2010, available at <www.china-spacenews.com/n435777/n435778/n674308/65983.html>.

42   Base 53 is headquartered in Kunming, Yunnan Province. The anti-ship ballistic missile brigade may be Unit 96219, headquartered in Qingyuan (Guangdong Province). Base 55 is headquartered in Huaihua (Hunan Province).

43   According to a former engineer, Unit 96637 is located in Kangzhuang. Formerly known as the 80809 Imagery Group, the unit shifted its mission toward operations support in 2002. In addition to providing imagery for land attack cruise missile brigades, the unit is also is said to carry out electronic reconnaissance, translation, and, in a crisis, battle damage assessment in direct support of strike operations. See, for example, Liu Feng and Wang Bingjun [刘峰, 王炳君], "Second Artillery 96637 Unit Establishes 'Warrior Culture'"[第二炮兵96637部队营造"尚武"文化], *Worker's Daily* [工人日报], August 3, 2006, available at <http://news.sina.com.cn/c/2006-08-03/01009640261s.shtml>.

44   The primary Second Artillery ECM Regiment is Unit 96620, home-based in Dingxing and commanded by Colonel Li Changwei [李长伟]. A newer regiment (Unit 96634) appears to have been formed in Nanchang.

45   Li Yanjie [李燕杰], "Live out the core values of the modern revolutionary soldier" [用生命践行当代革命军人核心价值观], *People's Daily* [人民日报], October 31, 2009, available at <http://paper.people.com.cn/rmrb/html/2009-10/31/content_372115.htm>; "Speech by a representative of the 'Study Comrade Liu Yiquan and Advance His Achievements Symposium'" [学习刘义权同志先进事迹座谈会代表发言], *China File News* [中国档案报], May 14, 2011, available at <http://www.qstheory.cn/tbzt/gzzg/lyq/shfxlyq/201105/t20110514_80668.htm>.

46   See Mark A. Stokes, "China's Nuclear Warhead Storage and Handling System," Project 2049 Institute, March 12, 2010, available at <https://project2049.net/documents/chinas_nuclear_warhead_storage_and_handling_system.pdf>; also see *Second Artillery Campaign Science*.

II

DOMESTIC CONTINGENCIES

China's Armed Forces Respond to Internal Disaster Relief: Assessing Mobilization and Effort

Jeffrey Engstrom and Lyle Morris

Responding to internal crises is among the most important day-to-day challenges that confront the Chinese armed forces—the People's Liberation Army (PLA), the People's Armed Police (PAP), and the militia. What does the involvement of these organizations in internal disaster relief operations reveal about broader military contingency response capacity?[1] This chapter argues that Chinese military participation in internal disaster relief provides important evidence about mobilization capacity and manpower effort that can inform an understanding of contingency response capacity across the spectrum of conflict. Larger scale and more violent contingencies are either infrequent (for example, border conflict) or do not generate useful public data (for example, internal unrest), but military responses to internal disaster relief occur regularly and are generally well publicized. With some important caveats, military participation in internal disaster relief provides a valuable and available means of quantifying the growing capacities and capabilities of China's armed forces to respond to contingencies.

Participation of the armed forces in internal disaster relief operations remains understudied. The few existing studies tend to focus on a single natural disaster, such as the 2008 Wenchuan earthquake.[2] There are no systematic comparisons across multiple cases.[3] Furthermore, without common metrics, cross-case comparisons are difficult to make between disasters, let alone across different types of contingencies. This chapter demonstrates the value of examining Chinese military internal disaster responses as a means of understanding China's overall contingency response capability. It also aims to provide a general approach on how to collect and categorize data from disaster relief contingencies that may be applied to future studies.

It is important to note that while internal disaster relief fits into broader conceptions of military operations other than war and diversified military tasks, Chinese armed forces have been participating in domestic disaster relief since the founding of the People's Republic of China (PRC) in 1949.[4] While recent doctrinally informed writings highlight the PLA's role in such tasks, it is so far unclear whether they fundamentally change it.[5] A general understanding of the legal underpinnings of military participation in disaster relief is nonetheless important for understanding how Chinese leaders conceive of their military forces as an increasingly important contributor to contingencies other than war. (Appendix A highlights several of these documents.)

This chapter is organized into three main sections. The first reviews the internal disaster "threat environment" that China's armed forces face. What types of disasters are most frequent, and how much damage do they cause? In which military regions do disasters occur most regularly? Next, by looking at empirical data, the chapter delves into both the mobilization capacity and total manpower effort in four disasters in which China's armed forces were deployed: the 2008 winter storms, the 2008 Wenchuan earthquake, the 2010 Yushu earthquake, and the 2010 Zhouqu mudslides. In particular, the analysis seeks to answer how quickly China's military was able to respond to the disasters, the size of forces projected, and the total manpower effort expended. The chapter concludes by exploring how these disaster relief contingency responses compare with actual warfighting by looking at mobilization capacity and manpower effort in the Korean War (1950–1953) and the Sino-Vietnamese War (1979). While the findings are preliminary in nature and further research is needed to track the evolution of China's armed forces' capacity to mobilize, data on various contingencies can be grouped by time to show mobilization levels at various historical periods. Data from future contingencies will aid empirical assessments of how Chinese mobilization capacity is developing.

Disaster Threat Environment for China's Armed Forces

This section briefly examines the scope and scale of natural and manmade disasters in China. This threat environment defines the context within which China's armed forces must plan, train, deploy, and operate to counteract the effects of disasters, while simultaneously fulfilling other tasks vital to China's national security. Not only do such disasters exact a serious toll in terms of human lives and suffering, but they also have the potential to become the source of social discord if not responded to in a timely and effective manner. Disaster response is one of the many ways that China's armed forces contribute to Chinese Communist Party (CCP) control and management of social stability.

Level of Impact of Natural and Manmade Disasters

China regularly suffers from large-scale natural and manmade disasters (see table 7.1). Based on data covering 27 years, China has faced a new natural or manmade disaster about every 2 months. Nearly 40 percent of such disasters have affected one million or more individuals (such as the Zhouqu mudslides or the Wenchuan earthquake).[6] Slightly over 16 percent of disasters have affected 10 million or more individuals (such as the Sichuan earthquake). In six cases (4 percent), disasters have affected at least 100 million persons: the 2010 floods (400 million persons), the 1998 floods (240 million persons), the 1991 floods (206 million persons), the 2003 floods (113 million persons), and the 1995 and 1999 floods (100 million persons each).[7]

Table 7.1. Instances of Disasters by Persons Affected in China, August 1985–October 2012

Number of Persons Affected	Number of Disaster Instances	Percent of Disaster Instances
<10,000	3	2
10,000–99,999	12	8.1
100,000–999,999	38	25.5
1,000,000–9,999,999	35	23.5
10,000,000–99,999,999	18	12.1
100,000,000–999,999,999	6	4
No Data/Unknown	37	24.8
Totals	149	100.0

Source: Data derived from Relief Web database, available at <http://reliefweb.int/country/chn>.

Location, Type, and Frequency of Disasters

Since late 1985, 75 percent of the disasters that have struck China have affected the Chengdu, Nanjing, and Guangzhou Military Regions (see table 7.2). If the Lanzhou Military Region is included, the total jumps to approximately 85 percent. As a result, China's armed forces likely focus the majority of their disaster relief preparations and efforts on these areas, which cover over 70 percent of China's geographic area. The Jinan, Beijing, and Shenyang Military Regions are comparatively less affected by disasters, accounting for only about 15 percent of the locations where disasters have struck.

Table 7.2. Types of Disasters and Affected Military Regions, August 1985–October 2012

Military Region	Various Manmade Disasters*	Various Natural Disasters **	Mudslide/ Landslide	Snow	Earthquake	Typhoon/ Tropical Storm	Floods	Total (%)	Total (#)
Chengdu	1%	2%	2%	3%	12%	1%	6%	26	52
Nanjing	0%	2%	0%	1%	1%	13%	9%	26	21
Guangzhou	0%	1%	1%	1%	0%	13%	8%	23	46
Lanzhou	1%	1%	1%	2%	5%	0%	3%	11	51
Jinan	0%	1%	0%	0%	1%	2%	3%	6	12
Beijing	0%	1%	0%	1%	3%	0%	1%	5	9
Shenyang	1%	2%	0%	0%	0%	1%	2%	5	9
Totals (%)	2	9	3	7	20	29	31		
Totals (#)	3	17	6	14	40	58	62		200

* Chemical spills, burst dams, and gas explosions.
** Droughts, local storms, tornados, fires, rainstorms, and hailstorms.
Source: Data derived from the Relief Web database, available at <http://reliefweb.int/country/chn>.

Floods constitute the most frequent natural disaster type (31 percent) and affect the greatest number of civilians. Instances of flooding are fairly evenly distributed over the various military regions, although they occur somewhat more regularly in the Chengdu, Nanjing, and Guangzhou Military Regions. Typhoons and tropical storms collectively constitute the second most frequent disaster type and occur most regularly in the Nanjing and Guangzhou Military Regions. Earthquakes are highly concentrated in the Chengdu Military Region and occur to a lesser extent in the Lanzhou and Beijing Military Regions. However, earthquakes rarely take the top spots in numbers of persons affected. The 2008 Wenchuan earthquake, which affected over 46 million people, is only the twelfth worst disaster in total number of affected individuals within the time period studied. Snowfalls constitute roughly 7 percent of natural disasters. The 2008 winter storms that affected roughly 78 million people were the most devastating non-flood disasters during this time period.

Disaster Contingency Case Studies: Mobilization Capacity and Manpower Effort

This section provides an overview of four case studies and then applies an approach to track and compare mobilization capacity and manpower effort across cases. The two large-scale and two smaller scale military responses presented below were chosen in a nonrandomized manner to highlight and compare the manpower and mobilization efforts at both ends of the disaster relief spectrum and focus on recent disaster events. The results, therefore, only offer a snapshot view. Future studies may build on the results of this initial exploration and further advance our understanding of Chinese armed forces participation in disaster relief.

2008 Winter Storms

China was hit by unusually cold weather and severe ice conditions from mid-January through February 2008, affecting large swaths of southern China. Heavy snow, ice, freezing rain, and subzero temperatures affected 14 provinces. Jiangsu, Jiangxi, Zhejiang, Anhui, Hunan, and Guangzhou provinces were hit the hardest. The severe weather and accumulations of ice on power lines cut off electricity, paralyzing civilian transportation and stopping the shipment of coal to power plants. The effects of the storms and cold weather on the transportation system were magnified by the fact that the crisis coincided with the Lunar New Year festival, one of the peak periods for domestic road, rail, and air travel. Millions of seasonal or migrant workers who were taking their annual trips home to the countryside became stuck in the major transportation hubs of southern China. Most notable was the Guangzhou railway station, which at one point saw 600,000 passengers stranded on trains and in waiting areas.[8] Twenty-four people died during the storms, and over 77 million persons were affected.[9]

On January 29, the CCP Central Committee Politburo held a meeting on deploying civilian and armed forces personnel for disaster relief. Immediately following the meeting, President Hu Jintao instructed units from all military regions to mobilize in support of disaster relief efforts. By February 10, 635,000 officers and 1.86 million militia and reservists were deployed, constituting the largest disaster relief effort since the Yangtze River floods of 1998.[10] However, the crisis differed from most other natural disasters in China in that rescue efforts were not concentrated on a single area. Dozens of crises spanned several provinces across thousands of kilometers, severely challenging rescue and coordination efforts.

2008 Wenchuan Earthquake

On May 12, 2008, a massive earthquake measuring 8.0 on the Richter scale struck Wenchuan County in Sichuan Province. More than 120 million people in Sichuan and the adjoining provinces of Gansu, Shaanxi, Yunnan, and Chongqing were exposed to the moderate to severe shaking effects of the earthquake. The quake left 88,000 people dead or missing and nearly 400,000 injured, damaging or destroying millions of homes and leaving 5 million people homeless. The earthquake also caused extensive damage to basic infrastructure, including schools, hospitals, roads, and water systems.

In just two days, China's armed forces had reportedly dispatched more than 100,000 soldiers and armed police to help with rescue operations in earthquake-hit areas, dividing their units into three geographical rescue zones. Chinese official media asserted that military transport aircraft and helicopters made 1,069 flights during the first week of operations, supplemented by 92 military trains and about 110,000 military vehicles, cranes, rubber boats, portable communication devices, and power generators.[11]

By the end of rescue operations on June 17, 140,000 PLA soldiers and reserves had been mobilized to the disaster areas by air and land from five of the seven military regions. Units from the army and armed police mobilized 4,696 helicopters, employed 340,000 pieces of various equipment, dispatched 96,800 medical personnel, and delivered over 940,000 tons of disaster relief materials. They dug out 3,338 survivors from the debris and rescued over 1.4 million trapped people.[12]

2010 Yushu Earthquake

The 2010 Yushu earthquake struck on April 14, 2010, registering 7.1 on the Richter scale. The epicenter was Shanglaxiu Township, about 800 kilometers from Xining, the capital of Gansu Province. The quake toppled houses and basic infrastructure, damaged roads, cut off power supplies, and disrupted basic telecommunications. A reported 2,698 people died in the quake, with 270 missing and 12,135 injured.[13] Over the following weeks, combat and engineering units from all of China's military regions joined the effort; a total of 16,000 PLA, PAP, and reserve troops were mobilized. Compared with rescue efforts during the Wenchuan earthquake, the location of the epicenter—on the Qinghai-Tibet plateau—proved especially challenging. Yushu has no railway and only one airport, making transportation of rescuers and supplies to the disaster zone difficult. Furthermore, the altitude of the Yushu quake zone averaged 4,400 meters above sea level, inducing high-altitude sickness among many troops.[14]

2010 Zhouqu Mudslides

The Zhouqu mudslides occurred in Zhouqu County, Gansu Province, on August 7, 2010. The mudslides occurred after the region had experienced heavy rainfall and flooding. It was the deadliest individual disaster among the series of incidents surrounding the 2010 floods. Following heavy rains, a buildup of water occurred behind a dam of debris blocking a small river to the north of the city of Zhouqu. When the dam broke, around 1.8 million cubic meters of mud and rocks swept through the town, creating a surge reportedly five stories high that covered more than 300 low-rise homes.[15] The mudslides killed more than 1,471 people; 1,243 others were rescued; in total, over 4.7 million civilians were affected.[16] A total of 6,281 PLA, PAP, and reserve troops from the Lanzhou, Chengdu, and Beijing Military Regions participated in rescue efforts, deploying 17 helicopters, 4 transport planes, 35 assault boats, and 140 sets of large machinery. They successfully treated more than 12,000 civilians.[17]

Disaster Contingency Mobilization Capacity

How can the mobilization of China's armed forces be compared across a number of seemingly disparate disaster responses? In order to make cross-case comparisons, this section defines mobilization capacity, develops and describes a simple model to assess it, and uses empirical data with the model to compare the cases and analyze the results.

Mobilization is "the act of assembling and organizing national resources to support objectives" whether "in a time of war or other emergencies."[18] Mobilization is a process, not an end state. The process begins once national command authorities recognize a need to use the armed forces and continues until those forces are employed to conduct the operation. Full mobilization, the ultimate goal of the process, occurs when the necessary means (various national resources) have been made available at the proper location (through organization and assembly) to carry out the policy ends. In other words, a fully mobilized force is one that is in place and ready to conduct the operation. The "mobilization clock" begins once the units involved in an operation receive orders or warning to prepare and continues ticking until the units and their equipment arrive at their operational locations and are ready to conduct the operation.

Mobilization involves a number of implicit tasks. Forces being mobilized either are or are in the process of being constituted, trained, organized, equipped, transported, and so forth, so as to be ready to commence operations at the proper locations. For internal disaster relief operations, the mobilization timeline is the time required to assemble and move necessary forces to the disaster area so they can commence relief operations. In a disaster, the mobilization clock starts almost immediately after the initial occurrence of the disaster, often with little to no warning. Assessments of the mobilization process and measures of mobilization capacity focus not on the quality or effectiveness of the operation itself but rather on the assembling and transport of forces and their equipment to operational areas.[19]

Mobilization capacity measures the speed with which a given quantity of forces can be mobilized—that is, ready to commence operations at a specific location. A highly efficient system can mobilize large numbers of trained and equipped forces in a short amount of time. This chapter develops a simple model to measure mobilization capacity. In our model, mobilization capacity is determined by two independent variables: *throughput capacity*, to measure number of forces in a certain time period, and *speed capacity*, to measure the movement of those forces in the same time period. Tradeoffs exist between force size and the distances those forces must travel. At one extreme, a large number of forces can be mobilized quickly if the distances to be traversed are short. At another extreme, only a small number of forces can travel long distances over the same time period.

The first independent variable is *throughput capacity*. Measured in days, this continuous variable measures the average number of military forces that are fully mobilized during an operation.[20] This simple model does this by taking the total number of troops ultimately mobilized (our proxy for military forces) and dividing it by the average time (in days) it takes those troops to arrive at the area or areas of operation. For example, if a unit consisting of 100 troops took 4 days to mobilize, the capacity of throughput demonstrated would equal 25 troops per day. Conversely, if the same unit of 100 troops were mobilized in half a day, demonstrated throughput capacity would equal 200 troops per day. Of course, in real contingencies, numerous units from multiple locations converge on a particular area. In these cases, the various times it takes different units to mobilize are averaged. Although troops often require contingency-specific equipment to operate, our simple model assumes that the units deploying take their equipment with them and does not attempt to separately capture the varying quantities of vehicles or supplies.[21] However, leaving out this explicit measure in our proxy does not mean that the model's outputs are necessarily unaffected by the amount of heavy equipment used in a particular contingency. Indeed, such aspects are implicitly captured by the proxy of troops themselves as, all things being equal, a unit traveling light will attain a higher throughput capacity rate than the same unit traveling with heavy equipment.

The second independent variable of the mobilization process is *speed capacity*. Also measured in days, this continuous variable seeks to capture how quickly mobilizing forces traverse distances to become fully mobilized. The model does this by taking the distance and dividing it by the average time (in days) it takes those forces to travel that distance. For example, if a unit takes 4 days to travel 100 kilometers, its demonstrated average capacity for speed is 25 kilometers per day. If a unit traveled 100 kilometers in 6 hours, its demonstrated capacity for speed is 400 kilometers per day. Similar to throughput capacity, numerous units from multiple locations will travel at different speeds to arrive at a particular area. In these cases, the various times it takes different units to mobilize in our simple model are averaged.

These variables allow measuring demonstrated mobilization capacity across a number of disaster relief operations that vary in scale and type and involve different force sizes and distances traveled. This simple model does not explicitly incorporate different or evolving mobilization plans or structures that might play a role in mobilization capacity. Similarly, it does not incorporate different levels of public interest or pressure brought to bear on Chinese authorities. These factors, to the extent they play a role, are also captured implicitly in the mobilization capacity demonstrated. This chapter highlights a number of these additional factors where relevant.

It also bears repeating that the analysis focuses solely on mobilization capacity. The model cannot shed light on how effective the Chinese armed forces are in relieving suffering or restoring public well-being. The data only presents a picture of how quickly Chinese armed forces responded and the total level of effort demonstrated. Both measures are necessary but not sufficient conditions for an effective response to a disaster. China's armed forces, or any military for that matter, could hypothetically arrive at a disaster scene quickly and with sufficient forces, only to botch the ensuing recovery and rescue efforts.

Table 7.3 summarizes the findings of the available empirical data from the four case studies. The calculations are based on data from Chinese press reports that specifically mention troop deployment departure and arrival times and location of departure.[22] This data was quantified into average distance traveled (in kilometers [km]), travel time (in days), average distance traveled per day (in km/day), and average total throughput (total number of troops deployed/day). For all four case studies, estimates are based on a subset of known data (shown in the last column of table 7.3). For example, of the 6,281 total troops known to be involved in the 2010 Zhouqu mudslides, mobilization data was available for 5,344 troops, or 85 percent, thus producing the highest confidence data of the four cases.

Table 7.3. China's Armed Forces Disaster Mobilization

Contingency	Total Number of Troops Mobilized	Average Distance Traveled (km)	Average Time of Travel (days)	Speed Capacity (km/day)	Throughput Capacity (troops/day)	Percent of Data Set Known
2008 winter storms	2,495,000	850	4.5	189	554,444	30
2008 Wenchuan earthquake	140,000	566	0.7	836	206,769	45
2010 Yushu earthquake	16,000	1,273	1.3	1,006	12,642	54
2010 Zhouqu mudslides	6,281	347	1.0	351	6,337	85

Sources: The following sources were exploited in calculating the data in this table as well as for all calculations involving troop mobilization and total man-days for the four case studies. For the 2010 Zhouqu Mudslides: "Zhouqu mudslides kill 1,364 people, rescue efforts wrap up" [舟曲泥石流灾害死亡1364人 搜救工作基本结束], Tencent News [腾讯新闻], August 19, 2010, available at <http://news.qq.com/a/20100819/001962.htm>; "PLA and PAP deploy 6,281 troops to Zhouqu mudslide disaster" [解放军及武警共6281人投入甘肃舟曲泥石流救援], Phoenix Satellite Television [凤凰卫视], August 16, 2010, available at <http://news.ifeng.com/mil/2/detail_2010_08/16/1961155_0.shtml>; "Lanzhou military region mobilizes a certain anti-chemical brigade, supports Zhouqu relief efforts after 6 hours" [兰州军区某防化团迅速行动 灾害发生6小时抵舟曲], *China National Radio* [中国广播网], August 20, 2010, available at <http://news.sohu.com/20100820/n274343763.shtml>; "Support, unfolding from midnight—Gansu PAP document relief efforts in Zhouqu" [救援, 从子夜展开——武警甘肃总队舟曲救灾纪实], *Guangming Daily* [光明日报], August 12, 2010, available at <http://military.people.com.cn/GB/12417424.html>; "A documentation of PLA and PAP relief efforts during the great mudslide of Zhouqu" [解放军武警部队舟曲特大山洪泥石流灾害救援纪实], Xinhua Online [新华网], August 11, 2010, available at <www.china.com.cn/military/txt/2010-08/11/content_20689382.htm>. For the 2008 Wenchuan Earthquake: Li Daguang [李大光], "PLA: The main force behind disaster relief efforts in mainland China" [解放军:大陆抢险救灾行动的主力军], *Life and Disaster* [生命与灾害] 9, (September

2009), 15–17; "Chinese military operations other than war since 2008," *PLA Daily*, September 5, 2011, available at <http://eng.mod.gov.cn/DefenseNews/2011-09/05/content_4295580_2.htm>; Li Shiming and Zhang Haiyang, "Vivid Earthquake Rescue Efforts Illustrate PLA's Ability to Complete Diversified Military Missions." For the 2010 Yushu Earthquake: Dong Qiang [董强], "Chinese military operations other than war since 2008," *PLA Daily*; "PLA and PAP achieve new stage of results in earthquake relief efforts" [解放军和武警部队抗震救灾获阶段性成果], *PLA Daily*, April 21, 2010; "Quake-Relief Troops Rescue 1,000-Odd People From Ruins" *PLA Daily*, April 16, 2010; "PLA Air Force Realizes Zero-Fault Air Rescue in Quake-Jolted Yushu," *PLA Daily*, April 20, 2010; "Documenting Yushu relief efforts by the reserves and militia of the PLA" [民兵预备役部队玉树抗震救灾实录], *PLA Daily*, April 25, 2010, available at <http://cpc.people.com.cn/GB/67481/187376/187506/11448209.html>; "Chinese armed forces provide quick response, quake relief to Yushu," Xinhua, April 20, 2010. For the 2008 Winter Storms: "Memorandum on relief efforts by the PLA and PAP during the 2008 Winter Storms" [2008 全军和武警部队抗灾救灾备忘录], *PLA Daily*, February 13, 2008, available at <www.chinamil.com.cn/site1/2008a/2008-02/15/content_1125040_3.htm>; "The Armed Forces Started a General Mobilization to Engage in a Fierce Battle with the World of Ice and Snow," Xinhua, February 3, 2008; "Composing epoch chapter of listening to the Party's command to serve the people while fighting against the snow and ice" [在抗击冰雪斗争中谱写听党指挥服务人民英勇善战的时代篇章], *PLA Daily*, February 25, 2008, available at <www.chinamil.com.cn/site1/zbxl/2008-02/25/content_1136127.htm>.

Figure 7.1 plots mobilization capacity and speed capacity for the four cases. The results of the scatterplot offer an important indicator of overall efficiency, as plots in the upper right-hand corner would signify high mobilization capacity, whereas plots in the lower right-hand corner would suggest the opposite. As the chart indicates, the 2008 winter storms were by far the highest in terms of throughput, with the PLA mobilizing an average of 554,444 troops per day, but moving them at the slowest average speed of 189 km per day (or 7.9 km per hour). For the 2008 Wenchuan earthquake, China's armed forces mobilized an average of 206,769 troops per day and traveled at an average speed of approximately 836 km per day. The other two case studies—the 2010 Yushu earthquake and 2010 Zhouqu mudslides—indicate that the Chinese armed forces mobilized an average of 12,642 and 6,337 troops per day, traveling at an average speed of 1,006 and 351 km per day, respectively. In other words, speaking in relative terms, the Chinese armed forces moved a large number of troops very slowly during the 2008 winter storms; moved a moderately large number of troops fairly quickly during the 2008 Wenchuan earthquake; moved a small number of troops very quickly during the 2010 Yushu earthquake; and moved a small number of troops fairly slowly during the 2010 Zhouqu mudslides. Of course, many of these discrepancies may be due to various factors (such as how widespread the damage was and whether the supporting infrastructure that China's armed forces might have relied on was affected).

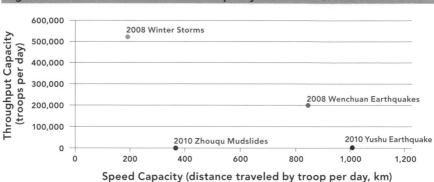

Figure 7.1. Demonstrated Mobilization Capacity of the Four Case Studies

Disaster Contingency Manpower Effort

Total man-days is another metric that is useful in quantifying and comparing the total manpower effort of the Chinese armed forces in disaster relief. Man-days allows comparisons to be made between contingencies that may be very dissimilar in terms of numbers of soldiers participating and the amount of time they are active. This variable is calculated by taking the sum of the number of troops active each day of an ongoing relief effort.[23] As figure 7.2 illustrates, the 2008 winter storms constituted by far the largest number of total man-days put forth by China's armed forces amongst the four case studies, at nearly 37 million. This is followed by the 2008 Wenchuan earthquake at around 4.9 million, the 2010 Yushu earthquake at around 114,000, and the 2010 Zhouqu mudslides at approximately 73,000.

Figure 7.3 superimposes the man-day timelines of each case study to provide a comparative analysis of mobilization across the different natural disasters. As the figure shows, although the 2008 winter storms represented the largest effort in terms of total man-days, the Chinese armed forces did not achieve peak troop levels with the same speed as the other three case studies, only doing so 12 days after initiation of relief operations. On the other end of the spectrum, the Chinese armed forces mobilized 100,000 troops on just the third day after the 2008 Wenchuan earthquake and achieved a peak level on the sixth day. Similarly, it took just 4 days to achieve a peak level of troops mobilized during the 2010 Zhouqu mudslides operations. Finally, it took 7 days to achieve peak mobilization for the 2010 Yushu earthquake. Figure 7.3 also illustrates not only the scale of troop involvement, but how sustained the effort was as well.

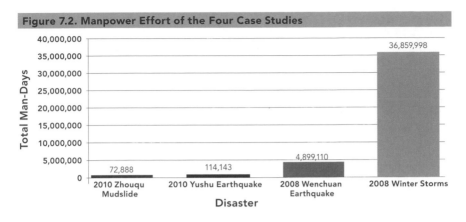

Figure 7.2. Manpower Effort of the Four Case Studies

The two notable results are the 2008 Wenchuan earthquake, representing the largest sustained effort among the four disasters, lasting approximately 37 days, and the 2008 winter storms relief operation, which lasted 19 days but required a far greater number of troops.[24]

One key qualitative factor differentiates the 2008 winter storms from the other case studies, however. While the 2008 winter storms presented a major infrastructure and transportation restoration challenge for the Chinese armed forces, it did not require urgent life-saving measures like the other three natural disasters. This might have influenced the speed and efficiency of mobilization during this event.

The results of the aforementioned tables and figures of the four case studies offer a rough analytic basis for examining Chinese armed forces effort and efficiency. If we define *total effort* using the metrics of average distance, time,

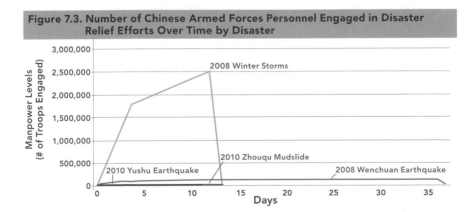

Figure 7.3. Number of Chinese Armed Forces Personnel Engaged in Disaster Relief Efforts Over Time by Disaster

speed, throughput, and man-days, the Chinese armed forces exhibited varying degrees of overall mobilization capacity across all examined case studies.[25] The data suggest that the Chinese armed forces were actually quite successful in mobilizing troops across long distances in a relatively short amount of time to the disaster areas. This conclusion contrasts with one article on the 2008 Wenchuan earthquake that noted, "PLA efforts . . . were overwhelmed in many ways by the devastated roads and ground-based access routes."[26]

Comparing Disaster Contingencies to Warfighting

This chapter has sought to demonstrate the usefulness of studying mobilization capacity and military effort as a way to both improve understanding of internal disaster relief response and track the evolution of the armed forces' capacity for broader contingencies. The chapter concludes by employing this approach to compare the four disaster relief case studies with two past warfighting contingencies: the 1950–1953 Korean War and the 1979 Sino-Vietnamese War. These two wars were chosen because they highlight both extensive amounts of mobilization and significant manpower levels.

Mobilization for warfare has many similarities to mobilization for disaster relief. Both types of contingencies require assembling a significant task-organized military force and sending it to a zone of operations. Of course, warfare mobilization can differ, especially under circumstances where the need for secrecy is high and the sense of emergency or need for immediate response is low. Given that disasters typically have little advance warning, they should stress the mobilization system much more than a hypothetical war of choice. On the other hand, military forces require significant amounts of equipment and supplies to conduct combat operations, increasing demands on the mobilization system.

In both the warfighting contingencies, Beijing tried to preserve a modicum of secrecy and conducted planned, rather than emergency, responses. To be sure, Beijing was seeking to react in a timely fashion against the United States and Vietnam, but there was leeway in exactly when operations would commence. Data on various contingencies can be grouped by time, producing curves showing levels of mobilization capacity at various historical periods.

As can be seen from table 7.4, China's armed forces initially mobilized more troops during the 2008 winter storms than it did for either the 1979 Sino-Vietnamese War or the 1950–1953 Korean War. Of course, natural disasters differ from warfighting in that they occur without warning, forcing China to respond quickly. In this way, instances of large-scale disaster relief present a highly significant and possibly even superior test of China's armed forces mobilization capacity. In terms of mobilization demands, internal disaster relief operations are more like responding to a theoretical surprise attack than conducting a deliberate, planned buildup toward war.

Table 7.4. Armed Forces Disaster and Warfighting Mobilization						
Contingency	Total Number of Troops Mobilized	Average Distance Traveled (km)	Average Time of Travel (days)	Speed Capacity (km/day)	Throughput Capacity (troops/day)	Percent of Data Set Known
2008 Winter Storms	2,495,000	850	4.5	189	554,444	30
1950–1953 Korean War	840,000*	1,897	74.8	25	11,226	33
1979 Sino-Vietnamese War	473,000*	1,304	13.1	100	36,207	45
2008 Wenchuan earthquake	140,000	566	0.7	836	206,769	45
2010 Yushu earthquake	16,000	1,273	1.3	1,006	12,642	54
2010 Zhouqu mudslides	6,281	347	1.0	351	6,337	85

* Denotes estimate of troops initially mobilized, not level of total troop participation

Note: Total troop numbers mobilized for the 1950–1953 Korean and 1979 Sino-Vietnamese War are derived from the number of group armies multiplied by the estimated number of troops in each group army. As a result, the number listed is very different than the total number of individuals that participated in the wars. This is specifically so for the Korean War, as it lasted over a period of years; attrition and reinforcements ballooned the total numbers of individuals who actually participated. See table 7.3 sources for earlier data on disaster mobilization.

Sources: Allen S. Whiting, *China Crosses the Yalu: The Decision to Enter the Korean War* (New York: The Macmillan Company, 1960), 64–67, 118–124; "PLA Armies in Korea 1950–1958: Dates of Service," Orbat.com, June 16, 2002, available at <www.orbat.com/site/history/historical/china/plakorea.html>; King C. Chen, *China's War with Vietnam, 1979: Issues, Decisions, and Implications* (Stanford, CA: Stanford University Press, 1986), 102–112; Edward C. O'Dowd, *Chinese Military Strategy in the Third Indochina War* (London: Routledge, 2007), 48, 50–55; *China's Military Policy and General Purpose Forces*, National Intelligence Estimate, NIE 13-3-72 (Washington, DC: Central Intelligence Agency, 1972), 64–66, available at <www.foia.cia.gov/docs/DOC_0001093704/DOC_0001093704.pdf>.

From these three cases, a *mobilization capacity curve* can be drawn (see figure 7.4), depicting a potential theoretical maximum or *frontier* of China's armed forces' present ability to mobilize. The dashed lines in the figure represent the tentative nature of our knowledge about China's mobilization efficiency from the limited set of nonrandomized cases examined.

How can we compare the evolution of capacity to mobilize from earlier historical contingencies? In the 1950–1953 Korean War and 1979 Sino-Vietnamese War, China's armed forces amassed significant forces yet were relatively slow moving those forces to their initial fighting positions, averaging an estimated 25 km and 100 km per day, respectively (see table 7.4). Figure 7.4 depicts these plots and draws highly approximated curves through them. While more data points, and more complete data for the existing data points, would be needed to increase confidence about the exact shape of such curves, the general trend is clear. The demonstrated mobilization capacity of China's armed forces to deal with internal and peripheral contingencies evolved significantly from the early 1950s to the late 1970s, increasing roughly three to four times. This capacity has taken an even more massive leap since that time to reach present levels. Combining data from other historical examples of Chinese mobilization, such as the 1962 Sino-Indian Border War or the various Taiwan Strait crises (1954–1955, 1958, and 1995–1996), would provide further evidence and more nuance about the evolution of conflict mobilization capacity over time.

While the findings presented here are preliminary in nature and further research is needed, we have demonstrated that data on disaster relief contingencies can be grouped by time to develop mobilization capacity curves showing levels of mobilization efficiency at various historical periods. Data from future contingencies could be used to track further developments of mobilization capacity. If the mobilization capacity curve continues to expand outward in the future, this would indicate that the PLA, PAP, and the militia are increasing their mobilization capacity. Lastly, if additional data about the disasters studied here becomes available (see table 7.4), we would have increased confidence in the actual shape of the mobilization curve.

One further note of caution: not every contingency will fully stress the Chinese mobilization system. With smaller or slower responses, the resulting data plot will be below the mobilization capacity curve. The 2010 Zhouqu mudslide is an example of such an event, as it is well inside the mobilization capacity curve (see figure 7.4).

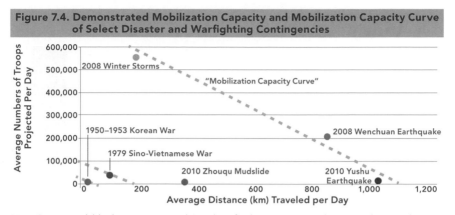

Figure 7.4. Demonstrated Mobilization Capacity and Mobilization Capacity Curve of Select Disaster and Warfighting Contingencies

Note: Gaps in available data are estimated. Numbers for the Korean War only capture the period between the official entry of Chinese forces (October 25, 1950) and their continued presence through the ceasefire armistice on July 27, 1953. It does not include the prior mobilization or the period after the ceasefire (July 28, 1953, to October 31, 1958) in which a number of Chinese forces remained in North Korea. Similarly, numbers for the Sino-Vietnamese War only capture the period in which Chinese forces operated within Vietnam, spanning from the conflict's official start date of February 17, 1979, to March 16, 1979. See table 7.3 for sources.

We can also assess manpower effort across the cases to make similar comparisons about overall effort and sustainment across very different contingencies (see figure 7.5). The 2008 winter storms are a good example of this. Indeed, as the figure demonstrates, more manpower effort was expended for this disaster than the 1979 Sino-Vietnamese War. Other large-scale, long-duration disaster responses will likely also demonstrate responses approaching or even exceeding efforts of certain military conflicts. As a result, with the abovementioned caveats, disaster relief is also an important indicator of the PLA's capacity to sustain military operations.

Conclusion

This chapter has depicted the enormity and importance of the internal disaster relief mission for China's armed forces, detailing the location and frequency of certain types of disasters. It also demonstrated an approach that enhances our understanding of mobilization capacity and manpower effort in China's disaster relief operations by conducting cross-case comparisons on the number of forces mobilized and length of time required to deliver forces to the point of operations. This approach can also be used to compare disaster relief contingencies to other contingencies China's armed forces

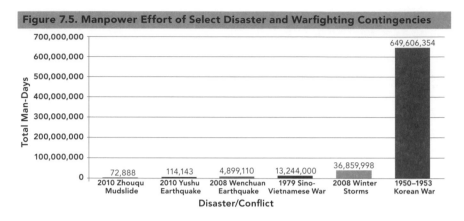

Figure 7.5. Manpower Effort of Select Disaster and Warfighting Contingencies

face. In terms of mobilization and manpower, disaster relief contingencies, with certain caveats, are comparable to a broad range of contingencies, including warfighting. The approach put forth here provides a useful means of tracking China's evolving capacities to respond to internal or peripheral contingencies over time.

Appendix A

Recent Chinese Government Documents Relating to Disaster Relief

The People's Liberation Army (the Ground Forces, Navy, Air Force, Armed Police, Second Artillery, and Reserve), the People's Armed Police, and the militia have regularly engaged in internal disaster relief contingencies for decades, if not since the founding of the People's Republic of China (PRC).[27] However, Chinese armed forces' participation in domestic disaster relief was only formally codified in the last decade in two PRC legal documents.

The first, "Regulations on the Army's Participation in Emergency Rescue and Disaster Relief" [*jundui canjia qiangxianjiuzai tiaoli*, 军队参加抢险救灾条例], passed on July 1, 2005, outlined in broad terms the legal authority as well as the principles, tasks, command, and support for the armed forces' participation in emergency rescue and disaster relief.[28] The regulations define *responsibilities* as:

> rescuing, transferring, or dispersing victims; protecting the safety of important targets; rescuing and transporting important materials; participating in specialized tasks including repair of roads, bridges, and tunnels, rescue at sea, nuclear, chemical, and biological rescue,

control of infectious disease, preventing or controlling other serious dangers or disasters, and when necessary, assisting local government in reconstruction.[29]

The second document, the "Contingency Response Law of the People's Republic of China" [*zhonghua renmin gongheguo tufa shijian yingdui fa*, 中华人民共和国突发事件应对法], passed by the National People's Congress Standing Committee on August 30, 2007, sought to streamline intraservice responses to sudden incidents [*tufa shijian*, 突发事件] across the different armed services and bureaucracies. The law states the military's role in quite flexible terms: "The Chinese People's Liberation Army, the Chinese People's Armed Police Force, and militia join in emergency response, rescue, and management in accordance with this law and other relevant laws, administrative regulations, and military laws and the commands of the State Council and the Central Military Commission."[30]

Finally, on May 12, 2009, on the anniversary of the 2008 Wenchuan earthquake, the State Council Information Office released its first white paper on disaster relief entitled *China's Actions for Disaster Prevention and Reduction*. The white paper reviews government policies related to disaster relief work and lays out broad policy objectives in alleviating the human and economic costs of natural disasters. The paper summarizes the effort in this way: "Given that many kinds of wide-ranging disasters frequently hit China and caused huge losses, China's main tasks were to strengthen its ability to manage potential risks of natural disasters, to monitor and forecast natural disasters, to prevent them, and conduct rescue and relief."[31]

Appendix B

Data on Troop Movement[32]

The four tables (7.5–7.8) represent the calculations based on Chinese reporting of the four case studies examined in the chapter. In the majority of cases, the Chinese reporting identified data points, such as units within various military regions, their time of departure and arrival at the disaster area, and the size of the unit involved, which allowed the authors to accurately calculate estimates of mobilization capacity. In some instances, only fragmentary information was revealed, such as the time of departure and the number of troops involved, without identifying the specific location of departure or arrival. In those instances, the authors undertook a subjective analysis of the proximate location that a given unit might have departed from based on the context of the article. In instances where the arrival location was not given, the authors assumed that the location was at or near the disaster zone.[33]

Table 7.5. 2008 Winter Storms						
Unit Name	Unit Size	Unit Military Region (MR)	Within Disaster Area MR[a]	Distance traveled (km)	Length of time to reach disaster area (hours)	Efficiency of mobilization (distance/ time)
Chengdu MR	499,000	Chengdu	Yes	700	120	5.83
Various PAP Branches	243,000	Unidentified	Yes	1,000	96	10.42
Total accounted	742,000					
Peak troop level	2,495,000					
Total % accounted	30					
Disaster date	January 25, 2008					
Order to mobilize came from Hu Jintao on January 29, 2008						
[a] Disaster area spanned Jiangsu, Jiangxi, Zhejiang, Anhui, Hunan, and Guangzhou provinces						

Table 7.6. 2008 Wenchuan Earthquake

Unit Name	Unit Size	Unit Military Region (MR)	Within Disaster Area MR	Distance traveled (km)	Length of time to reach disaster area (hours)	Efficiency of mobilization (distance/ time)
Chengdu MR units (various)	20,000	Chengdu	Yes	132	10	13.20
Chengdu MR reserves	15,600	Chengdu	Yes	132	40	3.30
Jinan MR units (various)	18,000	Jinan	No	1,000	12	83.33
4th or 3rd army aviation	9,000	Lanzhou or Jinan	No	1,000	3	333.33
Total accounted	62,600					
Peak troop level	140,000					
Total percentage accounted	45					
Disaster date	May 12, 2008					

Table 7.7. 2010 Yushu Earthquake

Unit Name	Unit Size	Unit Military Region (MR)	Within Disaster Area MR	Distance traveled (km)	Length of time to reach disaster area (hours)	Efficiency of mobilization (distance/ time)
Unidentified	218	Beijing	No	2,500	60.07[a]	41.62[a]
Unidentified	5,211	Lanzhou	Yes	1,028	24.70[a]	41.62[a]
Unidentified	283	Jinan	No	2,511	60.33[a]	41.62[a]
Unidentified	583	Chengdu	No	1,152	27.68[a]	41.62[a]
Unidentified	861	Second Artillery	No	1,273	30.60[a]	41.62[a]
Qinghai regiment (unspecified)	1,030	Lanzhou	Yes	800	19.00	42.11
Reserve engineer regiment (unspecified)	300	Chengdu	No	1,152	20.00	57.60
Second artillery unit (unspecified)	180	Lanzhou	Yes	814	24.00	33.92
Qumalai reserve corps	50	Lanzhou	Yes	230	7.00	32.86
Total accounted	8,716					
Peak troop level	16,000					
Total percentage accounted	54					
Disaster date and time	0749 on April 14, 2010					

[a] Extrapolated from data on other units responding to this disaster.

Table 7.8. 2010 Zhouqu Mudslides

Unit Name	Unit Size	Unit Military Region (MR)	Within Disaster Area MR	Distance traveled (km)	Length of time to reach disaster area (hours)	Efficiency of mobilization (distance/ time)
Longnan detachment	200	Lanzhou	Yes	77.30	2.35	32.89
Lanzhou anti-chemical corps	300	Lanzhou	Yes	387.00	5.80	66.72
Chengdu disaster relief corps	300	Chengdu	No	578.00	39.00	14.82
Various units	4,544	Various	Yes	347.43	48.00	7.24

Total accounted	5,344
Peak troop level	6,281
Total percentage accounted	85
Disaster date and time	2300 on August 7, 2010

Notes

1 Unless otherwise specified, the term *People's Liberation Army* (PLA) encompasses the PLA Ground Force, PLA Navy, PLA Air Force, Second Artillery, and Reserve. Information Office of the State Council, People's Republic of China, *China's National Defense in 2002* (Beijing: Information Office of the State Council, 2002).

2 For example, Kamlesh K. Agnihotri, "2008 Sichuan Earthquake and the Role of the Chinese Defence Forces in Disaster Relief," *Journal of Defence Studies* 6, no. 1 (2012), 30–43; James Mulvenon, "The Chinese Military's Earthquake Response Leadership Team," *China Leadership Monitor*, no. 25 (Winter 2008); Nirav Patel, "Chinese Disaster Relief Operations: Identifying Critical Capability Gaps," *Joint Force Quarterly* 51 (1st Quarter, 2009), 111–117.

3 Ding Dou's article on PLA participation in internal disaster relief presents four disaster relief case studies, but they are not systematically compared or analyzed. Ding Dou, "PLA's Disaster Relief Works: Review and Reform," *East Asian Policy* 2, no. 3 (July/September 2010).

4 Ibid.

5 For more on military operations other than war, see Harold M. Tanner, "The People's Liberation Army and China's Internal Security Challenges," in *The PLA at Home and Abroad: Assessing the Operational Capabilities of China's Military*, ed. Roy Kamphausen, David Lai, and Andrew Scobell (Carlisle, PA: Strategic Studies Institute, July 2010), 237–294.

6 This percentage is possibly greater based on the 24.8 percent of data that is unknown.

7 "Over 100 Dead or Missing After Floods Devastate NE China Province," Xinhua, August 1, 2010; United Nations Office for the Coordination of Humanitarian Affairs (OCHA), *China—Floods*, Situation Report no. 6 (August 7, 1998); World Vision, *Update on China Flood* (August 27, 1998); United Nations Disaster Relief Organization, *China—Floods*, Situation Reports 1–9 (June 25, 1991); International Federation of the Red Cross (IFRC), *China: Floods Information Bulletin No. 1* (May 21, 2003); IFRC, *China: Floods Information Bulletin No. 4* (July 9, 2003); Robert J. Saiget, "Death Toll in China Floods Hits 569," Agence France-Presse, July 11, 2003; OCHA, *China—Floods*, Situation Report no. 4 (September 24, 1999); United Nations Department of Humanitarian Affairs, *China—Floods*, Information Report no. 1 (July 7, 1995).

8 Howard W. French, "Snowstorms in China Kill at Least 24," *New York Times*, January 29, 2008, available at <www.nytimes.com/2008/01/29/world/asia/29china.html>.

9 "Heavy snow affects 77 mln people in 14 provinces," Xinhua, January 29, 2008, available at <www.china.org.cn/english/China/241079.htm>.

10   "Memorandum on relief efforts by the PLA and PAP during the 2008 Winter Storms" [2008全军和武警部队抗灾救灾备忘录], *PLA Daily* [解放军报], February 13, 2008.

11   "China Focus: China Deploys 113,080 Armed Forces for Earthquake Rescue," Xinhua, May 18, 2008.

12   Li Shiming and Zhang Haiyang [李世明, 张海阳], "Vivid Earthquake Rescue Efforts Illustrate PLA's Ability To Complete Diversified Military Missions" [抗震救灾斗争生动展示了我军完成多样化军事任务的能力], *Seeking Truth* [求是], no. 13 (July 1, 2008), 2, available at <www.qstheory.cn/zxdk/2008/200813/200906/t20090609_1338.htm>; Patel, 3.

13   "China Focus: At Least 67 Dead After 7.1-Magnitude Quake Hits China's Qinghai," Xinhua, April 14, 2010.

14   "Chinese armed forces provide quick response, quake relief to Yushu," Xinhua, April 20, 2010, available at <www.gov.cn/english/2010-04/20/content_1587929.htm>.

15   "Litany of Warnings Preceded Mudslide," *South China Morning Post*, August 10, 2010, available at <www.scmp.com/article/721756/litany-warnings-preceded-mudslides>.

16   "Zhouqu mudslide disaster anniversary: Zhouqu's past and present," *CCTV.com*, August 8, 2011, available at <http://english.cntv.cn/20110808/104160.shtml>.

17   "PLA and PAP deploy 6,281 troops to Zhouqu mudslide disaster" [解放军及武警共6281人投入甘肃舟曲泥石流救援], *Phoenix Satellite Television* [凤凰卫视], August 16, 2010, available at <http://news.ifeng.com/mil/2/detail_2010_08/16/1961155_0.shtml>.

18   Though this definition is U.S.-centric and somewhat vague, it suits the purposes of this chapter. Joint Chiefs of Staff, *Department of Defense Dictionary of Military and Associated Terms*, Joint Publication 1-02 (Washington, DC: The Joint Staff, February 2014), 175.

19   The efficacy of mobilization certainly has a large role to play in ultimate operational successes or failures. Likewise, inefficient or ineffective operations often require further mobilization to accommodate operational weaknesses.

20   Unlike the quantity of heavy equipment present (helicopters or cranes), troops are highly comparable over time and are a good barometer of a relief operation's scope and scale, as well as significantly easier to count in the open source literature. A more complex model might seek to incorporate quantities of heavy equipment though this metric may be more suited to another variable, explicitly not explored here, relating to relief operation efficacy.

21   One such example is an episode during the 2008 Wenchuan earthquake in which the PLA's lack of heavy-lift helicopters prevented vital equipment such

as excavators and cranes from being delivered. See Jake Hooker, "Quake Revealed Deficiencies of China's Military," *New York Times*, July 2, 2008, available at <www. nytimes.com/2008/07/02/world/asia/02china.html?pagewanted=all>.

22   Certain estimates were made if reporting did not mention specific locations. For example, some reports mentioned troops departing from the Chengdu Military Region without specifying the individual unit locations. In those instances, we used the Chengdu group army headquarters as the default point of departure. Likewise, certain assumptions had to be made when the exact time of departure or arrival was unclear. In instances when the reporting mentioned a unit leaving "in the early hours" on a certain date, for example, we estimated this time to be around 0300 hours, and so on.

23   Note the cut-off date of disaster relief operations is defined as the date the PLA concluded *rescue efforts*—extraction of victims from harm, delivery of life-sustaining supplies (blankets and food), and so forth. This does not include postdisaster construction efforts, which the PLA was also involved in but which continued well beyond the initial search and rescue phase of relief efforts.

24   The sudden drop-off in operations for this as well as for other case studies is due to the fact that we were unable to locate data on demobilization of troops from the disaster zone.

25   As noted earlier, a more complex model might take into account the political impact of effective and timely responses in mobilization capacity. This is a topic left for future research.

26   Patel, 116.

27   PLA participation is known to have occurred in the Tangshan earthquake of 1976 in which a 7.5 magnitude earthquake struck Heibei Province.

28   State Council and the Central Military Commission of the People's Republic of China, "Regulation on army participation in disaster rescue and relief" [军队参加抢险救灾条例], June 7, 2005, available at <www.gov.cn/yjgl/2005-10/09/content_75376.htm>.

29   Ibid., art. 3.

30   "Contingency response law of the People's Republic of China" [中华人民共和国突发事件应对法], passed by the National People's Congress Standing Committee on August 30, 2007, available at <www.gov.cn/flfg/2007-08/30/content_732593.htm>.

31   Information Office of the State Council of the People's Republic of China, *China's Actions for Disaster Prevention and Reduction* (Beijing: Information Office of the State Council, May 11, 2009), available at <www.gov.cn/english/official/2009-05/11/content_1310629.htm>.

32   See table 7.3 for sources.

33   Estimates were made if reporting did not mention specific locations.

CHAPTER 8

PLA Response to Widespread Internal Unrest in the Han Homeland

Ma Chengkun

If China were to experience widespread internal unrest, the People's Liberation Army (PLA) might be called upon to help restore order. However, an evolution in how the People's Republic of China (PRC) thinks about maintaining order has changed the PLA's responsibility from a frontline role in suppressing counterrevolutionaries to a secondary and supporting role in maintaining stability. This chapter begins by reviewing the evolution in Chinese leadership thinking about responding to unrest from Mao Zedong to Jiang Zemin. The second section considers PRC efforts to implement a reduction in the PLA's internal security role by constructing a legislative and regulatory framework defining the roles of the armed forces in emergencies and building the capabilities of the People's Armed Police (PAP) to respond to internal unrest. It also briefly reviews recent responses to internal unrest, noting that, in practice, Chinese authorities have relied on public security forces and the PAP and have avoided employing the PLA in internal security roles. The final section considers the impact of this shift, noting the use of political education and military "love the people" activities to try to ensure that the PLA will be a loyal tool if called upon by the Chinese Communist Party. However, the PLA does not relish an active role in stability maintenance. Few articles by military scholars discuss PLA participation in such operations, with most authors stressing that the PAP has the main responsibility to deal with internal unrest.

Evolution of the PLA Role in Responding to Internal Unrest

The evolution of the PLA's role in responding to internal unrest can be divided into three periods as Chinese leadership shifted from Mao Zedong to Deng Xiaoping to Jiang Zemin. In Mao's era, mass riots were viewed as the conspiracies of counterrevolutionary forces and suppression by the PLA was the only solution. Deng Xiaoping took a more pragmatic approach. He did not necessarily view all riots or protests as counterrevolutionary activities but still insisted that the PLA was the main force if it became necessary to suppress riots. Jiang Zemin viewed most unrest as people safeguarding their rights on the street. Accordingly, the PAP was a more proper and legitimate means to cope with these incidents, with the PLA role in riot suppression being reduced or eliminated.

Suppression of Counterrevolutionaries under Mao

After the founding of the PRC in 1949, responding to internal unrest was one of the PLA's principal missions. In 1950, when the CCP leadership started a nationwide land reform campaign, local riots arose along with sporadic armed conflicts between the PLA and residual Kuomintang (KMT) armed forces. Chairman Mao Zedong admitted that the situation had become severe because implementation of the CCP's land reform policy had been delayed by the civil war. After the PRC was founded, the negative impact of land reform became more notable because the civil war had ended and people could return their attention to the safety of their property.[1] To ensure the success of the land reform campaign, Mao decided to suppress the riots by initiating a policy of "Suppression of Counterrevolutionaries." The CCP regime issued the "Direction Concerning the Suppression of Counterrevolutionary Activities" in October 1950, declaring that the success of land reform and economic development required suppression of all the activities of counterrevolutionaries.[2] The PLA 3rd and 4th Armies were designated as the main forces to suppress land reform riots in eastern and southern China.[3] Party cadres went to the countryside, accompanied by PLA units, and entered villages to overcome opposition of landowners to the land reform policy.[4] During the revolutionary era, CCP leaders viewed the PLA as an effective tool for suppressing internal unrest, riots, and protests. The PLA was the only reliable coercive tool the party had in the initial period after the founding of the PRC when police forces were under military command. As a revolutionary force, the PLA could easily turn its guns against the Chinese people without hesitation, since the core mission of the PLA was to assure the security of the CCP regime rather than to protect the motherland.

The PLA used even more brutal means to suppress riots in Tibet and Xinjiang during the revolutionary era. During the Xunhua [循化] incident in the Qinghai-Tibetan Plateau in April 1958, CCP leaders mobilized the PLA 163rd and 165th Infantry Corps, the 306th Artillery Corps, and the 55th Engineer Division to suppress counterrevolutionaries gathered at a temple. After soldiers surrounded and rushed into the temple, they faced thousands of unarmed Tibetans. The PLA killed more than 700 and arrested the others.[5]

During the Cultural Revolution, when the power struggle between the conservatives and the radicals escalated from quarrel to armed conflict despite Chairman Mao's warning, Mao eventually decided to use the military to rein in the anarchical situation. He ordered the elite security guard force, the famous Unit 8341 troops, to be stationed at Tsinghua University to show his determination to regain control.[6] Under Mao's orders, the PLA suppressed workers and students cruelly. When student Red Guard groups refused to dissolve following a military ultimatum, PLA troops attacked them using regular combat tactics. The majority of the 500,000 victims of the Cultural Revolution were killed by the PLA's bloody suppression in 1968.[7]

Main Force of Riot Suppression under Deng

Two decades later, in June 1989, China's political leader, Deng Xiaoping, faced a severe situation in Tiananmen Square. Thousands of students protested and demanded political reform. The students refused to leave even after CCP Secretary General Zhao Ziyang went to the square and showed his sincerity in speaking to them. Like his predecessor Mao, Deng Xiaoping decided to use military forces to suppress the protests and restore social order. But because Deng was a pragmatist, he did not view all of the protesters as counterrevolutionaries. Deng mobilized military troops only after he concluded that the Beijing police were unable to restore social order in the capital.[8] Although Deng ultimately decided to suppress the protest by force, the first PLA troops, which received mobilization orders in mid-May, were ordered not to shoot even if they were provoked by protesters. Thus, many soldiers did not carry their weapons when they moved to Beijing.[9] At the beginning of the Tiananmen suppression, the PLA 38th Group Army attempted to use tear gas and rubber bullets to disperse the protesters. When these efforts failed, soldiers began to shoot people with AK-47 machine guns and to crush obstacles in the streets with tanks and armored vehicles.[10]

Deng Xiaoping eventually concluded that the essence of the protest was a threat to political and social stability that had to be suppressed as soon as possible to prevent it from escalating into an open challenge to the regime.[11]

However, the PLA was the last option, after the police and the PAP failed to suppress internal unrest. This contrasts with Mao Zedong, who viewed the PLA as an effective way to attack counterrevolutionaries and mobilized troops to suppress internal unrest without hesitation.

Secondary Force in Stability Maintenance under Jiang

Since this experience under Mao and Deng, the PLA has gradually moved from the frontline in suppressing internal unrest. The Tiananmen incident was a watershed moment in reducing the PLA's role in maintaining social stability. The PAP gradually replaced the PLA as the main coercive tool the regime could employ when challenges of social unrest arose.

In the Jiang Zemin era, internal unrest increased dramatically due to dislocations caused by rapid economic development. However, Jiang insisted that PLA troops should not be the frontline forces in suppressing riots. He emphasized the importance of the PAP in maintaining social stability and ordered the PAP to establish a contingency response capability.[12] In October 1999, 10 years after the Tiananmen incident, a robbery incident in Panzhihua City (攀枝花市) in Sichuan Province caused large-scale riots. People marched in the streets protesting collusion between local police and criminals. Chinese authorities mobilized 500 PAP troops to suppress the riots with tear gas instead of mobilizing PLA troops to shoot people.[13] According to official statistics, there were more than 100,000 mass riots in mainland China in 1999, a level that could have exhausted PAP forces. Considering the urgency of the situation, CCP leaders could have mobilized PLA troops to suppress riots and protests. However, the PLA continued to play a secondary role, backing up frontline PAP forces.

Implementing the Shift in the PLA's Role in Maintaining Social Order

Partly due to the traumatic impact of the Tiananmen incident on CCP leaders and on Chinese society, the PLA role in suppressing riots and maintaining internal stability has continued to decline over the last decade. The CCP regime has tried hard to rehabilitate its international and domestic image by civilizing its internal stability maintenance mechanisms. In this context, the PAP has gradually replaced the PLA as the main force responsible for coping with social unrest.

Legislative Framework

According to China's National Defense Law, the PLA's main mission is to conduct national defense operations. The PAP has direct responsibility for maintaining social order, though the PLA can offer assistance in this if necessary and authorized by law.[14] China has also used defense white papers to clarify the difference in the PLA and PAP missions. According to the 2013 Defense White Paper, China's armed forces assist the public security forces in maintaining social order and ensuring that the people live and work in peace and stability.[15] The white paper emphasizes that PAP forces, instead of the PLA, are the state's backbone and shock force in handling public emergencies. From 2011-2012 PAP forces handled 68 acts of serious violence and crime, including dealing with terrorist attacks and rescuing 62 hostages. The PAP also deployed a total of 1.6 million people to provide security during the 26th Summer Universiade and the China-Eurasia Expo in 2011 and the Shanghai Cooperation Organization Beijing Summit in 2012.[16]

The PLA has participated in emergency rescue and disaster relief operations, part of what the PLA calls military operations other than war (MOOTW) [*feizhanzheng junshi xingdong*, 非战争军事行动]. The 2013 defense white paper notes that China formed nine state-level professional emergency response units, boasting a total of 50,000 personnel, specializing in "flood relief, earthquake rescue, nuclear, biological, and chemical (NBC) defense, emergency airlift, quick repair of transportation and power facilities, maritime search and rescue, mobile communications support, medical aid and epidemic prevention, and meteorological support."[17] These units have been founded under the "Military MOOTW Capacity-Building Program" [*jundui feizhanzheng junshi xingdong nengli jianshe guihua*, 军队非战争军事行动能力建设规划] approved by the Central Military Commission (CMC) in 2008. These units include designated corps of engineers, nuclear-biological-chemical protection, pontoon bridge construction, hydropower, transport, communication, and medical service troops. Most are units from different services of the PLA, with only the hydropower unit drawn from the PAP. All of the units were operational by the end of 2010.[18]

The CMC approved and promulgated the "Regulations on Emergency Command in Handling Emergencies by the Armed Forces" in 2010 to establish the organization, command, force deployment, integrated support, and civil-military coordination of armed forces during their missions of maintaining social stability and handling emergencies.[19] The regulations make clear that China has separated armed force contingency responses into social stability and emergency rescue and disaster relief missions, with the PLA playing a much greater role in emergency rescue and disaster relief. This indicates that China has developed a mature division of labor for contingency response operations in different scenarios.

The relative importance of these missions is indicated by the increase in the annual budget for stability maintenance. The CCP regime has publicized the 2012 public security budget for central and local governments. Compared with 629.3 billion renminbi (RMB) in 2011, the total public security budget rose 11.5 percent to 701.8 billion RMB (U.S. $111.4 billion). Meanwhile, the defense budget rose 11.2 percent to 670.3 billion RMB (U.S. $106.4 billion).[20] This was the first time that the public security budget exceeded the defense budget. This trend continued in 2013 with the defense budget increasing 10.7 percent to 740.6 billion RMB (U.S. $119 billion) and public security spending increasing by 8.7 percent to 769.1 billion RMB (U.S. $123.5 billion).[21] Interestingly, when the 2014 budget was released, local budgets, which are used to calculate public security budgets, were not released. Because of this, only the central government's spending on public security is available, which was 205 billion RMB (U.S. $33 billion), while total defense spending was 808 billion RMB (U.S. $132 billion).[22] One consequence of the division of labor between the PLA and the PAP is that most of the funding for stability maintenance missions is carried in the PAP budget. This allows the PLA to use the defense budget to concentrate on building traditional military capabilities.

Buildup of PAP Forces and Capabilities

In addition to the legislation and official policies cited above, the expanded capabilities of the PAP have allowed the PLA to reduce its role in stability maintenance missions. Since Deng Xiaoping announced a cut of one million troops in the PLA and the formation of the PAP forces in 1985, some PLA infantry divisions have been transferred into the PAP. Most of these were reorganized into PAP Mobile Divisions responsible for counterterrorism, contingency response, and stability maintenance missions. PAP forces currently have 14 mobile divisions deployed nationwide, totaling 170,000 personnel. The PAP also has 31 corps in the Internal Security Force, which total more than 350,000 troops. At least one corps (averaging 6,000 soldiers, but varying in strength from

3,000 to 15,000) is stationed in each of China's 31 provinces, municipalities, and autonomous regions. An additional 80,000 troops are directly subordinate to PAP Headquarters and in charge of guarding official buildings, hospitals, airports, and other important transportation facilities. The 14 PAP Mobile Divisions, with an average of 12,000 soldiers each, can offer sufficient back-up troops to suppress mass riots within 24 hours.

The rapid increase in internal stability budgets has also allowed the PAP to purchase modern equipment necessary to suppress mass riots. This modern equipment includes Z-9 helicopters and ZSL92 wheeled armored vehicles.[23] The growth and maturation of the PAP contingency response capability has allowed the PLA to decrease its emphasis on stability maintenance missions.[24]

The Division of Labor in Practice

In practice, recent responses to internal unrest and operations to restore social order have been conducted mainly by the PAP. During the Wukan Village [乌坎村] incident from September to December 2011, the CCP contingency response working group in Guangdong included Public Security, PAP, and PLA Military District representatives. However, the authorities mobilized only police and PAP forces to block the village from the outside world.[25]

Compared to other mass riots in recent years, the Wukan incident was not large in scale; the largest street protest involved fewer than 5,000 people. But the scale is not the key element in CCP decisions about whether to deploy the PLA in suppressing riots. While Guangdong officials were negotiating with Wukan Village residents, another riot broke out in Haimen Town [海门镇], also in Guangdong Province. More than 30,000 people protested in the streets to oppose the construction of a power plant proposed by the local government. A third village, Daimei Village [岱美村], also experienced rioting, with more than 1,000 residents in the streets protesting against corrupt local officials. Guangdong CCP officials faced a severe situation, since most of the local PAP assets had already been mobilized to Wukan Village. After riots broke out in Haimen Town, Guangdong authorities mobilized the remainder of the local PAP forces to Haimen Town to maintain social order. Then the third riot occurred in Daimei Village. Even in these circumstances, Guangdong officials continued to rely on PAP forces to maintain order rather than calling on PLA forces stationed nearby. In Haimen, after residents occupied the town hall and blocked the highway in the morning, PAP forces did not arrive until evening.

In Daimei, when residents protested on the street and walked to the town hall, there were no riot police or PAP forces to confront them. The protesters were therefore able to blockade local officials inside the town hall.[26]

In October 2012, another large-scale mass riot occurred in Ningbo City [宁波市], Zhejiang Province. Ningbo residents took to the streets to protest the expansion of the PX Petrochemical plant located in the suburbs. Serious physical confrontations occurred between the protesters and the riot police, who dispersed the protesters with tear gas and made at least 10 arrests.[27] The riot happened only 10 days before the opening of the 18th CCP National Congress, a very sensitive political moment. Both the central and the local authorities wanted to stop the protest as soon as possible. Even then, local authorities did not use the PLA to restore order. Riot police took the leading role in suppressing the protest, with the PAP playing a backup role.

The only recent case involving social order in which the PLA participated was in hunting a criminal in Chongqing who had shot and killed 10 people in different provinces over the course of 8 years. The CMC authorized the Chengdu Military Region to mobilize 5,000 troops, including soldiers of the 37th Division of the 13th Army and the Special Forces Unit, to conduct joint operations with the local police and the PAP to round up this major criminal suspect.[28] The role the PLA played in this case was to protect people from a dangerous criminal, a very different operation than suppressing mass protests. In this case, residents welcomed the appearance of the PLA.

Analyzing the PLA's Residual Role in Responding to Internal Unrest

Internal unrest in the PRC is usually caused by violations of the rights and interests of the people. In most cases, collusion between local government and private enterprise and the accompanying official corruption are key factors.[29] Thus, when protests begin on the street, local officials usually seek to suppress them and restore social order quickly to prevent escalation. This response often makes protesters angry at local officials. For protesters motivated by violations of their legitimate rights and interests by local government policies and officials, the appearance of military forces to suppress demonstrations produces hostility toward the military forces, since they are viewed as thugs of corrupt officials and businessmen. Mobilizing troops to restore social order has the potential to provoke fierce reactions from the people and turn protests into riots.

Psychological Impact on Soldiers

Although the PLA has not played a frontline role in suppressing unrest in recent years, it plays a secondary role by providing transportation, communications, and logistic support to PAP forces suppressing mass protests and riots.[30] The negative reaction of the people thus extends to the PLA troops performing even such support missions. This reaction has caused a negative impact on PLA morale. Most of the soldiers participating in these missions do not know the real situation motivating the protesters because PLA troops are usually isolated from broader outside information sources and are legally restricted to obtaining their information through official media. Consequently, the protesters can affect soldiers by giving them information about their grievances that differs from official accounts. Such communication can potentially change the soldiers' attitude from confrontation to sympathy with the protesters.[31] Such sympathy could challenge the authority of military command and gradually undercut the principle of the party's absolute leadership over the military.

Exposure to contrary and conflicting information from the public can increase psychological pressure on soldiers tremendously. According to the "core values of contemporary revolutionary soldiers" [*dangdai geming junren hexin jiazhiguan*, 当代革命军人核心价值观] advocated by Hu Jintao, the PLA soldiers should love and serve the people as well as ensure that the people live and work in peace and stability. CCP mobilization of troops to suppress street protests creates contradictions between soldiers and the people. Investigation reports from the PLA's military medical system reveal that soldiers who participate in stability maintenance missions often suffer from psychological disorders ranging from anxiety to depression.[32] Although these PLA reports blame the psychological disorders on threats to the personal safety of soldiers and the effect of confrontations with the masses,[33] the contradiction between the messages received through propaganda channels and what soldiers learn from the people and personally see can also cause psychological stress.

Reinforcement of Political Education

The PLA seeks to provide political and psychological education to its troops, promoting loyalty to the party, preventing pollution of their minds by people with selfish intentions, and developing a clear understanding of the right way to increase the welfare of the people.[34]

Reiteration of the Core Values of Contemporary Revolutionary Soldiers. The number of mass riots occurring in China was roughly 90,000 in 2005 and increased to nearly 200,000 in 2010, according to Chinese sociologist Sun Liping of Tsinghua University.[35] The situation has forced the CCP to reinforce political education to ensure the loyalty of the military forces to the party. The PLA General Political Department (GPD) issued the document "Opinions on Widely Carrying Out Educational Activities on the Subject of Educating the Core Values of Contemporary Revolutionary Soldier in the Military" in January 2009, which increased political education in order to consolidate the loyalty of military members to the party and to prevent the emergence of psychological disorders.[36] In August 2009, the CMC held a "Forum on Psychological Service Work in the Military" in Beijing. One of the issues discussed was psychological counseling for soldiers who have symptoms of anxiety, gloom, or depression after participating in contingency response missions. In January 2010 and January 2011, the PLA GPD issued additional circulars on how to educate PLA soldiers on "the core values of the contemporary revolutionary soldier."[37] This repeated emphasis on political education indicates the desire of CCP leaders to ensure that the party still enjoys absolute loyalty from the armed forces.

"Love the People" Measures. CCP officials fully understand the negative impact of sending PLA troops to suppress mass protests. Such actions not only produce hostility between the people and the troops, but also brew suspicion among soldiers about the correctness of the party's orders to suppress protests. In addition to stressing the importance of political and psychological education of the troops, the PLA GPD has also sought to improve the social image of the PLA by conducting "love the people" measures. Such measures include military hospitals holding free clinics for local residents, military personnel donating blood regularly, donating money to victims of natural disasters or other emergency incidents, adopting children from poor families, and even having locally stationed troops adopt entire poor villages.[38] These measures differ from older PLA activities, which included helping people with manual labor, from barbering to filling potholes to repairing shoes. Today, the Chinese people appear to value cash donations and medical services more than labor from PLA troops.

In addition to these measures, the PLA and PAP have contributed substantially to poverty alleviation initiatives with the hope of developing rural areas as well as preparing for emergency rescue and disaster relief missions.

Over 20,000 small projects, such as the construction of irrigation and water conservation facilities, have been undertaken by joint PLA/PAP efforts. Roads have been constructed in rural areas and more than 1,000 industries have been developed. These projects, just in terms of poverty alleviation, have helped over 400,000 people escape from poverty.[39]

PLA and PAP forces have also undertaken emergency rescue and disaster relief missions. Based on the "Regulations on the PLA's Participation in Disaster Rescue," the PLA and PAP are assigned the tasks of rescuing and evacuating affected citizens, transporting disaster relief materials, quickly repairing roads, bridges, and tunnels, as well as assisting local governments in post-disaster reconstruction and other facets of disaster relief.[40] During the harsh winter in 2008, 1.26 million military and PAP personnel were sent to assist in relief efforts. Another 221,000 personnel were sent to assist in disaster relief and emergency rescue efforts after an earthquake in Wenchuan County, Sichuan. Since 2011, the PLA and PAP have contributed nearly 400,000 troops and mobilized nearly 900,000 militia and reservists to assist in disaster relief efforts ranging from floods to forest fires.[41] Both poverty alleviation and emergency rescue and disaster relief efforts have shown the PLA's and PAP's commitment to engage the populace and, in a way, win the hearts and minds of the people.

PLA Reluctance to Play a Stability Maintenance Role

The negative psychological impact of PLA participation in riot suppression has had a positive side effect. It has reinforced the viewpoint of Chinese military academics that the PLA should reduce its involvement in stability maintenance and leave this mission to the PAP. Most publications discussing contingency responses emphasize that the PAP is the main force to implement the stability maintenance mission. Only a few publications mention the PLA role in such missions. In these discussions, the PAP is described as the main force to face the people, with the PLA coordinating and cooperating with the PAP, while the police and CCP local officials play a supporting role.[42] Although a few PLA publications discuss countermeasures for suppressing mass riots, these articles cannot be viewed as evidence of PLA direct participation in riot suppression missions since PLA forces also need training and preparation to protect military barracks and facilities from attacks during mass riots.

These academic studies highlight the division of labor between the PLA and the PAP on contingency response missions. As a result, the legitimacy of mobilizing the PLA to suppress mass riots is declining. The PLA hides its reluctance to participate in riot suppression missions by asserting that the PAP forces are properly trained and better equipped to confront protestors and rioters. This division of labor helps the CCP improve management of social unrest by preventing the escalation of riots that might result from the appearance of PLA troops on the street.

Conclusion

Images from the Tiananmen incident have been deeply etched in people's minds since June 1989. The picture of a young man standing at East Chang'an Avenue to stop PLA tanks from entering Tiananmen Square inspired the world. The PLA has borne the bloody stigma of its actions since then.

The CCP regime is aware of this negative image of its armed forces and has sought to reverse this perception through a variety of means. In the mid-1990s, Jiang Zemin asked the PLA to respond to the Yangzi River flooding and resultant rescue mission, no matter the cost. Dozens of soldiers died fighting the flood. The CMC did not review the errors made by commanders during the mission but repeatedly praised the sacrifice of these soldiers and the contribution of the PLA in safeguarding the people.

After Hu Jintao succeeded Jiang, he worked to improve the PLA's image by implementing a division of labor between the PLA and the PAP through legislation and the buildup of PAP capabilities. The legislation was part of Hu's broader effort to institutionalize roles and responsibilities for the party and government. Throughout Hu's time in office, he strictly limited the mobilization of PLA troops for riot suppression missions. Despite some challenges, PAP forces have been capable enough to implement these missions.

Some observers suspect the CCP continues to rely on the PLA as the main force to suppress mass protests. This skepticism is a hangover from the Tiananmen incident. However, the PLA has been reborn as a modern and professional armed force focusing on safeguarding China's security, national sovereignty, and territorial integrity, leaving the riot suppression mission to the PAP.[43]

Although the PAP has taken charge of maintaining social order, the possibility of brutal suppression by military force still exists, since the PAP Mobilized Division Forces are equipped with the standard weapons of regular infantry divisions, including machineguns, artillery, rockets, armored vehicles, and helicopters. All of these weapons can be used to engage in traditional battlefield combat operations. Even though CCP leaders have moved the PLA away from the street, the PAP retains forces capable of treating the Chinese people as if they were enemies on the battlefield. The division of labor between the PLA and the PAP in stability maintenance missions has clarified which organization will play what role. However, there is still no clear justification for why the CCP needs heavily armed paramilitary forces to maintain social order.

The author would like to acknowledge Adam Jankowski and Phillip C. Saunders for their assistance in updating and editing this chapter.

Notes

1   The CCP Central Chairman Mao Zedong Articles Editing and Publication Committee, *Selected Works of Mao Zedong* [毛泽东选集], vol. 5 (Beijing: People's Press [人民出版社], 1977), 13.

2   "The CCP Central Authority Direction concerning Suppression of Counter-revolutionary Activities" [中共中央关于镇压反革命活动的指示], *Selected Important Documents Since the PRC Founding* [建国以来重要文献选编], vol. I (Beijing: Central Literature Publishing House, 1991), 420–423.

3   Qi Dexue [齐德学], *History of the War to Resist U.S. Aggression and Aid Korea* [抗美援朝战争史] (Beijing: Military Science Publishing House [军事科学出版社], 2000), 185.

4   Roderick MacFarquhar and John K. Fairbank, eds., *The Cambridge History of China,* volume XIV: *The People's Republic of China 1949–1965* [剑桥中国史：中华人民共和国史] (Beijing: Social Science Press [中国社会科学出版社], 1998), 85–89.

5   Li Jianglin [李江琳], *When the Iron Bird Flies in the Sky* [当铁鸟在天空飞翔] (Taipei: Lianjing Press [联经出版社], 2012), 177.

6   MacFarquhar and Fairbank, 188.

7   Maurice Meisner, *Mao Zedong: A Political and Intellectual Portrait* [毛澤東之政治與知識的圖像] (Taipei: Citadel Press [衛城出版社], 2012), 280.

8   Zhang Li Qun [张黎群], ed., *Yearning Yaobang* [怀念耀邦], vol. IV (Hong Kong: Asia-Pacific International Press [亞太國際出版公司], 2001), 277–278.

9   Ezra F. Vogel [傅高义], *Deng Xiaoping and the Transformation of China* [鄧小平改變中國], trans. Feng Keli [馮克利] (Taipei: Commonwealth Publishing Company [天下文化出版社], 2012), 817.

10   Ibid., 830.

11   Li Peng [李鹏], *Li Peng Tiananmen Incident Diary* [李鹏六四日记] (Hong Kong: New Century Press [新世纪出版社], 2010), referring to April 23, 1989.

12   Jiang Zemin [江泽民], "Speech in the Inspection of the PAP Force Training Outcome Report" [在视察武警部队训练成果汇报时的讲话], in *On National Defense and Military Building* [论国防和军队建设] (Beijing: PLA Press [中国人民解放军出版社], 2003), 103–105.

13   Gordon G. Chang, *The Coming Collapse of China* [中國即將崩潰] (Taipei: Valued Advice Publishing Corporation [雅言文化出版股份有限公司], 2002), 67.

14   *PRC National Defense Law* (中华人民共和国国防法), August 2009, Article 22.

15   PRC Information Office of the State Council, *The Diversified Employment of China's Armed Forces*, Beijing, April 2013, 6.

16   Ibid., 12.

17   Ibid.

18   See "Fully Establish National Team of Contingency Response Force" [全力打造应急力量国家队]," *PLA Daily* [解放军报], September 6, 2012.

19   The "Regulations on Emergency Command in Handling Emergencies by the Armed Forces" [军队处置突发事件应急指挥规定] are cited in PRC Information Office of the State Council, *China's National Defense in 2010*, Beijing, March 2011, 24.

20   "China's Stability Maintenance Budget Exceeds Defense Budget" [陆维稳经费超过国防预算], *udn.com*, March 6, 2012, available at <http://udn.com./NEWS/MAINLAND/MAI1/6942695.shtml>.

21   Ben Blanchard and John Ruwitch, "China Hikes Defense Budget, to Spend More on Internal Security," Reuters, March 5, 2013, available at <www.reuters.com/article/2013/03/05/us-china-parliament-defence-idUSBRE92403620130305?_ga=1.56494827.1308442095.1407506011>.

22   Edward Wong, "Beijing Goes Quiet on Rise of Local Security Budgets," *New York Times*, March 6, 2014, available at <http://sinosphere.blogs.nytimes.com/2014/03/06/beijing-goes-quiet-on-rise-of-local-security-budgets/?_php=true&_type=blogs&_r=0.

23   PAP Mobile Divisions are equipped with the standard equipment of a former PLA infantry division. In recent years, they have added more ZSL92 wheeled armored vehicles and Z-9 helicopters. See Dennis J. Blasko, "Politics and the PLA: Security Social Stability," *China Brief* 12, no. 7 (March 30, 2012).

24   The PAP has fewer than 700,000 troops, subordinated to 10 different forces including the PAP Headquarters and its directly subordinate forces, the Internal Security Force, the Mobilized Division Force, the Hydropower Facilities Force, the Traffic Policing Force, the Gold Mining Force, and the Forest Guarding Force. Eighty-five percent of PAP Forces, mainly the Internal Security Force and the Mobilized Division Force, can conduct contingency response missions involving maintenance of social stability immediately after a riot emerges.

25   After the residents of Wukan Village swore that they would break the blockade, Guangdong officials held an emergency meeting, with PLA and PAP participation, to find a solution. See "Wukan Village Residents Break Out Tomorrow" [乌坎村民明突围], *udn.com*, December 20, 2011, available at <http://udn.com/NEWS/MAIN-LAND/MAI1/6792569.shtml>.

26   Ibid.

27   See "The Protest in Ningbo Works" [宁波抗争奏功], *China Times*, October 29, 2012, available at <http://news.chinatimes.com/main-land/11050506/112012102900144.html>.

28   See "The First Time of Public Security History to Mobilize Ten Thousands Military and Police in the Mainland" [陆治安史首见 动员上万军警], *China Times*, August 15, 2012, available at <http://news.chinatimes.com/main-land/11050506/112012081500177.html>.

29   See Murray Scot Tanner, "China's Social Unrest Problem," Testimony before the U.S.-China Economic and Security Review Commission, May 15, 2014, available at <www.uscc.gov/sites/default/files/Tanner_Written%20Testimony.pdf>; and Carl Minzner, "Social Instability in China: Causes, Consequences, and Implication," in *The China Balance Sheet in 2007 and Beyond*, ed. C. Fred Bergsten et al. (Washington, DC: Center for Strategic and International Studies and the Peterson Institute for International Economics, 2007), 55–77, available at <http://csis.org/files/media/csis/pubs/070502_cbs_in_2007_and_beyond.pdf>.

30   Even during the serious riot in Lhasa in March 2008, the PLA troops stationed there only provided transportation and security guard support after the PAP quelled the riot. See Dennis J. Blasko, *The Chinese Army Today: Tradition and Transformation for the 21st Century*, 2d ed. (London: Routledge, 2012), 217–218.

31   In the 1989 Tiananmen incident, when the PLA troops entered Beijing in May, students and local residents surrounded them and offered soldiers information on the appeals of the students. Since this information obviously differed from the official statements they received, the soldiers were confused and became hesitant to suppress the protests. This forced Deng Xiaoping to withdraw the troops to a suburban area of Beijing and mobilize other PLA troops, which were not sympathetic to students, from the Jinan Military Region.

32   Several investigative reports produced by the PLA military medical department or related academic institutes have revealed the psychological conditions of soldiers who had participated in stability maintenance missions. See Wang Yin Hu [王引虎], "Investigation of the health conditions and prevention measures of one armed forces unit soldiers during the implementation of stability maintenance mission" [某部执行维稳任务期间官兵健康状况调查与防治对策], *Southwest National Defense Medicine* [西南国防医药] 21, no. 2 (February 2011), 222–223.

33   See Wang Xiaobo, Yu Xiaohua, and Liu Weiping [王晓波, 于晓华, 刘卫平], "Investigation of Incidence Situation at an Emergency Response Troop Depot during the Field Training in Fall" [某应急兵站秋季野外驻训期间发病情况调查], *Southeast National Defense Medicine* 10, no. 2 (April 20, 2008), 157–158.

34   Zhang Yang [张阳], "Always Insisting the Party's Absolute Leadership over the Military" [始终不渝坚持党对军队绝对领导], *People's Daily* [人民日报], June 6, 2012.

35   According to official statistics published by the PRC National Statistics Bureau, the total number of mass riots in the PRC was 90,000 in 2005. This is the last time China published such statistics on its social unrest. According to academic estimates, the number of mass riots in 2010 had doubled over 2005 levels. Thus, the situation of social unrest has deteriorated. See Damien Ma, "Before and After Hu," *Foreign Affairs*, November 7, 2012, available at <www.foreignaffairs.com/articles/138419/damien-ma/before-and-after-hu>; Andrew Jacobs, "Village Revolts Over Inequities of Chinese Life," *New York Times*, December 14, 2011, available at <www.nytimes.com/2011/12/15/world/asia/chinese-village-locked-in-rebellion-against-authorities.html?pagewanted=all&_r=0; "China's Spending on Internal Police Force in 2010 Outstrips Defense Budget," Bloomberg, March 6, 2011, available at <www.bloomberg.com/news/2011-03-06/china-s-spending-on-internal-police-force-in-2010-outstrips-defense-budget.html>.

36   PLA General Political Department, "Opinions on widely carrying out educational activities on the subject of educating the core values of contemporary revolutionary soldier in the military" [关于在全军广泛开展培育当代革命军人核心价值观主题教育活动的意见], January 2009.

37   PLA General Political Department, "Opinions on thoroughly carrying out educational activities on the subject of educating the core values of the contemporary revolutionary soldier" [关于深入开展培育当代革命军人核心价值观主题教育活动的意见], January 2010; PLA General Political Department, "Opinions on surrounding firm-ideal belief and loyally fulfilling mission to thoroughly carrying out educational activities on the subject of educating the core values of the contemporary revolutionary soldier" [关于围绕坚定理想信念、忠实履行使命深入开展培育当代革命军人核心价值观主题教育活动的意见], January 2011.

38   For example, the PLA troops stationed in Zhangjiakou City, Hebei Province, donated to 53 poor villages. See "Zhangjiakou Military Sub-District Coordinated Station Troops to Support Poor Villages" [张家口军分区协调驻军对口支持贫困村], *China's National Defense Press* [中国国防报], March 22, 2012, 1.

39   PRC Information Office of the State Council, *The Diversified Employment of China's Armed Forces*, Beijing, April 2013, 11.

40   Ibid.

41   Ibid., 12.

42   Some of these few articles distinguish between suppression of mass riots and management of mass collective incidents. PLA forces can operate independently during riot suppression missions that have the potential to escalate into large-scale social unrest or rebellion. See Liu Xiaoli [刘小力], ed., *Studies of MOOTW on the Response of Army to Major Emergencies and Crises* [军队应对重大突发事件和危机非战争军事行动研究] (Beijing: National Defense University Press [国防大学出版社], 2009), 119–131.

43   Even in the serious Lhasa incident, in March 2008, the PLA troops only played transportation and communication roles; they did not participate in direct suppression of riots in the street. See Roy Kamphausen, David Lai, and Andrew Scobell, eds., *Beyond the Strait: PLA Missions other than Taiwan* (Carlisle, PA: Strategic Studies Institute, 2009), 64–98.

III

BORDER CONTINGENCIES

CHAPTER 9

The PLA and Cross-Border Contingencies in North Korea and Burma

Thomas Woodrow

Addressing the potential for Chinese cross-border contingencies should begin with a clear assessment of China's current interests, the basis for those interests, and how they might change over the course of the next decade as China's economic presence expands and its diplomatic and military leverage increases. With respect to the Democratic People's Republic of Korea (DPRK) and Burma, as with all neighboring countries on China's land borders, Beijing desires stability and seeks to avoid crises that could threaten its economic development and internal stability. This is especially true now as Beijing attempts to transition to a demand-growth economy and the Chinese Communist Party (CCP) emerges from a difficult transfer of power.

The foundation of China's strength lies in its economy; CCP leaders continue to follow the model laid down by former leader Deng Xiaoping of focusing on economic development as the means to strengthen the state. Maintaining stability along China's periphery serves this interest, and the current focus on economic development is likely to continue for at least the next decade. However, as Chinese power grows, this will embolden nationalist tendencies to see the periphery as an extension of a greater China, particularly along its littoral, and to see a "return" to past imperial economic and military preponderance as a natural and positive development. Under such circumstances, China's current emphasis on nonintervention and noninterference in the internal affairs of other countries might change.

The trend toward a more active policy is evident in new leader Xi Jinping's signature "China Dream" vision of "the great rejuvenation of the nation."[1] The manifestation of the China Dream in foreign policy is already causing greater friction with some neighbors as Beijing embraces a more aggressive policy in disputed maritime areas. Since 2012, the People's Republic of China (PRC) has greatly expanded its military and civil maritime presence in the East China Sea near the Japanese-administered Senkaku Islands and in the South China Sea near the Scarborough Shoal (in dispute with the Philippines), the Spratly Islands (in dispute with multiple nations, including Vietnam), and the Luconia Shoals (in dispute with Malaysia).[2] China's announcement of an East China Sea Air Defense Identification Zone (ADIZ) in November 2013 that included the Senkaku Islands caught the region by surprise; in testimony to the U.S. House Select Committee on Intelligence in February 2014, Director of National Intelligence James Clapper stated China was becoming "quite aggressive about asserting what they believe is their manifest destiny."[3] The unprecedented dispatch of a Chinese submarine to the Indian Ocean in January 2014 and subsequent deployment of a three-ship People's Liberation Army (PLA) Navy task force to the Indian Ocean via the Sunda Strait startled Australia and India.[4] These actions reflect China's ambitions to project power along its borders, littoral, and beyond to protect economic and security interests.

In its 2012 report to Congress, the U.S. Department of Defense described China's leaders as currently perceiving a "generally favorable external environment" with a "low threat of major power war."[5] Chinese leaders describe national strategic priorities as "core interests." Based on a 2010 foreign policy overview by then–State Councilor Dai Bingguo, China's core interests include "the political stability of China" and the "sovereignty and security, territorial integrity, and national unity of China."[6] These core interests can also be viewed as red lines indicating a Chinese threshold for the potential use of military force. Even in a period defined by a generally favorable external environment, threats to sovereignty, territorial integrity, security, and political stability would be triggers for potential military action by the PLA, the People's Armed Police (PAP), or both. China's civilian maritime patrol and law enforcement entities, recently consolidated into the China Coast Guard, are also increasingly being integrated into a comprehensive strategy with the PLA in the East China and South China seas.[7] The border regions adjoining North Korea and Burma clearly qualify as areas where China's core interests could be threatened and thus are likely to generate requirements for PLA and PAP contingency planning.

North Korea and Burma both represent special interests for China, the former due to its historical alliance and role as a buffer state and the latter because of resources, longstanding economic and military cooperation, and its position as a strategic gateway to the Indian Ocean for Chinese-built oil and gas pipelines. Current Chinese plans for cross-border contingencies in North Korea and Burma probably focus on protecting stability and preventing refugee flows, although the PLA must also be ready to deal with issues involving North Korean weapons of mass destruction (WMD) and potential military intervention by the United States or South Korea in the event of a North Korean collapse. By the end of the current decade, however, existing contingency plans will likely be modified to reflect expanding Chinese economic and security interests and a greater Chinese willingness to act unilaterally to protect its national interests.[8]

North Korea

The PLA has prepared contingency plans to respond to a crisis on the Korean Peninsula. According to 2007 interviews with PLA officers and Chinese academics, the PLA has at least three contingency plans for North Korea: humanitarian assistance and disaster relief; peacekeeping; and "environmental control" missions to secure "loose nukes" and deal with contamination following presumed U.S. strikes on North Korean nuclear facilities.[9] In addition, the 1961 Treaty of Friendship, Cooperation, and Mutual Assistance between China and North Korea, which calls for military assistance in the event of an attack leading to war, remains in effect. China therefore likely also plans for a range of other military contingencies in the event of a full-scale war involving U.S., South Korean, and/or United Nations forces.

China's perceptions of North Korea appear to have changed in recent years. Following North Korean missile and nuclear tests, China voted for United Nations Security Council resolutions 1718 (2006) and 1874 (2009), which imposed sanctions against the North Korean regime.[10] During this period, Chinese authorities allowed sharp debate over North Korea to appear in authoritative journals and newspapers.[11] A series of interviews with PLA officers and Chinese scholars in 2007 reflected a variety of opinions on China's relationship with North Korea, with some respondents arguing for the continuing strategic importance of a "buffer zone," while others opined that the fundamental nature of the relationship had changed to the extent that the mutual defense treaty should be scrapped.[12] U.S. experts believed the variety of Chinese views expressed may have reflected debates and policy differences at senior levels of the Chinese government, PLA, and CCP.[13] However, following the sinking of the South Korean naval ship *Cheon'an* and the subsequent North Korean shelling of South Korea's Yeonpyeong Island in 2010, China refrained from criticizing North Korea and appeared to side with Pyongyang's version of events, exacerbating relations with Seoul.[14] If there was a policy debate over North Korea in Beijing during this period, it appears to have been settled by the spring of 2010 in favor of maintaining the status quo and upholding the North's value as a buffer zone against potential U.S. and South Korean encroachment.

China's North Korean policy appeared unlikely to undergo major changes and instead remain focused on maintaining close governmental, party, and military relations with Pyongyang and promoting economic development and reform in North Korea. However, the relationship has frayed due to North Korean leader Kim Jong Un's December 2013 execution of his uncle Jang Song Taek in what may have been a power struggle over economic issues.[15] Jang was North Korea's point man in dealing with China on cross-border economic relations, including the Rason Economic and Trade Zone and port complex in the northeastern DPRK being co-developed by China and Russia. Rason was specifically mentioned in official charges against Jang; he was accused of an "act of treachery" for "selling off the land of the Rason economic and trade zone to a foreign country for a period of five decades."[16] According to foreign businessmen, as of February 2014, all construction activity had stopped at the port following Jang's purge, and many Chinese and Russians are afraid to return.[17] The dispatch of Chinese Vice Foreign Minister Liu Zhenmin to Pyongyang in late February 2014 likely included discussions on economic issues and Rason.[18] China's long-term strategy for the peninsula appears to center on convincing Pyongyang to engage in meaningful economic reform along the lines of Deng's reforms for China. However, the execution of Jang Song Taek threatens the few economic initiatives that have been allowed in North Korea and could put the Rason port development at risk.

China has revealed few details about its contingency plans. However, the locations and dispositions of PLA and PAP troops and comments by PRC officials on potential crisis scenarios offer clues. Beijing's primary focus appears to be on securing the border area to prevent a mass flow of North Korean refugees into heavily Korean ethnic areas on the PRC side of the border, which could potentially destabilize the delicate balance in a region that has historically been Korean rather than Chinese. Chinese officials have been relatively open about their concerns about refugee flows in the event of an economic, political, or military crisis within North Korea. The first responders in the event of a border crisis would be the PAP, which was established in 1982 and later reinforced with downsized and redundant PLA units. While falling under the peacetime authority of the Ministry of Public Security and primarily devoted to internal security, the PAP also has ancillary missions of counterterrorism, rapid response, and border control. The Snow Leopard commando unit highlighted during the Beijing 2008 Olympic Games is perhaps the best known PAP outfit. The Ministry of Public Security and the PLA General Staff apparently share command and control over PAP border units.[19] During wartime, most PAP units ostensibly would shift to PLA control.

There are at least four PAP Border Defense Regiments along the Sino-DPRK border in the general areas of Dandong, Tumen (where there are two), and Linjiang.[20] These units are strategically located to respond to incidents near the two main border crossings at Dandong and Tumen. The area of China's northern border in Liaoning and Jilin Provinces is ethnically Korean, especially in the Tumen region, and North Korean refugees who successfully cross into China often find refuge with and receive support from their ethnic brethren.[21] In light of continuing tensions with South Korea (and probably North Korea) over Chinese control in an area that historically has been Korean (the ancient regimes of Goguryeo and Balhae), Beijing likely would be concerned that large numbers of North Korean refugees seeking shelter near the northern border could cause instability and potentially undermine Chinese authority.

PAP and PLA troops could potentially cross the border into North Korea to set up a "buffer zone" to contain and prevent Korean refugee flows into China and to provide humanitarian assistance to keep potential refugees in place inside North Korea. A Chinese presence on North Korean territory would be a necessary part of a peacekeeping operation there. China might also intervene across the border for other contingencies, such as controlling DPRK WMD stocks or protecting Chinese security interests in the event of U.S. or South Korean intervention. Beijing would almost certainly worry that South Korea and the United States could seek to take advantage of a regime collapse to change the status quo on the peninsula in ways that do not serve Chinese interests.[22] The trial of South Korean spy Park Chae-seo revealed the existence of a so-called PLA "Chick Plan" (as in a hen protecting its chick) in which PLA troops would cross the border if the situation in North Korea "deteriorated beyond repair."[23] The South Korean press has also reported that the PLA Academy of Military Sciences (AMS) examined various contingency scenarios in 2007, resulting in an AMS report that stated PLA troops could reach Pyongyang "in two hours" in the event of a disaster.[24]

The PLA is well positioned to respond to a variety of cross-border contingencies involving North Korea. The Shenyang Military Region (MR) contains the 39th Group Army (GA), which has its headquarters at Liaoyang. The U.S. Department of Defense assesses that the 39th GA has the primary PLA missions for regional rapid reaction and mobile offensive operations.[25] The 16th and 40th Group Armies, at Changchun and Jinzhou, respectively, would also probably have major roles in responding to any North Korea contingency.[26] PLA Air Force (PLAAF) assets in the Shenyang MR include three fighter divisions and one ground-attack division.[27] In total, roughly a quarter-million PLA troops could be rapidly mobilized in the Shenyang MR for a Korean contingency. In addition to these forces, the PLA Navy North Sea Fleet has at its disposal 3 nuclear attack submarines, 18 diesel attack submarines, 10 destroyers, 9 frigates, 2 amphibious ships, 5 medium landing ships and 19 missile patrol boats.[28] China's new aircraft carrier, the *Liaoning*, is also located in the North Sea Fleet. The North Sea Fleet PLA Navy Air Force provides an additional two fighter and fighter-bomber divisions.[29]

Other PLA units from the Beijing MR or elsewhere could be rapidly deployed into a Korean operational theater. The 2010 PLA Mission Action exercise involved group army–level units from multiple MRs in an unprecedented long-distance force mobilization using military and civilian transit means; the theme of a border conflict was the likely exercise scenario.[30] Smaller PLA river-crossing exercises with pontoon bridges occur annually in the summer along the Yalu River near Dandong.[31]

An environmental control contingency to secure "loose nukes" in North Korea or to decontaminate North Korean facilities offers another potential scenario in which China might seek to insert PLA troops into North Korea. PAP forces are not known to have decontamination units, whereas the PLA has practiced with them for decades (stemming from the belief from the 1960s through the 1980s that a nuclear strike would be a component of an attack from the Soviet Union). The PLA would face two challenges in executing plans for this contingency: first, knowing where North Korean nuclear facilities and weapons are located, and second, obtaining acquiescence from Pyongyang to enter DPRK sovereign territory and take control of its nuclear weapons. Any PLA incursion into North Korea that came uninvited would likely face stiff resistance from the highly nationalistic North Korean military, even given long-standing lip service to the "lips and teeth" relationship between the two sides.

The PLA likely also has a variety of contingency plans for a potential war on the Korean Peninsula. How the PLA would respond to a war would depend on the specific conditions of how the war started, whether Pyongyang requested activation of the Mutual Defense Treaty (which calls for military assistance in the event of an attack leading to war), and the level of involvement by the United States. China would almost certainly seek to prevent tensions from escalating to war but might misjudge the trajectory of a particular crisis or the danger of a crisis rapidly escalating out of control. The reactions of Beijing, Pyongyang, and Seoul to the sinking of the *Cheon'an* and the subsequent North Korean shelling of South Korea's Yeonpyeong Island in 2010 offer a case in point.

If the scenario involved potential regime collapse in North Korea, Beijing would probably be very suspicious that South Korea would seek to take advantage of the situation to change the status quo and/or unify the peninsula. China might institute a range of actions to support Pyongyang; direct military support would be heavily influenced by the response of Seoul and Washington to instability in the north and the status of South Korean and U.S. forces along the Demilitarized Zone (DMZ). Any crossing of the DMZ, even under the rubric of humanitarian assistance, would probably be seen by China as a threat to its interests unless understandings are reached in advance. Given increased economic and diplomatic China–Republic of Korea interaction over the past decade, any major instability in North Korea would surely precipitate high-level discussions between Beijing and Seoul. A likely Chinese demand under any crisis scenario would be the exclusion of U.S. troops from any role north of the DMZ.

In contrast, if Beijing were unable to prevent a war initiated by North Korea, either by Pyongyang acting against China's wishes or through lack of foreknowledge, there is no guarantee Beijing would activate the Mutual Defense Treaty, which stipulates in Article II that "in the event of one of the Contracting Parties being subjected to the armed attack by any state or several states jointly and thus being involved in a state of war, the other Contracting Party shall immediately render military and other assistance by all means at its disposal."[32] Thus, a conflict initiated by North Korea (or one assessed by Beijing to have been initiated by the North) probably would not automatically result in activation of the treaty. The Article II clause likely would be used by China as a lever of influence over Pyongyang's actions during rapidly rising tensions if Beijing had serious concerns over provocations by North Korea potentially dragging China into a war on the peninsula against its wishes.

In the event of a war initiated by South Korea (which China would almost certainly see as having at least tacit U.S. support), Beijing would begin to implement various operational contingencies, at least some of which would probably involve PLA troops crossing into North Korea and establishing positions to support Pyongyang and potentially repel South Korean/U.S. advances. Under this hypothetical scenario, China would see the conflict as an attempt to change the status quo and eliminate or reduce North Korea's role as a "buffer zone" protecting the PRC. Beijing's control over ethnic Korean areas in China could also be seen as under threat; Beijing's claims to legitimate control could be threatened under a scenario in which millions of Koreans flooded across the border. Thus, a military conflict would directly threaten several Chinese core interests (including security, sovereignty, and territorial integrity). Under such circumstances, the PLA would almost certainly initiate Korea-related operational contingency plans to protect Chinese interests.

A major unanswered question is whether a conflict on the peninsula could escalate into a situation where PLA and U.S. troops would face each other in a reprise of the Korean War. Such a scenario, while seemingly unlikely, should not be automatically discounted in the event of a rapidly escalating crisis. History books are littered with lessons on the unintended consequences of war.

Outlook for North Korea Contingencies

Over the course of the next decade, as China's economic, diplomatic, and military leverage increases and comprehensive Chinese power grows, it will probably embolden nationalist tendencies to see the periphery as an extension of a greater China. Growing Chinese economic development in North Korea likely will change the equation used to determine when to activate the PLA's plans for cross-border contingencies. The establishment in 2010 of the Hwanggumpyong and Wiwha Islands Joint Free Trade Area on the Yalu River estuary near Dandong and the Rason Economic and Trade Zone in North Korea's far northeast, if allowed to continue by Kim Jong Un, could greatly expand Chinese economic stakes in the DPRK.

While the Hwanggumpyong and Wiwha Islands Joint Free Trade Area has apparently received a lukewarm response from Chinese businessmen due to the unsuitability of the location for a trade center, China appears willing to embark on some level of development to keep Pyongyang happy.[33] A series of high-level PRC-DPRK meetings and steering group sessions in 2012 continued to lay the foundations for development of both economic zones.[34]

The Rajin Port and Rason Economic and Trade Zone is by far the more important of the two, for it will provide access to ice-free ports on the Sea of Japan and trade links with China's Jilin Province. An initial 2008 agreement with the Dalian-based Chuangli Group allowed this PRC firm to expand port facilities in Rajin and Sonbong (that is, Rason) and provided for a minimum 10-year lease.[35] A subsequent series of agreements in 2011 extended the Chinese lease to 50 years and paved the way for large-scale investment in railway and road links to China, an airport, additional port facilities, and a power plant.[36] Rason also has some Russian investment, but will be used by China to extend direct trade access for northeastern areas of the PRC. Beijing also hopes these investments will prod the Kim Jung Un regime into opening the North Korean economy for further development.

Within a few years, Rason is likely to become a strategic gateway and port facility, absent a major falling out between Beijing and Pyongyang. This would in effect create an economic extension of China and could prompt Beijing to include this area in any cross-border contingency planning. Improvements in rail and road access from China could improve China's capability to deploy and support PLA units in North Korea. Over time, the PLA could even be granted access to or use of the port facilities. An evolving PRC-DPRK economic dynamic and expanding Chinese investment inside North Korea will inevitably result in a concomitant expansion in PRC security concerns regarding the Korean Peninsula.

By the end of the current decade, Chinese cross-border contingency plans for North Korea, which currently are focused primarily on maintaining stability and preventing refugee flows, are likely to be modified to reflect expanding Chinese economic and security interests and Beijing's greater self-confidence to act unilaterally to protect and project its own interests.

Burma

Burma shares some commonalities with North Korea in terms of potential PLA contingency planning, especially China's focus on concerns about stability and cross-border refugee flows. Like North Korea, Burma has a history of extensive military and political ties with China. However, unlike North Korea, Burma does not have a mutual defense treaty or an alliance with the PRC. Recent leadership changes in both countries have increased tensions in relations with China and prompted Burma's leaders to try to move away from near-total dependence on Beijing.[37]

China currently has much more extensive economic interests in Burma than in North Korea. These interests (a massive Chinese economic presence and large-scale construction of dams, roads, pipelines, and ports linking the southwestern province of Yunnan to the Bay of Bengal through Burma) will over time make the northern portion of Burma, where the pipeline and road corridor connect southern China to the Indian Ocean, a vital strategic interest to China. This will give China incentives to try to draw Burma ever more tightly into the Chinese economic orbit. Many recent refugee issues stem directly from the massive Chinese economic presence and large-scale construction projects in Burma.

Concern over refugees flowing into China is another area where similarities exist. In both countries, non-Han ethnic groups are divided by a border, and instability south of the border has at times sent refugees fleeing into China. Concern about the impact on domestic stability of a long-term presence of displaced ethnic minorities in China is a driver for PLA planning for border contingencies in Burma. Unlike the China–North Korea border, where a single trans-border ethnic Korean community exists, the border between China and Burma divides multiple ethnic groups, including Christian Kachins, ethnic Chinese Kokangs, Buddhist Tibetans, Muslim Rohingya, Austroasiatic Blang, De'ang, and Va, Achang, Nu, and Zaiwa and a hodgepodge of at least a dozen other minorities, all of whom can be found on both sides of the border.[38] Disputes between any of these groups and the central government—or between different ethnic groups—could produce significant refugee flows into China. The maintenance of PRC authority in areas of Yunnan, where Chinese culture historically has not been dominant, is Beijing's overriding security concern in this region.

Unlike on the Korean Peninsula, China faces no serious threat of intervention from foreign military forces in the event of instability in Burma. In contrast with areas to the west and east, where the existence of large opposing Indian and Vietnamese military forces shape PLA security concerns, PLA and PAP forces along the border with Burma are focused on maintaining border security, preventing internal instability, and managing refugee flows. The PLA likely does not currently devote significant effort to planning for larger scale military contingencies in this area. However, this could change in the future as vital land trade and energy routes through Burma become more important as alternatives to the Malacca Strait.

There are two key challenges emerging from the complex situation along China's border with Burma: ethnic Kachins seeking refuge in China due to increased military pressure from the Burma Army in the far north, where major Chinese dam projects have exacerbated tensions, and ethnic Chinese Kokangs further south who have sought refuge in China due to fighting between the Burma Army and the semi-autonomous Shan State. In addition, although not a border issue, recent conflict between ethnic Buddhists and Muslims in the Rakhine area is also a concern for China, as the terminus of the huge road-rail-pipeline network linking Yunnan to the Bay of Bengal lies there.

The PAP currently has two Border Defense Regiments (BDRs) on the border with Burma: the 11th BDR located at Cangyuan, and the 12th BDR at Luxi.[39] An additional three BDRs are located within the Chengdu Military Region, and could be used for border or cross-border Burma contingencies: the 9th BDR at Diqing, the 10th BDR at Lincang, and the 8th BDR located near the border with Laos at Mengla.[40] PLA units within the Chengdu MR that would probably play a role in any expanded border contingency are located within the 14th Group Army, headquartered at Kunming.[41] The 13th Group Army is located farther north in the Chengdu MR but could be deployed south if needed.[42] The assessed missions of the 13th and 14th GA are defensive and offensive operations in complex terrain, and thus these group armies routinely train for mountain operations.[43]

PLAAF assets within the Chengdu MR include two fighter divisions and one transport division.[44] As noted, the PLA has in recent years focused on rapid mobility training to respond to border contingencies, as highlighted by the Mission Action group army–level exercises in 2010 and 2013.[45] Thus, the PLA could even today mobilize and deploy large numbers of troops to support a Burma contingency if required. The new Chinese superhighway 320 runs from Shanghai to the border with Burma at Ruili and will eventually be extended through Burma, all the way to Mandalay and down to the port city of Kyaukpyu.[46] The new rail and road networks would improve the PLA's ability to deploy forces into Burma and provide the logistics support necessary for them to operate.

Periodic offensives by Burmese government forces against ethnic minority militias and the displacements connected to Chinese economic development are both root causes of refugees crossing into China, facilitated by large-scale

Chinese development of road, rail, and pipeline links through northern Burma. Increased military pressure from the Burmese army in the far north where the Kachin reside has resulted in thousands of refugees fleeing into China to seek shelter with Kachin groups north of the border. Some 120,000 Kachin reside in China as PRC citizens, and at least 50,000 live in the Shan State region of Burma. The Kachin minority in Burma has fought for greater autonomy for decades, and the Kachin Independence Army (KIA) has waged a series of on-and-off battles over the years with Burma's military. The recent initiation of major dam projects along upper tributaries of the Irrawaddy River in northern Burma (in particular, the now-stalled Myitsone Dam) has exacerbated tensions with the Kachin and contributed to an increase in fighting between the KIA and central government forces. At least seven large dams are planned or in construction in the middle of Kachin territory to provide hydroelectric energy to China. Most of these projects are under Chinese control; construction has resulted in the forced dislocation of thousands of Kachin and stimulated anti-Chinese sentiment. This, together with Burma's attempts to force all ethnic separatist groups to give up their arms and submit to central authority, is responsible for ending a 17-year peace agreement between the KIA and the central government authorities in Naypyidaw in June 2011 and a major uptick in fighting and increased refugee flows into China.[47]

Up to 10,000 Kachin refugees crossed the border in 2011–2012 and currently remain in squalid camps on the PRC side of the border.[48] Beijing, however, refuses to acknowledge the status of these Kachin as refugees to avoid having to abide by sanctuary provisions contained in the 1951 United Nations (UN) Refugee Convention Agreement, of which China is a signatory. Instead, Chinese authorities, using the PAP and other internal security forces, regularly force Kachin refugees back across the border into Burma, where they face extreme hardship and even death at the hands of the Burma armed forces.[49] Human Rights Watch and Christian refugee support organizations have accused Beijing of systematic human rights violations against these Kachin minorities.[50] Following an expulsion of 5,000 Kachin in September 2012 by PAP and local militia, the UN Refugee Agency called on Beijing to abide by its commitments to protect and shelter displaced refugees.[51] Yunnan provincial authorities have stated that at least some of the PAP expulsions of Kachin came under direct orders from Beijing.[52] PRC leaders who ordered the expulsions likely became concerned over the presence of large numbers of ethnic Kachin in sensitive border areas; there may have also been an agreement with Burma to send the refugees back across the border.

A separate ethnic conflict further south on the China-Burma border involves the ethnic Chinese Kokangs and their armed resistance to the entry of central government forces into the semi-autonomous Shan State. An increase in fighting occurred in 2009 when the Burmese military attempted to bring the region under central control, which resulted in at least 50,000 Kokang fleeing across the border into China. Unlike the Kachin, the ethnic Chinese Kokang were treated well by Yunnan provincial authorities. Some Chinese claimed the offensive against the Kokang was driven in part by discrimination against Chinese businessmen in Burma and a reaction against the rapid penetration of Burma by PRC firms.[53] The PRC Ministry of Foreign Affairs issued a statement in August 2009 calling on Burma to "properly handle domestic problems and maintain stability in the China-Burma border region" and urging Burma to "protect the security and legal rights of Chinese citizens in Burma."[54] Subsequently, Beijing sent PAP and possibly PLA forces to the border area and dispatched a senior emissary to Burma for talks. Burmese authorities later "apologized" for causing instability along China's border.[55]

China's close relationships with the Kokang and the United Wa State Army located to the south of Kokang areas in Burma have important implications for potential future contingencies involving the border region. Burma's stepped-up military efforts since 2009 to bring the long-autonomous ethnic regions in northern and eastern Burma under central control have displaced tens of thousands of refugees who have crossed the border into China. Offensives against the Kokang and United Wa State Army appear designed in part to sever the close relationships these two ethnically Chinese minority groups have had with the PRC.

Outlook for Burma Contingencies

The network of highways, railroad, and gas and oil pipelines that China is constructing through Burma to link Yunnan to the port at Kyaukpyu will open the southern region of China to rapid economic expansion and serve as a vital gateway to African and Middle Eastern markets as well as a transit corridor for energy imports. The gas pipeline, capable of carrying 12 billion cubic meters of gas a year, became operational in 2013. Construction of an oil pipeline capable of carrying up to 440,000 barrels per day to China was completed in August 2014 and was expected to become operational by the end of 2014.[56]

The rapidly growing strategic importance of the trade network through Burma linking China to the Bay of Bengal, which will allow for an alternate transit route bypassing the Strait of Malacca, will change the dynamic of Beijing's strategic interests over the next decade and likely result in additional cross-border contingency planning for PLA forces stationed in the Chengdu Military Region bordering Burma. These contingencies, which now likely encompass border and internal security, will probably be expanded to address China's growing economic and strategic interests in Burma.

These road and rail networks will facilitate expanded Chinese economic penetration into Burma. The transit corridor that links Kunming to Kyaukpyu cuts through the heart of ethnic minority areas on the Burma side of the border. Beijing likely views the Kokang and Wa as natural allies for future security in an area that will assume increasing strategic importance for China. Although not strictly a border issue, recent conflict in the Rakhine area of Burma between ethnic Buddhists and Muslims is also a concern for China, as the terminus of the huge road-rail-pipeline network linking Yunnan to the Bay of Bengal lies at Kyaukpyu in Rakhine. The nearby offshore A-1 Shwe gas field is being exploited by the Chinese firm PetroChina and will be linked into the trans-Burma gas pipeline.

The recognition by the Burma central government of the dynamics of increasing Chinese influence likely precipitated the October 2011 suspension of the China Power Investment Corporation's $3.6 billion Myitsone Dam project and Burma's decision to engage in a limited democratic opening of the political system that resulted in a rapprochement with the international community and an end to many international sanctions.

Burma's military may also be having second thoughts about its relationship with the PLA, especially as alternative weapons suppliers become available. Army officers reportedly recently told a visiting academic from the London School of Economics that PLA-supplied hardware and weapons were of very low quality, with one officer stating, "The Chinese cheated us. They've given us all this crap and taken our resources."[57]

While Burma is unlikely to embark on an explicit strategic tilt toward the United States and against China, the visit of U.S. President Barack Obama to Burma in 2014 has compelled Beijing to regard its relations with Burma in a new light. The decision by Burma to reposition itself to shed its pariah image and balance Chinese and outside influence raises the stakes for Beijing. Given the long history of anti-China sentiment in Burma, the Chinese leadership cannot guarantee that huge Chinese investments in Burma will remain safe or that strategic transport links between Kunming and the Bay of Bengal will remain open in the event of a regional crisis. Thus, it is almost certain that the PLA will be tasked to plan for future cross-border contingencies to secure PRC strategic and economic interests in Burma.

Conclusion

In both North Korea and Burma, current PLA and PAP operations and contingency plans appear to focus primarily on maintaining border security and guarding against political or military developments that might send additional refugees across the border into China. Nearby PLA and PAP units assigned to these missions appear to have well-equipped forces; improvements in cross-border road and rail networks and in the PLA ability to transport and provide logistics support for deployed forces would probably be sufficient to support limited cross-border operations to contain refugee flows if greater instability breaks out inside North Korea or Burma. PLA units deployed near North Korea must also be prepared to cross the border to secure WMD in the event of a regime collapse and to prepare for potential higher end contingencies, such as peacekeeping or humanitarian assistance operations throughout the DPRK or (potentially) combat with U.S. or South Korean forces attempting to unilaterally reunify the two Koreas. These would be much more demanding missions. Although such higher end contingencies appear unlikely at present, the situation inside North Korea could change quickly. That is why contingency planning exists and why the PLA units with responsibility for Korean contingencies follow the situation in Korea closely.

Over the longer term, Chinese political relations with North Korea and Burma may deteriorate even as Chinese economic and security interests deepen. Chinese economic interests in North Korea are less critical than those in Burma, and strains in relations with Pyongyang may limit deepening of economic ties. However, if Kim Jong Un's international behavior and pursuit of WMD capabilities threaten to destabilize the region and damage China's burgeoning economic and political relationship with Seoul, there may come a point at which Beijing feels compelled to take action. In Burma, Chinese economic interests within the country and the strategic value of an alternative transit route for goods, oil, and natural gas that connects China and the Indian Ocean will only continue to increase. Burma's strategic value to Beijing will grow. If bilateral political ties remain strained and the central government appears unable or unwilling to protect the oil and gas pipelines and transit routes, a stronger China may relax its policy of noninterference in the internal affairs of other countries in order to protect its interests. Under such circumstances, the PLA may need to plan for and potentially execute a broader range of missions inside Burma, ranging from security assistance and counterinsurgency training up to deployments inside Burma to protect the pipelines and other Chinese interests. This would be a significant shift from today's more limited operations and contingency planning.

Notes

1   Xi Jinping's first expanded explanation of his China Dream vision was promulgated in March 2013. It remains a point of debate among scholars whether Xi's China Dream was influenced more by Thomas Friedman's October 2012 *New York Times* article or the nationalistic 2010 anti-U.S. book *China Dream: The Great Power Thinking and Strategic Positioning of China in the Post-American Age* [中国梦: 后美国时代的大国思维与战略定位] by PLA Col. Liu Mingfu [刘明福]. The PLA clearly interprets the China Dream as more aligned with Liu's prediction of an eventual power struggle with the United States for global supremacy.

2   Carl Thayer, "Tensions Set to Rise in the South China Sea," *The Diplomat*, February 19, 2014, available at <http://thediplomat.com/2014/02/tensions-set-to-rise-in-the-south-china-sea/>.

3   Ibid.

4   Henry Lawton, "Australia Startled by Chinese Naval Excursion," *The Diplomat*, February 15, 2014, available at <http://thediplomat.com/2014/02/australia-startled-by-chinese-naval-excursion/>.

5   Office of the Secretary of Defense (OSD), *Military and Security Developments Involving the People's Republic of China*, Annual Report to Congress, 2012 (Washington, DC: Office of the Secretary of Defense, May 2012), 2.

6   OSD, *Military and Security Developments Involving the People's Republic of China*, Annual Report to Congress, 2011 (Washington, DC: Office of the Secretary of Defense, 2011), 13.

7   See Linda Jakobson, "The PLA and Maritime Security Actors," in *PLA Influence on China's National Security Policymaking*, ed. Phillip C. Saunders and Andrew Scobell (Stanford: Stanford University Press, 2015), 300–323.

8   Mathieu Duchâtel, Oliver Bräuner, and Zhou Hang, *Protecting China's Overseas Interests: The Slow Shift away from Non-interference*, SIPRI Policy Paper No. 41 (Stockholm: Stockholm International Peace Research Institute, 2014).

9   Bonnie Glaser, Scott Snyder, and John S. Park, *Keeping an Eye on an Unruly Neighbor: Chinese Views of Economic Reform and Stability in North Korea*

(Washington, DC: Center for Strategic and International Studies and the U.S. Institute of Peace, 2008), 5.

10   Dick K. Nanto and Mark E. Manyin, *China-North Korea Relations*, CRS Report for Congress R41043 (Washington, DC: Congressional Research Service, 2010), 3.

11   Ibid., 3.

12   Glaser, Snyder, and Park, 8–9.

13   Ibid., 7.

14   Nanto and Manyin, 3–5.

15   Barbara Demick, "Purge of Kim Jong Un's Uncle Unsettles North Korean Businesspeople," *Los Angeles Times*, February 15, 2014; and Jayshree Bajoria and Beina Xu, "The China-North Korea Relationship," Council on Foreign Relations, February 18, 2014, available at <www.cfr.org/china/china-north-korea-relationship/p11097>.

16   Demick.

17   Ibid.

18   "China sends top envoy to N. Korea after purge, says official," Agence France-Press, February 17, 2014, available at <www.themalaymailonline.com/world/article/china-sends-top-envoy-to-n.korea-after-purge-says-official>.

19   Dennis J. Blasko, "PLA Ground Force Modernization and Mission Diversification: Underway in all Military Regions," in *Right Sizing the People's Liberation Army: Exploring the Contours of China's Military*, ed. Andrew Scobell and Roy Kamphausen (Carlisle, PA: Strategic Studies Institute, 2007), 360–373.

20   Ibid.

21   *National Geographic Atlas of China* (Washington, DC: National Geographic Society, 2010), 53.

22   Glaser, Snyder, and Park, 15, 19.

23   Kim Jong-dae, "The Chinese People's Liberation Army, the Taedonggang North Occupation," *Defence 21*, May 25, 2011, available at <http://defence21.hani.co.kr/9875>.

24   "China Can Enter P'yang in 2 Hours in Case of Contingency," *Dong-A Ilbo*, January 25, 2012.

25   OSD, *Military and Security Developments* (2012), 30.

26   Ibid.

27   Ibid., 32.

28   Ibid., 31.

29   Ibid., 32.

30   OSD, *Military and Security Developments* (2011), 5.

31   "China Conducts River Crossing Drill at North Korean Border," *Chosun Ilbo*, June 14, 2012, available at <http://english.chosun.com/site/data/html_dir/2012/06/14/2012061401080.html>.

32   "Treaty of Friendship, Co-operation and Mutual Assistance Between the People's Republic of China and the Democratic People's Republic of Korea," *Peking Review* 4, no. 28 (1961), 5.

33   Scott Snyder and See-won Byun, "China-Korea Relations: Managing Relations Amidst Power Transitions," *Comparative Connections* 14, no. 2 (September 2012).

34   Ibid.

35   "China's Jilin Wins Use of N. Korean Sea Port," *Chosun Ilbo*, March 9, 2010, available at <http://english.chosun.com/site/data/html_dir/2010/03/09/2010030900360.html>.

36   "China Agrees to Invest $3 Bln in N. Korea Trade Zone," Agence France-Presse, February 14, 2012.

37   See Yun Sun, "China and the Changing Myanmar," *Journal of Current Southeast Asian Affairs* 31, no. 4 (2012), 51–77.

38   *National Geographic Atlas of China*, 53.

39   Blasko.

40   Ibid.

41   Ibid.

42   OSD, *Military and Security Developments* (2012), 30.

43   Ibid.

44   Ibid., 32.

45   OSD, *Military and Security Developments Involving the People's Republic of China*, Annual Report to Congress, 2014 (Washington, DC: Office of the Secretary of Defense, May 2014), 5, 20.

46   Patrick Boehler, "China's Gateway to Myanmar Booming," *The Irrawaddy*, January 31, 2012.

47   Human Rights Watch, *Myanmar: Isolated in Yunnan* (New York: Human Rights Watch, June 2012), available at <www.hrw.org/sites/default/files/reports/china0612_forinsertForUpload_0.pdf>.

48   James Humphries, "Kachin/China Relationships," Kachin Wilderness Trumpeters blog, July 13, 2012, available at <www.kachinwildernesstrumpeters.com/2012/07/kachin-china-relationships.html>.

49   Ibid.

50   Ibid.

51   "China Chastised for Sending Kachin People Back to Myanmar," *Los Angeles Times*, September 7, 2012, available at <http://latimesblogs.latimes.com/world_now/2012/09/china-chastised-for-sending-kachin-people-back-to-myanmar.html>.

52   Human Rights Watch.

53   Larry Jagan, "Border war rattles China-Myanmar ties," *Asia Times*, September 1, 2009, available at <www.atimes.com/atimes/Southeast_Asia/KI01Ae04.html>.

54   "Kokang Fighters Flee to China," *Radio Free Asia*, August 31, 2009, available at <www.unhcr.org/refworld/docid/4a9fcd58c.html>.

55   Jagan.

56   Ilyas Sumar, "Oil News: Pipelines from Myanmar to China," *HEFFX Live Trading News*, February 7, 2014, available at <http://www.livetradingnews.com/oil-news-pipelines-from-myanmar-to-china-30232.htm#>; and "China-Myanmar joint pipeline starts delivering gas," CCTV, August 6, 2014, available at <http://english.cntv.cn/2014/08/06/VIDE1407301800241634.shtml>.

57   Evan Osnos, "The Burmese Spring," *The New Yorker*, August 6, 2012, 58.

PLA Contingency Planning and the Case of India

Larry M. Wortzel

Fifty years ago, China and India fought a brief but fierce war over disputed territorial claims in two major areas along their mutual border.[1] Today, despite decades of diplomacy and confidence-building measures, the basic conditions that led to war in 1962 have not changed. Each side refuses to yield on its basic territorial claims and mutual distrust remains high, although the intensity of concerns over the potential for conflict is probably higher in India than in China. Both the People's Liberation Army (PLA) and Indian armed forces train for border conflict, and each force ensures that lessons the respective militaries drew from the 1962 war are applied to planning for future contingencies.

Neither country had nuclear weapons when the Sino-Indian border war was fought. Cyber warfare did not exist; satellite communications and space-based surveillance were not yet part of normal military functions. There was no maritime involvement in 1962, and neither India nor China had a strong navy. Although air forces were moved near the border for contingency use in 1962, there was no conflict in the air. Today, although the likelihood of another border war is low, should one occur, the conflict would likely be wider than the ground battles fought in 1962. Air engagement, the use of ballistic missile forces, attacks in space, and cyber warfare would be part of any future conflict. Indeed, both sides plan for such contingencies. Both China and India would likely try to avoid the use of nuclear weapons, but both have nuclear arsenals. This study briefly examines the flashpoints that could lead to conflict as well as the domains of war where conflict may occur. Notwithstanding recent hype about maritime rivalry in the Indian Ocean, the most likely location for conflict between China and India is along the extended land-locked high-altitude border the two countries share.

This chapter first reviews the potential flashpoints and explains why a contingency between China and India is far more likely to involve land power than sea power. The chapter then examines five factors that will help determine the likelihood, nature, scope, and escalation potential of any future conflict between China and India. These factors are the deep mutual mistrust and enduring land border dispute between Beijing and New Delhi, civil-military relations, economic relations, nuclear postures, and lessons of Sino-Indian warfighting, notably those learned by China during the 1962 border war.

Potential Flashpoints: Maritime Hype and Himalayan Hotspots

China and India are both engaged in an increasing amount of naval activity in the Indian Ocean, the Pacific Ocean, and the South China Sea.[2] At least on the Indian side, there seems to be a lot of bluster about the possibility of hostile encounters with the PLA Navy.[3] In real-life encounters, however, the Indian side seems to understand that the closer they get to China, the more the PLA has the upper hand, a realization that keeps encounters from becoming conflicts.[4] Indian naval officers probably understand that as a relatively small navy without extensive force projection capabilities or experience, their ships would be outgunned and would be operating without strong logistics support on the eastern side of the Malacca Strait. Political leaders in New Delhi are likely to exercise restraint in the maritime domain, while not conceding India's economic interests or the right to conduct ship visits and transit the open seas.

Two recent Chinese military activities drew attention from India and demonstrate that there is some potential for conflict in the Indian Ocean. First, in late 2013, a Chinese *Shang*-class nuclear attack submarine conducted a 2-month patrol in the Indian Ocean, returning to its base on Hainan Island on February 20, 2014.[5] In addition, the PLA Navy conducted exercises in the South China Sea and then in the eastern Indian Ocean with a three-ship task force in February 2014.[6] During the course of a 23-day deployment, the amphibious ship *Changbaishan* and two destroyers, the *Wuhan* and the *Haikou*, operating as what the United States would call a surface action group or expeditionary strike group, passed through the Sunda Strait, conducted an antipiracy exercise near Bali, and then passed though the Lombok Strait back into the Western Pacific.[7] Chinese officials said the deployment was part of normal antipiracy patrols, but one retired Indian rear admiral saw it as "a reconnaissance probe, the prelude to a full-scale deployment."[8]

In the Indian Ocean, China is increasing its own naval presence, seeking places to refuel, reprovision, repair, and rest, and backing up its interests with investments.[9] China has deployed 20 small navy task forces to conduct counter-piracy operations in the Gulf of Aden. In the Persian Gulf, China has backed up its close relationship with Pakistan with investment in ports, increased trade, and ship visits.[10] Both the Chinese and Indian navies eye each other warily over China's investments in Myanmar and Sri Lanka and the potential for the PLA Navy to use ports there.[11] Moreover, as both China and India begin to operate aircraft carrier battle groups and perhaps start intermittent submarine patrols, there is always the possibility of maritime or air conflict.

However, when questioned about the potential for misunderstanding or conflict as China increases its expeditionary deployments and operations in the Indian Ocean, a senior PLA officer brushed off any concerns.[12] The officer opined that as long as China's naval forces operate in international waters and stay out of India's exclusive economic zone, exercises or deployments in or through the Indian Ocean would not be a matter of concern.

Neither China nor India will be capable of sustained air or naval operations at long distances from their homelands for some time, and certainly not before 2020. Both navies and air forces would have to operate on extended lines of communication in any conflict, and both would face logistics constraints. Leaders in New Delhi and Beijing are aware of these limitations. Over this period, there is a chance for some conflict, although not a high likelihood. Beijing is sensitive to the fact that Japan and Vietnam would like to see a greater Indian naval presence in the Pacific; New Delhi is sensitive to the growing Chinese naval presence in the Indian Ocean. However, the likelihood is low that China and India would engage in a major maritime or air conflict that would impede international shipping and aviation.

The Sino-Indian frontier, however, is another matter. Both countries are extremely sensitive to sovereignty issues along the border. China's support for Pakistan and the roads it has built are real irritants to India, while refuge for the Dalai Lama and India's support for the Tibetan exile government annoy China. China's border with India is some 3,380 kilometers long. China has two major claims and one smaller claim on what India considers its territory. In the western sector of the border, in the Ladakh District of Jammu and Kashmir, China claims the Aksai Chin.[13] In this western sector, the People's Republic of China (PRC) holds some 43,180 square kilometers of what India claims as its territory, including some 5,180 square kilometers of territory ceded to China by Pakistan in March 1963, through which China built the Karakorum Highway. Indo-Pakistani tensions have a strong influence on India's attitudes toward these conflicting claims, as do China's close strategic relations with Pakistan. In the middle sector of the border, southeast of the Aksai Chin, along the Xinjiang Uighur Autonomous Region and extending into Tibet, China claims some 2,000 square kilometers of what India considers its territory.[14] The middle sector borders the Indian states of Himachal Pradesh and Uttarakhand. In the eastern sector of the border, China claims some 90,000 square kilometers of the Indian state of Arunachal Pradesh, virtually the entire state.

The Aksai Chin area is strategically important to Beijing because it has a highway built by China connecting Xinjiang to Tibet. The middle sector is an area that has some key mountain passes between Tibet and India, on the western side of Nepal. The eastern sector is the most sensitive because it has a large Tibetan population.[15] China refuses to issue visas in passports to residents of Arunachal Pradesh, instead stapling them on pieces of paper, as a way to show that Beijing does not recognize India's claim.[16] The Dalai Lama fled to India in 1959, and India still gives the Tibetan government-in-exile sanctuary in Dharamsala, India.

The conflicting claims in the eastern sector are along the McMahon Line, a demarcation drawn by British Foreign Secretary Henry McMahon during the Simla Conference held in Northern India from October 13, 1913, through July 3, 1914.[17] In the western and middle sectors, the conflicting claims stem from a survey by British officials in 1846–1847 and another survey by W.H. Johnson, an officer of the British Survey of India, who traversed the Aksai Chin and Karakorum area in 1865.[18]

Successive British envoys to China between 1913 and 1947 continued to argue the border demarcation with China. When Great Britain relinquished its claim to the Indian empire in 1947, the British tried to translate these surveys into maps. However, the work was never completed and never agreed to by China, and the new Indian government began its own policy of completing this work while also moving forces forward.[19]

Factors Affecting Potential Conflict

To appreciate the likelihood, nature, scope, and escalation potential of a future conflict between China and India, five factors are examined in turn. Some of these factors make conflict more likely, some shape the nature and scope of the contingency, while others affect the potential for escalation.

Sino-Indian Mistrust and Border Dispute

Mutual mistrust and the territorial disputes increase the potential for conflict and ensure that the militaries of both countries continue to plan for border war contingencies. Each side anticipates hostile action from the other and possesses a heightened sense of vulnerability vis-à-vis the other. Moreover, when an incident or border violation occurs, the tendency is to assume malicious or nefarious intent on the part of the actor.

In 1960, India formulated its "forward policy," designed to place continuous pressure by Indian forces on Chinese troops along the disputed border.[20] Neville Maxwell cites an October 1959 editorial in the *Times of India* to explain the policy: "New Delhi must assert its rights by dispatching properly equipped patrols into the areas currently occupied by the Chinese, since any prolonged failure to do so will imply a tacit acceptance of Chinese occupation."[21] In China, Mao Zedong instructed the PLA in July 1962 to counter what he termed India's "nibbling policy" [*canshi zhengce*, 蚕食政策]. China's "anti-nibbling rules" instructed PLA troops to "never make a concession, but try to avert bleeding; form a jagged, interlocking pattern [of positions] to secure the border; and prepare for long-term, armed co-existence."[22]

For China, maintaining and defending definable borders is one of the most important missions of the PLA.[23] China's sovereignty over Tibet is tied up in Beijing's sensitivity over the border.[24] Further, the intensity of China's concerns over border security is exacerbated by the Tibetan presence harbored in Dharamsala, India.[25] This area is south of the middle sector of the disputed border. Chinese sensitivities also are heightened by the fact that the United States mounted a covert war to assist Tibetans in evicting the PLA and establishing an independent Tibet during the 1950s and early 1960s.[26]

In India, there is still political sensitivity to the losses of the 1962 war. The Indian Defense Ministry finally released casualty figures in 1965, acknowledging 1,383 troops killed, 1,696 personnel missing in action, and 3,968 personnel captured by Chinese forces.[27] Chinese casualties were considerably lower, with 722 Chinese soldiers killed, 1,697 wounded, and none captured.[28] In fact, the PLA captured three Indian brigades, including one brigade commander. China's close relations with and support for Pakistan as well as China's stance on

Kashmir, disputed between India and Pakistan, make relations between India and China particularly sensitive.[29] Indian military officers still characterize the 1962 conflict with China as a "serious debacle and ignominy suffered by the nation."[30]

These sensitivities make any settlement of the border dispute more difficult for both countries. That said, many articles in Indian newspapers and journals highlight the threat from China, whereas on the Chinese side, most commentaries focus on how the two sides can increase economic cooperation. On the Indian side, memories of the defeat in 1962 linger. According to one military analyst, the Indian Army assesses four levels of threat from China: "non-contact war (coercion and intimidation), low, medium and high."[31]

Some Chinese specialists on the border areas believe that further economic development in Tibet will strengthen China's control over the region and bind minorities to the PRC.[32] At the same time, these specialists advise that united front work [*tongzhan gongzuo*, 统战工作] is an important key to assimilating the Tibetan minority population.[33] That formulation implies that there is some enemy to unite against, suggesting that the Chinese Communist Party (CCP) and the PLA have strong motivation to continue to maintain some pressure on India over the shared border. There also are periodic propaganda reminders of the 1962 war and its justification aimed at the general populace, suggesting that the CCP is using the border dispute as a means to maintain a level of readiness to respond. One series reminds the populace about the reasons for the "self-defensive counterattack" and of Mao Zedong's goals in the 1962 Sino-Indian war, which Mao established in consultation with the Central Military Commission.[34]

In the wake of the 1986 Sumdurong Chu incident when the PLA seized a seasonal India observation post in the eastern sector, the Indian Army sent some 200,000 troops north of Tawang to respond to what it saw as an increased presence of Chinese infantry near the border and the construction by China of four helicopter landing areas.[35] Jonathan Holslag argues that even though China and India reached agreement to withdraw troops by 200 meters on each side of the border in 1996, the potential for conflict remains.[36] There also were arrests of an Indian intelligence team in Arunachal Pradesh by Chinese troops in July 2004, and some Indo-Tibetan border police were wounded by Chinese forces in 2009.[37] In April 2013, approximately 30 PLA troops crossed the Line of Actual Control (LAC) and pitched tents in the Depsang Plain of the

Western Section; a confrontation ensued for 3 weeks until both sides withdrew their forces. Another Chinese incursion took place in September 2014, prior to President Xi Jinping's visit to India; the incident escalated to involve more than 1,000 troops on each side.[38]

Further, in India, there is still a perceived sense of strategic vulnerability, even as there are plans to strengthen Indian capabilities on the border.[39] There have not been any Sino-Indian confidence-building military exercises since 2008, with the exception of some aerial acrobatics displays.[40] Even the last Sino-Indian exercise was a small-scale counterterrorism training exercise in Kunming. Many Indian analysts believe that Beijing intends to keep India on edge and unsure of the future. Arun Sahgal, joint director of net assessment, technology, and simulation at New Delhi's Institute of National Security Studies, opined that the 228 cases of "territorial intrusions" by Chinese troops in 2010 and the 213 cases in 2011 (by Indian count) are "Chinese pinpricks to keep India on tenterhooks."[41]

Observers in India are unhappy about the wave of infrastructure development along the Sino-Indian border. China did extensive construction in the early 2000s to improve the road network on its side of the border. India experts believe that India needs all-weather roads in order to ensure forces can reach the contested border, but only 15 of 73 planned roads were completed on time.[42] One estimate claimed that China had stationed some 300,000 PLA troops in Tibet and put six rapid reaction force units in Chengdu to respond to border crises.[43] On the Indian side, however, there are only some 120,000 troops in the eastern sector of the border.

The Indian side believes that in the event of a new border conflict, the PLA could move as many as 30 infantry division equivalents into the border area, overwhelming Indian forces.[44] At the Centre for Land Warfare Studies, Gurmeet Kanwal argues that "patrol face-offs are common as both sides patrol up to their perceptions of the LAC."[45] He believes a small incident is possible and, given the postures on both sides of the border, could escalate in scale.

Time does not heal all wounds, and some Chinese actions have opened deeper wounds. When the Panchen Lama, the second highest ranking Lama in Tibetan Buddhism, died in 1989, a controversy arose. The Tibetans and the Dalai Lama chose Gedhun Choekyi Nyima as the reincarnated Panchen Lama. However, in 1990 Beijing announced that a different Tibetan, Gyancain Norbu, was the Panchen Lama, and the Dalai Lama's choice disappeared from public view. When the current Dalai Lama, Tenzin Gyatso, eventually dies, Beijing is certain to pick its own candidate, while Tibetan monks in Dharamsala will carry out their own search for the new reincarnation. This will without question lead to closures of the Sino-Indian border and increased security in China.

Effect of Civil-Military Relations on Potential Conflict

Civil-military dynamics in China and India increase the possibility of conflict while mitigating the potential for escalation. Stovepiping in Beijing and New Delhi makes for poor bureaucratic coordination, thus increasing the likelihood of the two countries stumbling into war. Moreover, should a border crisis materialize, top political leaders such as President Xi Jinping and Prime Minister Narendra Modi, with strong nationalist credentials and reputations for being decisive and hardline, may feel it necessary to response with muscular assertiveness. However, once engaged in conflict, these insular institutional structures may tend to serve as brakes on horizontal or vertical escalation.

Arguably, civil-military relations in India affected the way in which the Indian Army prosecuted the 1962 border war. In 1961–1962, the civilian leadership pushed the Indian Army to pursue the "Forward Policy" aggressively when the military seemed to believe that the force balance was not in India's favor. The military wanted to use air forces in support of ground operations, but the civilian leadership was unwilling, fearing an escalation of the war.

Today, the Indian Army likely would still be constrained politically. The Indian government remains mired in bureaucratic silos and does not coordinate effectively across agencies. This is not a new problem. One restricted review of Indian actions before and during the 1962 Sino-Indian War complained of "the people's ignorance of military matters" and "total secrecy, unmindful of the needs of national security" of Indian government departments.[46] Based on the author's 30 years of experience, the diplomatic, intelligence, and military elements of the Indian security establishment have a great deal of difficulty in coordinating activities at both the national and the embassy levels. For example, members of India's external intelligence agency, the Research and Analysis Wing (RAW), report independently and seldom coordinate or share their reporting with foreign ministry officers and defense attachés at the embassy.[47]

One Indian military official, Major General Mrinal Susman, has described the military procurement process as "a national shame," with no holistic regime and confusion among defense, space, and atomic energy agencies.[48]

Other Indian security analysts have called for a comprehensive strategic defense review because elected representatives in Parliament, government ministries, and the military often have different geostrategic and geopolitical objectives.[49] In such circumstances, clear statements of policy and mission-type instructions from the highest levels of the Indian government are unlikely. In the event of a new border conflict, the Indian Army could well be in a position similar to the one in which it found itself in 1962.

China also faces huge bureaucratic coordination problems. The need to forge consensus among Central Military Commission (CMC) and Politburo Standing Committee (PBSC) members for major actions often delays decisionmaking.[50] That said, once the CMC conveys a set of combat orders to a theater command or military region, the commander seems to know the limitations on the scope of his action. Based on how the 1962 Sino-Indian War and the 1979 attack on Vietnam were orchestrated, the CMC defines timelines and the scope of action for an operation in advance. Finally, as slow as the consensus process may be in China, once senior political and military leaders make a decision, there is not much room for the PLA to misunderstand party instructions. From the standpoint of how civil-military relations may affect any future border conflict, the PLA may be in a better position than the Indian armed forces once hostilities commence and contingency plans enter the execution phase.

Economic Considerations and Potential Conflict

Burgeoning economic relations between China and India are unlikely to diminish mutual distrust, at least in the short to medium term. Moreover, these growing economic ties will not necessarily spill over into progress on resolving territorial disputes, nor even prevent the two countries from fighting a border war. However, these economic relations may be sufficiently consequential to serve as a factor limiting horizontal escalation. Both Beijing and New Delhi are likely to seek to contain hostilities to their respective frontier regions and avoid expanding the conflict to their heartlands.

Robert Abboud and Newton Minow, in a 2002 article in *Foreign Affairs,* made the argument that economic interaction leads to political adhesion, reducing the need for and likelihood of conflict.[51] Both China and India have made efforts to improve political relations and deepen economic interaction, but that does not seem to have reduced mutual mistrust or preparations for conflict.

Bilateral investment between the two countries is not vigorous. Chinese cumulative investment in India to December 2011 was $575.7 million, while Indian cumulative investment in China to the same time was $441.7 million. At a little more than a billion dollars, that economic interaction pales compared to, for instance, the $253.7 billion Japan has invested in the United States. Bilateral trade between China and India was $73.9 billion in 2011, with $23.41 billion in Indian exports to China and $50.49 billion in Chinese exports to India. In terms of content, the majority of trade is in electrical machinery, nuclear reactor equipment, boilers, machinery, ores, and organic chemicals.[52]

These economic interactions probably do not have the weight to affect political and security considerations between the two countries. Indeed, Yasheng Huang, writing in the *Journal of International Affairs*, argues that there is only a "groping for stability" between China and India based on forms of economic complementarity and investment flows.[53] Huang believes "that these economic interactions are not sufficient to solve the other tensions between the two countries."[54] Even if some of the trade is in civil nuclear materials and technology, there remains a shadow of nuclear conflict hanging over the disputed border.

The Nuclear Shadow

The fact that both China and India are nuclear powers might make conflict more conceivable but escalation less likely. Some research suggests that countries with nuclear arsenals may be more willing to engage in conventional conflict with each other, including proxy wars, because they rationalize escalation to use of nuclear weapons is all but unthinkable—what scholars Glenn Snyder and Robert Jervis dubbed the *stability-instability paradox*. Indeed, both Beijing and New Delhi are likely to be quite reluctant to cross the threshold to nuclear war. China has long maintained a *"no first use"* policy, with Chinese leaders insisting they will not use nuclear weapons except in the event that another state launches nuclear strikes on China. India, meanwhile, is well aware of the daunting nuclear imbalance it faces with China and cognizant of the need to maintain parity with its other nuclear neighbor, Pakistan.

In 1962, neither India nor China had nuclear weapons and neither had allies who could provide a nuclear umbrella. Beijing feared nuclear attack by both the United States and the Soviet Union, but both of those nations kept out of the Sino-Indian border war. Today, both China and India have nuclear arsenals. Even during a 1986 Sino-Indian confrontation in the Sumdorong Chu valley in the eastern sector of the border, Moscow remained silent about any nuclear umbrella for India.[55]

China has some seven brigades of intercontinental ballistic missiles, one brigade of intermediate-range missiles (which will soon be taken out of the inventory, if they have not been deactivated already), ten brigades of medium-range missiles, eight short-range ballistic missile brigades, and two brigades of land-attack cruise missiles.[56] India has a much smaller nuclear-capable missile force, with four groups of missiles (two medium-range groups and two short-range groups) but plenty of shorter range missiles that would be useful in a conflict.[57]

Most of the shorter range Indian missiles are capable of carrying both conventional and nuclear warheads, as are most Chinese shorter range missiles. Both countries have a declaratory policy that they will not be the first to use nuclear weapons in a conflict, although New Delhi has stated it may retaliate with nuclear weapons in the event of a biological or chemical weapons attack.[58] The Indian military and intelligence services are acutely aware of any shifts in the deployment of China's Second Artillery Corps missile forces and track them closely.[59] Such shifts might be interpreted by New Delhi as indications of impending conflict.

On the Chinese side, Second Artillery Corps forces have been integrated into exercises and operational plans in China's military regions, which may become war theaters in a conflict.[60] The integration of Second Artillery Corps missile units into a theater commander's operational forces is a natural evolution in military doctrine, but it increases the chances of miscalculation or escalation in a conflict.[61] The Indian armed forces believe that for nuclear-armed missiles, the chain of command in China runs from the overall authority of the CMC through the Operations Department of the General Staff Department to the Second Artillery Corps.[62] For conventional ballistic missile forces, however, the commander of the war theater has the authority to employ those missiles as part of a theater campaign.[63] What is not clear from Indian military sources or Chinese doctrinal publications, however, is whether the theater or war commander may employ those missiles outside of China's territory, where the use of even conventional ballistic missiles could be highly escalatory.

India probably does not have tactical nuclear weapons, although China might. A latent fear in Indian defense circles is that "if the PLA does not get a quick breakthrough [in any border conflict] against a determined Indian Army deployed with defenses in depth, what stops the PLA from threatening to use

TNW [tactical nuclear weapons] in the high altitude terrain with little collateral damage?"[64] Still, large-scale conventional ballistic missile strikes on the adversary's territory are the action most likely to escalate a conflict.

Indian concerns run deep, particularly because China has far more ballistic missiles and a much larger nuclear arsenal. Those concerns aside, Beijing is unlikely to initiate the use of nuclear weapons in a border conflict. However, there are contingencies for counterdeterrence nuclear operations in "high plateau frigid border regions" by the PLA. Chinese military writings discuss the need to "place a great emphasis on joint counternuclear intimidation operations" when conducting "informationized joint operations" in terrain that sounds a lot like Tibet.[65] The PLA expects enemy airstrikes in any future conflict in that area but also thinks it necessary to "actively deter enemy nuclear deterrence and conduct the right level of reasonable and constrained counternuclear intimidation operations to thwart enemy nuclear blackmail."[66] This kind of thinking raises the stakes in any conflict. When the PLA discusses *counterdeterrence,* the types of operations involved include unmasking weapons and moving them in ways the enemy can observe, conducting nuclear weapons exercises, and conducting conventional ballistic missile strikes—all potentially escalatory operational concepts.[67]

Lessons from the 1962 Conflict and Contemporary Doctrine

China appears to have learned the lessons of the 1962 war better than India. Nevertheless, this may tend to breed overconfidence in the victor's abilities five decades later and a tendency to underestimate the adversary. Indeed, one perceived lesson of the PLA's record of limited and contained conflicts around China's periphery since 1950 may be the predisposition to assume that the Chinese have mastered the art of escalation management—what the PLA dubs *war control.*[68] Meanwhile, the vanquished may be far less confident in its ability and prone to exaggerate the capabilities of its adversary. In terms of doctrine, the PLA's overarching concept of operations for decades has been that of *limited* or *local* war and an operational and tactical preference for seizing the initiative and engaging in proactive offensive actions even while ostensibly engaged in a strategically defensive posture under the flexible principle of active defense. These elements may on the one hand make Sino-Indian conflict more likely, while on the other hand serve to tamp down pressure for escalation.

Based on its analysis of operations in the 1962 Sino-Indian Self-Defense Counterattack Campaign, the PLA came away with a number of major lessons.[69] Most importantly, the PLA concluded that the best approach was to attempt to use peaceful means to settle boundary and border disputes through political discussions and diplomacy. The General Political Department also concluded that a good approach was to institute a propaganda campaign designed to educate opposing forces about the status of the border. But it was clear that the most critical area, according to PLA analysis at the time, was the eastern portion, which was the main direction of operations in the counterattack.[70] One reason was the Indian disposition of troops. The CMC also decided that the first order of business was to deal a "painful blow" to Indian forces that had intruded into China.[71] Surprise and speed in the counterattack were deemed to be extremely important to PLA success, and in both sections of the border, east and west, the PLA emphasized swiftness of operations. The PLA sought to follow up on combat successes and to pursue Indian forces that had abandoned border positions.[72] Establishing and maintaining good logistics bases and lines of transportation were deemed critical to the PLA's success. PLA analysis argues that a good policy toward minorities (Tibetan rural laborers and manual laborers) was important to operations. Finally, the PLA concluded that use of frontier troops and militia units around the border areas were keys to successful operations.

Other PLA officers argue that one of the most valuable lessons from the 1962 Sino-Indian war was about operating under conditions of high altitude and extreme cold.[73] Troops had to be acclimatized to these harsh conditions and properly equipped. Furthermore, in a discussion of how the self-defensive counterattack campaign contributed to PLA campaign thinking, the PLA's experience in the Sino-Indian war is given credit for planting the ideas that led to the development of combined arms campaigns.[74] Ultimately, however, the PLA did not seriously experiment with or implement combined arms operations until after the 1979 attack on Vietnam.[75]

None of these conclusions is a surprise. They constitute standard PLA campaign doctrine. However, these approaches have been updated and modernized to apply in 21st-century operations in border conflicts.[76] For its own operational planning, PLA doctrine seems to accept that "in times of peace (or lower tension), it is not necessary to deploy large forces along the border."[77] Further, PLA authors advise that when repelling intruding forces or defending against an enemy attack, the initial response is defensive. However, if an intrusion is in a limited area, defensive operations may be inadequate. In such circumstances, the best response is to use mobile units operating in depth as the main force responding to an enemy incursion and to "annihilate [*jianmie*, 歼灭] the enemy."[78]

The PLA text, *The Study of Ground Force* [Army] *Campaigns*, emphasizes that because of difficult terrain and special conditions in border areas [*zhanchang huanjing teshu*, 战场环境特殊], independent operations often have to be undertaken in different directions and areas. Border areas are characterized by limited mobility, limited lines of communication, and few transportation routes. Defensive operations are only the initial phase of border self-defense and are intended to prepare the contested area for offensive operations—the self-defensive counterattack.[79] The basic formula for contingency planning is defined as "impede the enemy while building the situation for one's own forces, conduct key point counterattacks, simultaneously annihilate and expel the enemy" [*zukang zao shi, zhongdian fanji, jian qu bing ju*, 阻抗造势, 重点反击, 歼驱并举].[80] In "key point counterattacks," the text notes the importance of concentrating "crack" or hand-picked troops at key points and that the main defensive orientation should be where the enemy's main force is concentrated.[81]

Most important for future contingency planning, the book advises that self-defensive counterattack campaigns should take full advantage of other arms and services, such as engineers, camouflage units, communications units, weather organizations, artillery and missiles, and specialized reserve forces.[82] A fully integrated force structure is important in coordinating border self-defensive counterattack campaigns. Commanders can maximize coordination by organizing forces into special forces groups, surface combat groups, surface warfare firepower groups, and air defense firepower groups.[83] The latter suggests that in future contingencies, the PLA expects its principal adversary (probably India) to use air forces and that the PLA Air Force (PLAAF) would be part of any campaign. Electronic reconnaissance, counterreconnaissance, information operations, and electronic deception measures would be important parts of any campaign, which also implies the use of cyber operations against enemy forces.[84]

The PLA expects that border self-defense will involve operations in very cold high-altitude areas where troops would be deprived of oxygen. To be ready for these contingencies, commanders should prepare for combat early, move forces into potential combat areas early, and prepare the battlefield for combat early.[85] With respect to terrain, *The Study of Ground Force Campaigns* advises that the PLA should control valleys and movement corridors using defensive fires and offensive electronic measures. It also is imperative for the PLA to control plateaus to facilitate offensive operations and use them for aircraft and helicopter operations. Finally, the text warns commanders to prepare troops to operate in extremely cold environments.

Cyber warfare would likely be employed by both Indian and Chinese forces. In the electronic and cyber realm, both China and India are developing robust capabilities to support military operations and intelligence gathering with computers and satellite surveillance. Both Beijing and New Delhi have space-based assets that could be targets in a conflict.

Neither side used combat aircraft in the 1962 war. Indian Air Force doctrine provides for close air support, but as one Indian assessment states, even though the army expected close air support, the air force was not ready to provide it.[86] An article on close air support in the 1962 war argues that even today, despite a doctrine calling for close air support, the Indian Air Force is still inept at providing it.[87] One senior Indian Air Force official, in discussions with a U.S. researcher, argued that a political decision by civilian authorities restricted the Indian Air Force from using airpower.[88] Several PLA officers have translated the restricted Indian history of the war, *History of the Conflict with China, 1962*,[89] which makes clear that political restrictions were placed on the Indian Air Force.[90] Prime Minister Jawaharlal Nehru apparently feared that China would widen the war if India used airstrikes. The Indian side did make extensive use of transport aircraft for troop movements and logistics.

The PLA tends to rely on massed indirect fire (artillery and mortar) along with preplanned airstrikes to support offensive operations. In the Chinese view, as a principle of war, mass not only means massing forces at critical points on the battlefield, but also massing fires to annihilate the enemy.[91] The PLAAF has at least three divisions of ground attack aircraft, including the Qiang-5, a variant of the F-6 updated with Italian help; the Xi'an FB-7, a fighter-bomber developed at home; and the Su-27.[92] There are two combat air divisions in the Chengdu Military Region. Some analysts note that although the PLAAF has provisions for close air firepower support for other services on the battlefield, it is not practiced much.[93] The PLAAF mostly conducts preplanned or on-call ground interdiction. Roger Cliff and his co-authors note in *Shaking the Heavens and Splitting the Earth* that doctrinal provisions call for a "target guidance small group" from the PLAAF to be sent to assist ground or other supported units, but Dennis Blasko has argued in *The Chinese Army Today* that such air support is still limited to cooperative planning at a headquarters level, which is a far cry from sending forward air controllers or air-naval gunfire coordinators into ground units the way the U.S. Air Force and Navy do with the Army and Marine Corps.[94] Even in descriptions of close air support by the PLAAF during an exercise on the Tibetan Plateau, it is not clear whether the "target guidance group" [*mubiao yindao zu*, 目标引导组] was operating at a headquarters or embedded in ground force units.[95] It is clear, however, that the PLA has begun employing army aviation units in direct ground attack support for infantry units.[96]

The Chinese military has learned that it must employ airpower in a future conflict, even if its effectiveness is limited. However, the PLA seems to prefer the use of artillery over air forces given the limitations of operations at high altitude.[97] This permits a more controlled and reliable massing of fires.[98] Also, PLA military doctrine makes it clear that missile strikes will be integrated with other forms of firepower. The PLA has exercised its conventional missile forces with ground forces under the control of the theater of operations commander.[99]

The PLA learned that operations at high altitude require special attention to acclimatizing personnel. While PLA forces have a number of personnel who were better acclimated because of longer service at high altitude, there still is a serious effort in China to study the effects of altitude on military operations at the General Hospital of the Tibet Military District.[100]

The PLA may have an advantage over Indian units in that its forces are deployed at high altitude for longer periods and train for operations on a regular basis.[101] China has three mechanized infantry brigades deployed in Tibet, two of them trained for mountain operations. There is also a reserve forces brigade and a People's Armed Police division in Tibet. There are six garrisons around Tibet, each of which probably is about brigade strength (approximately 4,000 men). Thus, there are probably several brigades of troops in Tibet and a division in Chengdu Military Region who are well acclimatized. PLA commanders seem to believe that it really takes about 6 months to get a unit fully acclimatized to operations in high altitude areas. This practical view comes from extended periods of training in Tibet.[102]

Preparing for Future Conflict: Exercises and Contingency Plans

China and India are both modernizing their armed forces and preparing for future conflicts in the information age. The PLA characterizes itself as modernizing in a number of ways in order to respond to Hu Jintao's 2004 charge to undertake "new historic missions" designed to provide strategic support for safeguarding national interests.[103] Part of this modernization is "informationizing" the armed forces, or ensuring that command, control, communications, computers, intelligence, surveillance, and reconnaissance (C⁴ISR) systems can operate across the domains of war and exchange data and targeting information.[104] Logistics, notably transportation, is a second area of interest. Over the last 4 years, the PLA has conducted a series of opposing force exercises around China that involved moving large numbers of troops from multiple military regions around the country to concentrate forces near potential conflict areas.

One indication that the PLA takes the potential for renewed conflict on the Sino-Indian border seriously is the attention it pays to Indian armed forces operational concepts. In a book that identifies and analyzes the concepts behind Indian military operations, the PLA Academy of Sciences has provided a detailed analysis of Indian military tactics, the organizational structure of the Indian armed forces, and Indian military exercises.[105] This detailed analysis covers everything from the strengths and weaknesses of the Indian military command and control system to how the Indian army constructs defensive positions. Books like this likely help frame PLA exercises in Tibet.

In autumn 2009, the PLA ran exercise Stride 2009 [*Kuayue* 2009] in four areas of China—northeast, northwest, central, and southeast. A year later, Mission Action 2010 [*Shiming* 2010] exercised corps-level strategic force projection in a joint campaign. In March 2011, an all-PLA training conference was run involving a cyber-networked exercise. In 2012, the PLA ran a live-fire, land-air integrated exercise in the Tibet Military District and Chengdu Military Region.[106] The PLA sought to orchestrate joint and integrated operations in the ground, air, space, maritime, and electromagnetic domains of war (the latter includes cyber warfare and electronic warfare). The 2012 exercise in Tibet is particularly important for this study because it focused on high-altitude operations in difficult terrain and cold areas, factors that characterize the Sino-Indian border.

Conclusion

Sensitivities are probably higher in India over the disputed border than in China, but the military forces on both sides of the border are watchful and stay on the ready. One reason for heightened Indian sensitivities is the sting that is still felt over the results of the 1962 conflict. A second reason is that the government has yet to make public its own internal review of the outcome of that war. The Indian press and analytic community spend a lot of effort analyzing every move by the PLA, but military journals and the press in China do not dwell nearly so much on the Indian army. Part of the reason is India's feeling that it lost the 1962 war. Indian military analysts seem to think that Chinese leaders believe that the preemptive use of force pays off when foreign leaders ignore warnings.[107] Chinese military doctrine may call the Chinese interventions in the Korean War, the Sino-Indian War, and the 1979 attack on Vietnam "self-defensive counterattacks," but to others they were each a massive use of force to preempt the other side in a growing conflict.

The likelihood of a border conflict is still low. Both New Delhi and Beijing regularly undertake diplomatic initiatives and military confidence-building measures to help maintain peace, even if it is an uncomfortable peace. With mutual distrust high in each country, civil-military relations serve on the one hand to increase the potential for unintended conflict, while on the other hand to limit or at least slow the horizontal or vertical escalatory potential once the two militaries are engaged in a contingency. Both sides also pursue economic links, and these help keep the potential of escalation lower, even if those ties are not deep. Should a conflict break out, it would probably expand beyond the land domain: cyber, airpower, and perhaps attacks on satellites are very likely to be part of any future conflict, but maritime conflict is less likely. If conflict crosses into one or more of these domains, then this increases the chance that a border clash may spread deeper into both countries and that the level of violence in combat operations may escalate. Although the specter of a nuclear exchange is likely to keep any conventional clash limited, the potential risk of nuclear escalation is always there if conflict should occur.

Notes

1   The seminal analysis of the Sino-Indian border war is Neville Maxwell, *India's China War* (New York: Pantheon Books, 1970). From the PLA's perspective,

perhaps the most complete assessment of the war is *History of Operations in the China-India Self Defensive Counterattack* [中印边境自卫反击作战史] (Beijing: Military Science Publishing House [军事科学出版社], 1994). From an Indian perspective, there are many studies and personal assessments. See, for instance, Shanti Prasad Varma, *Struggle for the Himalayas: A Study in Sino-Indian Relations* (New Delhi: Sterling Publishers, 1971); Lieutenant General B.M. Kaul, *The Untold Story* (New Delhi: Allied Publishers, 1967); Major General D. K. Palit, *War in the High Himalaya: The Indian Army in Crisis, 1962* (New Delhi: Lancer International, 1991).

2   "Gunboat Diplomacy: Indian Navy Ready to Set Sail to South China Sea," *RT News,* December 4, 2012, available at <http://rt.com/news/india-china-navy-oil-221/>.

3   Rajit Pandit, "Ready to Tackle China Sea Threat: Navy Chief," *Times of India,* December 4, 2012, available at <http://articles.timesofindia.indiatimes.com/2012-12-04/india/35594081_1_south-china-sea-accordance-with-international-al-laws-vietnam-coast>.

4   Ben Bland and Girjia Shivakumar, "China Confronts Indian Navy Vessel," *Financial Times,* August 3, 2011, available at <www.ft.com/intl/cms/s/0/883003ec-d3f6-11e0-b7eb-00144feab49a.html#axzz2I9e0dTD6>.

5   Sandip Unnithon, "Hidden Dragon on the High Seas," *India Today,* March 21, 2014, available at <http://indiatoday.intoday.in/story/china-nuclear-powered-at-tack-submarine-south-china-sea/1/350573.html>.

6   Ankit Panda, "Chinese Naval Exercise in Eastern Indian Ocean Sends Mixed Signals," *The Diplomat,* February 7, 2014, available at <http://thediplomat.com/2014/02/chinese-naval-exercise-in-eastern-indian-ocean-sends-mixed-signals/>.

7   U.S. China Economic and Security Review Commission (USCC), Staff Report, *China's Navy Extends its Combat Reach to the Indian Ocean* (Washington, DC: U.S.-China Economic and Security Review Commission, March 14, 2014), available at <http://origin.www.uscc.gov/sites/default/files/Research/Staff%20Report_China's%20Navy%20Extends%20its%20Combat%20Reach%20to%20the%20Indian%20Ocean.pdf>.

8   Ibid.

9   Jeremy Page and Tom Wright, "China's Military Considers New Indian Ocean Presence," *The Wall Street Journal,* December 14, 2011, available at <http://online.wsj.com/article/SB10001424052970203518404577096261061550538.html>; Andrew Miller, "Sri Lanka Defends China's Naval Presence in the Indian Ocean," *TheTrumpet.com*, December 28, 2012, available at <www.thetrumpet.com/article/10224.19.0.0/economy/trade/sri-lanka-defends-chinas-naval-presence-in-the-indian-ocean>.

10   Farhan Bokhari and Kathrin Hille, "Pakistan Turns to China for Naval Base," *Financial Times,* May 22, 2011; for background see Tarique Niazi, "Gwadar:

China's Naval Outpost on the Indian Ocean," *China Brief* 5, no. 4 (February 14, 2005), available at <www.jamestown.org/single/?tx_ttnews%5Btt_news%5D=3718>.

11 Saibal Dasgupta, "Eye on India? China Plans Naval Expansion, Woos Myanmar," *The Times of India,* May 28, 2011, available at <http://articles.timesofindia.indiatimes.com/2011-05-28/china/29594269_1_thein-sein-chinese-navy-myanmar-area>.

12 Bilateral seminar between the PLA and the United States, Carlisle, PA, March 17–18, 2014.

13 A good map can be found in Cheng Feng and Larry M. Wortzel, "PLA Operational Principles and Limited War: The Sino-Indian War of 1962," in *Chinese Warfighting: The PLA Experience since 1949*, eds. Mark A. Ryan, David M. Finkelstein, and Michael McDevitt (Armonk, NY: M.E. Sharpe, 2003), 175.

14 Sheo Nandan Pandey, and Hem Kusun, "Sino-Indian Border Talks and the Shifting Chinese Stance," *USI Journal Online* 142, no. 587 (March 31, 2012), 30–39, available at <www.usiofindia.org/Article/?pub=Journal&pubno=587&ano=891>. Also see Colonel Ravi Tuteja, "China-India Territorial Dispute: Moving towards Resolution," Article 1097, Center for Land Warfare Studies (India), May 22, 2008, available at <www.claws.in/index.php?action+details&m_id=88&u_id+5>.

15 See Andrew J. Nathan and Andrew Scobell, *China's Search for Security* (New York: Columbia University Press, 2012), 160–161.

16 "India and China: Unsettled for a Long Time Yet," *The Economist,* October 20, 2012, 37.

17 See Cheng Feng and Wortzel, 174–176.

18 Maxwell, 26–27.

19 Ibid., 61–62.

20 Cheng Feng and Wortzel, 178–179.

21 Cited in Maxwell, 22.

22 Xu Yan [徐焰], *The Historic Truth of the Sino-Indian Border War* [中印边界之战历史真相] (Hong Kong: Tian Di Books [文物天地], 1993), 87 as cited in Cheng Feng and Wortzel, 180, 196 (note).

23 Mao Zhenfa [毛振发], *On Frontier Defense* (边防论) (Beijing: Military Science Publishing House, 1996), 1. This point is forcefully made in Hu Jintao's December 24, 2004, speech on the "Historic Missions of the People's Liberation Army." See Hu Jintao, "See Clearly Our Armed Forces' Historic Missions in the New Period of the New Century" [认清新世纪新阶段我军历史使命], December 24, 2004, available at <http://gfjy.jxnews.com.cn/system/2010/04/16/011353408.shtml>. Also see an analysis of the speech in Daniel Hartnett, *Towards a Globally Focused Chinese Military: The Historic Missions of the Chinese Armed Forces*, Project Asia (Alexandria,

VA: CNA Corporation, June 2008), available at <www.cna.org/sites/default/files/9.
pdf>; and testimony by Hartnett to the U.S.-China Economic and Security Review
Commission, March 4, 2009, available at <www.uscc.gov/hearings/2009hearings/
written_testimonies/09_03_04_wrts/09_03_04_hartnett_statement.pdf>.

24   See "Note of the Ministry of Foreign Affairs of the People's Republic of China
to the Indian Embassy in China," December 26, 1959, in *The Sino-Indian Border
Question* (Enlarged Edition) (Peking: Foreign Languages Press, 1962), 51–92; also,
in the same volume, see "Statement of the Government of the People's Republic of
China," October 24, 1962, 1–5.

25   "Tibetan govt in exile to give fresh push to talks with China," *Times of India*,
September 2, 2012, available at <http://timesofindia.indiatimes.com/india/Tibetan-
govt-in-exile-to-give-fresh-push-to-talks-with-China/articleshow/16225103.cms>.

26   Kenneth Conboy and James Morrison, *The CIA's Secret War in Tibet* (Law-
rence: University of Kansas Press, 2002), 120–145; also see Pete Takeda, *An Eye at the
Top of the World: The Terrifying Legacy of the Cold War's Most Daring CIA Operation*
(New York: Thunder's Mouth Press, 2006).

27   Maxwell, 424.

28   Cheng Feng and Wortzel, 188.

29   Santosh Singh, "China's Kashmir Policy," *World Affairs, The Journal of International Issues* 16, no. 2 (April-June 2012), 100 112.

30   Lieutenant General Kamal Davar, "India Needs a Chief of Defence Staff,"
The Tribune Online Edition, August 21, 2012, available at <www.tribuneindia.
com/2012/20120821/edit.htm#6>.

31   Pravin Sawhney, "Unrestricted War: India is Far More Vulnerable than is
Generally Accepted," *Force* 9, no. 12 (August 2012), 42.

32   Zhang Hongnian [孙宏年], "Research Center for Chinese Borderland History
and Geography Opens Research and Discussion Conference" [中国疆史地研究中心问
题学术研讨会召开], Chinese Academy of Social Sciences [中国社会学院], December 2,
2010, available at <http://bjzx.cass.cn/news/133768.htm>.

33   Ibid.

34   Yi Ming [佚名], "Declassified: Behind the curtain on Mao Zedong's decisions
in the Sino-Indian Self-Defensive Counterattack" [解密: 毛泽东决策中印边界自卫反
击战内幕], *Dajunshi.com,* December 11, 2009, available at <www.dajunshi.com/Mil-
data/MilHistory/India/200912/36586_3.html>.

35   Jonathan Holslag, *China and India: Prospects for Peace* (New York: Columbia University Press, 2010), 120–121.

36   Ibid., 121–123.

37   Nitya Singh, "How to Tame Your Dragon: An Evaluation of India's Foreign Policy Toward China," *India Review* 11, no. 3 (2012), 150.

38   Ashok Malik, "Xi, Modi and the Chumar hijack," *Deccan Chronicle*, September 21, 2014, available at <www.deccanchronicle.com/print/140921/commentary-columnists/article/xi-modi-and-chumar-hijack>.

39   Ibid.

40   "Chinese, Indian Defense Ministers Hold Wary Meetings," *Los Angeles Times,* September 4, 2012, available at <http://latimesblogs.latimes.com/world_now/2012/09/chinese-and-indian-defense-ministers-meet-warily.html>.

41   Naomi McMillin, *Fiftieth Anniversary of the 1962 Sino-Indian Border War: An Interview with Arun Sahgal,* October 30, 2012, National Bureau of Asian Research, 6, available at <http://nbr.org/research/activity.aspx?id=290>.

42   V.K. Saxena, "House Panel Raps MoD for Slack Border Road Works," *Political and Defense Weekly* 11, no. 35 (June 12–18, 2012), 16–18.

43   Ibid.

44   Gurmeet Kanwal, "Military Threat from China," Article 2188, Centre for Land Warfare Studies, available at <www.claws.in/print_article.php?rec-No-1189&su_id=7>.

45   Ibid.

46   P.B. Sinha, A.A. Athale, and S.N. Prasad, eds., *History of the Conflict with China, 1962* (New Delhi: History Division, Ministry of National Defense, 1962), available at <www.bharat-rakshak.com/LAND-FORCES/Army/History/1962War/PDF/1962Main.pdf>.

47   Author's experiences based on extensive contacts with Indian defense attaches, intelligence officers, and diplomats.

48   Mrinal Suman, "Held to Ransom," *Force* 9, no. 12 (August 2012), 81.

49   Pravin Sawhney, "The Way Forward," *Force* 9, no. 12 (August 2012), 49–52.

50   Andrew Scobell and Larry M. Wortzel, *Chinese National Security Decisionmaking Under Stress* (Carlisle, PA: Strategic Studies Institute, 2005), 1–13, 56, 79, 110, 141–147; also see Ning Lu, *The Dynamics of Foreign Policy Decisionmaking in China* (Boulder, CO: Westview Press, 1997), 79; Alice Miller, "The CCP Central Committee's Leading Small Groups," *China Leadership Monitor,* no. 26 (Fall 2008), available at <www.hoover.org/sites/default/files/uploads/documents/CLM26AM.pdf>; and Sun Yun, "Chinese National Security Decisionmaking: Processes and Challenges" (Washington, DC: The Brookings Institution, May 2014), available at <www.brookings.edu/research/papers/2013/05/chinese-national-security-decision-making-sun>.

51   Robert Abboud and Newton N. Minow, "Advancing Peace in the Middle East: The Economic Path out of Conflict," *Foreign Affairs* 81, no. 5 (September/October 2002), 14–16.

52   The trade figures are from the Web site of the Indian Embassy in Beijing, available at <www.indianembassy.org.cn/DynamicContent.aspx?MenuId=3&SubMenuId=0>.

53   Yasheng Huang, "The Myth of Economic Complementarity in Sino-Indian Relations," *Journal of International Affairs* 64, no. 2 (Spring-Summer 2011), 111–124.

54   Ibid.

55   Andrew B. Kennedy, "India's Nuclear Odyssey: Implicit Umbrellas, Diplomatic Disappointments, and the Bomb," *International Security* 36, no. 2 (Fall 2011), 142–143.

56   The International Institute of Strategic Studies (IISS), *The Military Balance 2012* (London: IISS, 2012), 233–234.

57   Ibid., 243. Also see Dinesh Kumar, "India Militarily Take on China Today?" *The Tribune Online Edition*, October 20, 2012, available at <www.tribuneindia. com/2012/20121020/edit.htm#10>. This article has an excellent force comparison and documents the Indian short-range missile force.

58   Scott D. Sagan, "The Evolution of Pakistani and Indian Nuclear Doctrine," In *Inside Nuclear South Asia*, ed. Scott D. Sagan (Stanford: Stanford University Press, 2009), 245–246.

59   The author's experience dealing with Indian diplomats and military attaches in Beijing and Washington.

60   Jiang Ning and Guo Fengkuan [姜宁，郭丰宽], "A 'Live Show' of Integrated Air-Land Operations Performed 4,500 Meters Above Sea Level" [海拔4500米上，演空地一体战 "活剧"], *PLA Daily* [解放军报], August 15, 2012.

61   See Larry M. Wortzel, *China's Nuclear Forces: Operations, Training, Doctrine, Command, Control and Campaign Planning* (Carlisle, PA: Strategic Studies Institute, 2007), 8–12.

62   Pravin Sawhney, "The Iron Structure: China's Higher Defence Management," *Force* 9, no. 12 (August 2012), 36.

63   Ibid.

64   Sawhney, "Unrestricted War: India is Far More Vulnerable than is Generally Accepted," 45–46.

65   Cao Zhangrong, Wu Renbo and Sun Jianjun [曹正荣, 吴润波, 孙建军], *Informationized Joint Operations* [信息化联合作战] (Beijing: PLA Press [中国人民解放军出版社], 2006), 255–257.

66   Ibid.

67   Jingdong Yuan, *Chinese Perceptions of the Utility of Nuclear Weapons* (Paris: Institut Francais des Relations Internationales, May 2010), 14–15; see also "Conference on U.S.-China Joint Nuclear Dynamics," Conference Report, Beijing, June 20–21, 2006, organized by the Center for Strategic and International Studies, the Institute for Defense Analyses, the RAND Corporation, and the China Foundation for International Strategic Studies, available at <http://csis.org/files/media/csis/events/060620_china_nuclear_report.pdf>.

68   Lonnie D. Henley, "War Control: Chinese Concepts of Escalation Management," in *Shaping China's Security Environment: The Role of the People's Liberation Army*, ed. Andrew Scobell and Larry Wortzel (Carlisle, PA: Strategic Studies Institute, 2006), 81–104.

69   This section is drawn from a discussion of the lessons of the Sino-Indian campaign in *A History of Operations in the China-India Self Defensive Counterattack*, 391–423.

70   Ibid., 394.

71   Ibid., 397.

72   Ibid., 402–404.

73   Zhang Xingye and Wang Chaotian [张兴业, 王朝天], *A History of the Development of Campaign Thinking* [战役思想发展史] (Beijing: National Defense University Press [国防大学出版社], 1997), 327.

74   Ibid.

75   Larry M. Wortzel, *The Dragon Extends its Reach: Chinese Military Power Goes Global* (Washington, DC: Potomac Books, 2013), 83–98; and Li Jijun [李际均], *Military Theory and War Practice* [军事理论与争实践] (Beijing: Military Science Publishing House, 1994), 172, 194.

76   Chen Yong, Xu Guocheng, and Geng Weidong [陈勇, 徐国成, 耿卫东], eds., *The Study of Ground Force Campaigns Under High Technology Conditions* [高技术条件下陆军战役学] (Beijing: Military Science Publishing House, 2003), 303–322.

77   Ibid., 303.

78   Ibid.

79   Ibid., 304.

80   Ibid.

81   Ibid., 305.

82   Ibid., 308.

83   Ibid.

84   Ibid., 310.

85   Ibid., 321–322.

86   Group Captain A.G. Bewoor, "Close Air Support in the 1962 War," *Bharat Rakshak,* July 1, 2009, available at <www.bharat-rakshak.com/IAF/History/1962War/1019-Bewoor.html>. *Bharat Rakshak* is an unofficial Web site devoted to the Indian military.

87   Ibid.

88   Exchange between the author and Jeff Smith, American Foreign Policy Council, November 7, 2012.

89   Sinha, Athale, and Prasad.

90   Yao Yunzhu [姚云竹] et al., trans., *History of the Sino-Indian Conflict, 1962* [印度: 1962年与中国冲突的历史] (Beijing: Military Science Publishing House, 2010), 280–301.

91   Wortzel, *The Dragon Extends its Reach,* 90–97.

92   See Roger Cliff et al., *Shaking the Heavens and Splitting the Earth: Chinese Air Force Employment Concepts in the 21ˢᵗ Century* (Santa Monica, CA: RAND Corporation, 2011), 20, 76–78; "Qiang-5 Ground Attack Aircraft," *Sinodefence.com,* available at <www.sinodefence.com/airforce/groundattack/q5.asp>; also see "Xian JH-7 'Flying Leopard,'" available at <http://sinodefence.com/chinese-military-aircraft/bomber-ground-attack-aircraft/#JH7>.

93   Cliff et al., 76; Dennis J. Blasko, *The Chinese Army Today: Tradition and Transformation for the 21ˢᵗ Century* (New York: Routledge, 2006), 189–190.

94   Cliff et al., 76–77; Blasko, 190. Blasko reaffirmed this point in a discussion with the author on PLA air-ground support doctrine on October 20, 2012.

95   Jiang and Guo.

96   Ibid. In one description of the exercise, the *target guidance group* requested both air to ground attack from the air force and army aviation fire support.

97   Marcus P. Acosta, "High Altitude Warfare: The Kargil Conflict and the Future" (master's thesis, Naval Postgraduate School, June 2003), available at <www.nps.edu/Academics/Centers/CCC/Research/StudentTheses/Acosta03.pdf>.

98   Even if sufficient airpower can be brought to bear on a target, it is far more susceptible to the effects of weather than indirect artillery fire.

99   Ibid.

100 Yongjun Luo et al., "High Altitude Medicine Education in China: Exploring a New Medical Education Reform," *High Altitude Medicine and Biology* 13, no. 1 (March 19, 2012), available at <http://online.liebertpub.com/doi/abs/10.1089/ham.2011.1090>.

101 One example of this is "Various Branches of the Military Cooperate to Fight in Cold, High-Altitude, Mountainous Exercise in the Chengdu Military Region" [成都军区演练高寒山地夜间诸军兵种协同作战], *People's Daily* [人民日报], August 31, 2012, available at <http://news.xinhuanet.com/mil/2012-08/31/c_123653552.htm>; there are dozens of articles in Chinese newspapers about high-altitude training and operations in Xinjiang and Tibet.

102 The author has approached former regimental commanders, military district commanders, and a Xizang Military District political commissar with questions about their views on how long it takes to acclimatize troops at high altitudes. Between 1988 and 2008, there have been no variations from this time frame. While there is probably a lot of scientific research in China on ideal and minimum times for acclimation, unit leaders think it takes 6 months.

103 Xu Zhuangzhi [徐壮志], "Combat power leaps through transformation—Achievements of building national defense and military forces" [战斗力, 在变革中跃升—国防和军队建设成就综述], Xinhua Online [新华网], available at <http://news.xinhuanet.com/politics/2012-06/12/c_112201245.htm>. On the PLA's historic missions, see Hartnett, *Towards a Globally Focused Chinese Military,* and testimony by Hartnett to the USCC.

104 See Wortzel, *The Dragon Extends its Reach.* Chapters 2 and 8 address this matter. Also see Larry M. Wortzel, "PLA Command, Control, and Targeting Architectures: Theory, Doctrine and Warfighting Applications," in *Right-Sizing the People's Liberation Army: Exploring the Contours of China's Military*, eds. Roy Kamphausen and Andrew Scobell (Carlisle, PA: Strategic Studies Institute, 2007), 191–234.

105 Zou Hao and Qu Guixi [邹浩, 曲贵溪], *Analysis of Indian Military Operations* [印军作战透析] (Beijing: Military Science Publishing House, 2013).

106 See Xu; Jiang and Guo.

107 McMillin.

Like a Good Neighbor: Chinese Intervention Through the Shanghai Cooperation Organization

Ben Lowsen

entral Asia and Afghanistan are not the primary focus of China's security concerns. However, both rank high in one important area: they have the potential to nurture religious extremists, terrorists, and ethnic separatists whose activities might inflame separatism in Xinjiang. As the United States reduces its presence in Afghanistan, with unpredictable consequences, Beijing sees an increased risk of instability there that might spill into Central Asia and China. Under such circumstances, China may consider using some form of national power outside of its borders to ease the threat. This chapter examines how Beijing might intervene in Central Asia or Afghanistan to protect its interests. It begins by laying out Chinese interests, examining potential threats to those interests, and then analyzing China's potential use of strategic and tactical capabilities to protect them. Decisions about whether and how to intervene in Central Asia or Afghanistan would be tied to an assessment of China's interests, perceived threats, means available to ameliorate the situation, and political feasibility.[1] China has an array of means and approaches it might use: leveraging multilateral frameworks such as the Shanghai Cooperation Organization (SCO); supporting regional partners with economic and security assistance or with communications, intelligence, or space-based support; conducting military operations other than war such as training local military forces and participating in peacekeeping operations; and even intervening across its border with conventional forces. China is likely to seek to minimize its involvement, using indirect means before considering more direct methods. The difficulty and risks of military operations, along with Russia's special role in Central Asia, will temper China's willingness to intervene militarily.

Andrew Scobell and Andrew J. Nathan argue that "[l]imited interventions in countries around China's periphery are conceivable if vital interests such as the safety of Chinese citizens or access to energy resources come under threat."[2] China's interests in Central Asia and Afghanistan include both factors. However, Beijing's larger fear is that separatists, extremists, and terrorists (the "three evil forces") based in Central Asia and Afghanistan will support radical Uighurs inside China, destabilizing the Xinjiang Uyghur Autonomous Region or helping Uighurs there to secede. Chinese leaders worry that such a threat to territorial integrity could potentially cause a collapse of Chinese Communist Party (CCP) rule. Beijing also views the potential for Western incitement of Arab Spring–style "colored revolutions" with similar concern.

To prevent such scenarios and to promote domestic and regional stability, China has worked with Russia to create regional organizations in Central Asia to combat these threats, beginning with the Shanghai Five (China, Russia, Kazakhstan, Kyrgyzstan, Tajikistan) in 1996, which evolved into the Shanghai Cooperation Organization (SCO) in 2001 (adding Uzbekistan). Should China see acute threats to its interests in Central Asia or Afghanistan—particularly threats that might topple the government of one of the SCO members—it might be tempted to act, even if this violated Beijing's longstanding principle of non-interference in the internal affairs of other countries.[3]

China is more likely to intervene in Afghanistan than in Central Asia. The larger Central Asian states (Kazakhstan, Uzbekistan, and non-SCO member Turkmenistan) have remained relatively stable since the Soviet Union's dissolution and are unlikely to require extensive outside support to maintain stability. Kyrgyzstan and Tajikistan are less stable (according to the World Bank stability index), but their special relationship with Russia, which maintains military bases in both countries, means Beijing is unlikely to feel the need to intervene, although it may support or supplement Russian assistance should it become necessary. The combination of religious extremism, terrorism, and a shrinking U.S. and North Atlantic Treaty Organization (NATO) presence makes Afghanistan the place where Beijing is most likely to perceive a sufficiently serious threat to consider a cross-border intervention. This chapter, therefore, uses Afghanistan to examine Chinese threat perceptions and potential intervention through the SCO, of which Afghanistan became an observer state in 2012.[4]

China's military, the People's Liberation Army (PLA), has historically fought border wars using large, manpower-intensive forces, as it did in Korea, India, and Vietnam.[5] Today, it is building a force to fight and win "local wars under conditions of informationization [comprehensive digitization and networking]" with the operational concept of *active defense*.[6] The idea of fighting limited border wars has not changed, nor has the notion that these will be *defensive* in nature, even when Chinese forces cross the border.

What is changing is the dictate for the PLA to conduct "New Historic Missions" to meet an array of challenges, including protecting CCP rule and defending China's expanding national interests.[7] China's military is also shifting from its traditional reliance on quantitative superiority to a more balanced mix of numbers and qualitative improvements that can pressure even technically sophisticated militaries, especially if the fight is relatively close to China.[8] PLA capabilities are no longer limited to the traditional military domains of land, sea, and air but now cover a broad spectrum including space, communications, electromagnetic warfare, influence operations, and nuclear capabilities. China's capabilities in these areas are not uniformly state-of-the-art but are becoming more flexible and better able to respond to challenges to China's interests overseas. Despite these advances, there are questions about Beijing's logistical ability to sustain deployed forces, particularly at longer distances from China and in a combat environment.

Beyond military means, Beijing is linked into a network of likeminded states in the region. The SCO's framework established habitual collaborative bodies and cemented relationships to counter nontraditional security threats in Central Asia. The Regional Anti-Terrorist Structure (RATS) provides an information-sharing outlet to enhance cooperation in dealing with these threats. The SCO has also conducted a range of partnership exercises, most notably its Peace Mission series, which have developed a degree of comfort and interoperability between participating SCO members along with structures and experience that might come into play in future contingencies. Despite their prominent displays of traditional air and mechanized ground forces, the focus of these exercises has been *counterterrorism*, which to the SCO means fighting any nongovernment group threatening a member government. A group of scholars from the Chinese Academy of Social Sciences described the SCO's genesis and purpose in these terms: "Beginning with border talks among China, Russia, Uzbekistan, and other countries, the SCO has had the continuous goal of countering terrorism, separatism, and extremism. Counterterrorism has become the most important of all: member countries have since its foundation in 2001 conducted annual joint counterterrorism exercises."[9]

Interests, Threats, and Cooperation

Then–State Councilor Dai Bingguo gave a succinct account of China's "core interests" at a 2009 session of the U.S.-China Security and Economic Dialogue, defining them as "preserving China's basic state system and national security, national sovereignty and territorial integrity; and China's sustained, stable socio-economic development."[10] The U.S. Defense Department describes China's "overriding strategic objectives" as "preserving Communist Party rule, sustaining economic growth and development, defending national sovereignty and territorial integrity, achieving national unification, maintaining internal stability, and securing China's status as a great power."[11]

Concerning Central Asia and Afghanistan, there is broad agreement that Beijing's primary interests are domestic social stability and territorial integrity, in particular preventing ethnic separatist, religious extremist, and terrorist groups from coalescing to incite the Xinjiang Uyghur Autonomous Region to break away from the People's Republic of China (PRC).[12] China's 2011 Defense White Paper characterizes the task of the armed forces as follows:

> . . . to guard against and resist aggression, defend the security of China's lands, inland waters, territorial waters and airspace, safeguard its maritime rights and interests, and maintain its security interests in space, electromagnetic space and cyber space. It is also tasked to oppose and contain the separatist forces for "Taiwan independence," crack down on separatist forces for "East Turkistan independence" and "Tibet independence," and defend national sovereignty and territorial integrity.[13]

Although Beijing's primary focus remains to its east, Chinese leaders also devote significant attention to western China, seeing separatism as an existential threat common to both areas.

Beijing insists that terrorism, ethnic separatism, and religious extremism (which it labels the *three evil forces* or *three evils*) combine into a single movement that seeks to carve up China, a Chinese equivalent of the "axis of evil."[14] Beijing believes Xinjiang's Uyghur minority has produced a host of terrorist/ extremist organizations said to be responsible for over 200 "bombings and assassinations,"[15] killing at least 164 people and wounding 440, although there is some doubt as to the accuracy of these claims.[16] Chinese Academy of Social Sciences scholar Wang Haiyun describes common concerns about these threats as one factor holding the SCO together, and they are enshrined in the

SCO charter.[17] Emphasizing the threat posed by the three evils has also allowed the PRC to make common cause with the U.S. war on terror. However, Chinese official statements and writing make clear that Beijing's concerns are real and not just a pretense to gain U.S. support. Indeed, the SCO was formed to combat the three evils prior to the September 11 terrorist attacks in 2001.

China's and the SCO's conflation of terrorism, extremism, and separatism provides flexibility in justifying either individual or collective action; together they form a category broad enough to cover practically any hostile activity any of the governments might wish to suppress.[18] There is no theoretical obstacle to the SCO aiding its members in most any situation, although such support in Collective Security Treaty Organization (CSTO) states would likely require some form of CSTO mandate. The main issue would be mustering collective support or acquiescence for intervention.

China, Russia, and the other SCO members also have shared concerns about the entrance of a third great power into Central Asia: the United States after 9/11. China has a reflexive fear of U.S. encirclement along its Western border as a possible springboard for surveillance or efforts to destabilize Xinjiang. Beijing took the U.S. presence in Central Asia as proof of a unilateralist bent and as a possible military threat.[19] Beijing also fears a fourth evil: U.S. support for the "fifth modernization" of democracy and the potential to press for regime change. The United States has supported emerging democracies in Mongolia and Kyrgyzstan, as well as investing much capital in sweeping away the Taliban and attempting to install a more liberal government in Afghanistan. The Arab Spring and associated "colored revolutions" have intensified China's fears about the U.S. role in Central Asia. Beijing suspects itself to be the primary target for U.S. "peaceful evolution" and fights against this perceived political threat, including cooperating with Russia to form election monitoring groups that offer positive appraisals of "democratic" elections throughout the region.[20]

The SCO provides a forum and framework for mutual cooperation against the "three evil forces" (and by extension the fourth), in particular through its Regional Anti-Terrorist Structure. Because China focuses more on political and nontraditional security threats like terrorism in Central Asia and not on threats from other states, Beijing seeks to band together with SCO members against common enemies, which might be called "anti-state forces." Beyond fighting these forces, Beijing hopes that contact with Central Asian economies will actually help to stabilize Xinjiang.[21]

The SCO's principle of nonalliance reflects a longstanding Chinese preference, but it is also aimed at reducing Western and Russian perceptions of a potential threat of a Chinese bloc.[22] Russia lost direct control of the region when the five Central Asian Soviet republics broke away from the collapsing Soviet Union.[23] However, this did not alter Russia's significant connections throughout the region or its belief that it is entitled to a special regional role. The SCO's nonalliance principle thus avoids provoking Moscow's ire and helps Beijing avoid entanglement in an anti-NATO pact with Russia. Given that both China and Russia have primary concerns in other directions (Asia and Taiwan versus Europe and NATO, respectively), there is utility in an agreement that helps to preserve the status quo in each country's backyard.

For the Central Asian states themselves, having both Moscow and Beijing vie for their attention is advantageous.[24] In that regard, Russia's CSTO, a more traditional treaty alliance to which China does not belong, has existed in Central Asia since 1992. The Shanghai Five and later the SCO have provided Central Asian governments with additional support, while reminding Russia that it is not the only game in town. However, Central Asian states rely more on Russia and the CSTO for security assistance. Evidence includes a 2007 Memorandum of Understanding between the SCO and CSTO that nudged the SCO away from its nonalliance stance,[25] and a 2009 CSTO agreement establishing Collective Rapid Reaction Forces, a substantial joint force designated to combat both traditional and nontraditional threats. Thus, the five former Soviet republics now enjoy a strong, multilateral, and institutionalized stability enhancement mechanism, led by Russia. While this will not protect Central Asian rulers against all threats (it did not prevent two revolutions in Kyrgyzstan), it will probably help enhance overall stability.

The entry of the United States into Afghanistan and Central Asia after September 11, 2001, provided a third suitor to, and further support for, Central Asian governments. Because no one great power has sought absolute primacy or a radical change to the post-Soviet strategic landscape, all three great powers and the Central Asian governments have cooperated to protect their regional interests and share in the benefits. As the U.S. role and presence in Afghanistan decrease, the other players are working to maintain stability there—for example, by granting Afghanistan SCO observer status in June 2012.[26] Despite extensive U.S. security assistance, Afghanistan is still arguably the least stable state bordering China. Scholar Zhao Huasheng emphasizes that China's primary interest there mirrors its concerns for the other Central Asian states: "domestic concerns about the security and stability of the largely Muslim region of Xinjiang overwhelm all other [Chinese interests in Afghanistan]."[27]

Despite all its concerns about U.S. activities, China looks on the impending reduction of the U.S. presence in Afghanistan with a certain sense of trepidation. India, the European Union, and Iran may each lend some support to stabilize the country in their own way. China's future role may mirror its relationship with Pakistan, in which Beijing provides a modicum of support to its needy neighbor in return for it remaining a key security partner. Afghanistan's deep ethnic divides, complicated tribal politics, and entrenched disputes will give Beijing pause as it considers what sort of commitments, if any, it might make there.

Compared with Afghanistan, the Central Asian states hold only minor security issues for China. Kazakhstan and Turkmenistan, although authoritarian, have been relatively stable and prosperous. Uzbekistan appears to have settled its own domestic stability issues with a brutal crackdown at Andijan in 2005. Tajikistan, bolstered by a substantial Russian troop presence, has remained stable, in spite of tensions since the settlement of its civil war in 1997. Kyrgyzstan, also with Russian assistance, has managed to contain tensions that produced two forceful changes in government in 2005 and 2010. These are all CSTO countries, so any aid from China would likely be in coordination with the CSTO.[28] Turkmenistan and Kazakhstan both have substantial oil reserves, which provide resources to help their governments maintain stability.[29]

Given Beijing's emphasis on stability, the most salient threat involves a state collapse that gives Chinese extremists and/or separatists a foothold. The most prominent factors that might threaten collapse include an uncontrolled internal disturbance threatening China's interests, such as disorder or rebellion, likely along ethnic, religious, or national lines; the potential for lateral escalation or spread of conflict, especially into China; refugee issues; democratic uprisings; and threats to Chinese citizens or vital resources.

Finally, it is worth mentioning Beijing's longstanding articulation of the Five Principles of Peaceful Coexistence (in particular, mutual noninterference). In theory, noninterference prevents intervention in other countries' affairs except in self-defense. However, if Beijing can convince itself that it is threatened, it can disregard noninterference. Conversely, when Beijing does not want to act, noninterference provides a convenient rationale. China would prefer to keep a low profile in order to maintain the trade and economic development necessary for it to survive, but if Chinese leaders perceive direct threats to China's stability emanating from Central Asia or Afghanistan, they are likely to act.[30]

Strategic Options

China currently possesses the means to carry out a broad range of campaigns in support of Central Asian contingencies, including providing logistical, technical, political, and even moral support in any campaign against anti-government or terrorist forces. This includes deploying traditional military forces, although the PLA's ability to conduct and sustain such campaigns under adverse conditions is not clear. However, with the support of regional and/or international organizations and facing the right combination of threats and a manageable situation, Beijing might be willing to deploy a peacekeeping force. Deploying a peacekeeping force outside the United Nations (UN) framework would mark a significant advance in China's willingness to use force outside its own borders to defend its interests.

During his tenure as paramount leader, Hu Jintao made a concerted effort to get the PLA to broaden its mission set beyond Taiwan, multiplying and improving Beijing's options to protect its interests. Beijing can now apply varying levels of effort flexibly across multiple domains to mitigate perceived threats to stability. Because of the high material and political costs of using conventional military forces, China would likely first make every attempt to mitigate threats by less costly nontraditional means and other elements of national power.

Potential examples include the *DIME* grouping, which adds diplomatic, informational, and economic power to traditional military power; Qiao Liang's and Wang Xiangsui's magnum opus *Unrestricted Warfare*, which elaborated on lawfare, economic warfare, network warfare, and terrorism;[31] and the U.S. Army's counterinsurgency manual, which cites governance, combat and civil security operations, essential services, information operations, economic development, and host-nation security forces as areas critical to mission accomplishment in counterinsurgency.[32] Combining similar concepts and placing them alongside traditional domains of warfare yields the operational environment as shown in figure 11.1. While the traditional domains of land, sea, air, and intelligence remain prominent, the figure

Figure 11.1. Security Domains

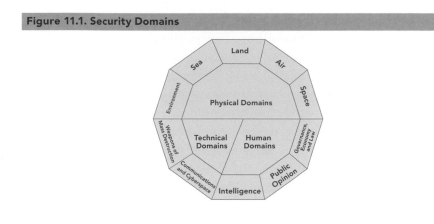

highlights the emerging importance of newer domains like space, communications and cyberspace, and weapons of mass destruction and the redis-
covered importance of domains such as the environment, public opinion,
and government, economy, and law.[33] China's government and military have
numerous ways to affect events across all of these domains.

In keeping with this expanded operational environment and Beijing's
broadening view of its own interests, Scobell and Nathan point out the PLA's
expansion of its primary mission set to include non-warfighting tasks, for
which it has adopted the U.S. military term "military operations other than
war" (MOOTW).[34] Hu Jintao raised the profile of this new era for the PLA with
his 2004 exhortation to take on new historic missions to protect expanding
interests including "counterpiracy and counterterrorism operations, humanitarian assistance and disaster relief, UN peacekeeping, sea lanes protection,
and securing space-based assets."[35]

The March 2011 evacuation of Chinese nationals from Libya by "commercial aircraft, ships, and buses, the guided missile frigate *Xuzhou* and four Il-76
transport aircraft" provides a practical example of Beijing's ability to combine
civilian and military assets to safeguard its interests.[36] Similar evacuation missions would be possible throughout Central Asia. Humanitarian and security
assistance could also lend critical support to a faltering neighbor in need. Such
capabilities provide more customizable, scalable options that take advantage
of emerging security domains to address security concerns.

Scobell and Nathan note that the PLA could be used in border control missions,[37] which might include China's borders with Central Asia and Afghanistan.

However, China's internal security force, the People's Armed Police (PAP), is more oriented toward quelling civil unrest, suggesting its greater usefulness in a Central Asian contingency. The PAP's organization and experience make it better suited to working with civil authorities. The Chinese government, however, might be reluctant to deploy significant numbers of PAP troops—its first line of defense against social disorder—outside Chinese territory.[38] Moreover, PAP units have no experience operating in a foreign environment. That said, their knowledge about maintaining social order might prove useful to a Central Asian government under threat of collapse. PAP cadres might be used inside or even outside China to provide training to increase the capabilities of indigenous constabulary forces.

China has several relevant laws that direct the state and military to perform a range of activities that might be useful in a Central Asian scenario, such as the 2010 National Defense Mobilization Law.[39] China's 2011 Defense White Paper also discusses the special PLA role in border defense:

> China practices an administration system of sharing responsibilities between the military and the local authorities in border and coastal defense. . . . The main responsibilities of the border public security force are as follows: border, coastal and maritime public security administration, entry-exit frontier inspection at ports; prevention and crackdown on illegal and criminal acts in border and coastal areas, such as illegal border crossing, drug trafficking and smuggling; and organization of and participation in counterterrorist and emergency-management operations in border and coastal areas.[40]

Thus, Beijing's capabilities are not necessarily limited to the PLA and PAP, but can be augmented with civilian assets. A certain amount of ambiguity is built into Chinese statements about border operations that might allow for operations across the frontier.

Even modest quantities of political and material support could be important to a government in difficult circumstances. China has been able to keep its ally in Pyongyang afloat relatively cheaply and with minimal blowback. Moreover, there is flexibility to modulate the level of support to gain leverage. Of course, Pyongyang's own actions have generated a significant backlash for Beijing, most notably following the sinking of the Republic of Korea Navy corvette *Cheon'an*. But Central Asia's governments are far less likely to provoke their neighbors. Countries in Central Asia and Afghanistan that are in crisis should be promising recipients for targeted political and economic support from China, although such support would be more effective for Kyrgyzstan and Tajikistan, with their smaller, less diverse populations, than for Afghanistan.

The SCO, the "cornerstone of Beijing's approach in Central Asia,"[41] provides a potential vehicle for Chinese intervention in Central Asia or Afghanistan. The SCO's most important institutionalized framework for military cooperation is the Peace Mission exercise series, although this is not the only military exercise conducted under SCO auspices, and its participants and activities vary from year to year. Table 11.1 lays out the participants and activities of major SCO military exercises. John Garver notes that 2002 marked the PLA's first ever exercise with foreign military forces: an antiterrorism exercise with Kyrgyzstan at their shared border under SCO auspices.[42] Contrary to common understandings of counterterrorism, some of these exercises have featured large displays of conventional heavy and air forces, suggesting a heavy-handed approach to maintaining government stability in the face of unrest, although it is unclear how closely such exercises correspond to what states would do in a real contingency.[43] China in 2012 promised a "fully fledged strategic development plan" at the SCO Heads of State Council in Beijing, including developing partnership networks with the UN, Commonwealth of Independent States, and CSTO.[44] Such networks could improve interoperability between China, Russia, and other Central Asian powers, allowing for more flexible joint employment of a broad range of capabilities.

Richard Weitz of the Hudson Institute has argued that the exercises:

> enhance the ability of the members' armed forces to deter and suppress regional terrorism as well as another popular rebellion . . . reassure Central Asian leaders that China and Russia will help them manage their security challenges . . . help the SCO militaries learn more about each other's evolving capabilities . . . [and] affirm to the U.S. and other extra-regional countries that Russia and China consider Central Asia as lying within their overlapping zones of security responsibility.[45]

The SCO thus includes a comprehensive stability guarantee, a joint commitment to cooperation and interoperability, and an assurance by China and Russia to negotiate their interests in the region and not come into direct opposition.

Table 11.1. Shanghai Cooperation Organization (SCO) Exercises

Cooperation 2003

- More than 1,000 troops in eastern Kazakhstan and China's Xinjiang region
- Several counterterrorism scenarios

Peace Mission 2005

- 8,000 Chinese troops, 2,000 Russian troops, and observers from all members
- Land maneuvers in Vladivostok
- Amphibious maneuvers in Shandong
- Russian Tu-160 and Tu-95 strategic bombers and some 140 warships

Peace Mission 2007

- 2,000 Russian troops, 1,600 Chinese troops, almost 6,500 troops and 80 aircraft
- Suppressing a major Islamist insurgency or popular rebellion in Urumqi
- Live-fire exercise at the Russian military training range near Chelyabinsk

Peace Mission 2009

- About 1,300 military personnel from each country
- Three days jointly planning and organizing for a combined antiterrorist campaign in northeast China
- Held at Taonan training base in China's Shenyang Military Region

Peace Mission 2010

- 5,000 troops, 300 major combat pieces, and over 50 combat planes and helicopters
- All full members of the SCO contributed at least one military unit to the exercise (except Uzbekistan, which pulled out at the last minute)
- PLA demonstration of network-centric capabilities
- PLA mid-air refueling of fighter aircraft during a rehearsal of precision strikes
- Exercise of various capabilities, including preparatory fire, mobilizing reserves, besieging residential areas, conducting breakouts, suppressing fire at night, intensive drill, live fire drills, and combat equipment display

Peace Mission 2012

- 2,000 personnel from China, Kazakhstan, Kyrgyzstan, Russia, and Tajikistan
- "New methods" of blocking and destroying "illegal armed groups"
- Coordination and interaction in combat missions in mountain areas
- Uzbekistan did not attend

Peace Mission 2013

- 646 Chinese and 600 Russian participants in Chelyabinsk, Russia
- Coordinating joint commanding organs and troop units of the two militaries to carry out military operations
- Antiterrorism exercise that included force planning and deployment, campaign planning, and campaign execution
- PLA and Russian air force participation

Peace Mission 2014

- 4,800 Chinese participants and 2,200 foreign participants in Inner Mongolia, China
- Multilateral antiterrorism exercise with all SCO full members except Uzbekistan
- Scenario involved an extremist or separatist group from abroad inciting people to join a terrorist insurgency in an SCO nation. The nation asked the SCO for assistance in suppressing the insurgency
- Chinese participation included infantry, aviation, airborne troops, and special forces, including fighter aircraft, airborne early warning aircraft, and unmanned aerial vehicles

Sources: Roger McDermott, "The Rising Dragon: SCO Peace Mission 2007," Occasional Paper (Washington, DC: Jamestown Foundation, October 19, 2007), available at <Document2www.jamestown.org/single/?no_cache=1&tx_ttnews%5Btt_news%5D=32>; Stephen Blank, "Peace-Mission 2009: A Military Scenario Beyond Central Asia," *China Brief* 9, no. 17 (August 20, 2009), available at <Document2www.jamestown.org/programs/chinabrief/single/?tx_ttnews%5Btt_news%5D=35433&tx_ttnews%5B-backPid%5D=25&cHash=201d76e87b>; Richard Weitz, "Military Exercises Underscore the SCO's Character," *Central Asia-Caucasus Institute Analyst* (May 25, 2011), available at <www.cacianalyst.org/?q=node/5565>; Roger McDermott, "China Showcases Expeditionary Military Power in Peace Mission 2010," *Eurasia Daily Monitor* 7, no. 174 (September 28, 2010), available at <www.jamestown.org/single/?no_cache=1&tx_ttnews%5Btt_news%5D=36955#.U2vbivmSwa8>; Zhang Zhichong, "On Shaping the Image of Our Military through Cooperation in Nontraditional Security Fields," *News World*, no. 11 (2011); Wang Dong; Medvedev; McDermott, "China Leads SCO Peace Mission 2012 in Central Asia;" "Peace Mission 2013: China-Russia Joint Anti-Terrorism Exercise," *China Military Online Special Report*, undated, available at <http://eng.chinamil.com.cn/special-reports/node_60757.htm>; and "Peace Mission 2014: SCO Joint Anti-Terrorism Exercise," *China Military Online Special Report*, undated, available at <http://eng.chinamil.com.cn/special-reports/node_72113.htm>.

As suggested by China's broad definition of terrorists, extremists, and separatists, the SCO's focus on counterterrorism is equivalent to support for government stability. The SCO's most basic function is to maintain five relatively stable Central Asian governments alongside their great power neighbors. Afghanistan's ethno-religious extremist movements have been a source of regional concern, particularly for China, as evidenced by the enshrinement of the three evils in the SCO's Shanghai Convention on Combating Terrorism, Separatism, and Extremism[46] and in the RATS agreement. In addition to setting up a permanent body headquartered in Bishkek, Kyrgyzstan, RATS specifically envisions multilateral coordination, government-to-government assistance, intelligence sharing (including a dedicated database), antiterrorism exercise coordination, antiterrorism operational assistance, and specialist, legal, and academic support.[47] Beijing could leverage any or all of these mechanisms, either bilaterally or with an SCO mandate, to support its neighbors' stability.

Another tool Beijing has used in the past is to offer political mediation, especially to reduce international pressure for U.S. or UN intervention. Because China maintains cordial relations with governments where the United States does not, it often finds itself in a position to mediate disputes. One example involves Syria, where the United States has been pushing for a UN Security Council resolution, while China has consistently refused to accept a resolution and offered to lead mediation efforts instead (proposing a four-point plan).[48] Beijing similarly lent its good offices to mediation efforts between factions in the Sudanese and Libyan civil wars.[49] Although reluctant to interfere in internal affairs, Beijing has built ties with some rebel factions that have become influential political forces. Beijing has already demonstrated some willingness to work with the Taliban in Afghanistan.[50] With its Central Asian neighbors, Beijing would be likely to support the government against threatening rebel groups, although mediation would remain an available tool.

China could also provide direct military assistance for threatened governments, via training, logistical support, technical support, or even by deploying PLA forces. China has been willing to use force internally when it sees its interests threatened. In the past 5 years, China has used PAP forces backed up by regular PLA units to suppress unrest in both Tibet and Xinjiang.[51] Such forces could potentially be used abroad, as discussed above. Even a relatively small force package, if well supported, might have a stabilizing effect in a particular area—for example, a capital city such as Kabul. Significant questions remain about China's ability to coordinate and support such an operation.[52] Furthermore, the presence of a foreign force might exacerbate the situation, particularly if it were operating without relevant training or adequate combat or logistical support.

Regular PLA ground forces have also performed their share of riot control missions. On multiple occasions (most recently and spectacularly in 1989), Beijing has called on the PLA to disperse large demonstrations. Since 1989, however, this has been the option of last resort due to the possibility of extensive bloodshed and international blowback. Beijing might be more willing to use a blunt instrument outside its own borders, but the potential for unintended consequences, damage, backlash, and mounting costs would almost certainly stay Beijing's hand.

Where its interests are involved, China has shown itself to be a willing and able partner in peacekeeping operations—for example, between Sudan and South Sudan and in Darfur.[53] Its interests in Central Asia and Afghanistan might make this an attractive option should other efforts fail. Several hurdles exist. First, a formal peacekeeping mission would mean recognizing the legitimacy of competing factions, which would make good sense in Afghanistan but not in other countries with more unified governments. Second, it would mean securing a mandate. The Western powers might be hesitant to support a UN authorization that gives China significant leeway, to say nothing of Russia. China could seek a mandate under the SCO, but the necessary consensus may be elusive. Finally, Beijing could seek to build its own "coalition of the willing" among nearby states, or else simply negotiate bilaterally or claim it intervened by invitation by some domestic actor in the neighboring state. Beijing has been known to obfuscate the boundary between sanctioned SCO activities and bi- or multi-lateral activities that happen to include SCO members.[54] Claiming a mandate outside the UN peacekeeping framework would mark a significant step forward in China's willingness to use force outside its borders. However, labeling an intervention as a peacekeeping operation would provide a moral high ground that might mitigate the less savory aspects of such an intervention.

Border missions such as interdiction and refugee management could likewise play a part in any scenario. China's border area forces, perhaps with reinforcements, would be able to prevent most antigovernment forces from crossing into China from Central Asia or Afghanistan, particularly considering the dearth of lines of communication, often impassable terrain, and security fences in place along the border. However, large refugee inflows might compromise border integrity and become a drain on the economy, as well as providing cover for infiltration of hostile elements. In certain situations, resettlement across a border might ease tensions on the other side, as with the Hoa migration from Vietnam into China in the late 1970s. But immigration by a non-Han minority would not evoke the same sense of fraternal responsibility in Beijing. It seems unlikely that large numbers of Central Asians would seek refuge in China or that China's border forces would have much difficulty holding them back if they did.

Beijing has long been able to conduct military campaigns to defend its borders. Some have been quite successful, as in India in 1962; others less so, as against the Soviet Union in 1969. Given that the last major instance of a Chinese cross-border conflict was the 1979 punitive expedition into Vietnam, these can hardly be taken as models, except that their scope and location defines what Beijing means by *local wars*. Several factors militate against China attempting such a campaign in Central Asia or Afghanistan: the possibility of unnecessary tensions or escalation with another power, especially Russia; the likely greater demand for and efficacy of support and stabilization forces; and the expense of sending a large force to do a small force's job. In Afghanistan's case, this sort of campaign would be a particularly poor fit and unlikely to accomplish much of value.

Tactical Capabilities

China possesses a broad range of options it could use in support of the SCO throughout Central Asia. These include traditional military force missions, peacekeeping operations, humanitarian assistance and disaster relief, police support to civil authorities, as well as a spectrum of other nontraditional capabilities such as cyber and communications operations, network support (including space assets), and focused economic engagement. Although China's legal framework for defense envisions domestic contingencies and not deployment abroad, the view that foreign turmoil generates domestic unrest may make the government more flexible about the distinction between foreign and domestic security threats. Any measure that involves putting "boots on the ground," however, would be difficult and potentially quite expensive due to longstanding problems with logistical coordination and joint operations, aside from potential political problems. Beijing's preferred option would be to offer support to enable partner governments to maintain stability on their own. Existing cooperative frameworks, such as the Peace Mission exercises, would provide a starting point for such enabling operations.

The PRC's legal framework designates specific tasks that may be performed in emergencies that it might apply to Central Asian or Afghan contingencies. The PRC's 2007 Emergency Response Law defines emergencies broadly enough to include not only events such as natural disasters but also threats to social stability, authorizing the PLA as necessary to set up security cordons and checkpoints, control traffic, guard key installations, control fuel, power, and water supplies, and use force to quell resistance.[55] There have been multiple opportunities to exercise most or all of these functions, most notably during the 2008 Wenchuan earthquake.[56] Other ground-level options the PLA might offer include facility security, impartial observers, riot control, logistical support, and presence patrolling. More advanced options might include base operations, leadership protection, staff support, and low-level mediation.

The 2009 People's Armed Police Law lays out both general and specific tasks for the PAP: "The PAP carries the national trust for the responsibilities of security protection as well as defensive operations, disaster and relief work, joining in national economic construction, etc."[57] Some of these tasks might be useful outside of China: area security and access control, civil patrolling and law enforcement, route security, social order and crowd control, and incident management. Woven into the law are multiple references to the authority of the "incident commander" [*xianchang zhihuiyuan*, 现场指挥员] to make on-the-spot calls, suggesting the desire of the government to empower subordinates to make the important decisions necessary for carrying out a civil-military campaign. That said, China faces significant institutional and cultural obstacles to delegating authority to subordinates.[58]

One of the biggest factors for any PLA deployment to Central Asia would be its ability to support a deployed force. This would be particularly difficult if the PLA were opposed and could not guarantee secure supply lines.[59] The PLA at present probably lacks sufficient lift assets to sustain opposed operations abroad indefinitely. Nonmilitary assets could help, as suggested by China's principle of civilian support to the military.[60] Setting up secure supply lines would be costly in the long run, likely causing Beijing to reassess the true threat of Uyghur terrorists and the means to deal with them. In an Afghanistan contingency, for instance, it might be simpler to contain the threat by partnering with neighboring countries rather than attempting to solve the problem unilaterally.

There are numerous roads between Xinjiang, Kazakhstan, and Kyrgyzstan that might enable the flow of military and supporting traffic.[61] There is likewise a road from Xinjiang into Tajikistan's Pamir Mountains and Afghanistan's Wakhan Corridor. Google Earth imagery and travel to the region suggest that all of these have trafficability and seasonal limitations. The "land bridge" and rail line between Urumqi, Xinjiang and Aqtoghay, Kazakhstan might enable robust, economical force projection capabilities into Kazakhstan[62] but would be of little use for most of Central Asia.

There are significant questions about the PLA's ability to conduct effective joint operations.[63] Bureaucratic interests and PLA culture might combine to hinder coordination, both within the PLA and among partner states. There is also some doubt about how well the PLA could tailor a combat force package. The PLA deployed a platoon of dedicated ground combat troops in support of UN peacekeeping operations for the first time in 2011.[64] Coordinating the activities of supporting arms (for example, cyber, space) is within Beijing's capability,[65] but organizing a viable package of deploying forces for operations abroad, along with a command structure and support plan, is more difficult. The PLA's emerging concept of brigade modularity might provide for a more tailorable force, although these forces seem to be optimized for diverse terrain, not necessarily diverse situations.[66]

The Peace Mission exercises, RATS, and the Collective Rapid Reaction Forces would provide convenient bases for China to support regional powers. Using these frameworks, Beijing could tailor support packages for partners in need. For example, using the experience in moving personnel and materiel into Kyrgyzstan via ground motorized maneuvers during Peace Mission

2012,[67] China might repeat such a maneuver during a crisis, especially with the agreement and support of the Kyrgyz government and perhaps in coordination with Russian forces or the Collective Rapid Reaction Forces. The 2013 and 2014 Peace Mission exercises also tested PLA planning and deployment capabilities within an SCO context. Information collected by RATS would be useful to any of the countries listed, including nonmember Afghanistan.

For SCO members, any collective deployment to Afghanistan would be limited. Tajikistan and Uzbekistan might look to provide limited support to the relatively peaceful enclaves where Tajiks and Uzbeks reside. Non-SCO member Turkmenistan might provide similar support. Russia's consent to the Northern Supply Route to support U.S. operations in Afghanistan shows both a concern for the security situation there as well as a willingness to provide indirect support. Russia might opt to use the Central Asian Five as a buffer instead of (again) moving forces into Afghanistan.

China would probably offer to negotiate a peaceful resolution[68] but would be extremely cautious about jumping into the fray with military forces. As long as its interests could be served through negotiation between subnational factions and the government in Kabul, Beijing would be unlikely to risk involvement in Kandahar or along the Pakistan border. While experience gained taking on "illegal armed groups" in the Peace Mission exercises might prove useful if applied tactically, Afghanistan's terrain and human environment would make operations challenging. The skills the PLA is gaining working with SCO members and Russia would not transfer directly into the more contentious environment in Afghanistan; China would require a significant investment to create forces able to operate effectively there. An assessment of the costs and possible outcomes might make Beijing reassess whether the threat of Uyghur separatists operating from Afghanistan justifies intervention.

China possesses numerous manned and unmanned aerial capabilities it could apply to a Central Asian or Afghan scenario. Airborne lift assets could evacuate Chinese citizens and perhaps be used to support threatened governments. The PLA Air Force and Army Aviation could conduct air presence missions such as reconnaissance, loitering, and flyovers. If antistate forces were present at or associated with a particular location, these forces could perform aerial interdiction, although this would require a good deal of intelligence support from RATS or another ad hoc intelligence sharing mechanism. Fighters, bombers, and helicopters equipped with precision strike munitions could conduct combat operations, although coordination challenges between air and ground forces would likely make joint air-ground operations unacceptably risky.

China could employ national-level space-based capabilities to support PLA operations and aid partners, including "space based surveillance, reconnaissance, navigation, meteorological, and communications satellite constellations." It also possesses counterspace assets such as "jamming, laser, microwave, and cyber weapons." [69] Despite reliability problems, these systems form what China sees as the basis for digital, "informationized" operations and as such may be of significant use to partners.

The Chinese government also possesses an array of communications and cyber capabilities. Jamming broadcasts, monitoring and blocking Web traffic, and undertaking computer network operations could allow Beijing to collect intelligence, deceive opponents, and disrupt antigovernment operations.[70] This might be particularly useful in shutting down social media and cell phone communications to prevent opponents from using these to spread their message. China has also previously conducted intelligence exchanges, arrests, extraditions, suppression of unfriendly groups, and internal security training, all of which could be useful in supporting a Central Asian government.[71] The habitual intelligence sharing structures within the SCO, namely under RATS, would provide a conduit to share information and coordinate with partners. Establishing a headquarters with authority similar to the PLA's "Incident commander" could remove the information stovepipe and allow a low-level exchange of actionable intelligence. However, governments may be uncomfortable delegating authority in this way.

Beijing could also support partners by providing direct medical, water, and other material aid during critical periods. It would also be likely to look the other way were its partner to distribute these items with political aims in mind, as in North Korea.[72] Nuclear weapons and other weapons of mass destruction would not be particularly effective and would produce extreme international opprobrium.

Conclusion

The Shanghai Cooperation Organization is more than a marriage of convenience. Its principal benefactors, China and Russia, each have reasons to want a peaceful, friendly, and stable Central Asia. The Central Asian Five have been relatively stable and do not appear to be moving toward either religious extremism or Arab

Spring–style uprisings. This is a boon for China because it lessens the threat of such an upheaval engulfing Xinjiang. Moreover, China has willing security partners in Central Asia. As long as Beijing respects Russia's special position in the region, it is free to invest in and work cooperatively with those powers. Maintaining the political status quo and pursuing shared economic development are commonly shared goals. Only a strategic reassessment of Central Asia might trigger one of the benefactors to reject this arrangement.

The ability of the Afghan government to work out a stable modus vivendi with its various ethnic groups and the Taliban is cause for some concern. China and the other powers are beginning to work through the SCO to see if Central Asia's relative stability can be extended there. Russia already maintains a sizeable footprint and extensive military relations throughout Central Asia, but it would probably avoid getting involved militarily in Afghanistan if at all possible. China will also proceed with great caution, concerned that the results of any Central Asian or Afghan adventure would not justify the costs in money and political capital. If necessary, however, Beijing would be able to supply support across a broad spectrum of domains and capabilities. In intangible domains such as cyberspace, economics, and public opinion, as well as in space, Beijing could provide a robust response if required. But logistical weaknesses and difficulties in executing joint operations would make an opposed ground force operation difficult, particularly in coordination with partners. Furthermore, the costs and political liabilities would make any such operation deeply unattractive. The nominally better-suited PAP forces are also unlikely to deploy outside China, although some sort of advisory role is imaginable. A relatively unopposed operation with some form of international mandate would also be possible, assuming the PLA could assemble a force package with skill sets matching the problem. In general, Beijing would prefer to help friendly governments build their capabilities and provide support rather than intervening with its own forces.

In pursuing stability, each of the Central Asian nations and Afghanistan would seek the help of its neighbors, great powers such as China, as well as organizations like the SCO. Although Beijing would feel some pressure to pursue its interests in neighboring countries through the SCO, it is likely to proceed cautiously, sensing a multiplication of dangers and few rewards for deeper involvement.

Notes

1   Graham Allison and Philip Zelikow allude to this formula in *Essence of Decision: Explaining the Cuban Missile Crisis* (New York: Longman, 1999).

2   Andrew Scobell and Andrew J. Nathan, "China's Overstretched Military," *The Washington Quarterly* 35, no. 4 (Fall 2012), 138.

3   Mathieu Duchâtel, Oliver Bräuner, and Zhou Hang, *Protecting China's Overseas Interests: The Slow Shift away from Non-interference*, SIPRI Policy Paper No. 41 (Stockholm: Stockholm International Peace Research Institute, 2014).

4   "China- and Russia-led Shanghai bloc eyes Afghan role," *BBC News*, June 7, 2012, available at <www.bbc.co.uk/news/world-asia-china-18349607>.

5   Andrew Scobell, *China's Use of Military Force: Beyond the Great Wall and the Long March* (New York: Cambridge University Press, 2003).

6   Office of the Secretary of Defense (OSD), *Military and Security Developments Involving the People's Republic of China* 2012, Annual Report to Congress (Washington, DC: Office of the Secretary of Defense, May 2012), iv, 3–4, available at <www.defense.gov/pubs/pdfs/2012_CMPR_Final.pdf>.

7   "The Military's Historic Missions in the New Period of the New Century" [*xin shiji xin jieduan wo jun lishi shiming*, 新世纪新阶段我军历史使命], shortened to "New Historic Missions."

8   James Hackett, ed., *The Military Balance: 2012* (London: Routledge, 2012), 213.

9   Gao Zugui, Wei Zonglei, and Liu Yu [高祖贵, 魏宗雷, 刘钰], "The Rise of the New Economic System and Its Influence" [新兴经济体的崛起及其影响], *International Data News* [国际资料信息], no. 8 (2009), available at <http://niis.cass.cn/upload/2012/12/d20121208101733441.pdf>.

10   Michael D. Swaine, "China's Assertive Behavior, Part One: On 'Core Interests,'" *China Leadership Monitor*, no. 34 (Winter 2011), 4; State Councilor Dai Bingguo in "Closing Remarks for U.S.-China Strategic and Economic Dialogue," U.S. Department of State, Washington, DC, July 28, 2009.

11   OSD, *Military and Security Developments*.

12   Wang Haiyun [王海运], "SCO Development Exceeds Western Expectations" [上合组织发展出乎西方预料], *Global Times* [环球时报], June 6, 2012, available at <http://euroasia.cass.cn/news/2012/06/494570.html>; Zhao Huasheng, *China and Afghanistan: China's Interests, Stances, and Perspectives* (Washington, DC: Center for Strategic and International Studies, 2012), 1; Alexander Cooley, *Great Games, Local Rules: The New Great Power Contest in Central Asia* (New York: Oxford University Press, 2012), Kindle edition, 74; John W. Garver, "China's Influence in Central and South Asia," in *Power Shift: China and Asia's New Dynamics*, ed. David Shambaugh (Berkeley and Los Angeles: University of California Press, 2005), 211;

and Liu Yuejin [刘跃进], *National Security Studies* [国家安全学] (Beijing: China University of Political Science and Law Press [中国政法大学出版社], 2004), 75.

13   Information Office of the State Council, People's Republic of China, *China's National Defense in 2010* (Beijing: Information Office of the State Council, March 2011).

14   "What Are the 'Three Evil Forces'?" [何为 "三股势力"?], Xinhua Online [新华网], July 13, 2009, available at <http://news.xinhuanet.com/politics/2009-07/13/content_11698031.htm>.

15   Cooley, 76; Information Office of the State Council, People's Republic of China, "East Turkistan Forces Cannot Get Away with Impunity," January 21, 2002, available at <http://news.xinhuanet.com/english/2002-01/21/content_247082.htm>.

16   Sean Roberts, "Imaginary Terrorism? The Global War on Terror and the Narrative of the Uyghur Terrorist Threat" (working paper, PONARS Eurasia, Elliot School of International Affairs, George Washington University, Washington, DC, March 2012), available at <www.gwu.edu/~ieresgwu/assets/docs/ponars/RobertsWP.pdf>.

17   Wang Haiyun; Cooley, 76–77.

18   The Shanghai Convention on Combating Terrorism, Separatism and Extremism, June 2001, art. 1, sec. 1, available at <https://www.unodc.org/tldb/pdf/Uzbekistan/Ratification_of_the_Shanghai_Convention_on_Combating_Terrorism_By_Uzbekistan.pdf>.

19   Cooley, 81; Bates Gill, *Rising Star: China's New Security Diplomacy* (Washington, DC: Brookings, 2010, revised); and David Shambaugh, "China Engages Asia: Reshaping the International Order," *International Security* 29, no. 3 (Winter 2004–2005), 64–99.

20   Cooley, 8.

21   Ibid., 78.

22   Wang Dong [王东], "Interpreting the 'Peace Mission' Counterterrorism Exercise" [解读 '和平使命' 反恐军演], *Observation and Ponderation* [观察与思考] (October 8, 2010), 48–49; Marcin Kaczmarski, "Russia Attempts to Limit Chinese Influence by Promoting CSTO-SCO Cooperation," *Central Asia-Caucasus Institute Analyst*, October 17, 2007, available at <http://cacianalyst.org/?q=node/4716>.

23   Ross H. Munro, "Central Asia and China," in *Central Asia: Kazakhstan, Uzbekistan, Tajikistan, Kyrgyzstan, Turkmenistan, and the World*, ed. Michael Mandelbaum (New York: Council on Foreign Relations Press, 1994), 228–229; Garver, 209–211.

24   Garver, 205–206.

25   Kaczmarski.

26 "China- and Russia-led Shanghai bloc eyes Afghan role," *BBC News.*

27 Zhao Huasheng, 1.

28 Cooley, 10, 74.

29 Central Intelligence Agency, "Crude Oil—Proved Reserves," *CIA World Factbook*, available at <https://www.cia.gov/library/publications/the-world-factbook/fields/2244.html#tx>.

30 See Duchâtel, Bräuner, and Hang.

31 Qiao Liang and Wang Xiangsui [乔良, 王湘穗], *Unrestricted Warfare* [超限战] (Beijing: PLA Literature and Arts Publishing House [解放军文艺出版社], February 1999).

32 Field Manual 2–24, *Counterinsurgency* (Washington, DC: Department of the Army, Marine Corps Combat Development Command, Department of the Navy, 2006), 4–5.

33 *Environment* refers to issues including water, food, and medical security, among others. It is distinct from the other physical domains in that, although it is not the domain of a specific military force, it significantly affects the overall security calculus. *Weapons of mass destruction* include all chemical, biological, radiological, and nuclear weapons. It is because of their destructive and disruptive potential and the resulting emphasis governments place upon them that they constitute their own domain.

34 Scobell and Nathan, 142.

35 OSD, *Military and Security Developments*, 4.

36 Ibid., 4.

37 Ibid., 3.

38 People's Armed Police Law of the People's Republic of China [中华人民共和国人民武装警察法], August 2, 2009, art. 1, sec. 2, available at <www.gov.cn/flfg/2009-08/27/content_1403324.htm>; and National Defense Mobilization Law of the People's Republic of China [中华人民共和国国防法], February 26, 2010, available at <www.gov.cn/flfg/2010-02/26/content_1544415.htm>.

39 National Defense Mobilization Law of the People's Republic of China.

40 *China's National Defense in 2010*, sec. IV.

41 Larry M. Wortzel, "PLA 'Joint' Operational Contingencies in South Asia, Central Asia, and Korea," in *Beyond the Strait: PLA Missions Other Than Taiwan*, eds. Roy Kamphausen, David Lai, and Andrew Scobell (Carlisle, PA: Strategic Studies Institute, 2009), 343–344.

42 Garver, 213.

43   Sergey Medvedev, "On the Road to 'Peace Mission 2012,'" *Moscow Krasnaya Zvezda*, May 24, 2012.

44   Roger McDermott, "China Leads SCO Peace Mission 2012 in Central Asia," *Eurasia Daily Monitor* 9, no. 121 (June 26, 2012), available at <www.jamestown.org/single/?no_cache=1&tx_ttnews%5Btt_news%5D=39538#.U2vRNfmSwa8>. McDermott cited *Krasnaya Zvezda*, June 18.

45   Weitz.

46   Shanghai Convention on Combating Terrorism, Separatism, and Extremism.

47   Agreement between the Member States of the Shanghai Cooperation Organization on the Regional Anti-Terrorist Structure, June 7, 2002, art. 6.

48   Neil MacFarquhar, "China Presents a Four-Point Proposal for Resolving the Civil War in Syria," *New York Times*, November 1, 2012.

49   Teddy Ng, "Beijing playing both sides in Libya," *South China Morning Post*, June 8, 2011; Daniel Large, "South Sudan Looks East: Between the CPA and Independence," Association of Concerned Africa Scholars, November 2011, available at <http://concernedafricascholars.org/bulletin/issue86/large/>.

50   Andrew Small, "China's Afghan Moment," *The Nation*, October 6, 2012.

51   Scobell and Nathan, "China's Overstretched Military," 137–138.

52   Hackett, 213.

53   Daniel M. Hartnett, staff memo, "China's First Deployment of Combat Forces to a UN Peacekeeping Mission—South Sudan" (Washington, DC: U.S.-China Economic and Security Review Commission, March 13, 2012).

54   Cooley, 79.

55   People's Armed Police Law of the People's Republic of China.

56   Jake Hooker, "Quake Revealed Deficiencies of China's Military," *New York Times*, July 2, 2008.

57   People's Armed Police Law of the People's Republic of China, art. 1, sec. 2.

58   Alison A. Kaufman and Peter W. Mackenzie, *Field Guide: The Culture of the Chinese People's Liberation Army* (Alexandria, VA: CNA China Studies, 2009), 25.

59   Hackett, 213.

60   *China's National Defense in 2010*, section IV.

61   Garver, 206–208.

62   Ibid., 206.

63   Kaufman and Mackenzie; Jane Perlez, "Corruption in Military Poses a Test for China," *New York Times*, November 15, 2012.

64   Hartnett.

65   For example, apparent Chinese "hacktivist" computer network attacks at the height of the Senkaku/Diaoyu Islands dispute. If loosely organized hackers can pose a threat to another government, it is reasonable to believe that governments themselves can organize attacks that are at least as effective; see also "Chinese cyber attacks hit Japan over islands dispute," Agence France-Presse, September 19, 2012, available at <http://www.theglobeandmail.com/news/world/chinese-cyber-attacks-hit-japan-over-islands-dispute/article4553048/>.

66   Jiang Daohong [姜道洪], "Targeting the 'Five Transformations': Opening Up the Pace of Military Transformation" [瞄准'五化': 迈开陆军建设转型步伐], *PLA Daily* [解放军报], July 14, 2011.

67   "Chinese troops participating in 'Peace Mission 2012' exercise arrive in Tajikistan," *PLA Daily*, June 7, 2012, available at <http://english.peopledaily.com.cn/90786/7838414.html>.

68   Small.

69   OSD, *Military and Security Developments*, 8–9.

70   Ibid., 9.

71   Garver, 211.

72   "UN to Resume Food Aid to North Korea," *RTT News*, August 4, 2012.

IV

MARITIME CONTINGENCIES

CHAPTER 12

The PLA and Near Seas Maritime Sovereignty Disputes

Alexander Chieh-cheng Huang

The "near seas" [*jinhai*, 近海] of the People's Republic of China (PRC) are the vast maritime areas between China's coastline and the first island chain, which runs from the Sea of Okhotsk in the northeast to the Strait of Malacca in the southwest. They include the Bohai Gulf [*bohai wan*, 渤海湾], the Yellow Sea [*huanghai*, 黄海], the East China Sea [*donghai*, 东海], the Taiwan Strait [*taihai*, 台海], and the South China Sea [*nanhai*, 南海]. Each of the five near seas areas is the subject of disputes involving different countries, with a different balance of naval and air power, and with different characteristics that would affect military contingencies.

The Chinese government considers the Bohai Gulf as an inner lake and the gateway to Beijing—China's political-military center of gravity. Adjacent to the Bohai, the Yellow Sea lies between the Chinese mainland and the Korean Peninsula and has historically been a contested area in the Sino Japanese competition for influence over Korea. The East China Sea, between China and the Japanese archipelago, serves as an important sea lane for shipping to China, Japan, and Korea, and is where China confronts the U.S.-Japan security alliance. The Taiwan Strait has served as a barrier dividing the Chinese mainland and Taiwan since the late 1940s, but in recent decades, it has connected the two sides via flourishing bilateral economic relations and cultural activities. The South China Sea is not only a battleground for disputes over sovereignty and maritime resources, but is also a critical sea line of communication for global maritime commerce.

These five contiguous segments of sea areas that constitute the PRC's near seas each have distinctive diplomatic, economic, and security features. To the Chinese, the near seas areas share some important commonalities. These five areas comprise all of China's claimed sovereign waters. Chinese thinkers view the near seas as the point of origin of more than 170 years of historical humiliation inflicted by foreign maritime powers. These areas are the subject of the inherited historical concept of "maritime defense" [*haifang*, 海防].

After more than 30 years of economic reform and opening up to the outside world, China's maritime interests have expanded along with its international influence, rapid economic growth, and military modernization. The expansion of these interests was formally recognized in November 2012, when Chinese Communist Party (CCP) General Secretary Hu Jintao stated in his work report that "we should enhance our capacity for exploiting marine resources, resolutely safeguard China's maritime rights and interests, and build China into a maritime power."[1] Even though China has interests around the globe, the maritime contingencies that pose the most direct threats to China's national security remain concentrated in the near seas areas.

This chapter describes five types of potential near seas contingencies and reviews three recent examples in which People's Liberation Army (PLA) naval forces have been involved. It then examines PRC naval strategy and the evolution of PLA Navy (PLAN) operational thinking and force modernization. Next, it describes the role of Chinese maritime paramilitary forces in near seas contingencies, reviewing Beijing's efforts to consolidate five separate maritime forces into a new China Coast Guard. The fourth section reviews the PLAN role in near seas contingencies, noting that the Coast Guard appears to have the leading role in the most likely contingencies, with the PLAN playing a supporting role. The chapter concludes with some thoughts on the PLAN's future role.

China's Near Seas Contingencies

Due to its relatively weak naval power projection capabilities, throughout the past century China's maritime contingencies have been entirely limited to the near seas areas. In its warfighting history, the PLAN has never engaged in a war with any modern Western navy. Until the end of the 20th century, the PLAN had encountered only two navies in combat—those of Taiwan and Vietnam, both small and weak forces.

The PLAN's warfighting experience has been conducted primarily in two geographic contingencies. From 1949 to 1965, the PLAN engaged in battles with Taiwan naval forces in gaining control of several dozen offshore islands located along the coast of Zhejiang, Fujian, and Guangdong. From 1974 to 1988, the PLAN engaged in several sporadic, small-scale skirmishes with Vietnamese naval forces in the Paracels [*xisha*, 西沙] and the Spratlys [*nansha*, 南沙] in the South China Sea. The PLAN has never fought a large-scale battle at sea with any strong maritime power.[2]

Past near seas contingencies involved mainly China's defense of its coastlines and maritime sovereignty claims. Today, however, with China's rapidly growing maritime commerce and military capabilities, the near seas areas have become venues of both prosperity and potential conflict. In these contested spaces, Chinese military maritime power may pivot from purely defensive roles to exhibit both defensive and offensive capabilities.

In reviewing recent Chinese maritime events and incidents, five types of near seas contingencies seem most likely:

- Encounters with foreign naval and air forces. With the large increase in China's defense expenditures and improved force projection capability, PLA forces now routinely fly and sail farther away from China's coasts to conduct training and exercises. This increases the probabilities of contact, including unplanned or even unfriendly encounters, with foreign forces operating in the near seas. The contact between the PLAN's *Han*-class submarine and the U.S. Navy's *Kitty Hawk* aircraft carrier battle group in the Yellow Sea in October 1994 and a near-collision between a PLAN vessel and the USS *Cowpens* in November 2013 illustrate the potential for such encounters.

- Freedom of navigation and the Chinese exclusive economic zones (EEZs). Different understandings and interpretations of the United Nations Convention on the Law of the Sea (UNCLOS) have led to quarrels between China and the United States on whether U.S. ocean surveillance ships and reconnaissance aircraft have the right to conduct operations within China's exclusive economic zones as defined by the UNCLOS. U.S. ocean surveillance ships equipped with low frequency active sonar systems operating in China's EEZs have raised suspicions and anxieties in China, which views their activities as worrying instances of sensitive military intelligence collection. The most notable naval incident occurred in March 2009 when Chinese PLAN ships and airplanes, law enforcement vessels, and some fishing boats tried to chase the USNS *Impeccable* away from China's EEZ.[3] Another major incident involved the collision of a PLA Navy Air Force J-8II fighter with a U.S. Navy EP-3 maritime reconnaissance aircraft in the South China Sea in April 2001.

- Maritime resources competition. Potential energy and mineral resources lying on or under the seabed in the near seas have caused or heightened maritime disputes in the region. Except for the territorial seas and adjacent areas, rival claimants have engaged in fierce competition in claiming islands and isles, defining the demarcation of EEZ lines, and attracting foreign energy companies for exploitation. China has disputes in numerous sea areas with its neighbors, especially with Japan over the Chunxiao gas field in the East China Sea where the Chinese and Japanese EEZ claims overlap, and with Vietnam and the Philippines over several offshore blocks opened for bidding by foreign companies.

- Disputed maritime claims. Since the end of the Cold War, China has engaged in negotiations with countries sharing land borders and has been able to settle most borderline demarcation and land border disputes.[4] In the case of maritime boundaries, however, overlapping claims over islands and waters are mostly unresolved due to conflicting national and maritime interests and interpretations of international law. These disputed claims have occasionally generated sporadic bilateral and multilateral conflicts among rival claimants.

- Disasters and crime at sea. Natural and manmade disasters at sea have been getting more attention in recent years. Ship collisions, oil spills, piracy, severe weather, and many other natural disasters have challenged the security of coastal states. As its international profile rises, China in recent years has been actively involved in humanitarian assistance and disaster relief (HA/DR) exercises in the near seas areas both individually and in tandem with its neighbors. Between 2002 and 2012, China participated in 54 nontraditional security joint exercises with foreign countries, including 22 joint HA/DR exercises with foreign navies at sea. Most were conducted as part of the PLAN's port call visits to other countries beyond the near seas areas.[5]

Four recent incidents illustrate the PLAN's actual or potential involvement in near seas contingencies involving maritime sovereignty disputes.

2010 Diaoyu/Senkaku Ship Collision

On September 7, 2010, the Japanese Coast Guard (JCG) ship *Mizuki* encountered the Chinese fishing boat *Minjinyu 5179* sailing in undisputed Japanese territorial waters. The Chinese fishing boat defied orders to stop and be inspected and attempted to flee from the scene. During the chase and interception, *Minjinyu 5179* collided with two JCG ships. On September 8, 2010, the JCG boarded the Chinese trawler and arrested its captain, Zhan Qixiong, for obstruction of performance of public duty and illegal fishing. The trawler, the captain, and 14 crew members were transported to the island of Ishigaki, Japan, for detention.

In response to the arrest, the Chinese government made a series of diplomatic protests demanding the immediate release of the trawler and all its crew. China summoned the Japanese ambassador to China six times. The trawler and 14 crew members (but not Captain Zhan) were released after the sixth summons on September 13, 2010. The captain remained in Japanese detention and was finally released on September 24, 2010.[6]

In this high-profile episode, there was little room for China to react militarily. However, the PLAN's North Sea Fleet and the East Sea Fleet conducted a series of naval exercises during and immediately after the dispute that may have been intended to support China's diplomatic protest by pressuring Japan. The exercises included ship maneuvers, missile firing, and combined arms training with the PLAN Air Force. The most noteworthy capability demonstrated was an amphibious landing "island seizure" [*duodao*, 夺岛] conducted by the East Sea Fleet on September 29, 2010.[7]

2012 Scarborough Shoal Standoff

On April 8, 2012, a Philippine Navy surveillance plane spotted eight Chinese fishing vessels docked at Scarborough Shoal. The Philippine Navy frigate *BRP Gregorio del Pilar* (former USCGC *Hamilton*) was sent on the same day to survey the vicinity of the shoal and confirmed the presence of the fishing vessels and monitored their activities. On April 10, the *BRP Gregorio del Pilar* came to inspect the catch of the fishing vessels. The inspection team discovered illegally collected corals, giant clams, and live sharks inside the first vessel boarded by the team. *BRP Gregorio del Pilar* reported that they attempted to arrest the Chinese fishermen but were blocked by two PRC maritime law enforcement vessels cruising in nearby waters. Following this initial confrontation, tensions continued for several months. During the course of the dispute, China mostly relied on its maritime law enforcement ships. However, according to Japanese sources, on May 2, the PLAN sent a large formation of combatants southward without a clear destination. The flotilla included five warships: two type 052B destroyers, the *Guangzhou* (168) and *Wuhan* (169);

two escort vessels, the *Yulin* (569) and *Chaohu* (568); and a type 071 landing ship, the *Kunlunshan* (998).[8]

2012 Japanese Nationalization of Diaoyu/Senkaku Islands

The most recent dispute on sovereignty over the Diaoyu/Senkaku Islands[9] was ignited by a speech at the Heritage Foundation in Washington, DC, on April 16, 2012, by then-Tokyo governor Shintaro Ishihara, a right-wing politician advocating a more proactive Japanese role in international affairs and a tough China policy. China and Taiwan were surprised when Governor Ishihara announced his intention to buy three of the disputed islands from their Japanese private land-owner.[10] Intending to curtail Ishihara's political maneuver and prevent a crisis, Japanese Prime Minister Yoshihiko Noda initiated a process of nationalization, by which the central government would purchase the three islands. Citizen activists across China, Taiwan, and Hong Kong organized public protests of varying sizes; some activists leased fishing boats to land on the Diaoyu/Senkaku Islands and were arrested (but soon released) by the Japanese Coast Guard. Taiwan's Yilan County Fishermen's Union orchestrated a massive boat formation to protest Japan's infringement of their fishing rights near the Diaoyu/Senkaku islands.[11]

The Japanese government signed a 2.05 billion yen contract on September 11, 2012, with the so-called owner of three of the five Diaoyu/Senkaku Islands in the East China Sea, effectively nationalizing the territory. This action immediately drew a strong protest from Beijing, which sent surveillance ships to the waters around the islands.[12] In addition to strong diplomatic protests, China began regularly sending maritime law enforcement ships to the vicinity of the islands and periodically entering the 12-nautical-mile territorial sea around them to assert Chinese sovereignty. There has been no direct evidence that the PLAN was employed to handle the situation. However, according to Japan's Joint Staff Office, between April and September 2012, Chinese military aircraft flew near Japan's air defense identification zone (ADIZ) 69 times, 54 of which were between July and September when tensions over the issue were at their peak.[13]

In addition, the PLAN also conducted distant water patrol and training exercises after the annual Sino-Russian Joint Sea 2012 exercise in the Yellow Sea. Though this may be routine activity, by passing through the Japan archipelagos into the Western Pacific, these actions did send strong messages to Tokyo over the dispute.[14] (See table 12.1 for a list of PLAN exercises and training that occurred while sovereignty disputes were heating up.)

Furthermore, on September 23, 2012, China's State Oceanic Administration (SOA) announced that it had approved a pilot program of using drones to undertake remote-sensing marine surveillance in Lianyungang, a coastal city in eastern Jiangsu Province. Using experience learned from the pilot program, the SOA intended to form a managerial system and issue technical regulations to set up unmanned aerial vehicle (UAV) surveillance and monitoring bases in provinces along China's coastline by 2015. The SOA also announced stepped-up efforts to enhance its surveillance of various islands and islets, including the Diaoyu/Senkaku Islands and Huangyan (Scarborough) Island.[15]

2013 PLAN South China Sea Deployment

From March 19 to April 3, 2013, a four-ship PLAN flotilla (including the amphibious transport dock *Jinggangshan*, destroyer *Lanzhou*, and frigates *Yulin* and *Hengshui*) deployed to the far waters in the South China Sea near the James Shoal, 80 kilometers from the Malaysian coast.[16] One of the highlights was a televised "oath-taking" ceremony by Chinese marines and sailors pledging "to defend the South China Sea, maintain national sovereignty, and strive toward the dream of a strong China." Rear Admiral Yin Zhou stated that the deployment was a "regular military exercise and not targeted at other countries" but noted that it was also intended to declare "China's determination to safeguard its sovereignty over the southernmost part of China's territory."[17] The fact that this deployment was approved by the civilian leadership was reinforced when Chinese President Xi Jinping subsequently visited Sanya on April 12 to inspect some of the ships involved in the deployment.[18]

Table 12.1. PLAN Activity in Times of Near Seas Sovereignty Disputes

Date	Exercise/Training Location/Area	PLAN Forces	Key Events
February 3, 2012	PLAN training East China Sea (ECS)/Japan, 130 kilometers (km) northeast of Miyako Island	054A x1 053H2G x1 053H3 x1	
April 22–27, 2012	Sino-Russian Joint Sea 2012 Yellow Sea/ECS	052 x1 054A x2	April 10, 2012: Scarborough Shoal/ Huangyanjiao dispute begins
April 30, 2012	After Joint Sea 2012 ECS/Japan, 430km west of Yaku Island	054A x2 Intel ship x1	
			April 16, 2012: Senkaku/ Diaoyu dispute begins
May 8, 2012	After Joint Sea 2012 ECS/Japan, 650km southwest of Okinawa	052B x2 054A x2 071 LSD x 1	June 21, 2012: Sansha City established
May 14, 2012	After Joint Sea 2012 ECS/Japan, 110km northeast of Miyako Island	054A x 2 Intel ship x 1	
October 18–21, 2012	Donghai Collaboration 2012 military and civilian joint maritime rights exercise in East China Sea	053H2G X1 053H3 x1 054 x1 054A x1 HH x1 MS+YZ x 6	September 11, 2012: Japan nationalizes Senkaku/Diaoyu islands
November 27–December 11, 2012	PLAN training ECS/Japan, near Miyako Island	DDG x 2 FFG x 2 AOR x 5	
January 29–February 14, 2013	PLAN training in Western Pacific	North Sea Fleet	
March 19–April 3, 2013	PLAN training 1 to north: ECS-Diaoyu-Bashi Channel 1 to south: South China Sea (SCS)-James Shoal-Bashi Channel	071 LSD x 1 052C x1 054 x1 054A x1	March 10, 2013: Reorganization and integration of maritime law enforcement agencies and forces
May 6–24, 2013	PLAN training W. Pacific/SCS	All 3 Fleets	
June 10, 2013	PLAN training W. Pacific	052 x1 054A x1 AOR x 1	
July 12–28, 2013	Sino-Russian Joint Sea 2013 ECS/Japan–pass through Soya Strait	051C x 2 054A x 2 AOR x 1	
October 8–November 1, 2013	Maneuver 5 joint exercise W. Pacific-SCS	051C x2 052A x1 052B x1 054A x5 AOR x 2	November 23, 2013: China announces East China Sea Air Defense Identification Zone November 29, 2013: China announces new maritime and fishery regulations for Hainan
November 26, 2013–January 1, 2014	Aircraft carrier training through Taiwan Strait-Hainan-SCS	CV x 1 051C x 2 054A x 2	December 5, 2013: PLAN ship almost collides with USS (CG 63) Cowpens

Table 12.1. PLAN Activity in Times of Near Seas Sovereignty Disputes (continued)			
Date	Exercise/Training Location/Area	PLAN Forces	Key Events
December 19, 2013	PLAN training W. Pacific/SCS	054A x 2 AOR x 1	
January 20–February 11, 2014	PLAN training SCS-Lombok Strait-Indian Ocean-Makassar Strait	071 LSD x 1 052C x 1 052B x 1	
February 28–March 12, 2014	PLAN training W. Pacific-Bashi Channel-SCS	052C x1 054A x2 AOR x 1	
March 2, 2014	Aircraft carrier training ECS	CV x 1	
May 20–24, 2014	Sino-Russian Joint Sea 2014 ECS/Japan	*Sovremenny* x 1 051C x 1 054A x 2 AOR x 1	

Chinese Naval Strategy and Near Seas Contingencies

Maritime sovereignty disputes are not China's only potential contingencies in the near seas area. Even though the PLAN has not taken the leading role to date, its fundamental roles and missions cannot be forgotten, and its growing warfighting and force projection capabilities cannot be overlooked.

In considering potential near seas contingencies today, it is helpful to review the basic assumptions underlying the PLA naval strategy adopted in 1985 and consider whether they remain true today. The PLAN's modern strategy was formulated under the leadership of Admiral Liu Huaqing during his tenure as navy commander during the 1980s. The PLAN's strategic concept of "active defense, near seas operations" [*jiji fangyu, jinhai zuozhan*, 积极防御, 近海作战] was first articulated in Liu's October 1983 speech "On Several Issues Related to the Navy's Implementation of the Strategic Guideline of Active Defense."[19] After consultations with his staff and the General Staff Department, he formally rolled out the new naval strategy of near seas defense [*jinhai fangyu*, 近海防御] at a PLAN tabletop exercise on December 20, 1985.[20] The strategy is sometimes translated as offshore defense, but Liu clearly distinguishes it from coastal defense [*jin'an fangyu*, 近岸防御] or distant ocean offense [*yuanyang jingong*, 远洋进攻] alternatives.

The strategy defined four strategic objectives [*zhanlüe mudi*, 战略目的] for the PLAN: to safeguard national unification and territorial integrity, to fight local war at sea [*haishang jubu zhanzheng*, 海上局部战争], to deter and defend against invasion from the sea by imperialists and hegemonies, and to maintain peace in the Asia-Pacific region. The PLAN's strategic missions [*zhanlüe renwu*, 战略任务] are divided into peacetime and wartime missions. Its peacetime missions are to realize and safeguard national unification including Taiwan, to serve the purposes of China's foreign policy, to deter invasion from the sea by potential enemies, to conduct potential local war at sea, and to support the state's socialist construction. The PLAN's wartime missions are to conduct operations independently or in coordination with the army and the air force, to protect China's own sea lanes of communication, and to participate in strategic nuclear counterstrike under high command orders.[21]

The PLAN's sea area of operations [*zuozhan haiqu*, 作战海区][22] was defined in the 1985 naval strategy, with the understanding that it would expand with time and increasing PLAN capability. The strategy stated that:

> from today [believed to mean the mid-1980s] to a relatively long period, the sea areas of operations would be the first island chain, its periphery, and the Yellow Sea, the East China Sea, and the South China Sea areas within the island chain. The extension of the area of operations from "coastal defense" to "near seas defense" would favor China in terms of conducting defense operations at sea [*haishang fangyu zuozhan*, 海上防御作战] in the "main operational directions" [*zhuyao zuozhan fangxiang*, 主要作战方向]. In the future, with a stronger economy and level of technology: gradually extend to the north Pacific and the second island chain.

From the promulgation of PLAN's near seas active defense strategy to today's maritime disputes in the East China Sea and the South China Sea, PLAN objectives, missions, and especially areas of operations remain largely the same—focused on near seas contingencies.

Advances in PLAN Operational Doctrine and Capabilities

The PLAN has been a major beneficiary of changes in China's military doctrine. To fight and win a local war under high-tech and informationized conditions, the PLAN has been given higher priority in resources and procurement to fulfill its expanded missions. Under the PLA's overall military strategic guidelines, the PLAN has engaged in massive efforts for more than a decade to adapt to new security environments and mission requirements and to develop new operational concepts to enrich and refine PLA doctrine. Key advances are described below.

Primacy of Technology

Since the promulgation of the new military strategic guidelines in 2004, the PLAN has emphasized the importance of being able to fight and win a local war at sea under modern, especially under high-tech, conditions.[23] In the new century, informationization has been identified as the core of modern naval warfare theory.[24] In parallel with the emphasis on "strengthening the army with science and technology" [keji qiangjun, 科技强军], the PLAN has advocated the importance of developing technologies and capabilities in electronic, electro-magnetic, and precision munitions and in advanced command, control, communications, computers, intelligence, surveillance, and reconnaissance, all of which aim to field new capabilities for future naval operations farther away from the Chinese coast.

Advocacy of Offensive

The PLAN continues to identify its strategy as defensive in nature, but many officers have advocated that offensive operations are necessary at the campaign and battle levels.[25] To fight a joint campaign at sea under informationized conditions, one PLA writer argues that the PLAN should establish an operational doctrine of "integration of offensive and defensive, but with offensive as the focus" [gongfang jiehe, yi gong wei zhu, 攻防结合, 以攻为主], insisting that the initiative [zhudong quan, 主动权] can only be obtained through preemptive and offensive actions in informationized operations at sea.[26]

Emphasis on Jointness

The PLAN recognizes that local war under informationized conditions can no longer rely on a single service but instead requires joint operations. Modern naval operations have to combine information, platforms, intelligence, communications, firepower, and logistics and must be conducted in the form of integrated joint operations.[27] Establishing an "information operations coordination and command center for joint campaign at sea" [haishang lianhe zhanyi xinxi zuozhan xietiao yu zhihui zhongxin, 海上联合战役信息作战协调与指挥中心] and numerous related recommendations have been put forth for fighting a better coordinated local war at sea.[28]

Expanded Area of Responsibilities

The PLAN sees the threats to China's maritime interests as growing in the new century, including maritime territorial disputes and demarcations, piracy and terrorist activities at sea, security of sea lines of communication, and threats to seaborne transportation of oil and natural gas.[29] Some analysts argue that China has been pursuing a "string of pearls" strategy, seeking to secure cooperation and gain access to ports in Pakistan, Sri Lanka, Bangladesh, Burma, Thailand, and Cambodia, along the energy sea lines of communication for East Asian countries.[30] Regardless of whether China truly has a string of pearls strategic concept, the PLAN has already begun sailing beyond the near seas areas of operations defined by Admiral Liu Huaqing.[31]

Strive for Access Denial

As the PLAN's offshore active defense strategy was being introduced, the depth of China's defense at sea was beginning to expand from China's coastal waters to the first island chain. Between 1995 and 2008, as China's fear of Taiwan moving toward de jure independence increased, discussions in the PLAN over strengthening antiaccess and area denial capabilities began to gain in prominence. Many argued that China should increase its long-range precision strike capability to dissuade possible third-party intervention in a conflict in the Taiwan Strait and to deny access to enemy forces seeking to project force against China.[32]

Robust Modernization Programs

Since the early 1990s, the PLAN has engaged in a robust modernization program, building large tonnage surface combatants equipped with modern sensors and weapons systems at an impressive pace, expanding its submarine fleet with better warfighting capabilities, improving antisubmarine warfare and fleet air defense capabilities, and acquiring aerial refueling and expanded underway replenishment capabilities.[33] All these increased assets and new capabilities have enabled Chinese strategists and war planners to develop and expand new strategic concepts and operational doctrines of the PLAN.

Maritime Law Enforcement Agencies

Although the PLAN would have a leading role in military contingencies involving major combat operations, since 2005 China's maritime law enforcement agencies began to serve as the first-response frontline units for maritime sovereignty disputes and contingencies. The Chinese government appears to have realized that using nonmilitary vessels is more acceptable to international public opinion and can help avoid escalation of maritime conflicts. During the 2004–2005 disputes over the Chunxiao gas field with Japan in the East China Sea, China sent PLAN ships to the area, about 290 nautical miles northwest of Kume Island, Okinawa Prefecture. The group consisted of a new *Sovremennyy*-class destroyer Number 137, two older *Jianghu*-class frigates, the new replenishment ship Number 886, and a new electronic/signals intelligence and space tracking ship Number 851.[34] Japan sent only Coast Guard ships, gaining a public relations advantage. Since then, China has rarely employed naval assets as its frontline response to maritime territorial disputes, preferring to keep PLAN forces in background roles.

Unlike in the United States, China did not have a unified institution to oversee and implement maritime affairs and law enforcement until 2013. For decades, the PRC had five major maritime law enforcement agencies (see table 12.2). The five agencies were under different ministries with diverse and complicated chains of command, funding resources, areas of responsibility, and personnel systems. Maritime law enforcement efforts were divided among rival bureaucracies and were so poorly coordinated that even in the official media, they have been derided as "nine dragons managing the sea" [*jiulong zhihai*, 九龙治海], a reference to the offspring of the Dragon King in Chinese legend.[35]

Table 12.2. PRC Maritime Law Enforcement Agencies (prior to 2013)		
Agency	**Ministry/ Department**	**Primary Missions/Ships**
China Marine Surveillance [*zhongguo haijian*,中国海监]	State Oceanic Administration (SOA)	Law enforcement within PRC's territorial waters, exclusive economic zones (EEZ), and shores; protecting maritime environment, natural resources, navigation aids and other facilities, and carrying out maritime surveys. Ship names: Haijian, HJ [海监] 1,000 tons: 38 36 1,000-ton ships to be built in 12th Five-Year Program Total: 400
Maritime Safety Administration [*zhongguo haishiju*,中国海事局]	Ministry of Transportation	Maritime traffic safety, coordinating maritime search and rescue in territorial waters. Ship names: Haishi, HS [海事] or Haixun, HX [海巡] 1,000 tons: 4 Total: 800+

Table 12.2. PRC Maritime Law Enforcement Agencies (prior to 2013) (continued)

Agency	Ministry/ Department	Primary Missions/Ships
Fisheries Law Enforcement Command [*zhongguo yuzheng*, 中国渔政]	Ministry of Agriculture Fisheries Management Administration	Law enforcement concerning fishing and maritime resources in PRC territorial waters and EEZ. Protecting Chinese fishing vessels and personnel, resolving disputes in fishing activities, preventing illegal fishing, and protecting maritime resources. Ship names: Yuzheng, YZ [渔政] 1,000 tons: 11 Under construction: 13 1,000-ton ships and 12 3,000-ton ships Total: 150+
China Public Security Border Control Maritime Police (or Coast Guard) [*zhongguo gong'an bianfang haijing*, 中国公安边防海警]	Ministry of Public Security People's Armed Police	Maritime security and fighting crime at sea. Ship names: Haijing, CG [海警] 1,000 tons: 3 Total: 480
China Custom Anti-Smuggling Police [*zhongguo haiguan jisi jingcha*, 中国海关缉私警察]	General Administration of Customs	Maritime antismuggling Ship names: Haiguan, HG [海关] 1,000 tons: 3 Total: 212+

Sources: Gao Zhiguo [高之国] et al., eds., "China's Maritime Law Enforcement," *China Maritime Development Report* [中國海洋發展報告] (Beijing: Ocean Press [海洋出版社], 2010), 441–456; National Institute for Defense Studies, *China Security Strategy Report 2012*, Japan Ministry of Defense; Yu Jianbin [余建斌], "Protection of Maritime Rights is Our Responsibility" [维护海洋权益 我们责无旁贷], *People's Daily* [人民日报], September 17, 2012. In 2013, 10 more 1,000-ton ships were built. "China to Build 36 Large- and Medium-sized Marine Surveillance ships" [中国将建36艘大中型海监船], SIMIC, January 3, 2013, available at <www.simic.net.cn/news_show.php?id=119321>;"China Marine Surveillance," available at <https://en.wikipedia.org/wiki/China_Marine_Surveillance>; Maritime Safety Administration, available at <www.msa.gov.cn/Static/zbjs>; National Institute for Defense Studies, *China Security Report 2011* [中国安全保障レポート2011], Japan Ministry of Defense, February 10, 2012, 6; "Building World's No. 1 Law Enforcement Fleet" [中国打造世界第一海上执法团队 辗压日本海保], January 24, 2014, available at <http://mil.huanqiu.com/mlitaryvision/2014-01/2725266.html>; Su Wanming, Wang Jun, Sun Honglei, and Li Junyi [蘇萬明, 王軍, 孫洪磊, 李俊義], "Fishermen Disputes over Fishing Zoning, Mismanagement by Multiple Agencies Unsustainable" [渔民网地争端上升 多头管理弊端愈显 不可持续], *People's Daily Online* [人民网], March 16, 2012, available at <http://politics.people.com.cn/BIG5/70731/17402446.html>; "Scholar: Coast Guard Integration with Mixed Blessing" [学者: 中国海警 整合令外界喜忧参半], Xinhua Online [新华网], August 9, 2013, available at <http://news.xinhuanet.com/world/2013-08/09/c_125139644.htm>; "Institute 708 Won Bid to Build Custom Anti-Smuggling Ship-building Project" [708所中标海关缉私舰艇设计建造项目], cnss.com.cn [中国海事服务网], January 5, 2013, available at <www.cnss.com.cn/html/2013/orders_and_cancellation_0105/89358.html>; "Ministry of Public Security Press Briefing Reports Custom Police Work Conditions," March 27, 2007, available at <www.mps.gov.cn/n16/n1237/n1432/n1567/136809.html>.

In terms of responsibilities, the Maritime Safety Administration, the Coast Guard, and the Customs Police primarily cover inner waters, territorial seas, and contiguous zones. The Marine Surveillance [*haijian*, 海监] and the Fisheries Law

Enforcement Command [*yuzheng*, 渔政] cover waters in China's EEZ and continental shelf. These two agencies were designated to manage China's maritime sovereignty disputes and respond to peacetime contingencies in the near seas.[36]

To address problems of overlapping functions, wasted resources, and diplomatic misunderstandings, on March 10, 2013, the National People's Congress passed the State Council Institutional Reform and Functional Transformation Plan [*guowuyuan jigou gaige he zhineng zhuanbian fang'an*, 国务院机构改革和职能转变方案]. According to the plan, four of the five maritime law enforcement agencies are to be integrated into a new China Coast Guard [*Zhongguo haijing*, 中国海警] under the State Oceanic Administration (SOA) [*guojia haiyang ju*, 国家海洋局].[37] The plan also established the State Oceanic Commission [*guojia haiyang weiyuanhui*, 国家海洋委员会] as a new high-level consultative and coordinating body on maritime affairs.

The revamped SOA carries out missions defined by the State Oceanic Commission, reports to the Ministry of Land and Resources [*guotu ziyuan bu*, 国土资源部], and executes maritime law enforcement duties under the operational guidance of the Ministry of Public Security. Since the promulgation of the State Council Institutional Reform and Functional Transformation Plan on March 28, 2013, maritime law enforcement ships were given new designations as part of the China Coast Guard.[38]

PLA and Near Seas Contingency Planning

Despite the view that the PLA always favors a hard line on sovereignty disputes, the PLAN appears to have accepted the strategic logic of giving the Coast Guard the lead role in maritime sovereignty disputes, and it obeys CCP orders when leaders decide to resolve disputes through dialogue rather than force. For example, in the midst of the 2012 Scarborough Shoal dispute, the deputy director of the contingency office in the PLA's General Staff Department publicly stated that "China is opposed to the use or threat of use of force" to resolve disputes, and Ministry of National Defense spokesman Geng Yansheng stated that the South China Sea issue should be resolved through bilateral negotiations between the parties concerned.[39]

On the other hand, when the CCP leadership wants to emphasize the seriousness of a crisis, the PLA supports the party line with both words and deeds. For example, in the early stages of the Diaoyu/Senkaku nationalization crisis, Chinese Defense Minister Liang Guanglie told U.S. Secretary of Defense Leon

Panetta that Japan's stated intention to "nationalize" the Diaoyu Islands was to blame for heating up the dispute and said that China "firmly opposes the U.S. position that the U.S.-Japan Security Treaty applies to the Diaoyu Islands."[40] Similarly, the declaration of a Chinese ADIZ in the East China Sea in November 2013 was the product of a PLA Air Force proposal to increase pressure on Japan over the Diaoyu/Senkaku confrontation.

Retired officers are freer to express their views. For example, former chief of the PLAN's equipment and technology department, Rear Admiral Zheng Ming [郑明], used an interview to raise five critical questions for further study by Chinese experts:[41] Should China deploy troops on strategically important but currently uninhabited islets and shoals? Should China build up a "production and logistics base" on the Spratly Islands to support fishing and maritime scientific research activities? What support infrastructure is necessary in order to maintain regular patrols of PLAN and maritime surveillance and law enforcement ships in the South China Sea? What are the most effective ways to create a fait accompli against the other claimants to South China Sea islands or to prevent those states from annexing China's claimed maritime features piece by piece? Should diplomatic measures and negotiations always be the first priority in dealing with future maritime disputes? Admiral Zheng's views suggest that some PLAN officers may sometimes favor a more assertive approach than civilian leaders are willing to endorse in China's South China Sea contingency planning.

Analyzing China's management of maritime sovereignty disputes can provide useful insights into Chinese civil-military relations between the PLAN and the civilian maritime affairs agencies. Though the PLAN may not be in the lead on handling maritime disputes, it nonetheless definitely maintains a close operational relationship with its civilian partners in at least three areas. First, the PLAN is the ultimate guarantor for civilian maritime operations at sea and can serve as a deterrent as well as the back-up force. Second, the PLAN can provide logistical support for civilian agencies, transfer decommissioned navy ships to maritime law enforcement agencies, facilitate professional education and training, and supply materials and munitions.[42] Third, civilian maritime agencies can be advocates for PLAN modernization, with the SOA, for example, having voiced support for acquisition of an aircraft carrier for over 20 years.

Immediately after Japan "nationalized" the Diaoyu/Senkaku Islands on September 11, 2012, the PLAN collaborated with its civilian counterparts in

October 2012 to conduct the first joint civil-military maritime exercise in China's history—Donghai Collaboration 2012 [东海协作 2012], simulating scenarios of protecting China's maritime rights against adversaries in the East China Sea.[43] According to reports, a total of 11 vessels, 8 aircraft, and more than 1,000 personnel from the PLAN's East Sea Fleet, China's fishery administration, and marine surveillance agency took part in the exercise. The exercise was commanded by Rear Admiral Shen Hao [沈浩], the deputy chief of staff of the East Sea Fleet, with two deputy commanders—Zhou Tong [周彤], inspector of East Sea Fishery Bureau, and Liu Zhendong [刘振东], deputy chief of SOA's East Sea Bureau.[44] This "military-local joint maritime rights protection exercise" [*jun-di haishang lianhe weiquan yanxi*, 军地海上联合维权演习] may serve as a reference point for near seas contingency planning and as evidence of the PLAN's key role in the maritime law enforcement and rights protection.

Similarly, when the China National Offshore Oil Corporation (CNOOC) deployed the HD-981 oil exploration platform into waters claimed by both Vietnam and China in May 2014, the oil platform was reportedly accompanied by both China Coast Guard and PLAN ships to defend against possible Vietnamese interference or attack.[45] The operation required extensive coordination across multiple ministries, the Coast Guard, and the Chinese military, something that would have been unlikely in the previous stovepiped system.

Conclusion

China's near seas can be the venue for economic prosperity, regional cooperation, sovereignty disputes, and even military conflict. In recent years, China has significantly strengthened its comprehensive capabilities to deal with near seas contingencies in military, administrative, legal, law enforcement, and diplomatic areas to defend and protect its maritime interests.

As stated in China's 2013 Defense White Paper, the PLAN "provides security support for China's maritime law enforcement, fisheries, and oil and gas exploitation. It has established mechanisms to coordinate and cooperate with law enforcement organs of marine surveillance and fishery administration, as well as a joint military-police-civilian defense mechanism."[46] Given growing Chinese maritime interests, the roles, missions, and areas of responsibility of the PLA, and especially the PLAN, have expanded considerably. Though not usually taking a frontline role in dealing with maritime sovereignty disputes, the PLAN is very likely to increase its presence and roles in the near seas in the future.

Notes

1   "Hu calls for efforts to build China into maritime power," Xinhua [新华], November 8, 2012.

2   Alexander Chieh-cheng Huang, "The PLA Navy at War, 1949–1999: From Coastal Defense to Distant Operations," in *Chinese War-fighting: The PLA Experience Since 1949*, ed. Mark Ryan and Michael A. McDevitt (Armonk, NY: M.E. Sharpe, 2003), 241–269.

3   Mark Valencia, "The *Impeccable* Incident: Truth and Consequences," *China Security* 5, no. 7 (2009), 26–32.

4   See M. Taylor Fravel, *Strong Borders, Secure Nation: Cooperation and Conflict in China's Territorial Disputes* (Princeton: Princeton University Press, 2008).

5   Tang Cheng, "PLA and Foreign Military Joint Exercise: non-traditional security cooperation," *Chinese Communist Studies* [中共研究] 45, no. 7 (July 2011), 85.

6   Justin McCurry, "Japan-China row escalates over fishing boat collision," *The Guardian*, September 9, 2010, available at <www.theguardian.com/world/2010/sep/09/japan-china-fishing-boat-collision>. Also see Wikipedia, available at <http://en.wikipedia.org/wiki/2010_Senkaku_boat_collision_incident>.

7   *Chinese Communist Yearbook 2011* [2011年中共年報] (Taipei: Chinese Communist Studies Magazine Press [中共研究雜誌社], 2011), 3-110– 3-112.

8   "China sends five warships to the disputed Scarborough Shoal," *What's on Shenzhen*, May 10, 2012, available at <www.whatsonshenzhen.com/news-2423-china-sends-five-warships-to-the-disputed-scarborough-shoal.html>.

9   Taiwan uses the name Diaoyutai to refer to the islands.

10   "Ishihara thumbs his nose at the central government," *The Asahi Shimbun*, April 18, 2012, available at <http://ajw.asahi.com/article/behind_news/politics/AJ201204180054>.

11   "Chinese activists land on Senkaku islet; Japan arrests 14," *Japan Times*, August 16, 2012, available at <www.japantimes.co.jp/news/2012/08/16/national/chinese-activists-land-on-senkaku-islet-japan-arrests-14/#.U1UYO_mSx6M>. Also, "Japanese water cannon attack on Taiwanese fishing boats over Senkaku dispute," *The Telegraph*, September 25, 2012, available at <www.telegraph.co.uk/news/worldnews/asia/taiwan/9564421/Japanese-water-cannon-attack-on-Taiwanese-fishing-boats-over-Senkaku-dispute.html>.

12   Masami Ito,"China enraged, sends ships: ¥2 billion deal nationalizes the Senkakus," *Japan Times*, September 12, 2012.

13   "Chinese military aircraft frequently appear in Diaoyu Islands airspace" [中国军机频繁出现钓鱼岛空域], *Japan News Networks*, October 19, 2012, available at <www.ribenxinwen.com/html/g/201210/19-14526.html>.

14   A Chinese PLA Navy fleet passed through Yaku Islands, Okinawa Islands, and Miyako Islands during the tension over Diaoyu/Senkaku. See table 12.1.

15   "China to promote drones for marine surveillance," Xinhua, September 23, 2012, available at <http://news.xinhuanet.com/english/china/2012-09/23/c_123750476.htm>.

16   Bai Ruixue, Gao Yi, and Gan Jun [白瑞雪, 高毅, 甘俊], "From South China Sea to West Pacific: Complete Record of Navy Task Force's Distant Sea Training of Combat-Readiness Patrol" [从南海到西太平洋:海军编队战备巡逻远海训练全记录], Xinhua, April 3, 2013.

17   CCTV-4 "Focus Today" [今日关注] program, March 28, 2013.

18   Teddy Ng, "Xi Jinping Calls on Navy To Be Prepared for Struggle," *South China Morning Post*, April 12, 2013.

19   Liu Huaqing [刘华清], *The Memoirs of Liu Huaqing* [刘华清回忆录] (Beijing: PLA Press [中国人民解放军出版社], 2004), 434.

20   Ibid., 435.

21   Ibid., 437–438.

22   The term *sea area of operations* here can be understood as parallel to the concept of area of responsibility (AOR) in the West.

23   "PLA Navy Commander Shi Yunsheng on Naval Development Strategy" [解放军海军司令员石雪生: 縱論海軍發展戰略], *Zijing Monthly* [紫荆月刊], no. 130 (August 2001), 6–9.

24   Liu Shengru, Liu Zheng, and Wang Lei [刘胜如, 刘政, 王磊], "Innovation and Development of Naval Operations Doctrine under Informationized Conditions" [信息化条件下海军作战理论的创新与发展], *National Defense University Journal* [国防大学学报], no. 11 (2004), 44.

25   Quan Jinfu [全金富], "Innovative Development of Our Naval Strategic Theory in the New Century" [新世纪我国海军战略理论的创新发展], *Journal of Nanjing Institute of Politics* [南京政治学院学报] 20, no. 3 (2004), 82–83.

26   Wang Zheng [王政], "Some Issues Concerning Information Operations in the Joint Naval Campaign" [海上联合战役信息作战的几个问题], *National Defense University Journal*, no. 10 (2004), 44.

27   Liu Shengru, Liu Zheng, and Wang Lei, 44.

28   Wang Zheng, 45.

29   Wu Shengli and Hu Yanlin [吴胜利, 胡彦林], "Forge a Powerful People's Navy that Can Adapt to Its Historical Mission" [锻造适应我军历史使命要求的强大人民海军], *Seeking Truth* [求是], no. 14 (2007), 32. This issue of *Seeking Truth* is a special edition in commemoration of the 80th anniversary of the PLA.

30   For discussion and analysis of the concept of a *string of pearls* strategy, see Christopher D. Yung and Ross Rustici with Scott Devary and Jenny Lin, *"Not an Idea We Have to Shun": Chinese Overseas Basing Requirements in the 21st Century*, China Strategic Perspectives 7 (Washington, DC: National Defense University [NDU] Press, 2014).

31   See Christopher H. Sharman, *China Moves Out: Stepping Stones Toward a New Maritime Strategy,* China Strategic Perspectives 9 (Washington, DC: NDU Press, 2015).

32   Du Chaoping [杜朝平], "The Island Chain and Its Impact on Chinese Navy" [岛链—对中国海军的影响有多大], *China's Navy Today* [舰载武器] (May 2004), 40.

33   For the analyses of the massive modernization of the PLAN's platforms and systems in the past decade, see Bernard Cole, *The Great Wall at Sea: China's Navy in the Twenty-First Century* (Annapolis, MD: Naval Institute Press, 2010). Also, Ronald O'Rourke, *China Naval Modernization: Implications for U.S. Navy Capabilities*, CRS Report for Congress RL33153 (Washington, DC: Congressional Research Service, December 23, 2014).

34   Richard Fisher, Jr., "Growing Asymmetries in the China-Japan Naval Balance," International Assessment and Strategy Center, November 22, 2005, available at <www.strategycenter.net/research/pubID.83/pub_detail.asp>.

35   "Dragons unite: To protect its maritime interests, China is setting up a civilian coastguard," *The Economist*, March 16, 2013, available at <www.economist.com/news/china/21573607-protect-its-maritime-interests-china-setting-up-civilian-coastguard-dragons-unite#sthash.yPwuLSjm.dpbs>.

36   State Oceanic Administration, Institute of Oceanic Development Strategy, *China's Ocean Development Report, 2013* [中国海洋发展报告, 2013] (Beijing: Ocean Press, 2013), 261–262. Measuring the capacity of China's maritime law enforcement agencies would require numerous sets of studies on their operational doctrines and tactics, professional education, training, promotion, and logistics, as well as operating sequence, duration, shifts, and operational coordination.

37   "China will reorganize State Oceanic Administration and execute maritime law enforcement under the name of Coast Guard" [我国将重组国家海洋局 以海警局名义海上执法], *Tencent News* [腾讯新闻], March 10, 2013, available at <http://news.qq.com/a/20130310/000281.htm>. In the reorganization of the five maritime law enforcement agencies in 2013, the Maritime Safety Administration [海事局] of Ministry of Transport [交通运输部] was not integrated into the State Oceanic Administration, due in part because one of its functions is international shipping management. See "State Oceanic Administration Insiders Talks About the Birth of China Coast Guard: It's Not Just a Uniform Issue" [海洋局内部人士谈海警局诞生：不只是统一服装的问题], available at <http://big5.china.com.cn/gate/big5/ocean.china.com.cn/2013-04/07/content_28464179.htm>.

38   Additional details on "China Maritime Law Enforcement Activities During Near Seas Sovereignty Disputes" and on "Hull number changes of China's law enforcement ships since reorganization under State Oceanic Administration 2013" are available for download from the NDU Press Web site at <ndupress.ndu.edu/huang.pdf>.

39   Chi Le-yi [亓樂義], "PLA Opposes Resolving South and East China Sea Disputes by Force" [共軍：反對動武解決南、東海爭議], *China Times* [中國時報], May 10, 2012.

40   "Liang Guanglie: Japan is fully responsible in the Diaoyu Island dispute" [梁光烈：釣魚島問題升溫責任完全在日方], *China Review News Online* [中國評論新聞網], September 19, 2012, available at <www.chinareviewnews.com/doc/1022/4/0/0/102240076.html?coluid=7&kindid=0&docid=102240076>.

41   Zheng Ming [郑明], "Diaoyudao and Huangyandao Incidents Might Be the Cut-in Point for the Formation and Implementation of Maritime Development Strategy" [钓鱼岛、黄岩岛事件或可成为我国制定和实施海洋发展战略的一个切入点], *Modern Ships* [现代舰船], no. 10 (2012), 16–17.

42   For details, see Linda Jakobson, "The PLA and Maritime Security Actors," in *PLA Influence on China's National Security Policymaking*, ed. Phillip C. Saunders and Andrew Scobell (Stanford: Stanford University Press, 2015), 300–323.

43   "Air-Sea Cooperation, Witnessing 'East Sea Collaboration–2012' Exercise" [海空协同 直击 "东海协作—2012" 演习], Xinhua Online [新华网], October 21, 2012, available at <http://news.xinhuanet.com/mil/2012-10/21/c_123849340_2.htm>.

44   "Exercise in East China Sea, Protecting Rights with Strength" [東海練兵 實力維權], *Ta Kung Pao* [大公報], available at <http://paper.takungpao.com/html/2012-10/20/content_2_1.htm>.

45   See Carl Thayer, "China's Oil Rig Gambit: South China Sea Game-Changer?" *The Diplomat*, May 12, 2014, available at <http://thediplomat.com/2014/05/chinas-oil-rig-gambit-south-china-sea-game-changer/>.

46   Information Office of the State Council, People's Republic of China, "The Diversified Employment of China's Armed Forces," Xinhua, April 16, 2013, available at <http://news.xinhuanet.com/english/china/2013-04/16/c_132312681.htm>.

The PLA and Far Seas Contingencies: Chinese Capabilities for Noncombatant Evacuation Operations

Michael S. Chase

This chapter assesses the Chinese military's perspectives on evacuation operations, the capabilities required to perform them, the challenges the People's Liberation Army (PLA) is likely to face in conducting such operations, and the broader policy implications of these developments. The chapter first provides background and context to frame the discussion of PLA preparations for far seas contingencies. Next, a case study is presented that examines the evacuation of Chinese citizens from Libya. Future evacuation operations may differ from this one in important respects, but as the largest, most recent, and highest-profile evacuation China has conducted to date, it is worthy of close examination. Then, PLA assessments of the nature and likelihood of future evacuation contingencies are considered. This is followed by an examination of relevant PLA capabilities, which could include China's large amphibious ships, the newly commissioned aircraft carrier of the PLA Navy (PLAN), and the large transport aircraft of the PLA Air Force. This section also covers doctrine, training, and coordination challenges involved in evacuating large numbers of People's Republic of China (PRC) citizens from a distant location. Finally, conclusions and broader policy implications are offered.

Background and Context

China's rapidly growing overseas interests create a number of new challenges for leaders in Beijing. This is an unavoidable consequence of China's "going out" strategy and its increasingly global economic and political profile. Over the past few years, however, the challenges have been growing, as political upheavals in a number of foreign countries have increased the risks associated with China's expanding overseas interests. This has been especially true in North Africa, including Egypt, Libya, and Sudan, where, as Chinese scholars point out, recent violence and turmoil have threatened the interests of Chinese companies and the safety of Chinese citizens, raising calls for China to do more to protect its overseas interests.[1] Within this context, as Mathieu Duchâtel and Bates Gill point out, the problem of "overseas citizen protection" [*haiwai gongmin baohu*, 海外公民保护] is not entirely new for Chinese leaders and officials, but it is emerging as an increasingly serious concern.[2] One important way in which China may need to address this problem is by evacuating its citizens from foreign countries in times of turmoil. As PRC Ministry of Foreign Affairs official Yue Yucheng noted in a November 2011 review of recent events in Chinese foreign affairs, "The three overseas evacuations from Egypt, Libya, and Japan evacuated a total of 48,000 Chinese citizens—five times the number of Chinese personnel evacuated from overseas over the last 30 years."[3]

Two trends are contributing to the increasing likelihood that China will need to execute such evacuation missions in the future. First, Chinese workers are going abroad in growing numbers, with many concentrated in potentially dangerous and unstable areas of the globe. Second, the Chinese government faces rising domestic pressure to protect its citizens overseas, and Beijing wants the Chinese public to see it as willing and able to meet these rising expectations.[4] Consequently, not only is the frequency of evacuation operations likely to grow, but their domestic political importance also seems set to increase. As one Chinese writer puts it:

> Protecting the safety and security of the lives and property of Chinese overseas and other such interests has become a practical issue facing China's government. If protection is effective, it will be conducive to strengthening the centripetal force, cohesiveness, and sense of identity of the state and the people, but if protection is ineffective, it may not only result in harm to the stability of the state and the unity of the people, it may also have an influence on China's international status and international image.[5]

This has important implications for the Chinese military. According to Gu Weijun, a researcher with the PLA Academy of Military Sciences (AMS), "Economic 'going global' requires military 'going global' as escorts, and in the future, it will be inevitable for China to use its troops overseas."[6]

Within this context, one important trend concerns the role of the PLA in evacuation operations. A broad range of Chinese institutions is involved in the protection of Chinese citizens overseas in general and in evacuation operations in particular. The lead role in many respects belongs to the Ministry of Foreign Affairs (MFA). For example, when China decided to evacuate its citizens from the Solomon Islands in April 2006 following rioting that led to the destruction of numerous Chinese businesses, leaders in Beijing turned to the MFA. The Chinese embassy in Papua New Guinea arranged for chartered aircraft to withdraw 325 people as the security situation in the Solomon Islands deteriorated.[7]

Yet the prominence of the PLA in such activities appears to be growing. Noncombatant evacuation operations (NEOs) are among the diversified military tasks [*duoyanghua junshi renwu*, 多样化军事任务] the PLA is expected to be able to perform in support of the Communist Party leadership's domestic and international objectives. Indeed, China's 2013 Defense White Paper highlights evacuation of Chinese nationals as one of the ways in which the PLA is responsible for protecting China's growing overseas interests.[8] Such operations are likely to become an increasingly high-profile mission as well, as suggested by the extensive coverage of the Libya evacuation in Chinese media. The PLA's unprecedented involvement in the Libya evacuation, which included the deployment of a PLAN frigate and four PLAAF Il-76 transport aircraft to the region, may foreshadow an even larger role in future evacuation operations. As PLAN researcher Li Jie writes, as more and more Chinese go abroad, "providing maximum protective measures" for them when they are in danger, including by evacuating them when necessary, is becoming an increasingly critical mission that the PLA is duty-bound to perform.[9] Methods such as chartering civilian aircraft to evacuate citizens have been adequate in many cases, but some PLA scholars clearly expect the military to play a more central role in future operations. As Gu Weijun of AMS puts it, "During recent riots in southern Kyrgyzstan, the Chinese government dispatched chartered planes to withdraw our citizens who were living there. But the protection of overseas citizens and expatriates cannot do without military measures. China can refer to the methods of foreign nations and employ armed protection and evacuation measures when its overseas citizens and expatriates face large-scale attacks."[10] Indeed, Chinese publications are replete with general discussions of the importance of protecting citizens overseas and conducting NEOs when necessary.

China's accomplishments in evacuating its citizens have been impressive in some respects. By most accounts, for example, the PLA performed its limited role in the Libya evacuation quite effectively. The PLA is also developing and deploying a number of capabilities that could prove useful for future evacuation missions. At the same time, however, it is less clear that the PLA's doctrine, training, and ability to coordinate effectively with the MFA and other organizations are equally advanced. Moreover, in future NEOs, the degree of difficulty may be higher than was the case in the Libya example. As Andrew Scobell and Andrew Nathan point out, all of the evacuation missions China has conducted to date "were modest in scope, involved no fighting, and sought only to protect economic interests and personnel. But as China's investments increase outside of Asia, there may be more locations where such missions become necessary, and these missions may require force."[11] This raises some questions about how effectively China could respond to the challenges that would likely be involved in more taxing evacuation scenarios.

Case Study: PLA Involvement in Libya Evacuation

As the security situation deteriorated in Libya early in 2011, imperiling the interests of Chinese companies with investments in the country and the safety of tens of thousands of Chinese nationals working there, Beijing prepared to launch an unprecedented evacuation operation to bring them home safely.[12] PRC official media described the ensuing late February and early March 2011 evacuation of Chinese citizens from Libya as the "largest and the most complicated overseas evacuation ever conducted by the Chinese government."[13] In about 10 days, according to official media reports, China evacuated almost 36,000 of its own citizens and about 2,100 citizens of 12 other countries.[14]

According to one official media report, as soon as it became clear that the situation in Libya would require the evacuation of Chinese citizens, the PRC government established a task force led by Vice Premier Zhang Dejiang. Its mission was "to ensure effective evacuation of all the stranded Chinese, including those from Hong Kong, Macao and Taiwan."[15] Following establishment of this task force, Beijing made what official media reports describe as "an all-out effort" to extract its citizens from Libya.[16] In all, according to one official media report, "From February 22 to March 5, the Chinese government organized an overseas evacuation of citizens by air, land and sea—its largest since 1949, involving 91 domestic chartered flights, 12 flights by military airplanes, 5 cargo ferries, 1 escort ship, as well as 35 rented foreign chartered flights, 11 voyages by foreign passenger liners, and some 100 bus runs."[17]

As for the specific mechanisms used to evacuate Chinese citizens, the PRC government relied heavily on chartered aircraft and ships.[18] For example, the Chinese embassy in Malta chartered four ships to help evacuate Chinese nationals to Malta, where they waited for chartered flights to take them back to the PRC.[19] In contrast to some past evacuations, however, China did not rely exclusively on such assets. Beijing also directed the PLAAF and PLAN to participate in the evacuation. On February 28, China dispatched four PLAAF Il-76 transport aircraft to Libya via Khartoum. China also sent the *Jiangkai II*–class frigate *Xuzhou* to the area to provide support and protection for the evacuation of Chinese citizens from Libya. The frigate had been participating in counterpiracy operations in the Gulf of Aden and waters off of Somalia.[20]

The MFA played a crucial role in organizing the evacuation and obtaining international assistance,[21] but this was clearly an important operation for the Chinese military as well. Although more than 90 percent of the Chinese citizens withdrawn from Libya had already been evacuated on chartered aircraft and ferries before the PLAN and PLAAF arrived on the scene,[22] their participation was an important development in that it was the first time the PLA has deployed military assets to support a NEO. As Gabe Collins and Andrew Erickson point out, the dispatch of the four PLAAF transport aircraft was particularly significant in that it marked "the first use of long-range military transport aircraft to rescue Chinese citizens from a foreign conflict zone," while the participation of the *Xuzhou* in the evacuation of Chinese citizens from Libya set "a major precedent because it marked the first time China has sent military assets to a distant part of the world to protect its citizens there."[23] Accordingly, the *PLA Daily* has highlighted the significance of the Libya evacuation as "the first time for China to utilize military force to evacuate Chinese personnel overseas" and named it as one of the "top ten firsts in Chinese military diplomacy from 2002 to 2012."[24] The evacuation mission is clearly seen as important from a service perspective as well. For example, PLAN researcher Li Jie highlights the PLAN's role in particular: "China's dispatch of a navy ship to provide support and protection for the citizen evacuation operation is not only a major breakthrough in terms of execution of an overseas action, but also a major breakthrough in terms of the military's execution of non-war military operations overseas and the PLA Navy's concepts for execution of diversified military tasks."[25]

Given that the evacuation involved withdrawing Chinese nationals on chartered vessels, chartered aircraft, military aircraft, and buses, it required a considerable amount of interagency coordination and cooperation with a number of other organizations. Accordingly, PRC Foreign Ministry officials highlighted the importance of coordination between related ministries, local authorities, the PLA, and Chinese enterprises, as well as cooperation with a number of other countries in successfully completing the evacuation of Chinese nationals.[26] Indeed, as Collins and Erickson point out, "The NEO operation involved an intricate level of interagency coordination, with the Ministries of Commerce, Foreign Affairs, and Public Security working closely with the Civil Aviation Administration of China and consular officials. In addition, Chinese companies operating in Libya, including the China National Petroleum Corporation (CNPC) and China Rail Construction and shippers like COSCO who helped evacuate Chinese citizens from Libya, coordinated closely with the government agencies listed above."[27]

Chinese media accounts suggest that leaders in Beijing viewed the operation as successful in practically all respects. Perhaps unsurprisingly, Chinese media reports tended to portray the evacuation as highly successful. Official media reporting highlighted several aspects of the story, including the role of the PLA and cooperation with international partners. In addition, a number of reports characterized it as indicative of the importance the Chinese government attaches to protecting its citizens abroad, suggesting that addressing domestic political concerns was among the most important considerations for party leaders in Beijing.[28]

Nonetheless, other Chinese assessments of the Libya evacuation were more critical. For example, even as Wang Yizhou praised the MFA for arranging charter flights, renting a Greek ferry, and obtaining international assistance, he indicated that this approach "also revealed that China has some weaknesses."[29] For instance, according to Wang, "the PLAAF used Russian-made transport planes, not the domestically produced large aircraft the Chinese public hopes to see." In addition, Wang notes, the situation encountered in Libya reflected another problem that has emerged as Chinese businesses have expanded internationally: "the assessment of and response to security risks by Chinese companies as they go global has been insufficient."[30] Other observers pointed out that the PLA's involvement was relatively limited and suggested that China should not have to rely on international help when evacuating its citizens from dangerous areas.[31]

Looking ahead, the Libya evacuation underscored some key questions Beijing will need to address over the next few years. As Collins and Erickson point out, these issues include "how to manage the growing Chinese expatriate presence in Africa and other volatile regions where security problems are almost certain to arise and how to handle popular nationalist pressures for intervening when Chinese citizens abroad are threatened."[32] China's experience in Libya also suggests that the PLA will play a major part in addressing those questions, even though its contribution to the Libya NEO was rather modest as a result of its limited capabilities. The Libya NEO underscores the importance of studying how the PLA is likely to approach future evacuation missions.

PLA Assessments of Future Evacuation Contingencies

For Chinese analysts, the need to protect or evacuate Chinese living overseas is a function of growing threats to their security. According to Gu Weijun, "For reasons such as political struggles, terrorist attacks, labor disputes, and natural disasters, Chinese citizens and expatriates living abroad have encountered more and more attacks in recent years."[33] It is also consistent with demands for the PLA to handle nontraditional security threats. Indeed, Chinese military publications on diversified military tasks and military operations other than war (MOOTW) [*feizhanzheng junshi xingdong*, 非战争军事行动] highlight the importance of a number of types of such operations for the PLA, including noncombatant evacuation operations [*cheli feizhandou renyuan*, 撤离非战斗人员]. Foreshadowing the PLA's participation in the 2011 evacuation of Chinese citizens from Libya, one book published in 2009 indicated that such operations would involve dispatching military aircraft or ships to rescue Chinese citizens and overseas Chinese from countries where the security situation was deteriorating rapidly or major incidents of anti-Chinese violence or turmoil were taking place.[34] As a result of China's expanding overseas interests, according to PLAN researcher Li Jie, "Undoubtedly, evacuation and escort incidents like the one in Libya will continue to occur in the future, and will be an increasing trend . . . and the duty of the people's army to provide emergency rescue and protection of the masses will clearly grow larger."[35]

Relevant PLA Capabilities

This section provides a brief overview of the specific assets most likely to be involved in future noncombatant evacuation operations. Chinese military authors suggest that the PLAN and PLAAF probably will play particularly important roles in future evacuation operations.[36] Chinese writers highlight a number of naval and air capabilities—including large amphibious ships, aircraft carriers, and transport aircraft—as particularly important assets that will be required to ensure the successful execution of future evacuations of Chinese citizens. In addition, PLAN marines, airborne troops, or special operations forces could be required to provide security, especially in environments less permissive than the ones China has confronted in its previous NEOs, such as the evacuation of its citizens from Libya. PLA capabilities are clearly improving in many of these areas but are still limited in some important respects. Some Chinese authors tend to focus on past accomplishments and the PLA's recent capability improvements, but others acknowledge the limitations and constraints the PLA will still face in performing future NEOs.

Large Amphibious Ships

Large amphibious ships may be designed primarily for combat operations, but they can also be useful for missions such as NEOs. Indeed, notwithstanding the prominent role of the *Xuzhou* in the Libya evacuation, one of the naval capabilities that Chinese authors highlight as most directly relevant to future evacuation operations is large amphibious ships. Chinese authors indicate that evacuation operations are one of several potential military operations other than war that could be carried out by the PLAN's large amphibious ships. As one article in *Modern Navy* points outs, large amphibious ships are an "excellent choice" for operations such as international assistance, evacuation of citizens, and escort missions.[37] Similarly, in an article highlighting the accelerated development of new dock landing ships, Li Jie suggests that the PLAN's *Yuzhao*-class amphibious transport docks (LPDs) are relevant to a number of potential scenarios, including protection of Chinese citizens overseas, arguing that:

> In future struggles to safeguard our nation's territorial sovereignty and maritime rights and interests in the near seas, the security of our international strategic channels in the intermediate or far seas areas, and even in non-war military actions, which will gradually increase, including protection of the interests of overseas Chinese nationals and international humanitarian assistance, dock landing ships . . . will have an impressive performance.[38]

China currently has three Type 071 *Yuzhao*-class LPDs. Beijing launched the PLAN's first *Yuzhao*-class LPD, the *Kunlunshan*, in 2006. According to the Office of Naval Intelligence, it was commissioned in 2007, "signaling a developing capability for expeditionary warfare and over-the-horizon amphibious assault."[39] The second *Yuzhao*-class LPD, the *Jinggangshan*, was launched in July 2011.[40] The third was launched in September 2011.[41] The PLAN's *Yuzhao*-class LPDs can carry troops, amphibious vehicles, helicopters, and *Yuyi*-class air-cushioned landing craft.[42]

Aircraft Carrier and Other PLAN Capabilities

The PLAN's newly commissioned aircraft carrier also figures prominently in some Chinese discussions of capabilities relevant for executing noncombatant evacuations in distant waters. In particular, Li Jie highlights the role the aircraft carrier could play in future non-war military actions far from China's shores, including "fighting terrorists and pirates, maintaining the security of maritime transportation lines, and evacuating overseas citizens."[43] More broadly, some Chinese military writers argue that planning for future evacuation operations should influence naval equipment development and procurement. PLAN informationization expert and strategist Rear Admiral Yin Zhuo suggests that missions such as protection and evacuation of overseas Chinese should be taken into account in equipment planning by ensuring adequate accommodation aboard large amphibious ships, supply ships, and hospital ships.[44]

PLAAF Large Transport Aircraft

Large transport aircraft can be a critical capability for NEOs instead of or in addition to chartered commercial flights. Accordingly, the PLAAF is also an important player with significant capabilities relevant to noncombatant evacuation operations. For example, a PLAAF assessment of Hu Jintao's direction to build a "powerful people's air force" lists evacuation of Chinese citizens from global hotspots as one of the tasks the PLAAF must be prepared to carry out as it becomes a more globally capable force.[45] Other Chinese authors also highlight the importance of transport aircraft for future evacuation missions. This is one of several missions for large transport aircraft, which are seen as crucial to enhancing the "strategic projection" capabilities China needs in order to protect its increasingly far-flung interests.

The PLAAF currently relies on imported Il-76 transport aircraft for its strategic airlift capabilities. China, however, is not content with its limited strategic airlift capabilities. Indeed, according to the U.S. Department of Defense, "In response to the new historic missions' requirements to protect China's global interests, the PLA Air Force is attempting to increase its long-range transportation and logistics capabilities, to achieve greater strategic projection."[46] Specifically, Beijing is working to enhance the PLAAF's strategic airlift capabilities with a domestically produced large transport aircraft, the Y-20 strategic transport, which conducted its first flight test in January 2013 and currently remains under development.[47]

Interservice Rivalry?

There appears to be some dispute about which service is most capable of withdrawing Chinese citizens from global hotspots. According to Li Jie, the PLAN is uniquely well suited to participate in evacuation missions. Moreover, Li writes, the PLAN enjoys several inherent advantages when compared to the PLAAF. Although this judgment presumably reflects bureaucratic interests and interservice competition more than anything else, Li's reasoning is worth highlighting. Specifically, according to Li, the Libya withdrawal highlighted the PLAN's advantages relative to the PLAAF because:

> In this evacuation action, the air force also dispatched four Il-76 military transport aircraft, which flew over five countries and made a number of important breakthroughs. By comparison, however, the overseas actions of air force troops are rather limited. For example, this time the air force flew across five countries and crossed six time zones, so they had to discuss and negotiate with these countries and had to fly in accordance with stipulated flight paths, altitudes, times, and so on. But the navy's ships navigated on the high seas and in international waters for the most part, so they faced fewer constraints. . . . The navy's ships are also less susceptible to the effects of weather and sea conditions, which is not so for the air force's aircraft. Specifically, the aircraft cross a relatively large area, and in adverse weather they are susceptible to having trouble or even serious problems. There is one more important point, which is that the navy's ships, and especially the medium and large surface ship formations, can sail to the waters

facing the location where an incident is taking place, producing real deterrence and effects, and giving the other side a powerful demonstration of deterrence, and this is something the aircraft are unable to accomplish.[48]

The PLAAF would undoubtedly beg to differ with Li's less than generous assessment of its relevance in such scenarios, as its transport aircraft actually evacuated Chinese citizens from Libya, whereas the PLAN frigate appears to have been present mainly to show the flag and to offer some level of protection if needed.[49] Indeed, the PLAAF has consistently highlighted the important role of its transport aircraft in evacuating Chinese citizens from Libya. PLAAF officers have pointed out that the deployment was unprecedented in many respects, including setting a record for the longest distance flown by the PLAAF's large transport aircraft. Moreover, according to one PLAAF officer, although civilian aircraft can be chartered to evacuate citizens from dangerous areas, China sent military transport planes not only due to the large number of people that needed to be withdrawn from Libya, but also because as military aircraft they have an attribute that civilian planes cannot replicate—notably, their power as a symbol of the Chinese government's determination to protect its citizens overseas.[50] This thinking about the strategic symbolism of global airlift capabilities appears to reflect a growing "air mindedness" in China.[51] In addition, the PLAAF could certainly point out that however limited its strategic airlift capabilities may be, aircraft can arrive on the scene much more quickly than ships. In addition, the PLAAF's capabilities would be much more relevant than those of the PLAN in a scenario involving evacuation of Chinese citizens from one of any number of landlocked countries where China has people, investments, and related interests to protect.[52]

Relevant Doctrine and Training Activities

Doctrine that covers noncombatant evacuation operations and realistic training that focuses on the challenges involved in conducting such operations are crucial to ensuring that the PLA is properly prepared to carry out these kinds of operations when called upon to do so by China's leaders. The U.S. military provides a useful example in this regard; it has published joint doctrine specifically focused on planning and conducting joint noncombatant evacuation operations.[53] The United States has a detailed planning process for NEOs that takes into account many factors, such as security considerations and coordination between the military and the Department of State. In addition, the U.S. Marine Corps has a compressed version of its normal planning process, known as the rapid response planning process (R2P2). When an urgent situation does not permit employment of the standard planning process, a U.S. Marine Expeditionary Unit (MEU) can use the R2P2 approach to begin planning and executing operations in a matter of hours.[54]

Moreover, the U.S. military regularly conducts training for NEO operations to make sure troops are ready to evacuate U.S. citizens, and in some cases nationals of other countries, when the need arises. For example, in October 2012, U.S. Marines took part in a NEO exercise that simulated the evacuation of a U.S. Embassy. The training, which took place in Yuma, Arizona, and at the Marine Corps Air Ground Combat Center in Twenty-Nine Palms, California, focused not only on tactical activities such as establishing a security perimeter and flight operations, but also on the type of interagency coordination required to successfully execute a NEO in the real world. To that end, a State Department consular affairs officer took part in the exercise to help the Marines learn to work as a "unified U.S. military and State Department team."[55] It is unclear how well prepared the PLA is in these respects. Not only is it uncertain whether the PLA has promulgated doctrine that covers evacuation operations, but it is also difficult to judge, based on Chinese publications, the extent to which the PLA conducts training focused specifically on such operations.

Interagency Coordination

As Collins and Erickson have observed, evacuation missions present significant operational challenges for the PLA, as NEOs can be "very demanding in terms of coordinating air and sea platforms operating far from their home bases and in potentially hostile areas."[56] Coordination with the MFA and other organizations is another potential challenge. Indeed, interagency coordination is especially critical in overseas evacuation operations, as is emphasized in U.S. joint doctrine and training. This is no different for China. The PLA must be prepared to communicate and coordinate with the MFA and other governmental and nongovernmental organizations.

The involvement of a large and likely growing number of actors in evacuation operations makes coordination very challenging for China. How well the PLA prepares to carry out such operations in cooperation with the MFA and other organizations is difficult to assess in much detail based on available Chinese publications. For this reason, Duchâtel and Gill conclude that "coordination between government ministries, the armed forces, state-owned enterprises and private businesses—problematic under most circumstances—remains unclear when it comes to protecting citizens abroad."[57] This is apparently a work in progress for the PLA.

Conclusion

The evacuation of Chinese citizens from Libya likely signals a growing requirement for Chinese government and military involvement in the protection of Chinese nationals abroad, quite possibly to include future evacuation operations. Indeed, because of the increasing number of Chinese working overseas, many of whom are located in politically volatile and potentially dangerous areas, and because of the need to appear responsive to domestic concerns about China's ability to protect its citizens overseas, Beijing must ensure that it is capable of handling similar crises in the future.[58]

All of this suggests that Beijing will need to find ways to more actively ensure the protection of Chinese citizens residing abroad. Exactly how Beijing will approach this problem remains to be seen. When the security situation is relatively permissive, the United States generally prefers to rely on civilian assets for NEOs because it is less expensive than using the military. Will China follow suit, or will Beijing conclude that using PLA assets to show the flag is important enough to justify the extra expense even when it is not really necessary? China's evacuation of its citizens from Libya could be instructive in this regard. A key question is why the Communist Party leadership ordered the PLAN and PLAAF to participate in the evacuation. It is difficult to judge with certainty whether military involvement was motivated primarily by a desire to ensure the successful evacuation of Chinese citizens. It could also have been a function of other considerations, such as a perceived need to satisfy domestic concerns about China's ability to protect its citizens or a desire to burnish China's international image. These possibilities are not mutually exclusive, of course, and China's overall approach to the Libya evacuation suggests one possibility is that such situations are likely to remain primarily the responsibility of the MFA but may increasingly involve at least limited participation by the PLA as well. If so, this will require the PLA to work in cooperation with the MFA and other organizations to plan and carry out future evacuation operations.

From an institutional perspective, the PLA benefits from its growing role in protecting China's overseas interests in general and from its role in evacuations in particular. For example, the success of the Libya evacuation and the perceived need to be prepared to rescue Chinese nationals from other crisis-torn areas afford the PLA an opportunity to display its growing capabilities to domestic and international audiences. At home, it allows the PLA to show its value by protecting Chinese citizens overseas. Abroad, it enables the PLA to portray its growing capabilities as ones that China can employ constructively and responsibly. The PLA's participation in evacuation operations may also further strengthen its position in terms of internal arguments over the allocation of resources by showcasing its ability to contribute to China's desired image as a responsible global power.

Yet there are risks for the PLA as well, especially given the domestic requirement of being seen as capable of protecting Chinese citizens overseas and the importance the party leadership appears to attach to China's international image. One possibility is that planning and doctrine exist primarily in internal channels; another is that they may not be fully developed at this point. Moreover, in future evacuation missions, the PLA may have to face more difficult challenges than those it has handled thus far. However, it is unclear how much attention the PLA has devoted to the myriad factors that would be involved in preparing for less benign situations, including the intelligence, surveillance, and reconnaissance requirements for NEOs under such circumstances. Whether PLA capabilities, doctrine, training, and ability to coordinate with the MFA and other organizations will be adequate to handle more taxing scenarios is unclear.

Notes

1   See, for example, Liu Linzhi [刘林智], "Turbulence in North Africa and China's Overseas Interests Protection" [北非地区动荡化与中国海外利益维护], *Contemporary International Relations* [现代国际关系], no. 5 (May 2012), 46–51; and Tang Hao [唐昊], "Strategic Thought on Protection of China's Overseas Interests" [关于中国海外利益保护的战略思考], *Contemporary International Relations*, no. 6 (June 2011), 1–8.

2   Mathieu Duchâtel and Bates Gill, "Overseas citizen protection: a growing challenge for China," *SIPRI Newsletter*, February 2012, available at <www.sipri.org/media/newsletter/essay/february12>. According to the authors, "Between 2006 and 2010, a total of 6,000 Chinese citizens were evacuated from upheavals in Chad, Haiti, Kyrgyzstan, Lebanon, Solomon Islands, Thailand, Timor-Leste and Tonga," and in

2011, China not only withdrew almost 36,000 PRC citizens from Libya but also evacuated a substantial number of its nationals from Egypt and Japan.

3   Yue Yucheng [乐玉成], "Chinese Diplomacy in the Context of World Change" [世界大变局中的中国外交], *Foreign Affairs Review* [外交评论] (November 2011), 1–6.

4   On growing domestic pressure to protect Chinese abroad, see Jacob Zenn, "Chinese, Overseas and Insecure," *Asia Times*, September 6, 2012, available at <www.atimes.com/atimes/China/NI06Ad02.html>. For an example of an attempt to assure its domestic audience and Chinese living overseas that the Chinese government is responding effectively, see Nie Chuanqing, "China Makes Great Efforts to Protect Overseas Citizens," *People's Daily Overseas Edition*, April 24, 2012.

5   Wang Tao [王涛], "Viewing the Protection of China's Overseas Interests from the Perspective of the Civil War in Cote d'Ivoire" [由科特迪瓦内战看中国的海外利益保护], *Conmilit* [现代军事], no. 6 (June 5, 2011), 26–29.

6   "Gu Weijun: China Should Research Ways to Use its Troops Overseas" [古伟俊: 中国要研究海外用兵之道], *Global Times* [环球时报], June 29, 2010.

7   See, for example, Qin Jize and Liang Qiwen, "310 Chinese Back Home from Solomons," *China Daily*, April 25, 2006, available at <www.chinadaily.com.cn/china/2006-04/25/content_575798.htm>.

8   Information Office of the State Council, People's Republic of China, *The Diversified Employment of China's Armed Forces*, 2013 defense white paper (Beijing: Information Office of the State Council, April 2013).

9   Li Jie [李杰], "In the Overseas Evacuation Operation, the Navy Is as Impressive as Before!" [海外撤侨行动, 海军依然给力!], *Modern Ships* [现代舰船] (April 1, 2011), 54.

10   "Gu Weijun: China Should Research Ways to Use its Troops Overseas."

11   Andrew Scobell and Andrew J. Nathan, "China's Overstretched Military," *Washington Quarterly* 35, no. 4 (Fall 2012), 143.

12   On the threat to Chinese companies and workers, see, for example, Leslie Hook and Geoff Dyer, "Chinese Oil Interests Attacked in Libya," *Financial Times*, February 24, 2011.

13   "35,860 Chinese nationals in Libya evacuated: FM," Xinhua, March 3, 2011, available at <http://news.xinhuanet.com/english2010/china/2011-03/03/c_13758221.htm>.

14   Ibid.; "35,860 Chinese evacuated from unrest-torn Libya," Xinhua, March 3, 2011, available at <http://news.xinhuanet.com/english2010/china/2011-03/03/c_13759456.htm>; Li Xiaokun, "Chinese nationals set to be evacuated from Libya," *China Daily*, February 23, 2011, available at <www.chinadaily.com.cn/china/2011-02/23/content_12061077.htm>; "China's successful evacuation

from Libya completed," Xinhua, March 4, 2011, available at <http://news.xin-huanet.com/english2010/video/2011-03/04/c_13761456.htm>; "China's evacuation of citizens from Libya is impressive: U.S. observer," *People's Daily*, March 5, 2011, available at <http://english.people.com.cn/90001/90776/90883/7308976.html>; and "China evacuates 12,000 from Libya, sends frigate to help," *China Daily*, February 25, 2011, available at <www.chinadaily.com.cn/china/2011-02/25/content_12075249.htm>.

15   "35,860 Chinese nationals in Libya evacuated: FM." Xinhua.

16   Ibid.

17   "China's miraculous evacuation from Libya widely applauded," *People's Daily*, March 7, 2011, available at <http://english.peopledaily.com.cn/90001/90776/90883/7310717.html>.

18   "Chartered planes take off to evacuate Chinese from Libya," *People's Daily*, February 25, 2011, available at <http://english.people.com.cn/90001/90776/90883/7301087.html>.

19   "Four Vessels on Libya Evacuation Mission for Chinese Nationals," *People's Daily*, February 26, 2011, available at <http://english.people.com.cn/90001/90776/90883/7300925.html>.

20   For brief discussions of the frigate's participation in the evacuation operations as one of the highlights of the PLAN's involvement in responding to "multiple types of security threats" and completing "diversified military tasks," see Wu Chao, Cai Nianchi, Yu Zhangcai, and Qian Xiaohu [吴超, 蔡年迟, 虞章才, 钱晓虎], "Braving the Wind and Waves: On the Spot Report on How the PLAN has Accelerated the Promotion of Unit Transformation, Construction, and Development During the 11th Five Year Program" [长风破浪正当时: 海军 "十一五" 时期加快推进部队转型建设发展纪实], *PLA Daily* [解放军报], December 5, 2011; and Li Tang and Qian Xiaohu [李唐, 钱晓虎], "Chinese Navy Makes Contributions to Peaceful Development on Oceans" [中国海军为和平发展建功大洋], *PLA Daily*, September 3, 2012.

21   For a brief discussion, see Yue Yucheng, 1–6.

22   See Daniel J. Kostecka, "From the Sea: PLA Doctrine and the Employment of Sea-Based Airpower," *Naval War College Review* 64, no. 3 (Summer 2011), 25–26.

23   Gabe Collins and Andrew Erickson, "Implications of China's Military Evacuation of Citizens from Libya," *China Brief* 11, no. 4 (March 10, 2011). See also Gabe Collins and Andrew Erickson, "China dispatches warship to protect Libya evacuation mission: Marks the PRC's first use of frontline military assets to protect an evacuation mission," *China SignPost*, no. 25 (February 24, 2011), available at <www.chinasignpost.com/2011/02/24/china-dispatches-warship-to-protect-libya-evacuation-mission-marks-the-prcs-first-use-of-frontline-military-assets-to-protect-an-evacuation-mission/>.

24   "Top ten firsts of Chinese military diplomacy from 2002 to 2012," *PLA Daily*, September 26, 2012, available at <http://english.peopledaily.com.cn/90786/7960693. html>.

25   Li, 54.

26   "35,860 Chinese nationals in Libya evacuated: FM." Xinhua. This report mentions offers of assistance from Greece, Malta, Egypt, Tunisia, Turkey, and Jordan and commends two Chinese companies that were operating in Libya—China Communications Construction Group and China Railway Construction Corporation—for their contributions to the organization of the withdrawal of Chinese citizens.

27   Collins and Erickson, "Implications of China's Military Evacuation of Citizens from Libya."

28   "China's Libya evacuation highlights People-First nature of government," Xinhua, March 3, 2011, available at <http://news.xinhuanet.com/english2010/ indepth/2011-03/03/c_13759953.htm>. According to this report, "The massive, orderly and extraordinarily efficient evacuation is widely regarded as a vivid reflection of the Chinese government's motto of 'putting people first and running the government in the interest of the people.'" Moreover, "the swift evacuation also benefited from China's growing national power and equally important, the advantage of the socialist system enabling the whole country to mobilize all of the necessary resources needed for an arduous mission."

29   Xu Ming [徐明], "Wang Yizhou: China should be 'Creatively Involved' in World Affairs" [王逸舟：中国应'创造性介入'国际事物], *International Herald Leader* [国际先驱导报], December 20, 2011.

30   Ibid.

31   Shen Fan, Ma Dongfeng, and Cui Dong [沈凡, 马东锋, 崔冬], "Analysis of Materials Support for Our Army's Overseas Rescue" [我军海外救援物资保障分析], *Logistics Sci-Tech* [物流科技], no. 10 (2011), 94–96.

32   Collins and Erickson, "Implications of China's Military Evacuation of Citizens from Libya."

33   "Gu Weijun: China Should Research Ways to Use its Troops Overseas."

34   Gai Shijin and Zhang Peizhong [盖世金, 张培忠], *On Diversified Military Tasks* [多样化军事任务论] (Beijing: Long March Press [长征出版社], 2009), 68.

35   Li, "In the Overseas Evacuation Operation," 54.

36   Gai and Zhang, 157–158. According to the authors, in these types of operations, the air force and navy may need to work jointly to establish air safety corridors [*kongzhong anquan zoulang*, 空中安全走廊] and set up safety zones [*anquan qu*, 安全区], as part of the overall effort to withdraw Chinese citizens from the threatened areas.

37   Ye Qi [叶顼], "A Brief Discussion of the Future of China's Large Amphibious Warfare Ships" [浅谈中国大型两栖作战舰艇的未来], *Modern Navy* [当代海军], no. 11 (November 2011), 42–44.

38   Li Jie, "China's Accelerated Development of New-Model Dock Landing Ships Follows Overall Trends" [中国加速发展新型船坞登陆舰乃是大势所趋], *Modern Ships* (May 2012), 54. According to Li, the advantages of the *Kunlunshan*-class dock landing ships include "advanced design, outstanding performance, and extensive applications." They can be employed to conduct amphibious operations, to provide command, control, and communications support, or to function as a mobile command post for an amphibious task force.

39   Office of Naval Intelligence (ONI), *The People's Liberation Army Navy: A Modernizing Navy with Chinese Characteristics* (Suitland, MD: Office of Naval Intelligence, August 2009), 20.

40   See "China launches largest dock landing ship," United Press International, July 22, 2011, available at <http://www.upi.com/Business_News/Security-Industry/2011/07/22/China-launches-largest-dock-landing-ship/64291311369476/>.

41   For photos, see "071 YUZHAO Class Amphibious Transport Dock LPD Number Three Launched," *China Defense Blog*, September 26, 2011, available at <www.china-defense.blogspot.com/2011/09/071-yuzhao-class-amphibious-transport.html>.

42   See Wendell Minnick, "China Bolsters Lift as Regional Tensions Increase," *Defense News*, October 18, 2012; and Richard D. Fisher, Jr., "China's Gathering Amphibious and Airborne Expeditionary Capabilities," presentation for Institute for Defense and Government Advancement's Amphibious Operations Summit, May 21, 2012.

43   Li discusses the potential missions of China's aircraft carrier in "Naval Expert: Aircraft Carrier Will Play a Major Role in Settlement of Islands Disputes," *People's Daily*, September 24, 2012, available at <http://english.peopledaily.com.cn/90786/7957606.html>. For more on his views, see Li Jie, "If China has an Aircraft Carrier Formation, what will it be able to do?" [倘若中国有航母编队，将能干啥?], *Modern Ships* (June 2011), 54.

44   See Zhu Mengqin and Yuan Zhenjun [朱梦勤, 袁珍军], "Dialogue with Yin Zhuo: Escort Mission is an Epoch-Making Symbolic Event" [对话尹卓: 护航是划时代标志性事件], *Modern Navy*, no. 12 (2011), 22–25.

45   Shang Jinsuo, Li Zhen, Li Liguang, and Ye Haiyuan [尚金锁, 李振, 李黎光, 叶海源], "A Study of Hu Jintao's Thinking on Building a Powerful People's Air Force" [胡锦涛关于建设强大的人民空军思想研究], *China Military Science* [中国军事科学], no. 5 (2011), 13–17.

46   Office of the Secretary of Defense (OSD), *Military and Security Developments Involving the People's Republic of China*, 2012, Annual Report to Congress (Washington, DC: OSD, May 2012), 6.

47   "Test flight frequency of Y-20 heavy-duty transport aircraft sets new record," *China Military Online*, March 5, 2014, available at <http://eng.chinamil.com.cn/special-reports/2014-03/05/content_5796131.htm>.

48   Li Jie, "In the Overseas Evacuation Operation," 54.

49   I would like to thank Dan Kostecka for raising this point.

50   Dong Ruifeng and Guo Hongbo [董瑞丰, 郭洪波], "Sharp Weapons of a Great Power: Visiting the Air Force's Strategic Transport Aircraft Unit" [大国利器: 探访空军战略运输机部队], *Outlook* [瞭望], no. 34 (August 20, 2012), 48–49.

51   I would like to thank Dan Kostecka for raising this point and for highlighting an instructive quote from former U.S. Air Force Chief of Staff General Ronald Fogleman: "as our big 'T' tail aircraft, with the American flag painted on them, fly around the world, they not only represent America, but they are America." See Ronald R. Fogleman, "Core Competencies—New Missions: The Air Force in Operations Other Than War," *Airman*, no. 39 (April 1995), 2–9.

52   I would like to thank Dan Kostecka for raising this point.

53   Joint Publication 3-68 *Noncombatant Evacuation Operations* (Washington, DC: The Joint Staff, December 23, 2010), available at <www.dtic.mil/doctrine/new_pubs/jp3_68.pdf>.

54   Marine Corps Warfighting Publication 5-1, *Marine Corps Planning Process* (Washington, DC: U.S .Marine Corps, August 24, 2010).

55   For a brief account of the exercise, see Sean Dennison, "Marines Simulate U.S. Embassy Evacuation in Yuma, Twenty-nine Palms," October 25, 2012, available at <www.dvidshub.net/news/96708/marines-simulate-us-embassy-evacuation-yuma-twentynine-palms>.

56   Andrew Erickson and Gabe Collins, "Looking After China's Own: Pressure to Protect PRC Citizens Working Overseas Likely to Rise," *China SignPost*, no. 2 (November 7, 2010).

57   Duchâtel and Gill.

58   See, for example, Erickson and Collins, "Looking After China's Own."

CHAPTER 14

PLA Navy Planning for Out of Area Deployments

Kristen Gunness and Samuel K. Berkowitz

The People's Republic of China (PRC) is a power with global interests. Those interests have led the Chinese defense establishment to invest in a range of military capabilities that will enable its military reach to extend far beyond China's borders. Recognition of China's expanding national interests and the need to protect those interests was first articulated in Hu Jintao's "New Historic Missions" speech in 2004.[1] As these global interests face various threats, requirements to secure them primarily fall on China's military, the People's Liberation Army (PLA), and in many cases specifically on the PLA Navy (PLAN). Chinese naval developments in the years since the New Historic Missions speech have laid the foundation for an increasing range of "expeditionary" roles that have taken the PLAN farther abroad more frequently and on lengthier deployments. The longest and best observed of these expeditionary missions began in 2008, when the PLAN embarked on its first major long-term out of area operation off the coast of Somalia to counter piracy in cooperation with a multinational task force.

Preparing for the counterpiracy mission and for a more diverse mission set far beyond China's borders has required extensive planning by China's defense bureaucracy. This chapter discusses the PLAN's deployment planning efforts. First, it describes some of the broader Chinese military doctrinal and operational changes that laid the groundwork for the PLAN's ability to conduct longer deployments. Next, it outlines the key missions that take the PLAN beyond China's periphery to the far seas. It then uses counterpiracy operations as a case study of PLAN deployment challenges and solutions, and, finally, it discusses the implications for future PLAN deployments.

Laying the Foundation for Longer Deployments: PLA Doctrinal and Operational Changes

Before the PLAN's first deployment to the Gulf of Aden, the PLA leadership paved the way by making several modifications in PLA doctrine and operations, including changes to doctrine, training, personnel, and logistics.

Preparing for Diverse Military Tasks

The concepts that the PLA needed to perform "diversified military tasks" and to prepare for "military operations other than war" (MOOTW) were raised in importance in PRC and PLA official speeches and documents from the mid-2000s onward. For example, MOOTW was emphasized as an important component of China's national defense policy in official PRC documents such as the 2006 and 2008 white papers on China's national defense.[2] The 2008 Defense White Paper in particular contained more detail than past editions on PLA training efforts with regard to MOOTW. The official recognition of the importance of developing the capability to deploy abroad allowed the PLA and PLAN to engage in serious planning for such missions.

Revising Training Methods and Regulations

The PLA has also embarked on a comprehensive program to enhance the quality of military training. While not tied solely to the PLA's preparations for deploying abroad—better training is an important aspect of the PLA's overall military transformation—it has been a critical contributor to successful longer PLAN deployments and is an area of continuing focus for the PLA and PLAN. The 2008 Defense White Paper emphasized the need for better training to prepare for modern warfare, which included the need to train under informationized conditions, conduct more realistic training that mirrors combat conditions, train in complex electromagnetic environments, conduct joint training, and better evaluate the results of exercises.[3]

In addition to the Defense White Paper, the PLA issued a new version of its Outline for Military Training and Evaluation (OMTE) [*junshi xunlian yu kaohe dagang*, 军事训练与考核大纲], a set of authoritative long-term training instructions. The 2009 document reflected the training priorities listed above and also emphasized "stepping up research and training on non-war military actions," training for a variety of security threats, diverse military tasks, and MOOTW.[4] In September 2011 the PLA's General Staff Department (GSD) released an "Overall

Plan for Military Training Reform during the 12ᵗʰ Five Year Program," which discussed reforms to increase force integration, establish better multi-service (joint) training, integrate a "system of systems" approach, and develop new training mechanisms to increase combined arms and multi-service competencies. A revised OMTE and these new training methods, according to PLA open source writings, should be in place by 2015, though at the time of publication of this book an official revision had not yet appeared.[5]

Very little is discussed in open sources about specific PLAN training of ships for deployments abroad. PRC and PLA leaders have called for increased PLAN far seas training in the past several years, though specific distances are generally not given. For example, East Sea Fleet Commander Admiral Du Jingchen stated in 2010 that "you can't exercise a fine horse in a courtyard," and called for:

> regular training far out on the ocean. . . . In every one of the recent years, the Navy has arranged for units to go far out to sea and onto the oceans to train sailors. Surface ships going to the tactical setting of the island chain to train in tactical subjects, submarines training on long voyages, groups of aircraft making long-distance raids in complex weather conditions, surface ships, submarines, and aircraft in joint confrontational training, etc., have tempered Navy units, tested equipment, made crews familiar with environments, and boosted units' all-round operational capabilities.[6]

Given the PLA's overall emphasis on training for MOOTW and out of area operations, it can be assumed that specific guidelines exist for training PLAN ships for particular missions abroad. Recent work by Bernard Cole on PLAN training and exercises indicates that the PLAN follows a "building-block approach, with [individual ship] training progressing in both complexity and scope until a unit is qualified to join fleet-level operations. Such building-block events include training in small-craft maneuvering, sea-lane interdiction, reconnaissance, submarine positioning and navigation, landing ship formation steaming, weapons and sensor systems exercises, and aviation unit familiarization with new equipment."[7] It is plausible that the PLAN follows a similar model when preparing certain flotillas for deployment abroad, particularly when they will work with foreign navies (as in the Gulf of Aden counterpiracy missions).

In addition to domestic exercises, the PLAN has gained some of the skills it needs for longer deployments by working and exercising abroad with foreign navies. While the PLAN has conducted search and rescue and humanitarian assistance/disaster relief (HA/DR) exercises with various countries, the counterpiracy operations and subsequent exercises have provided the most benefit in terms of increasing PLAN knowledge of capabilities of ships operating at sea for sustained periods of time, logistics management, and development of personnel who know how to interact with foreign navies and operate independently far from home.[8] In September 2012, the U.S. Navy and PLAN conducted their first bilateral counterpiracy exercise, including a combined visit, board, search, and seizure. The focus of the exercise was on "bilateral interoperability in detecting, boarding and searching suspected vessels as well as the ability of both Chinese and American naval assets to respond to pirated vessels."[9] The PLAN also participated in the 2014 multinational Rim of the Pacific (RIMPAC) exercise, including conducting a gunnery exercise with U.S. Navy ships. More Chinese lessons learned from the counterpiracy mission will be discussed in the case study below.

Searching for Better Educated, More Professional Personnel

The third area the PLA has sought to reform is its professional military education (PME) system.[10] Like training, PME reform has been part of the PLA's overall military modernization program over the past decade and has implications for the success of its deployments abroad. The PLA's most recent efforts to educate and recruit the "right" type of officer can be traced back to the "Strategic Project for Talented People" implemented by the Central Military Commission (CMC) in 2003. The project was broadly aimed at recruiting and educating a technologically savvy contingent of officers capable of directing informationized wars and of building informationized armed forces in one to two decades; later versions added the requirement for officers who can command and take part in joint operations (essential for winning future wars, in the PLA's view).[11]

In addition to education, the PLA has sought to develop a more "professional" force to send abroad that could interact with foreign officers as well as a force that could mentally withstand longer deployments. This involves political work to ensure loyalty to the party and cultural training, with the PLAN receiving particular attention as the main service to bear the brunt of deployments abroad. For example, in October 2012, then–Vice CMC Chairman Xu Caihou toured the Dalian Naval Academy and emphasized the importance of the cultural training center located on its grounds.[12] In April 2012, the PLAN's training ship, the *Zheng He*, embarked from Dalian on a round-the-world voyage to teach naval cadets "professional sailing theories, methods and skills, and cultivate good nautical working styles" in addition to expanding the maritime, cultural, and diplomatic awareness of the PLA naval cadets on board.[13]

The importance of political work in longer deployments and far seas training is a continuous theme in PLA writings. For example, in January 2012, *People's Navy* [人民海军] published a lengthy article that described the importance of political work during long voyages, using the PLAN East Sea Fleet Submarine Flotilla's multiple long-voyage training as an example. The article described the use of political work in maintaining unit cohesiveness and a "positive fighting spirit" during a long voyage, the role of political cadres on board, the decision-making process of the "submarine interim party committee" during a weather emergency, and the role of self-criticism in ensuring that equipment and operations work properly.[14] Another article states that because far seas tasks are so complex and the environment subject to change, political work is a major component of ensuring PLAN forces are able to complete missions abroad.[15]

Developing a More Sustainable Logistics System

Finally, the PLA must be able to sustain a long-term operation abroad logistically. This has required some revamping of the logistics system, though the changes thus far have not been as wholesale as with training and PME. The PLA realizes that in order to carry out an increasingly diverse set of military missions, it must have a logistics system that is flexible, far-reaching, and able to respond quickly to natural disasters or emergencies abroad. The PLAN has already had to confront many of these issues to sustain its operations in the Gulf of Aden: logistical challenges cited include lack of reliable access to port facilities, lack of adequate food preparation (absence of fresh food), lack of crew time in port, procurement issues, lack of continuous communications, and various maintenance issues.[16]

Some of the solutions the PLAN has employed for maintenance, personnel, and procurement challenges include negotiating more regular access to ports to resupply and provide leave for crew members and decreasing red tape and procurement/shipping times through increased cooperation with civilian companies such as the Chinese Ocean Shipping Company (COSCO) Logistics and Shipping. In addition, the United States and China have considered an agreement to share logistical resources such as fuel, food, supplies, and vessel parts to support joint operations in counterpiracy and HA/DR missions.[17] While the agreement has not yet been fully adopted, in 2013 the United States and China conducted joint counterpiracy exercises in the Gulf of Aden, paving the way for potentially broader cooperation.[18]

Communications issues have been somewhat remedied by providing continuous satellite communications for all out of area deployments.[19] On this last point, China has been working on building a network of modern communications and navigation satellites that will help support future out of area missions.

Various analysts have pointed out that the PLAN's logistical capabilities will be limited as long as it lacks significant numbers of oilers and resupply ships capable of operating at great distances. These capabilities will likely take some time for the PLAN to build. In addition, the PLA's logistical network is limited by its lack of overseas bases and inability to preposition equipment abroad.[20]

Sailing the Far Seas: PLA Navy Roles and Missions Abroad

To better understand how the PLAN plans for deployment, it is instructive to look at where it deploys and what missions it seeks to accomplish. Beyond goodwill cruises and port calls around the world, which mainly serve to wave the flag and promote exchanges with foreign navies, three primary missions have taken the PLAN on longer deployments to execute specific tasks.

The first such mission is humanitarian assistance and disaster relief (HA/DR). As of the end of 2014, the PLAN had completed five humanitarian voyages with its hospital ship, the *Peace Ark*.[21] During the Harmonious Mission 2010 deployment, the ship sailed through the Malacca Strait and into the Indian Ocean to make port calls in Djibouti, Kenya, Tanzania, the Seychelles, and Bangladesh.[22] For the second deployment, Harmonious Mission 2011, the hospital ship journeyed through the Panama Canal and conducted port calls in Jamaica, Cuba, Trinidad and Tobago, and Costa Rica.[23] During both of these voyages, the medical staff aboard the ship provided examinations portside. In November 2013, after international criticism over China's slow response to a natural disaster in its region, the *Peace Ark* sailed to the Philippines to assist in the aftermath of Typhoon Haiyan.[24] In 2014, the *Peace Ark* participated in RIMPAC in June and then visited Tonga, Fiji, Vanuatu, and Papua New Guinea for the medical service mission Harmonious Mission 2014.[25]

The second mission that will take the PLAN farther abroad is noncombatant evacuation operations (NEOs). The PLAN conducted its first NEO in Libya in February 2011. The Libya NEO was primarily managed by the Chinese Ministry of Foreign Affairs, and most of the 35,000 Chinese nationals were evacuated by sea on chartered merchant vessels, chartered and military aircraft (PLAAF Il-76 transports), and buses. However, the PLAN directly participated by sending four military transports and a navy frigate, the *Xuzhou*, which had been part of the 7th Flotilla in the Gulf of Aden, to the Mediterranean Sea to escort and provide overwatch for the chartered shipping.[26] In all, the PLA directly provided or assisted in the evacuation of almost 3,000 Chinese citizens.[27] The deployment of the *Xuzhou* set a major precedent because it marked the first time China has sent military assets to a distant part of the world to protect its citizens there and demonstrated Beijing's growing capability to conduct long-range operations that it had been incapable of performing only a decade ago.

Finally, the missions of counterpiracy and protection of sea lines of communication (SLOCs) will require longer deployments. The Chinese consider piracy to be an increasing threat to their shipping. A number of SLOCs important to China run through areas affected by piracy, including routes in the South China Seas and the Malacca Strait, West Africa, and more recently the Gulf of Aden. The PLAN sent its first flotilla to the Gulf of Aden in December 2008 to counter piracy as part of a multinational task force. As of April 2015, the PLAN had sent 20 task forces to the Gulf of Aden. The Chinese ships are mainly focused on protecting their respective merchant shipping vessels transiting the area, though some coordination is occurring among the various navies. The counterpiracy case study discussed later in this chapter provides further details.

Developing Capabilities to Support the Missions

While in-depth analysis of PLAN capabilities is beyond the scope of this chapter, it is worth briefly discussing the capabilities that the PLAN, in coordination with other PLA services, has developed or is in the process of developing to support the above missions. These include investing in aircraft carrier(s), which could support HA/DR and SLOC protection operations (in addition to playing a role in regional combat operations), expeditionary airlift and sealift, and at-sea replenishment capability. In addition, space-based assets such as communications satellites are necessary for PLAN ships operating far from home as they enable instantaneous communication for command and control from higher echelons. China already has a number of communications satellites in geostationary orbit that allow both voice and data transfer to moving units. Navigation satellites are a crucial component of overseas operations, and China currently has at least 11 of these satellites in both geostationary and geosynchronous orbits.[28] Intelligence, surveillance, and reconnaissance satellites provide maritime surveillance for the PLA.[29]

Finally, the PRC government and the PLA have continued to successfully negotiate port access to support operations around the world. The prospect of Chinese "bases" abroad is the subject of much speculation. Locations in the Indian Ocean such as Hambantota (Sri Lanka), Gwadar (Pakistan), and most recently the Seychelles have been mentioned as possible future ports where the PLAN could negotiate access. Even without official bases, the PLAN has already effectively used a network of commercial ports in the Gulf of Aden to support its counterpiracy mission, providing a remarkably footprint-free way for China to conduct such operations far from home.[30] As will be discussed in the case study below, the PLAN is already making regular use of Aden in Yemen, Djibouti Port in Djibouti, and Salalah in Oman for rest and replenishment of its flotillas. Local ports have provided fuel, food, and water to the at-sea replenishment ship dispatched with each flotilla.[31]

Case Study: PLAN Deployment Planning for Gulf of Aden Counterpiracy Missions

The PLAN's deployment to the Gulf of Aden is the longest and best documented of the Chinese navy's expeditionary missions and thus provides a window through which to observe deployment planning efforts. This section will look at specific preparations the PLAN undertook prior to the Gulf of Aden deployments, as well as some of the issues they encountered throughout the missions and lessons learned for future deployments. For this case study, we examined several hundred PLA open source articles and analyses from 2008 to 2012 to determine how the PLAN went about preparing for these missions and the challenges they encountered along the way. Findings are divided into several areas: logistics and replenishment, equipment and maintenance, training, care for personnel, and communications.

It is worth noting that because the PLA announced that it would be carrying out counterpiracy missions in the Gulf of Aden less than 2 weeks before the first deployment, the amount of open source information on the earliest stages of planning for this endeavor is fairly limited. However, some assumptions can be made based on the capabilities that the PLAN has shown over its first dozen missions off the coast of Somalia.

Logistics and Replenishment

Deployment planning related to food and fuel issues evolved considerably over the course of the first few deployments to the Gulf of Aden. On the eve of the first naval escort task force's departure, PLAN leaders expressed pride about the rations that they had procured for their sailors. In an interview with *Xinhua*, Captain Long Juan, commander of the missile destroyer *Wuhan*, said that the soldiers aboard his ship would be enjoying "self-service meals, eggs and milk at breakfast, fruit at all three meals, [and] beverages with the evening meal." Moreover, he boasted, they would be able to eat sea cucumber or abalone, both highly nutritious delicacies, once a week while at sea.[32] This was no doubt possible due to special refrigeration equipment aboard the ships capable of preserving leafy green vegetables for a full month and melons and other fruits for several months.[33] Additionally, the supply ship *Weishanhu* that accompanied the two destroyers on the first task force carried a total of 680 tons of dry goods and ammunition, a large part of which was presumably nonperishable food, as well as 250 tons of drinking water.[34] The Chinese authorities estimated that these supplies would be sufficient for a "few months' consumption."

The *Weishanhu* berthed in Aden, Yemen, on February 21, 2009, to procure more food and water just under 2 months into the mission. This could indicate that initial estimates of how long the food supply would last may have been overly optimistic, or Aden might simply have been a convenient stopping point for replenishment.[35] Replenishment at sea using merchant ships appears to have become standard procedure fairly quickly. In a September 2009 interview with state media, Yu Chang, deputy director of the materiel and fuel department of an unspecified support base for the South Sea Fleet, indicated that Chinese merchant ships were highly reliable, more likely to provide sailors with food that they enjoy eating, and offered cheaper prices than local alternatives.[36] By the time the fifth naval escort task force deployed to the Gulf of Aden, Chinese merchant vessels like the *Guyuhe* were delivering up to 20 tons of fruits, vegetables, seasoning, staple foods, and other replenishment materials at a time.[37]

Fuel was also a major deployment planning priority for PLAN leaders during the initial task force deployments. When the *Weishanhu* departed from Hainan with the first task force on December 26, 2008, it took 10,500 tons of oil to refuel the missile destroyers *Wuhan* and *Haikou*.[38] This supply was presumably dwindling by the time the *Weishanhu* docked in Aden to resupply in late February of 2009.

It is also clear that the PLAN was still very much in the process of refining its at-sea refueling procedures during the first several naval escort task forces. On the first task force, PRC media eagerly reported that the destroyers *Wuhan* and *Haikou* were refueled by the supply ship *Weishanhu* in the Strait of Malacca on December 30, 2008, only 5 days after they had left China for the Gulf of Aden.[39] Similarly, Chinese papers reported that the *Weishanhu*, which stayed on after the first task force returned to Hainan, rendezvoused with the destroyer *Shenzhen* and the frigate *Huangshan* of the second task force for refueling on April 11, 2009, 2 days before the two new warships arrived in the Gulf of Aden.[40] By the time of the fourth task force deployment, however, the PLAN had clearly refined its overseas fuel management capabilities to the point where the Chinese military press no longer felt the need to report every refueling. Subsequent reporting on refueling seems to have depended largely on if the task force fleet made friendly port calls or participated in international joint exercises on the way to its patrol area first.[41]

Port access is an undeniably critical issue for navies hoping to replenish their ships far from home. There has been substantial discussion in Chinese policy circles about the need for overseas bases, or at least supply points, in recent years. Interestingly, however, it appears as though China sent its first naval escort task force out to sea before it had finalized agreements to ensure access to onshore resupply points in the countries near the Gulf of Aden. At a Ministry of National Defense press conference on the eve of the first deployment to Somalia's coastal waters, Rear Admiral Xiao Xinnian, deputy chief of staff of the navy, touched on the port access as he described the PLAN's replenishment strategy for the upcoming mission:

> The replenishment of their supplies . . . will be dominated by self-support and self-supply. When the ships are on duty in the region over a long period of time, we need to approach some ports in the nearby countries and territories to replenish their supplies. This issue is being negotiated with the coastal countries through relevant channels. Our military will send advance men to liaise and negotiate. Communication with relevant ports over some specific details is needed.[42]

That the Chinese were willing to send two large warships and a replenishment vessel to Somalia prior to finalizing port access agreements with nearby nations suggests a certain level of confidence that Chinese military leaders and diplomats would be able to get these deals done in time, but it also shows that the priority for the PLAN in this case was to start conducting naval escort operations as soon as possible without getting bogged down in the specifics of predeployment planning for on-shore replenishment.

Eventually, ships in the naval escort task forces did begin to stop at foreign ports. The first such port call was when the replenishment ship *Weishanhu* of the first naval escort fleet docked in Aden, Yemen, in late February 2009 to resupply. Before the ship arrived in Aden, an advance group made up of Chinese representatives from the Naval Headquarters, the Political and Logistics Departments, the Foreign Affairs Department, and the Transportation Department worked with employees of COSCO to procure locally the necessary goods for the replenishment operation.[43] Subsequent task forces continued to use to the model of PRC government coordination with Chinese enterprises to coordinate on-shore resupply efforts as the PLAN established port access agreements with additional countries such as Oman (during the second task force), Djibouti (during the fourth task force), and Singapore (after the fifth task force's mission concluded).[44]

Though the warships of the first naval escort task force remained at sea while the *Weishanhu* resupplied in Yemen, beginning with the second task force, Chinese destroyers and frigates also began to conduct port visits, presumably to provide weary sailors with shore leave.[45] Though not directly related to the issue of deployment planning, it is also worth noting that beginning with the second task force, the fleets began making friendly and official military visits to other countries en route back to China after having completed their missions in the Gulf of Aden. Countries visited include Algeria, Australia, Bulgaria, France, Italy, Portugal, Turkey, Israel, Pakistan, India, Malaysia, the Philippines, Vietnam, Djibouti, Sri Lanka, the United Arab Emirates, Egypt, Greece, Myanmar, Saudi Arabia, Bahrain, Kuwait, Morocco, Tanzania, South Africa, and the Seychelles.[46] While the purpose of these visits has been largely to encourage friendly relations with the host countries, some of the port calls, notably those to the Seychelles, presumably were carried out in order to explore the possibility of establishing permanent supply points or even formal military bases abroad.[47]

Equipment and Maintenance Issues

Given that China did not announce its intention to send ships to patrol the Gulf of Aden until shortly before the deployment of the first naval escort task force, there is not a great deal of open source information about how equipment decisions factored into predeployment planning for the first counterpiracy missions. A March 2010 interview with China People's Political Consultative Conference member retired Rear Admiral Yin Zhuo, however, sheds some light into the PLAN's early discussion about which ships to deploy. Explaining the naval leadership's thought process, Yin explained that:

> we sent out two destroyers in the first batch for the escort mission, we sent out one destroyer and one frigate in the second batch, and we sent out all frigates in the third batch and the fourth batch. Why did we do things like this? We did that from the military economy perspective. When we went to the Gulf of Aden the first time, we were not familiar with that sea area, and we were not familiar with the wind and wave situation there either. However, the escort operations in the Gulf of Aden mainly relied on helicopters. Therefore, we sent out destroyers to go there in the beginning. They were large destroyers. One was 5,000 tons to 6,000 tons, while the other one was 6,000 tons to 7,000 tons. Also, they brought one to two helicopters with them. At that time, we did not know much about the sea area there, so we would rather send bigger ships there first.
>
> During the second time, we sent out the second formation, with one large ship, one destroyer and one frigate. We wanted to see whether a frigate would work there or not. Therefore, we sent it there to have a try, and we found out that it did not have a great difference with a destroyer. During the third and fourth batches, we sent all frigates there. Frigates burn diesel oil, while destroyers use gas turbines, with a relatively large amount of oil consumption. Both kinds burn RMB [renminbi], and it is the money of our taxpayers. Of course, for the same task, the less money we spend, the better.[48]

Yin's explanation illustrates that the Chinese leadership approached predeployment ship selection as a performance maximization problem that required a careful balancing of firepower and costs. Over the course of the first few task force deployments, the PLAN gradually realized that it could achieve the same results with smaller, less expensive vessels, so it ultimately shifted toward including at least one frigate on every task force beginning with the second deployment.[49] The one exception to this trend was the sixth task force, during which a destroyer accompanied a *Yuzhao*-class large landing vessel to the Gulf of Aden.[50] Given that this was the first time such a landing vessel had been deployed to the area, however, this decision largely fits the trend of initially using maximal firepower to ensure operational success before whittling fleets down to smaller, more cost-efficient sizes.

Chinese naval officers and experts do not tend to discuss maintenance issues in great detail in the open source literature, but as some Western PLA analysts point out, capabilities in this area seem to have improved substantially. On the eve of the inaugural deployment to the Gulf of Aden, Rear Admiral Du Jingchen, commander of the first task force, stated: "To ensure reliability, all of the formation's equipment has undergone thorough inspection, repair, and maintenance, and backup equipment is available for key items such as motive power, communication, and navigation equipment."[51] Not only did the PLAN leadership take predeployment measures to ensure the reliability of equipment, but it also made preparations to carry out repairs under way if necessary. Indeed, a September 2009 article on the replenishment ship *Weishanhu*, which had just returned from servicing the first two task forces, reported: "In the course of performing its escort mission, the *Weishanhu* ship not only accomplished a large number of tasks for replenishment, but also played the role of a 'hospital ship' and 'repair workshop.' It carried out duties to treat the injured, make emergency equipment repair, and so on."[52] This report seems to confirm speculation of increased self-sufficiency with regard to repairs and maintenance.

This is not to say, however, that the predeployment plan to carry out repairs using replenishment ships as workshops has always been sufficient. During the first few missions, the task force fleets used port calls as opportunities to carry out maintenance and overhaul in Oman, Djibouti, and Yemen.[53]

Training

Developing a comprehensive understanding of predeployment planning with regard to training is difficult using only the open source literature. Having said that, these sources do allow several important observations.

First, much of what the PLAN has done in terms of training over the past decade prepared the members of the first few task forces for their missions to the Gulf of Aden. In a predeployment interview, Rear Admiral Du Jingchen emphasized this point. A December 2008 *Xinhua* article summarized his argument:

> Du Jingchen said the components of the formation are well trained and have strong and comprehensive capabilities. They have played important roles in preparation for military struggle and in exercises in recent years. Also, since the Chinese Navy's first circumnavigation of the earth in 2002, its presence has been seen on the five great continents and the four great oceans. That has not only tempered the Navy's long-distance sailing capabilities, it has also boosted its ability to carry out diversified military tasks. So the Navy certainly has the experience to carry out missions.[54]

In addition to the general training alluded to by Admiral Du, members of the first task force also underwent specialized counterpiracy and escort training prior to their deployment, though the specifics of this training are somewhat unclear. In his *Xinhua* interview, Du mentioned that the training focused on "characteristics such as the small size of pirate targets, their strong ability to conceal themselves, their determination to commit these crimes, and the flexible tactics."[55] At a Ministry of National Defense press conference around the same time, Rear Admiral Xiao Xinnian also emphasized that the men of the first task force had received "necessary preoperational training in light of this mission" without getting into specifics. He also expressed confidence that the mission would pose "no problem" for the well-trained PLAN sailors.[56]

Perhaps the most notable thing about PLAN training for the first few task force deployments is that a great deal of it (or at least of the training that was reported in the state media) took place either in or on the way to the Gulf of Aden. A December 29, 2008, *PLA Daily* article describing the first task force's voyage to the coast of Somalia stated: "Two days into the mission, antipiracy training is already a daily occurrence aboard the ships." Noting that the sailors only got the order to deploy 2 weeks before leaving China, the article mentioned that many of the troops had been getting seasick, perhaps a sign that they had not undergone extensive training in simulated realistic conditions before leaving for the Gulf of Aden.[57]

Part of the reason for this is presumably that some types of operations are difficult to simulate in normal conditions. Several state media outlets carried stories about special forces troops practicing rappelling from helicopters at sea for the first time ever during the voyage to the first task force's patrol area.[58] It is interesting, however, that this seemingly last-minute training continued to be part of PLAN deployment planning long after the first handful of task forces concluded their missions. As part of the sixth task force, the *Kunlunshan* amphibious transport dock carried out numerous exercises on its way to the Gulf of Aden. Reporting on this ship's training regimen, one article noted: "This is the first time a PLA Naval amphibious transport dock conducted floatation-immersion drills in the open sea, making up for the lack of such abilities in relevant fields."[59] Given that the deployment of naval escort task forces had become fairly routine by this point, it is unclear why the crew of the *Kunlunshan* did not find time to conduct this training well before deploying. There are other examples of soldiers attempting complex operations for the first time on the way to the Gulf of Aden on later task forces, including a February 2011 *Xinhua* story about an eighth task force helicopter pilot, for the first time ever, landing at sea during the night on a ship that was under way.[60]

One aspect of training that the PLAN leadership certainly considered carefully during deployment planning was how to help newly arrived task force fleets learn from their predecessors. According to PLAN officers, the PLAN Command College in Nanjing held meetings to capture lessons learned from officers leading counterpiracy deployments and incorporated this material in predeployment training for subsequent task forces.[61] This concern manifested itself in the form of joint escort missions carried out by overlapping task forces. In general, the model was that the two task forces would carry out two joint escort missions, the first led by the outgoing task force and the second headed by the newly arrived fleet.[62] At least during the earliest missions, some members of the outgoing task force would stay on for a period of time to help the new fleet get accustomed to its tasks. A March 2009 *China Daily* article featuring an interview with Rear Admiral Zhang Deshun mentions that some personnel from the first naval escort task force would stay on after the rest of the fleet departed in order to ensure the "consistency and effectiveness of the mission."[63]

In addition to emphasizing training on technical military capabilities, PLAN leaders in charge of the naval escort task forces also included soft skills like legal expertise and foreign language proficiency in their early training plans. Each of the 800 members of the first counterpiracy fleet received four handbooks emphasizing psychological knowledge, security knowledge, knowledge of international law, and instructions on how to apply international law in military situations.[64] Additionally, a number of state media articles have pointed out that even early in the history of the PLAN's counterpiracy missions, the task forces often incorporated spoken English into their training regimen.[65]

Likely as a result of successful training, the PLAN gradually began to entrust command of the task forces to less experienced officers after the initial missions. The commander of the first task force was then–Commander of the South Sea Fleet Rear Admiral Du Jingchen. Du's previous experience included stints as deputy commander at the North Sea Fleet's Lüshun Naval Base in Dalian and assistant chief of staff of the PLAN.[66] The PLAN's selection of such an experienced leader as the first task force commander probably indicates the importance that the military leadership placed on a successful outcome for the first mission.

By the seventh Gulf of Aden mission, slightly lower ranking officers were leading the task force. Rear Admiral Zhang Huachen, at the time the deputy commander of the East Sea Fleet, led the mission.[67] Zhang's previous major roles had included an assignment as the commander of the East Sea Fleet's Fuzhou Naval Base.[68] While Zhang held the same rank as Du at the time of his deployment to the Gulf of Aden, unlike Du, he had never held the most senior command position in a PLAN fleet. The PLAN's willingness to deploy a less experienced commander on the seventh task force suggests a high level of leadership confidence in its commanders' capabilities as well as an increased routinization of this particular mission.

Care for Personnel

The well-being of personnel was a priority for the PLAN leadership during the deployment planning processes for the first task forces. The ships featured recreation facilities for sailors including libraries, computer study rooms, and gymnasiums, and the vessels were equipped with local area networks.[69] By the time of the third task force, a protocol had been established to allow sailors to have relaxation time onshore while their ships made port calls for replenishment.[70] For the fifth task force, concerns about sailors' mental health led to the inclusion of staff psychiatrists aboard the ships for the first time.[71] Efforts were also made to ensure that the men had access to email as well as the ability to phone home twice a month.[72] Beyond these quality of life issues, access to trained medical staff and the ability to execute emergency medical evacuations were concerns. For example, in 2010, an ill sailor ended up being flown to hospitals in Salalah and Muscat before finally being flown back to China for medical treatment.[73]

Communications

Communications have steadily improved between the first and current counterpiracy task forces. In December 2008, while discussing how merchant vessels in the Gulf of Aden should contact the naval escort task force fleet on the eve of the inaugural counterpiracy deployment, Rear Admiral Xiao Xinnian said:

> Chinese vessels should go through the notification channel first. This is more reliable. They can notify the Ministry of Transport and the Maritime Safety Administration of the time and location of their upcoming passage through the dangerous waters. The Ministry of Transport should be informed of the relevant factors, so that there will be a channel available for distress calls even in emergency. For distress calls in emergency, they can either make a direct call via the international channel, Channel 16, which we will keep open, as the position of our ships will be disclosed; or make their call via satellite communication or other relevant means of communication. The same method applies to foreign vessels that require emergency help and convoy cover.[74]

This top-down approach to communications, whereby the ships needed to first inform the Ministry of Transport before having a channel open to them, proved problematic, particularly when trying to coordinate and communicate with other navies in the same area. As a result, continuous satellite communications have been provided to the counterpiracy task forces, as well as an improved network of modern communications and navigation satellites that China has steadily deployed over the past several years. Finally, while the utility of centralizing versus decentralizing the task forces' command and communications systems still appears to be up for debate, there is some evidence that current PLAN task force commanders do carry out more autonomous decision-making than their counterparts from the earlier task forces.[75]

Length of Deployment

Though length of deployment was certainly an issue that the PLAN decision-makers considered during predeployment planning, fleet commanders and their superiors appear to have taken a wait-and-see approach to the exact number of days that the earliest task forces spent at sea. A Xinhua article announcing the departure of the first naval escort task force fleet reported: "The first phase of the mission will last for three months and the Navy will send new ships to relieve the fleet at an appropriate time, depending on the situation and the UN [United Nations] Security Council."[76] Even as the first task force was winding down operations, the exact timeframe for its return remained unclear. Interviewed for a March 9, 2009, *China Daily* article, Rear Admiral Zhang Deshun was unable to give an exact date for when the first round of ships would be replaced, stating only that it would probably be sometime in late April or early May. He did, however, indicate the level of detail of Chinese naval planning when he mentioned that the leadership was considering emergencies such as the potential failure of a warship and an upcoming monsoon in the Indian Ocean as it tried to pinpoint ideal replacement dates.[77]

Chinese aversion to scripting exact dates for the fleets to deploy and return continued into the second task force. In an early April 2009 interview with the *PLA Daily*, second naval escort task force fleet commander Rear Admiral Yao Zhilou said that it was not yet set how long the mission would last. The *PLA Daily* interview noted: "China will act strictly in accordance with the international laws and the related resolutions of United Nations Security Council (UNSC) and make the decision according to the actual condition in escort waters off Somalia."[78] While Chinese leaders cited international law and the "actual condition" of the waters off the coast of Somalia, it is clear that as the PLAN gained more experience in counterpiracy naval escort and expanded the network of overseas ports that it could use for replenishment, the length of the early task force deployments increased gradually, though only slightly.

Challenges Encountered, Lessons Learned, and Changes Made for Future Deployments

Evaluations of China's counterpiracy missions in the open source literature tend to be very positive and rarely discuss setbacks or failures, so it is difficult to paint a completely representative picture of the challenges that the PLAN has encountered and the changes that it has made as it expanded its reach to include the Gulf of Aden. There are, however, several issues that the Chinese have publicly identified as being challenges. These are issues that would affect any long-term deployment, so the solutions made or proposed to these challenges would probably pertain to future PLAN deployments to other parts of the world.

Well-Being of Personnel

A major concern for PLAN planners has been the health, both physical and mental, of the sailors deployed on the naval escort task forces. An April 2009 *PLA Daily* article discussing the performance of the first task force as it prepared to return home emphasized just how grueling the mission had been for the first cohort of Chinese sailors to patrol the Gulf of Aden: "During the last period of the escort mission, the sailors, worn out both physically and mentally, are apt to slack off. . . . But all the servicemen of the escort task force are making all-out efforts to fulfill every escorting task successfully."[79] Despite the paper's praise of the sailors' efforts to work through their exhaustion, it is clear that the 3 ½-month deployment had taken quite a toll on the men. Later that year, after the third task force had deployed to the Gulf of Aden, Li Jie of the Chinese Naval Research Institute commented: "Some measures should also be taken to help naval servicemen stay in good physical and psychological shape."[80] These statements hint at how the first escort missions proved surprisingly physically and mentally taxing for the hundreds of sailors onboard.

The PLAN leadership has been fairly quick to respond to these calls for better conditions for escort personnel. While the destroyers of the first task force fleet stayed at sea for the duration of their deployment, by the second deployment, Chinese naval planners had realized the importance of rest in ensuring the health of personnel. In late June 2009, roughly 7 weeks into the second task force's deployment, personnel aboard the fleet's three ships were given brief shore leave in Oman, a practice that PLAN has continued to carry out on subsequent task forces.[81] Chinese naval planners have also attempted to keep troops physically and mentally fit in a variety of other, more subtle ways discussed in previous sections, including stationing psychiatrists on task force ships, improving entertainment facilities onboard, and increasing access to communications with sailors' families. In a particularly creative show of innovation, the PLAN provided each member of the tenth naval escort task force with special "heat-proof" (lightweight) clothing after acknowledging persistent complaints about the hot, humid climate in the Gulf of Aden.[82]

Ongoing Logistics Challenges

The PLAN was also quick to recognize deficiencies in its logistics planning, particularly with regard to replenishment and food storage issues. Issues with the quality of goods procured during the first on-shore replenishment of the first naval escort task force seem to have been largely solved by the time the *Weishanhu* returned to China following the second task force. Additionally, initial struggles with food preservation seem to have been mitigated by the development and refinement of advanced refrigeration techniques in coordination with several PLAN departments. Finally, as mentioned earlier, more frequent access to a greater number of ports in the region have contributed to smoother logistics and replenishment during long deployments.

More Permanent Bases or Places

Despite improved access to ports around the world, the chorus of calls for permanent overseas supply points (or perhaps even bases) has only grown louder over the past few years, indicating that replenishment (and logistics more generally) remains an issue in the eyes of a substantial part of the PLAN leadership. Indeed, the PLAN's reliance on access to friendly ports—and a stable political and security environment to support that access—severely limits what it can count on in both peacetime and during conflict. A less stable or friendly environment would limit China's reach and thus its capabilities to perform various expeditionary tasks.

Better Communications

While not discussed nearly as much as other issues related to counterpiracy operations, there is clearly still room for improvement in communications, particularly communications with foreign navies. As mentioned earlier, China has increased the number of communications and navigation satellites substantially over the past decade. In terms of communications with foreign navies, there are indications that the PLAN is willing to work with others. In January 2012, China entered into an agreement with India and Japan to share their naval assets in the counterpiracy operations. This includes exchanging piracy-related information over the Internet, as well as sharing information about warship movements and escort schedules.[83] Nevertheless, a senior PLAN officer has cited the PLAN's command, control, and communications system as an obstacle to cooperation with other navies conducting counter-piracy operations.[84]

Conclusion

Although the PLAN has made remarkable strides in its expeditionary capabilities and its ability to plan for long-term deployments over the past 10 years, outstanding issues and challenges remain, particularly with logistics and communications. The PLAN will undoubtedly continue to use the Gulf of Aden counterpiracy deployments to hone its skills and refine the solutions to these challenges for use in deployments in the future. However, questions remain as to how well the lessons learned from the Gulf of Aden deployments will translate to other deployments elsewhere in the world. Depending on the mission and task, it is likely that many of the challenges mentioned above would persist or even worsen if the PLAN were to attempt a long-term deployment to another part of the world. How the PLAN will grapple with these challenges in the future remains to be seen.

Notes

1   The New Historic Missions as stated by Hu Jintao include ensuring military support for continued Chinese Communist Party rule; defending China's sovereignty, territorial integrity, and national security; protecting China's expanding national interests; and helping to ensure a peaceful global environment and promote mutual development.

2   Michael Chase and Kristen Gunness, "The PLA's Multiple Military Tasks: Prioritizing Combat Operations and Developing MOOTW Capabilities," *China Brief* 10, no. 2 (January 21, 2010).

3   Bernard D. Cole, "China's Navy Prepares: Domestic Exercises, 2000–2010," in *Learning by Doing: The PLA Trains at Home and Abroad*, ed. Roy Kamphausen, David Lai, and Travis Tanner (Carlisle, PA: Strategic Studies Institute, November 2012), 19–80.

4   Ibid. See also Wu Dilun and Liu Feng'an [吴弟伦, 刘逢安], "Highlights of Military Training in First Half of 2009" [上半年全军军事训练亮点纷呈], *PLA Daily* [解放军报], July 9, 2009; and Wu Dilun and Liu Feng'an, "General Staff Department Lays out Plan for Military Training Throughout the Armed Forces in the New Year" [总参部署全军新年度军事训练工作], *PLA Daily*, January 7, 2009.

5   Liu Feng'an and Hu Junhua [刘逢安, 胡君华], "Describing the '12th Five-Year Program' Period Military Training Scientific Development Blueprint" [描绘 "十二五" 时期军事训练科学发展蓝图], *PLA Daily*, September 23, 2011.

6   Du Jingchen [杜景臣], "Regard the Distant Seas and Oceans as Training Areas" [把远海大洋当作「练兵场」], *People's Navy* [人民海军], May 18, 2010.

7   Cole; also see Christopher D. Sharman, *China Moves Out: Stepping Stones Toward A New Maritime Strategy*, China Strategic Perspectives 9 (Washington, DC: NDU Press, April 2015).

8   Michael McDevitt, "PLA Naval Exercises with International Partners," in *Learning by Doing: The PLA Trains at Home and Abroad*, ed. Roy Kamphausen, David Lai, and Travis Tanner (Carlisle, PA: Strategic Studies Institute, November 2012), 81–126.

9   U.S. Navy Public Affairs Office, USS *Winston S. Churchill*, "US and China Team Up for Counter Piracy Exercise," September 18, 2012, available at <www.navy.mil/submit/display.asp?story_id=69643>.

10   The PLA does not use the term *professional military education*, referring instead to *military education*.

11   "Chinese Military Steps Up Training for Talented Soldiers," Xinhua, December 27, 2004, available at <http://english.sina.com/china/1/2004/1227/15352.html>. For an in-depth description of personnel reform in the PLA, see Roy Kamphausen, Andrew Scobell, and Travis Tanner, eds., *The People in the PLA: Recruitment, Training, and Education in China's Military* (Carlisle, PA: Strategic Studies Institute, September 2008).

12   "Xu Caihou Tours Troop Units in Dalian and Qingdao," *PLA Daily*, October 16, 2012, available at <http://english.peopledaily.com.cn/90786/7978019.html>.

13   Li Qinwei and Cao Jinping [李秦卫, 曹金平], "Zheng He Training Ship's Round-the-World Navigation Boasts Four Features" [郑和舰环球航行有四大特点], *PLA Daily*, April 18, 2012.

14   Wu Hanyue and Cao Jieyu [吴寒月, 曹结余], "Strong Guarantee for Moving Out Into the Deep Blue Sea—Record of a Certain Submarine Flotilla of the East Sea Fleet Using the Main Theme and the Main Line to Guide Ideological and Political Work During Long Voyages" [走向深蓝的坚强保证：东海舰队某潜艇支队用主题主线引领远航中思想政治工作纪实], *People's Navy*, January 9, 2012.

15   Zheng Lei [郑雷], "Exploration of Political Work in Distant-Sea Tasks" [远海任务中政治工作探索], *People's Navy*, November 9, 2011.

16   Christopher D. Yung and Ross Rustici with Isaac Kardon and Joshua Wiseman, *China's Out of Area Naval Operations: Case Studies, Trajectories, Obstacles, and Potential Solutions*, China Strategic Perspectives 3 (Washington, DC: NDU Press, December 2010).

17   Donna Miles, "U.S., China to Consider Sharing Resources During Joint Missions," American Forces Press Service, October 12, 2012.

18   Office of the Secretary of Defense, *Military and Security Developments Involving the People's Republic of China*, Annual Report to Congress, 2014 (Washington, DC: Office of the Secretary of Defense, 2014), available at <www.defense.gov/pubs/2014_DoD_China_Report.pdf>.

19   Yung and Rustici with Kardon and Wiseman.

20   Abraham M. Denmark, "PLA Logistics 2004–2011: Lessons Learned in the Field" in *Learning by Doing: The PLA Trains at Home and Abroad*, ed. Roy Kamphausen, David Lai, and Travis Tanner (Carlisle, PA: Strategic Studies Institute, November 2012), 297–336; and Christopher D. Yung and Ross Rustici with Scott Devary and Jenny Lin, *"Not an Idea We Have to Shun": Chinese Overseas Basing Requirements in the 21st Century*, China Strategic Perspectives 7 (Washington, DC: NDU Press, October 2014).

21   For an excellent description of the *Peace Ark* and its missions, see Peter Mackenzie, *Red Crosses, Blue Water: Hospital Ships and China's Expanding Naval Presence* (Alexandria, VA: CNA Corporation, September 2011), available at <www.cna.org/sites/default/files/research/Red%20Crosses,%20Blue%20Water%20D0025784%20A1%20(2).pdf>.

22   Ju Zhenhua and Wang Lingshuo, "PLA Navy 'Peace Ark' Hospital Ship Leaves Kenya," *PLA Daily*, October 19, 2010; Joy Nabukewa, "Jubilations as Chinese Medical Ship Docks at Kenyan Port," Xinhua [新华], October 13, 2010.

23   Wang Zhenjiang and Dai Zongfeng, "Peace Ark Hospital Ship to Visit Latin America," *PLA Daily*, September 16, 2011, available at <www.china.org.cn/world/2010-10/14/content_21122285.htm>.

24   Jane Perlez, "China Offers Hospital Ship to the Philippines," *New York Times*, November 19, 2013, available at <http://sinosphere.blogs.nytimes.com/2013/11/19/china-offers-hospital-ship-to-the-philippines/?_php=true&_type=blogs&_r=0>.

25   Zhang Tao, ed., "Chinese navy sails out for 2014 RIMPAC," Xinhua, June 9, 2014, available at <http://eng.chinamil.com.cn/news-channels/china-military-news/2014-06/09/content_5948932.htm>; "'Peace Ark' hospital ship arrives in Papua New Guinea," *China Military Online*, September 12, 2014, available at <http://eng.chinamil.com.cn/news-channels/china-military-news/2014-09/12/content_6134725.htm>.

26   Gabe Collins and Andrew S. Erickson, "Implications of China's Military Evacuation of Citizens from Libya," *China Brief* 11, no. 4 (March 10, 2011).

27   Embassy of China in South Africa, "Chinese Naval Warships Visit Durban on 4 April 2011," March 29, 2011, available at <www.chinese-embassy.org.za/eng/sgxw/t810585.htm>.

28   For a comprehensive overview of China's space-based intelligence, surveillance, and reconnaissance capabilities, see Mark A. Stokes and Dean Cheng, *China's*

Evolving Space Capabilities: Implications for U.S. Interests, paper prepared for the U.S.-China Economic and Security Review Commission (Arlington, VA: Project 2049 Institute, April 26, 2012), available at <http://project2049.net/documents/uscc_china-space-program-report_april-2012.pdf>.

29 Andrew S. Erickson, "Satellites Support Growing PLA Maritime Monitoring and Targeting Capabilities," *China Brief* 11, no. 3 (2011), 13–19.

30 Daniel J. Kostecka, "The Chinese Navy's Emerging Support Network in the Indian Ocean," *China Brief* 10, no. 15 (July 22, 2010), 5; "Seychelles Invites China to Set Up Anti-Piracy Base," Agence France-Presse, December 2, 2011; Jeremy Page and Tom Wright, "Chinese Military Considers New Indian Ocean Presence," *Wall Street Journal*, December 14, 2011; Li Xiaokun and Li Lianxing, "Navy Looks at Offer From Seychelles," *China Daily*, December 12, 2011.

31 Yung and Rustici, 30.

32 Bai Ruixue [白瑞雪], "Chinese Navy's Ship Protection Formation All Set for Departure" [中国海军护航编队准备就绪], Xinhua, December 25, 2008.

33 Ibid.

34 Liu Yanxun, Chen Xiaoshu, Wang Jing, He Jing, Li Haoran, and Yao Yijiang [刘炎迅, 陈晓舒, 王婧, 何婧, 李赫然, 姚忆江], "Background of Expedition to Somalia—Chinese Push Forward to Dark Blue," *China News Magazine* [远征索马里背后—中国海军挺进 "深蓝"], January 5, 2009, 20–26.

35 Tian Yuan and Qian Xiaohu, "'Weishanhu' Ship Accomplishes First Replenishment at Foreign Port," *PLA Daily*, February 25, 2009.

36 Sun Zifa [孙自法], "Chinese Navy's 'Weishanhu' Supply Ship Sets New Records in Maritime Support" ["微山湖"舰护航: 创造中国海军远洋保障新纪录], China News Agency [中国新闻社], September 13, 2009.

37 Li Jianhong and Zhang Qi [李建红, 张旗], "Chinese Naval Escort Taskforce Entrusts Merchant Ship with Replenishment for First Time" [海军第五批护航编队首次依托商船进行补给], *PLA Daily*, May 31, 2010.

38 Liu Yanxun et al.

39 "Chinese naval fleet completes first at-sea replenishment," Xinhua, December 30, 2008.

40 Xia Hongping and Cao Haihua, "Second Chinese Naval Escort Taskforce Meets Supply Ship Weishanhu," *PLA Daily*, April 13, 2009.

41 Yin Hang and Yu Huangwei, "6th Chinese naval escort taskforce arrives in Gulf of Aden," *PLA Daily*, July 14, 2010; Li Jianwen and Fang Lihua, "Seventh Chinese naval escort taskforce arrives in Gulf of Aden," *PLA Daily*, November 18, 2010; Liu Yiwei and Hou Rui, "8th Chinese naval escort taskforce leaves Pakistan for Gulf of Aden," *PLA Daily*, March 14, 2011.

42   Central People's Government of the People's Republic of China, "Ministry of National Defense Briefing on Navy's Deployment to Gulf of Aden/Somali Waters to Provide Convoy Cover and Other Information" [国防部介绍海军赴亚丁湾, 索马里海域护航 情况等], December 23, 2008.

43   "Our Naval Escort Ship Docked at a Foreign Port for Necessary Daily Support for the First Time" [我海军护航军舰首次停靠外港补给生活用品], Xinhua Online [新华网], February 24, 2009.

44   Kostecka.

45   Ibid.

46   "Chinese missile frigate 'Xuzhou' visits Malaysia," Xinhua, December 7, 2009; "Chinese Naval fleet makes port call in Manila," Xinhua, April 13, 2010; Andrew S. Erickson, statement before the U.S.-China Economic and Security Review Commission, Panel III: "China's Political and Security Challenges in the Middle East," "China and the Middle East" hearing, Washington, DC, June 6, 2013; Andrew S. Erickson and Austin Strange, "China's Blue Soft Power," *Naval War College Review* 68, no. 1 (Winter 2015), 81–82; "China proud of her role in ensuring maritime safety," *Seychelles Nation*, April 18, 2011; and Li Jianwen and Fang Lihua, "Chinese warships visit South Africa," *PLA Daily*, April 6, 2011.

47   Peter Simpson and Dean Nelson, "China considers Seychelles military base plan," *The Telegraph*, December 13, 2011, available at <www.telegraph.co.uk/news/worldnews/africaandindianocean/seychelles/8953319/China-considers-Seychelles-military-base-plan.html>.

48   "Yin Zhuo: Maritime Hegemony of the United States Threatens China's Security" [尹卓:美国海上霸权威胁中国安全], *China Online* [中国网], March 8, 2010.

49   *NIDS China Security Report 2011* (Tokyo: National Institute for Defense Studies, February 2012), 32.

50   Ibid., 32.

51   Bai Ruixue.

52   Sun Zifa.

53   Kostecka.

54   Bai Ruixue.

55   Ibid.

56   "Ministry of National Defense Briefing on Navy's Deployment to Gulf of Aden/Somali Waters to Provide Convoy Cover and Other Information."

57   Qian Xiaohu and Tian Yuan, "Anti-Piracy Training Becomes Required Daily Training Subject," *PLA Daily*, December 29, 2008.

58   Li Tang [李唐], "Escort is carrying out anti-piracy exercise" [海军护航编队边

航行边进行反海盗演练], *China Youth Daily* [中国青年报], January 3, 2009.

59   Hai Tao and Liang Jiawen [海韬，梁嘉文], "The 'birth' record of China's first aircraft carrier" [中国首艘航母"诞生"记], *International Herald Leader* [国际先驱导报], July 9, 2010.

60   Qiu Junsong and Tang Shifeng [邱俊松，唐诗风], "Chinese Navy Eighth Escort Formation Conducts First Comprehensive Anti-Piracy Drill" [中国海军第八批护航编队首次举行反海盗综合演练], Xinhua Online [新华网], February 25, 2011. It is important to note, however, that PRC media often publicize events for propaganda purposes; in this case, it seems unlikely that such training had never been conducted before, given the routine nature of the deployments.

61   Thanks to Phillip C. Saunders for this information, derived from 2013 and 2014 meetings with PLAN officers.

62   See, for example: "Two Fleets of Chinese Naval Escort Ships Meet in Gulf of Aden," *China View*, April 13, 2009, available at <http://news.xinhuanet.com/english/2009-04/13/content_11180769.htm>; "Commander of USCTF 151 Visits 'Zhoushan' Frigate," *China Defense Mashup*, November 4, 2009, available at <www.china-defense-mashup.com/commander-of-usctf-151-visits-zhoushan-frigate.html>; Li Jianwen and Liu Yiwei,"Chinese Navy Fights Pirates," *China Military Online*, March 17, 2011, available at<http://eng.chinamil.com.cn/special-reports/2008hjdjhd/2011-03/17/content_4407525.htm>.

63   Cui Xiaohuo, "Somali mission fleet to be replaced, navy official says," *China Daily*, March 9, 2003, available at <www.chinadaily.com.cn/cndy/2009-03/09/content_7552551.htm>.

64   Liu Yanxun, Chen Xiaoshu, Wang Jing, He Jing, Li Haoran and Yao Yijiang.

65   Qian Xiaohu and Cao Haihua [钱晓虎，曹海华], "'Chaohu' Warship Sets Multiple Ocean-Going Escort Records" ['巢湖'舰 创我战斗舰艇远洋护航多项纪录], *PLA Daily*, December 15, 2010.

66   "In adjustment of high-level Navy officers, Di Jingchen to become commander of the East Sea Fleet" [海军高级将领调整 杜景臣出任东海舰队司令员], *People's Daily Online* [人民网], December 29, 2009, available at <http://news.xichu.net/folder111/folder209/2009/12/2009-12-2963853.html>;"China begins anti-piracy mission," BBC News, December 26, 2008, available at <http://news.bbc.co.uk/2/hi/africa/7799899.stm>

67   "Chinese escort taskforce commander meets EU counterpart," *PLA Daily*, February 16, 2011, available at <http://eng.chinamil.com.cn/news-channels/china-military-news/2011-02/16/content_4385740.htm>.

68   "Zhang Huachen comes to tour Zhucheng" [张华臣来诸城参观], *People's Daily Online* [人民网], February 17, 2007.

69   Bai Ruixue.

70   Zhang Qingbao [张庆宝], "Resolutely protect the safety of the nation's strategic corridor—interview with Rear Admiral Wang Zhiguo, Commander of the Third Naval Escort Taskforce bound for Gulf of Aden, Somalian waters" [坚决维护国家战略通道的安全—访第三批赴亚丁湾索马里海域护航编队指挥员王志国少将], *People's Navy* [人民海军], August 5, 2009.

71   Ai Yang, "Navy beefs up anti-piracy effort," *China Daily*, March 4, 2010, available at <www.chinadaily.com.cn/china/2010-03/04/content_9534852.htm>.

72   Ibid.

73   Michael McDevitt, "PLA Naval Exercises with International Partners."

74   "Ministry of National Defense Briefing on Navy's Deployment to Gulf of Aden/Somali Waters To Provide Convoy Cover and Other Information."

75   Yung and Rustici with Kardon and Wiseman, 22.

76   "Chinese Navy Sets Sail for Anti-Piracy Mission off Somalia," Xinhua, December 26, 2008.

77   Cui Xiaohuo.

78   Xia Hongpin and Cao Haihua [夏洪平, 曹海华], "The coherence and effectiveness of protective ship escort operations" [确保护航行动的连贯性和有效性], *PLA Daily*, April 2, 2009.

79   "First Chinese naval escort taskforce keeps good performance before leaving," *PLA Daily*, April 9, 2009.

80   Li Jie, "China's Navy Still Has Far to Go," *China Daily*, August 14, 2009.

81   Huang Shubo and Su Yincheng, "Chinese naval escort taskforce berths in Port Salalah for rest," *PLA Daily*, July 2, 2009.

82   Gao Fei and Yang Kai, "Chinese naval escort taskforce sees heat-proof clothing introduced," *PLA Daily*, November 16, 2011.

83   Nitin Gohkale, "India, China, and the Pirates," *The Diplomat*, March 6, 2012, available at <http://thediplomat.com/2012/03/06/india-china-and-the-pirates/>.

84   2014 comments by a senior PLAN officer who has deployed on counter-piracy missions. Thanks to Phillip C. Saunders for providing this information.

Andrew Scobell is a Senior Political Scientist at the RAND Corporation. He was previously an Associate Professor of international affairs at the George H.W. Bush School of Government and Public Service at Texas A&M University. He is the author of *China's Use of Military Force: Beyond the Great Wall and the Long March* (Cambridge University Press, 2003) and co-authored *China's Search for Security* (Columbia University Press, 2012). In addition to editing or co-editing 12 books, Dr. Scobell has written dozens of reports, monographs, journal articles, and book chapters. He holds a Ph.D. in political science from Columbia University.

Arthur S. Ding is a Distinguished Research Fellow and Director of the Institute of International Relations at National Chengchi University in Taipei. His research focuses on China's security and defense policy, including civil-military relations, defense strategy, defense industry, and arms control. His publications include *China's Changing Military Theory, 1979–1991*, *PRC's Defense Industry Conversion*, and numerous journal articles and chapters in edited books. He received his BA in anthropology from the National Taiwan University and his Ph.D. in political science from the University of Notre Dame.

Phillip C. Saunders is Director of the Center for the Study of Chinese Military Affairs and a Distinguished Research Fellow at the Center for Strategic Research, both part of National Defense University's Institute for National Strategic Studies. Dr. Saunders previously worked at the Monterey Institute of International Studies, where he was Director of the East Asia Nonproliferation Program from 1999 to 2003, and served as an officer in the U.S. Air Force from 1989–1994. He is co-author of *The Paradox of Power: Sino-American Strategic Restraint in an Era of Vulnerability* (NDU Press, 2011) and co-editor of books on PLA influence on Chinese national security decisionmaking, China-Taiwan relations, the Chinese navy, and the Chinese air force. Dr. Saunders attended Harvard College and received his MPA and Ph.D. in international relations from the Woodrow Wilson School at Princeton University.

Scott W. Harold is a Full Political Scientist and Deputy Director of the Center for Asia-Pacific Policy at the RAND Corporation, where he specializes in Chinese foreign policy, East Asian security, and international affairs. In addition to his work at RAND, Dr. Harold is an Adjunct Associate Professor of Security Studies at Georgetown University's Edmund A. Walsh School of Foreign Service, where he has taught since 2006. Prior to joining RAND in August 2008, Dr. Harold worked at the Brookings Institution from 2006 to 2008.

Samuel K. Berkowitz is a Research Assistant at the RAND Corporation. He holds a BA in economics with a minor in East Asian Languages and Civilizations from the University of Chicago. Prior to joining RAND, he studied in Beijing at Tsinghua University with the Inter-University Program for Chinese Languages Studies.

Michael S. Chase is a Senior Political Scientist at the RAND Corporation and an Adjunct Professor in the School of Advanced International Studies (SAIS) at The Johns Hopkins University. He was previously an Associate Professor at the U.S. Naval War College in Newport, Rhode Island. Prior to joining the faculty there, he was a Research Analyst at Defense Group, Inc., and an Associate International Policy Analyst at RAND. He is the author of the book *Taiwan's Security Policy: External Threats and Domestic Politics* (Lynne Rienner, 2008) and numerous chapters and articles on China and Asia-Pacific security issues. He holds a Ph.D. in international affairs and an MA in China studies from SAIS.

Dean Cheng is the Senior Research Fellow for Chinese political and security affairs in the Asia Studies Center at the Heritage Foundation. He specializes in Chinese military and foreign policy and has written extensively on Chinese military doctrine, technological implications of its space program, and "dual use" issues associated with China's industrial and scientific infrastructure. Before joining the Heritage Foundation, he was a Senior Analyst with the Center for Naval Analyses, a Federally funded research and development center, and a Senior Analyst with Science Applications International Corporation (now Leidos). He has testified before Congress, spoken at the U.S. National Defense University, U.S. Air Force Academy, and National Space Symposium, and has been published in the *Wall Street Journal* and *Washington Post*.

Mark Cozad is a Senior Defense Analyst at the RAND Corporation. He has written on Chinese military planning and strategy, intelligence analysis, and global strategic warning issues. Before joining RAND, he served in both the military and Intelligence Community at the strategic, operational, and tactical levels as well as in a variety of functional areas including intelligence analysis, targeting, operational planning, and strategy development. In his final assignment in the Intelligence Community, he served as the Assistant Deputy Director of National Intelligence for the President's Daily Brief. Immediately preceding his assignment to the Office of Director of National Intelligence, Mr. Cozad was the Defense Intelligence Officer for East Asia, the senior intelligence officer on that issue within the Department of Defense.

Jeffrey Engstrom is a Senior Project Associate at the RAND Corporation. He was previously a Defense Policy Analyst at Science Applications International Corporation. He is a co-lead author of *China's Incomplete Military Transformation: Assessing the Weaknesses of the People's Liberation Army* (RAND, 2015) and is the author or co-author of numerous reports and articles focused on Chinese military capabilities, disaster relief, power projection, and partnership capacity-building. Mr. Engstrom received his BA in political science and international studies from the University of Nebraska-Lincoln and an MPP from the University of Chicago.

Kristen Gunness is Adjunct Senior International Policy Analyst at the RAND Corporation, where she specializes in Chinese military and foreign policy issues. Formerly, Ms. Gunness served as the Director of the Navy Asia Pacific Advisory Group at the Pentagon, where she advised the Chief of Naval Operations on security and foreign policy trends in East Asia. Ms. Gunness has written extensively on Chinese security affairs and is the co-editor of *Civil-Military Relations in Today's China: Swimming in a New Sea* (M.E. Sharpe, 2006). She holds an MA in security studies from Georgetown University's Edmund A. Walsh School of Foreign Service.

Alexander Chieh-cheng Huang is a Professor at Tamkang University's Institute of Strategic Studies, Chairman of the Council on Strategic and Wargaming Studies, and Secretary-General of the Council of Advanced Policy Studies in Taiwan. He is also a Nonresident Senior Associate at the Center for Strategic and International Studies in Washington, DC. Dr. Huang previously served in the Taiwan government as Deputy Minister of the Mainland Affairs Council, and has been working closely with consecutive governments on foreign and security policy matters. He specializes in Asian and Chinese foreign and security affairs. His recent publications include "Taiwan in an Asian 'Game of Thrones'" in *Asia Policy* and "East China Sea Peace Initiative: From Principle to Practice" in *A Bridge over Troubled Waters: Prospects for Peace in the South and East China Seas* (Prospect Foundation, 2014).

Ben Lowsen is an Assistant Army Attaché in the U.S. Defense Attaché Office in Beijing. He has been an Active-duty officer since 1998, serving as a Field Artilleryman in Germany, South Korea, and Qatar and as a China Foreign Area Officer on the Army Staff in Beijing. He received an MA in East Asian regional studies from Harvard University.

Ma Chengkun is Professor and Director of the Division of PLA Studies at Taiwan's National Defense University. Professor Ma received his Ph.D. in China's war behavior study from National Taiwan University and specializes in People's Liberation Army affairs. His articles include "China's security strategy and military development" and "China's three warfares against Taiwan." Professor Ma is currently researching China's military strategic thinking and military transformation and participates in international academic exchanges about China's military modernization with various countries.

Lyle Morris is a Project Associate at the RAND Corporation with over 5 years of experience researching issues and leading projects related to Asia-Pacific security, Chinese defense and foreign policy, and U.S.-China relations. Prior to joining RAND, Mr. Morris was the 2010–2011 Next Generation Fellow at the National Bureau of Asian Research and a Research Intern with the Freeman Chair in China Studies at the Center for Strategic and International Studies. From 2004 to 2008, Morris lived in Beijing, where he studied Mandarin Chinese at Peking and Tsinghua universities and later worked at Dentsu Advertising and the *China Economist Journal*. Mr. Morris received an MA in international affairs from the Columbia University School of International and Public Affairs and a BA in international business from Western Washington University.

Lieutenant Colonel Mark A. Stokes, USAF (Ret.), is Executive Director of the Project 2049 Institute. During 20 years of Air Force service, Mr. Stokes was assigned to a variety of electronic warfare, intelligence, planning, and policy positions. In 1989, Mr. Stokes entered the Air Force's foreign area officer training program, and from 1992 to 1995, he served as the Assistant Air Attaché in the U.S. Defense Attaché Office in Beijing. Mr. Stokes subsequently was assigned to Headquarters U.S. Air Force's Plans and Operations Directorate, where he was responsible for operational and strategic planning for the Asia-Pacific region. Between 1997 and 2004, he served as Senior Country Director for the People's Republic of China, Taiwan, and Mongolia in the Office of the Assistant Secretary of Defense for International Security Affairs, with responsibility for developing, coordinating, and managing U.S. defense policy with respect to China. Mr. Stokes holds a BA in history from Texas A&M University, an MA in Asian studies from the Naval Postgraduate School, and an MA in international relations and strategic studies from Boston University.

Marcelyn L. Thompson is a Federal employee with a BA in Sino-Russian Studies from Vanderbilt University and MPA from the Monterey Institute of International Studies. She holds a Certificate in Chinese Studies from the Hopkins-Nanjing Center and was an Asia-Pacific Leadership Fellow at the East-West Center. Using a Fulbright Scholarship and Freeman Foundation grant, she conducted postgraduate research on labor migration and human trafficking in Northeast Asia. She is also a graduate of the Joint and Combined Warfighting Course at the Joint Forces Staff College.

Jonathan Walton is a Ph.D. student and Katzin Scholar at the University of California, San Diego. His research focuses on state-society relations, social control, and religious policy in China, combined with a longstanding interest in analog simulations and game design as methods for modeling and exploring complex issues. He previously worked for 7 years in the policy world with the National Bureau of Asian Research and Long Term Strategy Group. Mr. Walton has an MA in China studies from the University of Washington and a BA in East Asian studies from Oberlin College.

Catherine Welch is an Asia Analyst at the CNA Corporation. Before joining CNA, Ms. Welch worked at the Greater Cincinnati Chinese Chamber of Commerce and at an energy consulting firm in Washington, DC. Her research interests include China's approaches to crisis management, U.S.-China cyber security cooperation, China's political and military cooperation in Asia, and U.S.-China relations. Ms. Welch is the author or editor of a number of publications about China and the People's Liberation Army including *China's New Media Milieu: Commercialization, Continuity, and Reform* (CNA, 2010). Ms. Welch holds an MA in global affairs from George Mason University and a BA in Asian and Middle Eastern studies from the University of Pennsylvania.

Thomas Woodrow served at U.S. Pacific Command in Honolulu, Hawaii, from 2003–2014, where he was most recently the Senior Intelligence Analyst for the Joint Intelligence Operations Center China Division. Mr. Woodrow previously worked at the Defense Intelligence Agency as a Senior Expert in Chinese and Russian military, and nuclear forces. He is the author of numerous studies on Chinese political, military, and economic policies. Mr. Woodrow received an MS in national security strategy from the National War College and an MA in international public policy from the Paul H. Nitze School of International Studies at The Johns Hopkins University.

Colonel Larry M. Wortzel, USA (Ret.), served two tours of duty as a Military Attaché in China. He was a faculty member and Director of the Strategic Studies Institute at the U.S. Army War College. After retirement, he was Asian Studies Director and Vice President for Defense and Foreign Policy at the Heritage Foundation. Dr. Wortzel served for seven terms on the U.S.-China Economic and Security Review Commission. He has written or edited 10 books and numerous articles about China and East Asia. His latest book is *The Dragon Extends its Reach: Chinese Military Power Goes Global* (Potomac, 2013). A graduate of the U.S. Army War College, Dr. Wortzel earned his Ph.D. in political science from the University of Hawaii-Manoa.